THE
HISTORY OF
Ships

THE HISTORY OF
Ships

Peter Kemp

GREENWICH EDITIONS

This edition published in 2000 by
Greenwich Editions
10 Blenheim Court, Brewery Road
London N7 9NT
First published in 1978 by Macdonald & Co
Copyright © 1978, 1988, 2000
Little, Brown and Company (UK)

A CIP catalogue record for this book is
available from the British Library
ISBN 0-86288-345-8

Little, Brown and Company (UK)
Brettenham House
Lancaster Place
London WC2E 7EN

Production by Omnipress
Printed in The Slovak Republic
52185

Endpapers: the schooner *Alert* (right) lying
in Whitby upper harbour, North
Yorkshire, photographed by Frank
Meadow Sutcliffe in 1880.
Page one: Trial run of USS *Connecticut* off
Maine, 1907, by E. Muller.
Page two: The oil tanker *Tactic*.
Page four: Ships of the French-Genoese
fleet of 1390 from a late fifteenth-century
French manuscript.
Page six: One of the entries in the Tall
Ships Race, New York, 1976.

Contents

Foreword

'Ships and the sea, there's nothing finer made.' Thus did John Masefield express what countless shiplovers have felt for centuries. Today, when old sea ways are giving place to new, interest is greater than ever before, and the thirst for information has led to such a spate of books that their very number is bewildering, making wise choice daily more difficult.

The history of ships is a vast subject, extending for over five thousand years of man's endeavour, and to cover it fully is a daunting challenge. The knowledge needed is encyclopaedic and calls not only for an awareness of every stage in the development of the ship, from the age of the Pharaohs to that of the nuclear submarine, but also for a detailed understanding of the changes in man's lifestyle and habitat that have led to each new maritime advance. The author must supplement the expertise of the naval architect with the scholarship of the historian.

Additionally, and this is of the utmost importance, no man can truly evaluate or write convincingly of ships unless he is himself a seaman. And finally, the author must be somebody of vision and imagination who can explain a subject of immense complexity in words the reader can understand, and do this so powerfully that the story, as it unfolds, becomes difficult to lay down.

The success of this book, the best of its kind that I know, stems from the fact that in its author all these requirements are superbly, perhaps uniquely, combined. Add to this the wealth of illustration, illuminating every important detail of the text, and you have within the covers of a single magnificent volume what is in effect a distillation from the resources of a whole maritime university. A book to enjoy, a book to study, and a book to treasure.

FRANK CARR
Former Director of the National Maritime Museum

Chapter One
The Cradle of Seafaring

No contemporary picture of a truly primitive boat exists. The oldest known pictures of boats, in rock carvings or on pottery, show them at a much later stage of their development. Such knowledge as we have of earlier craft can only really be surmise. There is plenty to suggest what they were like, in present-day vessels in some less developed parts of the world. Men still bind branches together to make crude rafts beside some of the lakes and rivers of Africa; in South America people still take to the water in tree trunks, hollowed out with the aid of primitive implements or with fire. But the earliest actual pictures of boats that we have show them at a comparatively recent stage in their history. They date from about 6,000 years ago, and there were many thousands of years before then during which man ventured upon the water.

The rock carvings and pottery decorations which are the oldest known pictures of boats come from the Nile valley. They generally show some sort of long, narrow craft, with a steering paddle over the stern and men paddling amidships. Most are boats made of papyrus reed, since wood suitable for boatbuilding was scarce in the Nile valley, but some of them are constructed of numerous short wooden planks, held together with pegs or rope binding.

The earliest ship – for she was a great deal bigger than a boat – about which we have real knowledge is the funeral ship of the Pharaoh Cheops, the builder of the great pyramid at Giza, the first of the three pyramids built by his dynasty at Giza. It is generally accepted that he lived about 2600 B.C.

His funeral ship was carefully and lovingly made in prefabricated sections to be buried in

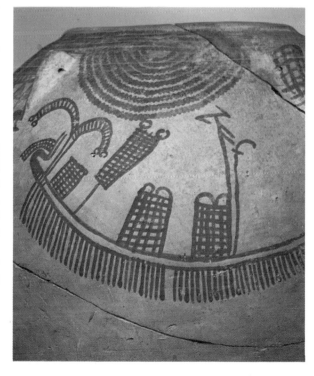

Left: Model of boat used by Tutankhamun on the Nile.
Above right: Earliest known picture of a vessel under sail, from an Egyptian pottery decoration of 3100 B.C.
Right: Egyptian river boat of 3300 B.C. on pottery.

a great pit hewn from the solid limestone of the Giza plateau, and when assembled was covered over by forty-one slabs of rock, each weighing around 18 tons. There she remained in her pit, ready to be used by Cheops if his soul should wish to embark on a voyage to the celestial regions. Since she was built more than forty centuries have gone by; 250 generations of men and women have lived and died. But this funeral ship of an ancient Pharaoh, preserved by the dry Egyptian air, has come to us out of the depths of time.

She is a wooden ship, constructed out of 600 separate pieces of wood, and considerably larger (133 ft (40·5 m) by 26 ft (7·9 m)) than any other ship of her day. This was undoubtedly because she was built purely as a funeral ship, and for the most powerful Egyptian ruler of his time. She was not built to go to sea, and, in fact, if she had tried to do so she would have been broken up by any moderate waves. Her importance in the history of the development of ships lies in the evidence that she furnishes about the skill of the Egyptian shipwright of 5,000 years ago in the working of wood to form a ship's hull. She was built with a made-up timber, rather like a keel, to which was attached a curved sternpiece and stempiece, but as yet there were no ribs, or timbers, to which to fasten the hull planking. In this ship they are held in place partly by wooden pegs and partly by small, shaped blocks of wood. The wood itself is cedar, imported for the purpose from Phoenicia.

Above: The interior of the cabin shows the fine workmanship.

Far right: The funeral ship of Cheops is the oldest and largest ancient ship to survive. It has been rebuilt from 600 parts and a further 624 fittings which had been carefully buried.

Right: Sewn cedar planks with elaborate scarfs held in position by rope fastenings.

Right: Relief from the tomb of Sahuré (about 2500 B.C.). It shows a keel-less boat with longitudinal bracing provided by a stout rope or hogging truss above the deck.

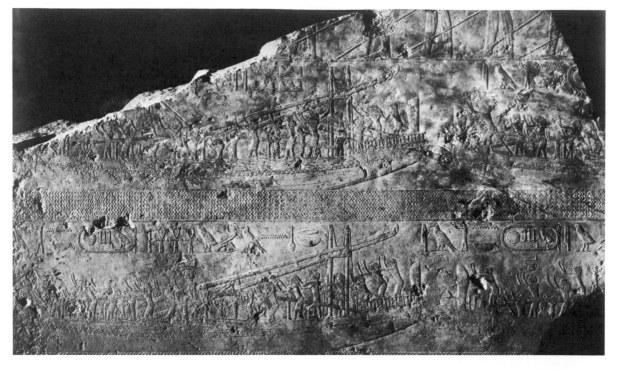

If we date Cheops's funeral ship at about 3000 B.C., we know from stone reliefs and hieroglyphics that by this time Egyptian ships were trading in the Mediterranean with Crete and Syria, and similar evidence records a war expedition to Phoenicia in 2700 B.C. We know also from these reliefs that the ships carried a single square sail on a bipod mast which could be lowered when the rowers took over. From the fact that this bipod mast was stepped well forward in the ship it is evident that the sail could only be used with a following wind, though early pictures on rock faces and pottery show ropes attached to the ends of the yard, which indicate that the yard could to some extent be braced round to the wind. There were still no ribs rising from the keel to support the outside hull planking and no deck beams to maintain the upper hull shape. Longitudinal support was provided by a large rope stretched from stem to stern and tensioned by a bar of wood in the manner of a Spanish windlass, and athwartship support by two ropes taken tightly round the whole upper hull and tensioned by a series of zig-zag racking turns with a smaller rope. Paddlers had by now given place to rowers, since the discovery of how to attach the oar to the ship's gunwale and use it as a powerful lever.

The rock temple at Deir el-Bahari at Thebes contains a long series of reliefs which tell the story of Queen Hatshepsut's expedition of five ships to the land of Punt, in search of such exotic imports as monkeys and greyhounds, myrrh and ivory. She was the co-regent and sister of Pharaoh Thotmes II, and the date is 1500 B.C. Judging from the temple reliefs, these ships were

Right and below: Modern
reconstruction and relief
of one of the ships from
Queen Hatshepsut's
expedition to Punt.
(Deir el-Bahari)

Left: State progress down
Egypt's main highway, the
River Nile.

fairly large, around 100 ft (30 m) in length. They
had fifteen rowers a side, thirty in all, and set one
large square sail on a yard. The land of Punt is
now thought to have been the present Somalia,
or possibly even Rhodesia, a long voyage from
Egypt down the Red Sea and around the horn of
Africa, and an expedition undertaking a voyage
of such long duration as this would obviously
require larger ships than were necessary for the
shorter Mediterranean voyages, since they had
to accommodate larger crews. But the reliefs in
the temple, which are remarkably detailed, show
two points of interest which transcend the mere
increase in size. They show the mast now stepped

amidships instead of forward, which meant that
the yard could be braced to a beam wind, instead
of only to a following wind, and they also show
a row of deck beams carried through the hull
planking, providing the essential athwartships
stiffness which every ship needs if she is to be
able to sail in any but the calmest of waters.

The temple reliefs at Deir el-Bahari also give a
picture of another remarkable Egyptian vessel, a
purpose-built ship for transporting obelisks,
which were hewn straight from the granite at
Assuan, down the Nile to Luxor. The obelisks
stood about 95 ft (29 m) high when erected, and
each weighed about 350 tons. The ship built to

carry them loaded two at a time, and was about 180 ft (55 m) long with a beam of 60 ft (18·3 m), if we can believe the figures of a court official of Thotmes, though probably she had in fact to be somewhat larger if she was not to sink under the weight of the obelisks, possibly up to 200 ft (61 m) in overall length with a beam of about 75 ft (23 m). The temple reliefs show three levels of deck beams to provide support athwartships.

All these pictures of Egyptian ships provide evidence that, as long ago as 1500 B.C., the basic design of a ship was very similar to that of ships today. The long central keel had been developed, shaped stem and stern pieces had been attached at either end, and deck beams had been evolved to support the hull. All that was still missing were ribs, rising from the keel and shaped to take the hull planking.

Below: Egyptian river craft from the fifteenth century B.C. (Tomb of Sennefer)

It should not be thought that the Egyptians were the only Mediterranean people who built and used ships. It is convenient to describe the evolution of their ships only because a greater wealth of illustration remains, in the shape mainly of rock carvings and reliefs, recording Egyptian achievements at sea. There can be no doubt that, simultaneously, ships were being built and developed in Crete, Syria, Phoenicia and Greece, as well as outside the Mediterranean in a host of other lands which bordered the sea.

If it is possible to generalize about Mediterranean ships of this early period, it could be said that those of Crete and Greece leant more towards the making of war, and those of Egypt and Phoenicia more towards seaborne trade, although there were at the same time undoubtedly Cretan and Greek ships built as traders and Egyptian and Phoenician vessels built as warships. On certain circumstantial evidence it seems that much of the Egyptian trading around the shores of the eastern Mediterranean was carried out under the protection of Cretan warships, and the fact that the ancient Cretan cities were built without defensive walls has been attributed to the extent of Cretan control of the surrounding seas, denying their use to invaders.

That Egypt, too, had ships built for war is certain from the evidence of rock carvings, but their main purpose was to escort merchant ships in their search for trade, or to seize and hold a trading port on the Palestinian coast. In the fifteenth century B.C. the Pharaoh Thutmose III fought eighteen small wars to capture ports on the Phoenician coast, though the ships he used were probably large merchantmen temporarily adapted for purposes of war. Three hundred years later Ramses III, the last of the great pharaohs, won a significant naval battle against 'the northerners of the isles', and details of the action are depicted on the walls of his temple at Medinet Habu. The ships are shown with the traditional bipod mast, but now there is a distinct crowsnest at the masthead, though whether for a lookout or an archer is unknown. The square sail is fitted with brails so that it can be furled up to the yard when the rowers were required at their oars, and around the sides of the ships are high washboards to protect the rowers. There were no thwarts for them, indicating that they stood to their oars. But the most important feature of the ships as depicted on the temple walls is the absence of the usual girdle of two ropes to provide athwartships support for the sides. This would seem to indicate that the last step towards what has been basic shipbuilding practice ever since may by then have been taken, with the introduction of timbers, or ribs, rising at intervals from the keel to support the hull planking. (There is evidence that these ships of Ramses III were copied from the ships of his enemies.)

Left and below: Modern reconstruction and relief of Ramses III's great naval victory over the 'northerners of the isles'. (Medinet Habu)

Above: A fresco dating from about 1500 B.C. sheds new light on Minoan naval power. This is the first detailed representation of their seagoing ships. (Thera)

Evidence of the form of construction of Cretan ships is scarce, as it is only in comparatively recent years that the remains of the Minoan civilization have been uncovered, and there is nothing like the wealth of Egyptian rock carvings and temple decorations to provide any details of design or building. According to Thucydides, the Minoan kings were the first to build fighting navies, and since, unlike Egypt, there was no shortage of trees on the islands of the Aegean Sea we assume that they built their warships of wood. Such pictures as we have, mainly on rings, seals and scraps of pottery, show Cretan ships with a single mast and a bank of oars, and with a pointed bow which could have been used as a ram in battle. What does seem certain is that Cretan warships during the period of the Minoan civilization controlled much of the waters of the eastern Mediterranean and used their fighting power to clear those seas of the pirates who preyed upon the peaceful trade of the islands.

Some time before 1450 B.C. – the exact date is uncertain – the Cretan empire was invaded by the Mycenaeans from the mainland of Greece and completely and utterly overthrown. The entire Minoan civilization was obliterated; their cities burned to the ground. To mount an invasion such as this across the seas argues a very considerable development in the size and strength of the ships used, for this was a major operation of war, a far greater undertaking than any of the maritime battles in which the Egyptians had taken part. There is plenty of detailed evidence about the size and development of later Greek ships, both trading ships and warships, and it is probably safe to assume that, even by this early date, the Greeks had made significant advances in ship design and construction. They would hardly have ventured their attack on the Minoan empire if they had not.

A clear distinction between the ship built expressly for war and the ship built for trade emerged with the Greeks, if at this stage we consider the Mycenaeans as Greek. They engaged in a long series of wars before finally they had to surrender their mastery of the Mediterranean to the Romans. The first of them was the Trojan War, of which we have many accounts in the writings of Homer. It is a nice, romantic idea that Agamemnon fought this long war against Troy in order to recover his brother's wife Helen, but it is much more likely that he did so to keep open the Greek trade routes in the Aegean Sea. Greece was by then trading extensively by sea. Her ships called regularly at the Black Sea ports for shipments of grain, and protection of the merchant shipping certainly called for a large navy. Homer talks about 1,200 ships engaged in the Trojan War. No doubt this was poetic exaggeration, but, whatever the exact number, there can be no doubt that there were a great many of them. Homer even provides some descriptions: almost all were 'black', which means that their hulls were covered, or payed, with pitch to make them watertight; they were 'hollow', which indicates that they still had no deck; they were 'benched', which shows that the rowers sat on thwarts at their oars. The largest of them rowed 50 oars, making them perhaps 80 ft (24·4 m) in overall length, and they lay low in the water, with a short wickerwork screen set forward to keep out the spray. There is some evidence that the largest were fitted with an *embelon*, or bronze beak for ramming an enemy, and, if this is so, they were the direct forerunners of the war galley which was to be the principal warship of the Mediterranean for the next 2,500 years.

However, for the next three or four hundred years, before the Greek bid for sea power, it is to the Phoenicians that the sea story of the Mediterranean really belongs. Centred on the ports of Tyre and Sidon, their ships ranged throughout the length of the Mediterranean and beyond, in search of trade. The Bronze Age had arrived, and the Phoenicians were notable workers in metal, so tin and copper (the ingredients of bronze) were the raw materials most in demand during the years of their maritime supremacy. At sea, the Phoenicians were, above all, great traders, though as their trade expanded over the seas they also had to build war galleys to protect their merchant vessels. They had a great reputation, too, as practical and skilled seamen. They built two types of merchant ship: the relatively small *gaulus*, for trade in and around the Aegean Sea, and the bigger *hippo*, or ship of Tarshish, for longer voyages. It was largely in their search for sources of tin that the Tarshish ships were built. Copper was obtainable locally from the mines in Cyprus, and could be brought to the ports of Sidon and Tyre in the smaller ships, but the nearest source of tin was Spain, and when the Spanish supplies began to run short, tin had to be brought from Cornwall and the Scilly Islands.

There were two distinct types of Tarshish ship, the earlier being a large ship with a single square mainsail set between upper and lower yards on a central mast, and with a steering oar on each quarter. The ship was decked, with two hatches for cargo and crew. The hull was built deep and roomy, on a length-to-beam ratio of about $2\frac{1}{2}$ to 1, with high, curved stempieces and sternpieces. There were no bulwarks, but along the gunwales were what today we would call stanchions and rails, to provide protection for the crew in rough weather and to keep the deck cargo from sliding overboard when the vessel rolled in a seaway. Cargo was normally carried both above and below the deck. (A mural painting in a thirteenth century B.C. tomb at Thebes, showing Phoenician ships at anchor in an Egyptian harbour, provides the details of this ship.)

It was with ships such as this that the Phoenicians traded the length of the Mediterranean and beyond, to southern Britain and the Canary Islands. There is evidence, too, that they operated them in the Red Sea and Indian Ocean, a canal between the River Nile and the head of the Red Sea providing the means of access to those waters. But, no matter in which direction they traded, their ships were always known as Tarshish ships. The site of this city has never been discovered, though references to it abound in the ancient records of all Mediterranean countries, and it was recognized as the richest city-state in the world. It almost certainly lay somewhere on the Iberian peninsula, probably outside the Mediterranean on the Atlantic coast of Spain or Portugal. It could be that even the Phoenicians never reached it, in spite of the fact that their ships were named after the city. For it is certain that they settled a colony at Gadir, now known as Cadiz, on the Atlantic coast of Spain and built it up into a rich and prosperous centre from which to stretch their trading tentacles into even more distant lands, but Gadir was not Tarshish.

The second type of Tarshish ship, a good deal later than the *hippo*, is of particular interest in the history of the development of the ship. Details of its rig were revealed on a carved marble sarcophagus which was discovered in 1914 in the Old Harbour at Sidon. It has two masts — or possibly one mast and a very high-steeved bowsprit — each carrying a sail laced to a single yard, the foresail being very similar to the spritsail set

below the bowsprit carried by sailing ships up to about the seventeenth century A.D. Both yards could be braced to the wind, and there is no apparent provision for rowers. It seems unlikely at this very early stage that any ship was built exclusively for sailing, but with the two-masted rig as shown in the carving it is not entirely impossible. Alternatively, it may be that the carver of the sarcophagus had not the skill or the space to show oars as well as sails. The usual twin steering oars are shown, but a point of considerable interest is a sort of low aftercastle projecting beyond the sternpost, very reminiscent of the sterns of the typical Spanish carracks of 1,800 years later. Another interesting feature is a raised cargo hatch, as is generally found on merchant vessels today. The mainmast shrouds appear to be tensioned by deadeyes — another modern touch — and the carving shows a small ship's boat carried on deck.

To protect their merchant ships on their long voyages the Phoenicians built war galleys with two banks of oars, the forerunners of the Greek bireme. Indeed, they were the first true biremes, and the Greeks copied them almost exactly. On the waterline or just below it, they were fitted with a bronze, or occasionally wooden, beak, or ram, the traditional main weapon of the galley throughout most of its history. Unlike the merchant ships, they were built long and slim, with a length-to-beam ratio of 5 or 6 to 1, or sometimes even as much as 8 to 1, and under oars they were fast and very manoeuvrable. They carried archers on a central upper bridge for attacking enemy ships, and were rowed by slaves. The earliest known representations occur in two Assyrian reliefs of about 700 B.C., and these show a curious arrangement of the two banks of rowers. The rowers pulling the lower oars sit below the narrow central bridge which runs the whole length of the galley, while those pulling the upper oars sit in outrigger extensions to the hull on either side. The design shows not only considerable shipbuilding skill, but also an improvement on earlier designs in understanding of the principles governing a ship's stability in a seaway. The long, narrow hull ensured greater speed and power if the ram was to be used, while the outrigger extensions, which were fully planked, provided a reserve displacement and an effective counter to the risk of capsizing through excessive rolling, which is inherent in any long vessel of minimum beam. A typical square sail, set on a mast stepped in the longitudinal centre of the galley, gave relief to the rowers with a following wind, and the two traditional steering oars, one over each quarter, ensured adequate directional control. For their day, these biremes were formidable vessels of war.

Right: Two-banked
Phoenician warship of
about 700 B.C., showing
ram. (Palace of
Sennacherib)

Below: A Tarshish ship.
(From a sarcophagus found
in the Old Harbour, Sidon)

Even the Greeks, their traditional enemies, admitted that the men who manned the Phoenician ships were magnificent seamen. Their long voyages in search of trade, particularly of tin, proved that. They are reputed to have made an even longer voyage, circumnavigating Africa during the reign of Pharoah Necho II (the pharoah who started the construction of the canal to connect the River Nile with the Red Sea). It was, in fact, an Egyptian-organized expedition, though the men who undertook it were all Phoenician. Herodotus, who travelled in Egypt 150 years later, was doubtful about the authenticity of the story, but the reason he gave for his doubts is at least an indication that it could well have taken place. His account runs:

'Libya [the original name of all Africa] shows that it has sea all round except the part that borders on Asia, Necho a king of Egypt [610–594 B.C.] being the first within our knowledge to show this fact; for when he stopped digging the canal which stretches from the Nile to the Arabian Gulf he sent forth Phoenician men in ships, ordering them to sail back between the Pillars of

Right: Phoenician merchant ship of about 700 B.C., loading and towing timber. Cedarwood was a staple Phoenician export. (Palace of Sargon)

Below: Eighth century B.C. Greek warship. Opinion is divided about whether it is one- or two-banked.

Hercules until they came to the Northern [Mediterranean] Sea and thus to Egypt. The Phoenicians therefore setting forth from the Red Sea sailed in the Southern Sea [the Indian Ocean], and whenever autumn came they each time put ashore and sowed the land wherever they might be in Libya as they voyaged, and awaited the reaping-time; having then reaped the corn they set sail, so that after the passing of two years they doubled the Pillars of Hercules in the third year and came to Egypt. And they told things believable perhaps for others, but unbelievable for me, namely that in sailing round Libya they had the sun on the right hand. Thus was Libya known for the first time.'

Herodotus can be excused for doubting the truth of the story, for all Mediterranean men knew that at midday the sun lay to the south of them, or on their left hand when they faced the sunset. If the Phoenicians did make this voyage, they sailed about 14,000 miles (23,000 km), a prodigious feat in 600 B.C., yet quite possible, even though it was to be nearly another 2,000 years before the magnetic compass was available to guide mariners across the seas. In those days few ships ventured out of sight of land during their voyages if they could help it, creeping round the coast by day and anchoring at night.

Unfortunately, Herodotus, in recounting this story which he picked up in Egypt, says nothing about the ships in which the Phoenicians sailed. We can only guess, but it is reasonable to assume that they were not designed specifically with this voyage in view, and, in fact, were the normal merchant ships of the period, still with the single central mast and square sail, and rowing probably 12 to 15 oars each side. The typical Phoenician *hippo*, in which they made their long voyages to the Canary Islands and southern Britain, was of exceptionally solid construction and would be the best ship available for such a voyage round Africa, particularly as they were built with a crowsnest at the masthead for a lookout, almost essential on a voyage such as this where it was necessary to keep the coastline in sight.

During the period of Phoenician dominance at sea, the city-state of Tyre was the richest in the world, and built mainly on extensive maritime trade. For three centuries Tyre, Sidon and the smaller Phoenician ports were the great clearing houses of world trade, importing great quantities of linen, cotton, wheat and papyrus from Egypt, silver, tin, iron and lead from 'Tarshish' (including Cornwall and the Scilly Islands), cedar and other timber from Cyprus and the Lebanon, brassware and slaves from Greece and Asia Minor. Their exports were mainly bronze articles, glassware (the Phoenicians are believed to have discovered the method of glass manufacture by fusing sand and nitre) and coloured dyes, of which the most desirable was Tyrian purple, reserved for the robes of emperors, caesars, and the richest and most desirable whores. To service this great trade not only was a great number of ships required, but also the finest and most robust ships that could be built, manned by the best seamen in the world. The Old Testament, in the words of the prophet Ezekiel, gives some of the details. Speaking of Tyre, Ezekiel says: 'They have made all thy ship boards of fir trees of Senir; they have taken cedars from Lebanon to make masts for thee. Of the oaks of Bashan have they made thine oars; the company of the Ashurites have made thy benches of ivory, brought out of the isles of Chittim. Fine linen with broidered work from Egypt was that which thou spreadest forth to be thy sail; blue and purple from the isles of Elishah was that which covered thee. The inhabitants of Zidon and Arvad were thy mariners; thy wise men, O Tyrus, that were in thee were thy pilots. The ancients of Gebel and the wise men thereof were in thee thy calkers [a Bible commentary translates this as 'stoppers of chinks' or, in the modern term, 'caulkers']; all the ships of the sea with their mariners were in thee to occupy their merchandise. . . . The ships of Tarshish did sing of thee in thy market; and thou wast replenished and made very glorious in the midst of the seas.'

All this was true enough, but Ezekiel was merely building up the picture for a prophesy of doom: 'Thy riches, and thy fairs, thy merchandise, thy mariners, and thy pilots, thy calkers, and the occupiers of thy merchandise, and all thy men of war, that are in thee, and in all thy company which is in the midst of thee, shall fall into the midst of the seas in the day of thy ruin. The suburbs [another version gives 'waves' for 'suburbs'] shall shake at the sound of the cry of thy pilots. And all that handle the oar, the mariners, and all the pilots of the sea, shall come down from their ships, they shall stand upon the land; and shall cause their voice to be heard against thee, and shall cry bitterly, and shall cast up dust upon their heads, they shall wallow themselves in the ashes. And they shall make themselves utterly bald for thee, and gird them with sackcloth, and they shall weep for thee with bitterness of heart and bitter wailing. . . . The merchants among the people shall hiss at thee; thou shalt be a terror, and never shalt be any more.'

Ezekiel prophesied that Nebuchadnezzar, king of Babylon, was to be the instrument of Tyre's downfall. Phoenicia was never a nation as such,

Above: The dock entrance at the old Phoenician port of Motya, Sicily, is so narrow that it confirms the small size of ancient warships.

merely a collection of independent city-states which never learned to combine against their enemies. Nebuchadnezzar subdued them one by one with great ferocity, but, although he besieged Tyre for thirteen years and captured the outer city whose inhabitants he put to the sword, he failed to take the harbour area. Nevertheless, Tyre took many years to regain its trading supremacy, and only did so through the constant realization that wealth depended on mastery of the sea. By building larger and better ships, and maintaining a yet more powerful force of warships, the Tyrians at last won back to their former trade pre-eminence.

But, many years later, Ezekiel's prophecy finally came true. The instrument of the city's fall was Alexander of Macedon – better known as Alexander the Great – who succeeded in breaching the city's walls after a siege of nine months. The slaughter of Tyrians was immense, and 30,000 of them were sold into slavery.

It was the end of Tyre as a city-state, the end of Phoenician mastery of the seas. For close on seven centuries their ships had ventured into waters as yet not penetrated by any other Mediterranean power, and had shown that the old belief of Mediterranean sailors that a ship sailing into the unknown ocean beyond the Pillars of

Hercules would fall over the edge of the world into the abyss was false. They had done this partly by building fine, strong ships and partly by an understanding of some of the rudiments of celestial navigation, an understanding not generally possessed by the seamen of other Mediterranean nations. Of their methods of navigation, and of the early attempts to map the ocean, an account is given at the end of this chapter; of their shipbuilding skills, the proof lies in the long voyages which they undertook.

They were probably the first of the Mediterranean nations to give their ships a continuous upper deck with hatches cut for the loading of cargo. The Egyptians had taken the first step, it is true, when they gave their ships transverse beams to provide athwartships support, but it was the Phoenicians who developed the idea to its logical conclusion, by raising the transverse beams to deck level and thus producing the basic pattern of keel, stempiece, sternpiece, possibly ribs, and deck beams to which every modern ship is built. Unlike the Egyptians, they were fortunate in having close at hand plenty of suitable timber for their ships. They were the first to experiment with two masts, for though the second mast looked perhaps more like a bowsprit than a mast it was cocked up, or steeved, so high that it acted more as a foremast than a bowsprit. On this they set a spritsail on a yard, which enabled them to sail with the wind on the beam, a tremendous advance on the single square sail of the Egyptians and Cretans that could only be hoisted and used to advantage with a following wind. They caulked the seams of their ships with wool and pitch to make hulls and decks watertight. They also realized that an expanding maritime trade could not be sustained without an efficient navy to protect the merchant ships, and so they developed the bireme with a bronze ram and an upper bridge deck for archers, so that the two banks of rowers below could pull their oars unhindered by the fighting men. The long, slim lines of the galley hull, with the added stability of the two outrigger extensions, either shows that the Phoenicians knew more about the modern science of hydrodynamics than many other seafaring nations a thousand years later or that they had a remarkable piece of good fortune, in hitting upon a design that was not simply revolutionary, but also ideal for the calm waters of the Mediterranean. Given the known skills of the shipbuilders of Tyre, Sidon, Gebel and Arvad, it seems reasonable to discount the element of luck and to assume that this particular design was the result of study of what a ship was required to do.

More important than the advances in shipbuilding and design which the Phoenicians initiated was the example that they set to the rest of the world by their trading ventures. By opening up new trade routes, first to the western Mediterranean and then out into the Atlantic, even as far as the green seas and grey skies of northern Europe, they proved that man had it in his power to overcome obstacles hitherto thought to be unassailable. Wherever their ships went, whether to Cornwall and the Scilly Islands or, by way of Red Sea ports, to India and perhaps beyond, their enterprise and courage formed the first link of a chain of maritime achievements which in the end was to lead man to the very last outposts of the earth. The sea was their dominion. They learned to be fine seamen, and their practical ability enabled them to profit by that learning in building fine, robust ships. But behind their skill lay the spirit of adventure and a determination to discover what filled the great unknown spaces of the world, by daring the wild waters. One of the great periods of maritime expansion came to an end with the fall of Tyre.

For a time the Phoenician tradition of trade was carried on by Carthage, a sister city-state colonized by the men from the Levant. But the true heirs to Phoenician sea power were the Greeks, whose maritime domination of the Mediterranean was about to begin. For a long time they did no more than follow closely the pattern set by the Phoenicians, both in their methods of trade – though they never ventured outside the Mediterranean, except to the Black Sea – and in the design of their ships. Only later in their history did they prove themselves to be even better seamen than the Phoenicians.

The Greeks traded to and from colonial settlements which they set up in Italy, Sicily, southern France, North Africa and the Black Sea. This last colony is interesting: not only was it a wheat-producing area which supplied most of the homeland of Greece, but there was gold in the rivers. The method of extracting the gold from the fast-flowing rivers was to pin down sheepskins on the river beds to catch the grains of gold washed down by the current. And here we find the basis of the legend of the Golden Fleece, the Argonauts and their ship, *Argo*.

We know quite a bit about the *Argo*. She was built of pine felled on the slopes of Pelion, the pine trunks being shaped into planks with an axe. She was built as a galley and her top strakes were pierced for fifty oars. Her whole hull was covered with pitch inside and out, except for her bows which were painted vermilion, the standard colouring for all Greek ships, and on either bow there was the traditional eye, so that the

Left: Model of
Phoenician trireme,
about 300 B.C.

23

ship could see her way across the waters. She was built on a beach, and when she was completed she was too heavy for the fifty Argonauts to run her down into the water, her keel sinking deep into the sand. So they cut more pines to make rollers, and got her up onto the rollers and so down to the water.

This is the traditional story of the building of the *Argo*, and it matches almost exactly the normal construction of a Greek *penteconter*, a sixth-century B.C. galley, with 50 oarsmen, a length of about 80 ft (24 m) and a beam of about 10 ft (3 m). Although the *Argo* was obviously built for trade – the fact that she was going to the Euxine (Black) Sea for the Golden Fleece, or, in other words, for a cargo of sheepskins which had been pinned down in the rivers to catch grains of gold, is evidence of this – we know from Herodotus that on many Greek trading voyages

the ships used were 'not the round-built merchant ship, but the long *penteconter*'. They were used not for defence against pirates, with whom the Mediterranean waters abounded, but for attack; for the Greeks were, above all, buccaneers in their trading ventures, and never averse to running a merchant ship aboard, plundering her cargo, and either enslaving her crew or leaving them to drown in their sinking ship.

The *penteconter*, based on the original design of the Phoenician galley, had a long history of buccaneering during the centuries of Greek dominance in the Mediterranean. They were of light construction and, pulling 25 oars a side, were fast enough to overtake any other vessel that they encountered. When the wind was favourable they set the usual square sail, laced to a yard hoisted on a central mast which was always lowered when the wind came ahead.

Below: Greek vase decoration showing Ulysses and the Sirens. The ship is of the *penteconter* type.

They were open ships, undecked except for a storming bridge (*kakastroma*, in Greek) which ran from stern to bow, providing the longitudinal strength needed for fighting purposes and making possible the light construction of the hull. The normal steering oars, one on each quarter, gave them their manoeuvrability.

The *penteconter*, built for the sort of aggressive trade which the Greeks pursued, was not the sole type of merchant ship used by them. There are few illustrations – no doubt Greek artists preferred to depict the more prestigious biremes and triremes – but one vase decoration shows a ship with an overhanging bow, not unlike a modern clipper bow, high bulwarks and a light central bridge running the length of the ship. She is shown under sail and with no oars visible. It is difficult to estimate her size, but if the length of the yard and the size of the sail approximate to

those in more detailed illustrations she would be 45 to 50 ft (13·7 to 15·2 m) long, and one would guess at a beam of about 14 ft (4·3 m). The vase shows her fairly high out of the water, and her distinct bulwarks indicate that she would carry a deck cargo in addition to that stowed in her hold. The clipper-like bow is interesting: a very similar shape of bow is found in Mediterranean fishing craft today, particularly in the waters around Italy and Malta. It would be wrong to conclude from this one illustration that all Greek trading vessels, except of course the *penteconters*, followed this pattern – each district no doubt had a more or less traditional design based on the type of cargo to be carried – but in general it could be said with some confidence that they were small, tubby ships built to carry the maximum amount of cargo with the minimum length of keel.

Above: A high-sided Greek merchant ship with deep draught. Contrast the lightly built war-galley on the left.

A whole series of wars, initially between the individual Greek states, against Carthage, against Persia, and finally against Rome, made it necessary for the Greeks to concentrate on warship building. The Phoenicians had already developed the bireme, the galley with two banks of oars on either side, and, with the *penteconter* proving too light in construction for purposes of outright war, the Greeks took the bireme as their warship. However, they built it lighter than the Phoenician model, with only a skeleton outrigger, instead of a solid one, on either side to provide a fulcrum for the upper bank of oars. The lower bank were pivoted on the edge of a round hole cut in the side planking. The upper and lower rowers sat on different thwarts, the upper rowers having a thwart level with the gunwale, the lower having one level with the holes in the sides. The main weapon of the bireme was the beak, or ram, fixed to the bow on or just below the waterline, and archers or stone-slingers were carried in addition to the rowers, using the *kakastroma* as their action station. To enable the hull to absorb the shock of ramming an enemy, the keel was slightly prolonged beyond the hull line aft and the thick wales, fixed to the hull near the waterline, were similarly prolonged to meet the end of the keel, where they were brought up together into a point or bunch, often decorated with the head of a bird or a stylized acanthus. The biremes all carried a mast, which was always lowered when the wind was ahead, and the traditional square sail on a long yard, with brails to furl it to the yard when not required.

26

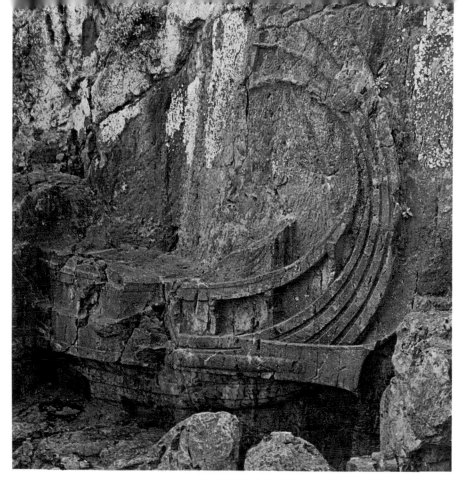

Above: Large rock carving at Lindos, Rhodes. The ship had to beach stern first, with steering oars raised.

Above left: Greek biremes under sail, sixth century B.C.

Left: Greek trireme of first century B.C. (Graffito from Delos)

Below left: Detail of an Athenian trireme, showing the upper oarsmen rowing through an outrigger. (Relief from Athens)

struced in sets of three, with the thranite sitting on the top bench, his zygite sitting on a bench 2 ft (60 cm) lower and 1 ft (30 cm) behind him, and the thalamite on a bench another two feet lower and another foot behind. A different theory envisages only two benches, with thranites and zygites sitting side by side on the upper bench, their oars extending through two separate holes in the outrigger planking, one above the other, with the thalamite sitting on a lower bench, behind them and between them to give him space to swing his oar. The recent construction of a full-sized trireme by the Greek Navy has dissolved many uncertainties over the trireme's propulsion under oars.

But how the rowers were actually seated is of less importance than the design and structural details of the trireme herself. Once again the waterline wales were brought up to a point with the keel to form a decorated sternpost. The stern rose from the keel at an angle of about 70 degrees and curved backwards up to the level of the forecastle, or raised fighting bridge, then rose above it and curved forwards to finish in the *acrostolion* or ornamental decoration. The beak projected about 10 ft (3 m) beyond the stem, reinforced by the thick wales, and formed a three-toothed spur, with the centre tooth longer than the others. This was covered in metal, usually bronze. Above it, but not so long, was a second beak, formed by the upper wales meeting in a point. This, too, was covered in metal, and frequently shaped like a ram's head. The object of the upper ram was to give the *coup de grâce* to an enemy, after she had been pierced by the lower beak.

The trireme was rowed by 31 thranites, 27 zygites and 27 thalamites each side, giving a total of 170 rowers. Five officers and twenty-five petty officers and other specialists made up the total ship's company of 200. In the Greek triremes a few marines, fighting men in heavy armour, were stationed on the deck in battle. The captain had a sort of small deckhouse aft, just forward of the flagstaff. The discovery of the foundations of dry docks at Munychium and Zea give some idea of the overall dimensions of a trireme. The docks measure about 150 by 20 ft (46 by 6 m), and, allowing for a certain amount of spare room at the sides and each end, suggest figures of about 130 ft (40 m) for length, including the ram, and 16 ft (5 m) for beam. One would expect such a vessel to be capable of a maximum speed of around 7 to 8 knots in short bursts with the rowers giving their best. The trireme had two masts, or possibly one mast and a bowsprit steeved at an angle of about 70 degrees to the horizontal and called the *artemon*, but never used sail in battle, both masts being lowered before battle was joined.

Over the course of a series of wars fought on the Mediterranean against increasingly powerful enemies, the Greeks discovered that they needed something stronger and heavier than the bireme, if they were to retain their control of the sea. Who it was that designed and built the first trireme is unknown. Thucydides suggests that it was the Corinthians, and that they used them in battle in 664 B.C. He may have been referring to some other form of warship, possibly using oars on three levels instead of two – his text is imprecise on this point – since 664 B.C. seems a very early date for the full development of this most famous of Greek warships. Much of the strength of the trireme was attributable to the solid outrigger. If we date this innovation sometime during the sixth century B.C., as is generally done, we arrive at a date for the first appearance of the trireme which is about a hundred years later than that given by Thucydides.

The arrangement of rowers in the trireme has been a matter for argument for centuries. Unhappily, there is no illustration or drawing to settle the doubts. We know that the three banks of rowers had separate names: the rowers of the top bank were known as 'thranites', and the length of their oars has been put at 14 ft (4·3 m); the middle bank rowers were 'zygites', pulling an oar 10½ ft (3·2 m) long; and the lower bank rowers were 'thalamites', and the length of their oars was 7½ ft (2·3 m). How their benches were arranged is not known for certain, but one popular theory, put forward after considerable research by Dr. Graser, is that they were con-

Greek trireme
(c. 480 B.C.)

Length 130 ft (39·6 m) *Beam* 16 ft (4·9 m) *Complement* 200

The trireme, the capital ship of her day, was developed from the bireme during the sixth century B.C. Her principal weapon was the long ram projecting about 10 ft (3 m) from her bow. This was formed by bringing together the thick wales which ran down either side of the vessel to meet the keel. In this way the shock of ramming an enemy could be absorbed by the whole structure of the ship, not simply the keel. In addition to her 170 rowers, she had one or two masts with square sails, used when the wind was astern but lowered when the trireme went into battle. The most famous engagement in which triremes took part was the battle of Salamis in 480 B.C.

The reconstruction is of a Greek trireme of about the time of Salamis. The side is cut away to show the raised platform, or *kakastroma*, running the length of the ship. The diagram shows two possible arrangements of rowers.

The battle of Salamis, fought in 480 B.C. against a Persian fleet, much superior in numbers, commanded by Xerxes, saw Greek triremes in action. The Greek fleet was commanded by Themistocles and he had drawn up his ships in the bay of Eleusis in the island of Salamis in the Aegean Sea. There they were trapped by the Persians who closed the two channels leading into the bay. It was the narrowness of these channels, combined with the great number of Persian ships, which led to the Persian defeat. Unable to use their numerical superiority in such restricted waters, and too impetuous in attack they jammed themselves in the narrow entrances, presenting a perfect target for the Greek triremes. After some hours of battle, over 200 Persian warships had been destroyed for the loss to the Greeks of about 40 vessels. Aeschylus, in his play *The Persae*, compares the Persian fleet with tuna fish, the traditional method of catching them being to drive them into shallow water where they could be killed with any available weapon.

Aeschylus was serving as a marine on board one of the Greek triremes and his words are those of an eyewitness. In Gilbert Murray's translation there is a graphic description of the battle, given by the messenger who brought the news of the defeat to Xerxes's mother:

'The first rammer was a Greek
which sheared away a great Sidonian's crest;
then close, one on another, charged the rest.
At first the long-drawn Persian line was strong
and held; but in those narrows such a throng
was crowded, ship to ship could bring no aid.
Nay, with their own bronze-fanged beaks they
      made
destruction; a whole length of oars one beak
would shatter; and with purposed art the Greek
ringed us outside, and pressed, and struck;
      and we –
our oarless hulls went over, till the sea
could scarce be seen, with wrecks and corpses
      spread.

One of the mysteries of Greek, also of Roman and Carthaginian, warships is the evolution of the trireme into the quadrireme and quinquireme. Until comparatively recently, the doctrine of 'one oar, one man' was widely accepted, and these vessels were visualized as rowing four and five banks of oars. But, on this theory, there are records of ships built with up to 16 banks of oars, which is plainly ridiculous. There is even an account of a 40-banked vessel, a *tesseraconteres* built for Ptolemy Philopator, which is even more ridiculous, if we accept the 'one oar, one man' theory. The upper rower in a *tesseraconteres* would be pulling an oar 53 ft (16 m) long (the longest oar used in the British navy is 18 ft (5·5 m)).

Today it is considered that the terms quadrireme and quinquireme referred to the number of men on each set of three oars. For example, two thranites, two zygites, and one thalamite on each set would make the ship a quinquireme.

These vessels were, of course, larger and more unwieldy than the trireme, and required larger crews. Ptolemy's *tesseraconteres* was said to be 400 ft (122 m) long with a beam of 50 ft (15 m), needing 4,000 oarsmen without counting the fighting men. It seems most unlikely that this immense ship ever existed, except in Ptolemy's imagination. Not unnaturally, perhaps, there came a revulsion against the big warship on the grounds of the expense of building and upkeep, and, even more, her unwieldiness, and by the third century B.C. the bireme was coming back into fashion.

Inevitably, as trade developed in the Mediterranean, there were other powers ready to challenge the supremacy of Greece. Carthage was always a thorn in her flesh, and Rome was growing into a major power, ready to expand east and west as the number of her legions grew. Although essentially a land power, Rome quickly discovered that she needed control of the seas if she was to keep her expanding empire. This lesson was learnt during the First Punic War when, in 269 B.C., the Carthaginians sent a fleet to invest the island of Sicily and threaten the coastal towns and ports into quick surrender. Fortunately for the Romans, a Carthaginian quinquireme was wrecked on the Italian coast and revealed the secrets of her construction. Using her as a model, the Senate in Rome decided to build a fleet of 100 quinquiremes and 20 triremes, the ships being built by Greek shipwrights who had settled in Italy. Always a methodical race, the Romans constructed rowing benches on scaffolding ashore and trained teams of rowers to be ready to man the ships as soon as they were launched.

Being soldiers rather than sailors, the Romans built their warships large and heavy, adapted more for a military style of action than conventional naval warfare. Not for them the swift galley relying on its ram to pierce an enemy's hull; not for them the *dickplous*, the sudden charge on a given signal to break through the enemy line of battle, wheeling right and left after breaking the line to take the enemy galleys in the rear; or the *periplous*, a move to outflank the enemy's line and fold it up on itself. The Romans preferred a straight fight, using marines as soldiers to capture enemy ships by boarding. For this purpose Roman triremes were fitted with a gangway 36 ft (11 m) long, hinged below and held vertical against the mast. Forcing their way alongside an enemy, they would let go the gang-

Above: First century B.C. Roman galley with two banks of oars. This was probably a quadrireme or larger ship. (Relief from Praeneste)

Right: Roman galley on a coin from the second century B.C.

For this purpose, the number of marines on board was increased from 40 to 120 or more.

This type of military warfare at sea was immensely successful at first, possibly because of its novelty and the unpreparedness of the Carthaginian fleet to counter such tactics, and at the battle of Mylae, fought in 260 B.C., Gaius Duillius shattered the Carthaginians, sinking or capturing more than forty of the enemy. A column adorned with the beakheads of the captured Carthaginian ships was erected in Rome to celebrate this.

Mylae set the pattern of Roman maritime dominance of the western Mediterranean, and by the end of the First Punic War there was no other navy to challenge her. She relied on the big galley, massively constructed, to maintain her power, accepting the loss of speed and manoeuvrability as of lesser importance than the weight of attack so heavy a galley could mount. When Roman galleys were sent into the eastern Mediterranean to meet the challenge of Philip of Macedon, they established control of those waters, too, in spite of the hordes of pirates who attacked at every opportunity. It took a naval

way from the masthead and it would fall across the enemy ship, a spike at the end, known as a *corvus*, holding it firmly on the enemy's deck like a grappling iron. The gangway was 4 ft (1·2 m) wide and across it poured the marines, armoured and carrying the Roman short sword.

Above: Part of the hull of a huge Roman ship raised from Lake Nemi, showing the beams that supported the lower deck.

force of more than 500 ships and a military force of many legions to clear the sea and hold the shores for Rome, but Pompey, in a masterly campaign which was begun in 67 B.C., achieved it.

The dominance of the extremely heavy warship, however, was not to last. Rome was torn apart by a struggle for internal power with Octavian's bid to become emperor. He selected Agrippa as his commander at sea, and at the battle of Actium, fought in 31 B.C., Agrippa was able to demonstrate that victory did not always go to the bigger, heavier ship. Mark Antony's ships were considerably heavier and slower than those of Agrippa, and that day proved that the relatively small, fast ship had little to fear from sheer weight, if handled intelligently. Agrippa concentrated not so much on ramming his enemies as running alongside their galleys and shearing off their oars.

Actium, having disposed of the challenge to Octavian, set the seal on Rome's naval control throughout the entire Mediterranean. For the next two and a half centuries, Roman galleys kept the peace at sea and Roman merchant ships carried the bulk of seaborne trade. In 1932 a chance came to examine Roman ships, when the Lago di Nemi in the Alban hills was drained. In the mud at the bottom of the lake lay two enor-

mous hulls, one of a warship and one of a merchant ship. They were dragged up out of the mud onto the shore and a museum constructed around them. The warship was about 235 ft (72 m) long with a beam of 110 ft (33·5 m). These dimensions suggest that it could have been a '15-banked' galley, or a trireme with 15 rowers for each set of oars. There was a recognizable ram, and the traditional inward curve of the bow was still intact, with part of the starboard outrigger and the starboard steering oar. But the main interest of the warship hull lay in the construction, which indicated a very considerable skill in building, with a keel, keelson, frames very closely set, and the strakes of the hull planking pinned to each other and attached to the frames. The underwater part of the hull was sheathed in lead, an innovation in shipbuilding usually dated several centuries later. The ship almost certainly had two decks, a lower deck on which the rowers sat, supported by pillars mounted on bilge stringers at about waterline level, and an upper deck near the top of the frames. No trace of the upper deck remained when the ships were recovered, but the frames rose so high above the lower deck that a second must surely have been included.

The merchant ship, about 240 ft (73 m) long with a beam of 47 ft (14 m) had the lines of typical Mediterranean trading vessels. The hull which was recovered was less complete than that of the warship and there were no clues as to her rig, but

Above: Relief at Ostia showing Roman merchant ship with twin triangular topsails, entering harbour.

there is other evidence that the two-mast rig (main and *artemon*) was being supplemented about this time by a third mast aft, eventually to be called a 'mizen'. A contemporary account of a Roman grain ship gives her size as about 180 by 45 by 44 ft (55 by 13·7 by 13·4 m), somewhat stubbier than the Lake Nemi merchant ship. But that Roman merchant ships were large by the standards of the time is well documented: the ship in which St. Paul was wrecked is recorded as carrying 276 passengers and crew.

There are a number of contemporary illustrations of Roman merchant ships, the most interesting and detailed being that found at Ostia. They are thought to be ships of the third century A.D., and the illustration shows two triangular topsails set on the mast above the square sail. It also shows a strong forestay led to the stemhead and shrouds tensioned through deadeyes. The vessel herself looks broad and deep. She is two-masted, with mainmast and *artemon*, but no sign yet of a mizen. But perhaps more interesting still is the description given by Lucian of a Roman grain ship which he inspected when she put into the port of Piraeus during the second century A.D. 'What a tremendous vessel it was,' he wrote, '120 cubits [180 ft (55 m)] long, as the ship's carpenter told me, and more than 30 cubits [45 ft (14 m)] across the beam, and 29 cubits [44 ft (13 m)] from the deck to the deepest part of the hold. And the height of the mast and the

yard it bore, and the forestays that were necessary to keep it upright. And how the stern rose in a graceful curve ending in a gilt goosehead, in harmony with the equal curve of the bow and the forepost with its picture of Isis, the goddess who had given the ship her name. All was unbelievable: the decoration, paintings, red topsail, the anchors with their windlasses, and the cabins in the stern. The crew was like an army. They told me she could carry enough grain to satisfy every mouth in Athens for a whole year. And the whole fortune of the ship is in the hands of a little old man who moves the great rudders with a tiller no thicker than a stick. They pointed him out to me, a little, white-haired, almost bald fellow: I think they called him Heron.'

Just why the two ships discovered in the mud in 1932 were built on a lake high up in the Alban hills is a mystery. One opinion is that they were constructed as playthings of the Roman court. But, be that as it may, they revealed a great deal about the skill of contemporary Roman shipwrights in building large ships. It is a pity that the upperworks of the galley did not survive, since they might have revealed the reason for the one or two small wooden turrets, usually painted to resemble stone, which the Romans erected on the decks of their galleys. The museum for the two ships built on the shore of Lake Nemi was destroyed by fire during World War II, and the

Right: Two-banked *liburnian* depicted in a mosaic at Palazzo Barberini at Palestrina.

Far right: Roman shipwright shaping a rib before inserting it into the completed shell – a reversal of modern practice.

Below right: Trajan's Column showing the Emperor standing in the stern of a trireme flanked by two *liburnians*.

ships perished in the flames before the full extent of their secrets could be revealed. An attempt to date them on the basis of the earliest Roman coins discovered in them suggests that they were built during the reign of Caligula, the latest coin found being one of A.D. 164.

As the Roman empire consolidated and expanded, new forms of armament were provided for the heavier galleys. Catapults to sling stone and lead were erected on the upper deck, and it is recorded that the catapults of a large galley could throw up to half a ton of lead a distance of 600 to 700 yards. Greek fire (a mixture of naphtha, sulphur and pitch) was another new weapon. It was blown through long copper tubes with ends shaped like the jaws of savage monsters, or launched by hand by the marines onto the decks of enemies, as a sort of hand grenade.

Although the Romans continued to build large galleys for their fleet, the lessons of Actium were not ignored. At the same time they developed a smaller, faster galley, based on a design first produced in the Adriatic, to protect their merchant ships from the incessant attacks of pirates. This vessel was known as a *liburnian*, originally pulling 25 oars in a single bank on each side. But in a later version, illustrated in a mosaic in the Palazzo Barberini at Palestrina, she had become a bireme, with two banks of oars. A larger version, known as a *dromon*, built to a length of 150 ft (46 m) and pulling 50 oars a side in two banks, was armed with catapults and fighting towers for the marines. Smaller, and possibly built for reconnaissance or as a fleet lookout, was the *galea*, though she was heavily enough armed to hold her own should need arise.

As Rome expanded her empire through north-west Europe, Roman ships penetrated northern waters. A fleet of warships was stationed in the English Channel during much of the Roman occupation of Britain; Roman merchant ships brought supplies and reliefs to the legions that held the land in sway. There was no competition for control of these seas as yet: northern European peoples were not yet awake to the wonders and riches that lay beyond the seas. Nor does it appear, when the northerners did at last begin to carve a way to new lands across the sea, that the Roman ships which they had seen had any influence on local design and construction. Development was entirely indigenous to the region, designs emanating from the Baltic out into the North Sea and more distant waters.

The Birth of Navigation

Navigation (a term derived from the Latin *navis*, a ship, and *agere*, to drive) is the art of taking a ship from one place on the earth's surface to another by sea, safely, speedily and efficiently. Today it is done by means of charts, compasses, logs (to record a ship's speed and distance run), accurate sextants (to measure the angle of heavenly bodies), automatic sounding machines to gauge the depth of the water, broadcast time signals, and a host of electronic aids, which give the navigator his exact position on the surface of the globe; the first navigators in history had none of these aids. It took hundreds of years for the first seaman to evolve as simple an implement as a lead and line to measure the depth of water under his ship. Usually, in this very early period of travel by sea, ships always sailed by day, and within sight of land, hugging the coast, then anchoring as night fell. When, occasionally, they were blown · out to sea beyond sight of the shore, they were lost until they had the good fortune to make a landfall somewhere else. We read that, even as late as A.D. 61, when the ship in which St. Paul was voyaging from Caesarea to Rome was driven out to sea in a storm, no one on board knew where the ship was until the wind blew the ship to Malta and safety.

It is thought that it was the Phoenicians, during their voyages in the first millennium B.C., who first learned how to use the stars, or, at least, one of them, in plotting a course at night, though it is possible that the knowledge came from Eastern navigators. The Greek poet Aratus, writing about the constellation of the Little Bear, says, 'By her guidance the men of Sidon steer the straightest course,' 'the men of Sidon', of course, being Phoenicians. *Ursae Minoris*, the Little Bear, contains *Polaris*, the Pole Star, which always lies to the north, and this knowledge gave the Phoenicians a fixed point of reference by night. They knew, too, that at local noon the sun always lay due south, and this was especially useful knowledge when combined with another navigational aid – the wind-rose.

The wind-rose was a circular card, in the shape of a compass card, on which were drawn the directions of certain named winds. It is not known who first introduced it, but it is certain that by the time of Homer, around 900 B.C., Greek seamen used four particular winds, which blew from the four quarters, as their principal means of navigation. These were Boreas, the north wind, Euros, the east wind, Notos, the south wind, and Zephinos, the west wind. Later, as voyages became longer and a greater degree of accuracy was needed to reach a given destination, four more winds were added. After one of the original four had been moved through 45°, the eight winds were (clockwise from the north) Boreas, Kaikias, Apeliotes, Euros, Notos, Lips, Zephuros and Skiros. By reference to the sun at noon or the Pole Star by night, a navigator would identify which wind was blowing, and shape his course accordingly.

The eight wind system was adopted by the Romans, who gave their own names to the winds which became Tramontana, Greco, Levante, Sirocco, Mezzodi, Garbino (later changed to Affricone), Ponente and Maestro. The system was later expanded to twelve winds, then sixteen, and finally thirty-two.

It is surprising that, in a developing world where more and more trade was being carried by sea and men were inquiring more and more into the shape and nature of the earth, very few attempts were made to map the sea. Homer, in his poems, envisaged the world as an immense disc surrounded by a broad, flowing river known as Okeanus. The earliest known map, moulded in clay and now in the British Museum, dated about 700 B.C., follows Homer's model, with Babylon at the centre of the disc. The earliest Greek maps share the disc concept, though they have Delphi at the centre. Later Greek geographers, noting the overall shape of the Mediterranean, thought that the world must be longer along the east-west axis than the north-south, and so drew the earth as a rectangle, with a prime meridian and a prime latitude passing through Rhodes, then considered to be the maritime centre of the world.

But even before these Greek geographers got to work, the idea that the earth was a sphere had already taken hold. Pythagoras, in about 580 B.C., was the first man to grasp this. Using the Pythagorean theory, a Greek from Cyrene in Libya, named Eratosthenes,

Above: Ptolemy, the Greek mathematician, astronomer and father of cartography.

set out in 200 B.C. to discover the circumference of the earth by calculation. He measured the length of the shadow of a gnomon, cast by the sun in Alexandria at the summer solstice, and, taking the distance due south to Aswan, on the Tropic of Cancer, where the sun is directly overhead (this distance was known from the existing cadastral surveys of the Nile valley), he arrived at a figure for the circumference of the earth which differs by less than 4 per cent from the modern one.

On the basis of this calculation Eratosthenes constructed a new world map, using meridians of longitude and parallels of latitude, adjusted to pass through places of importance, such as Meroe (in Abyssinia, the farthest known point to the south) and the Pillars of Hercules (the farthest known place to the west). These meridians and parallels were based on Rhodes.

Eratosthenes was followed by Marinus of Tyre, who in the first century A.D. began drawing charts for seamen. His meridians and parallels were equally spaced, though he still used Rhodes for the intersection of his prime meridian and prime parallel.

There was, therefore, by this time a considerable body of knowledge about the real shape of the earth and sea, at least in the Mediterranean and in Arabian waters. Where the great difficulty lay, so far as charts for navigators at sea were concerned, was in accurately translating a curved surface (the earth) into a flat surface (a chart). This problem was solved by Ptolemy, whom we recognise today as the real father of cartography. Although born a Greek, he lived and worked in Alexandria, as a mathematician and

Above: The earliest map of the world with the oceans and Babylon at its centre.

astronomer. In about 130 A.D. he evolved a simple conic projection whereby the features of a curved surface could, with reasonable accuracy, be projected onto a flat surface. Later he evolved a more sophisticated method of doing it with his equal-area projection. Using this projection he drew a map of the world, showing it as contained within 180 degrees of longitude, from the Canary Islands in the west to China in the east. The whole of the Mediterranean Sea, Red Sea and Persian Gulf are shown with fair accuracy, although he portrays Africa as a huge continent bending round to the east and finally joining up with China to enclose the Indian Ocean as a vast lake.

Only in one respect did Ptolemy really fail: for his world maps he accepted a figure, given by Poseidonius who lived in the first century B.C., of 18,000 miles for the earth's circumference, instead of the earlier and much more accurate measurement of Eratosthenes. This made one degree of latitude, the basis of all measurement of distance at sea, equivalent to 50 miles, instead of 60 miles as it should be, and led to considerable distortion.

Left: Ptolemy's world map drawn in 130 A.D. His works, rediscovered at Constantinople in 1400, formed a basis for the rebirth of ocean mapping in the two succeeding centuries, stimulated by the discoveries of navigators like Columbus, Diaz and da Gama.

Chapter Two
The Ship in Northern Waters

There are, in Norway, Sweden and Denmark, rock carvings of boats which, if not stretching so far back in time as those of Egypt, date back at least to the Stone Age. Some of them closely resemble the oldest Greek representations of boats, and this similarity has led to a theory that Mediterranean practice and design spread northwards through Europe and that this was how the boat found its way to northern waters.

Nothing could be further from the truth. The oldest Scandinavian rock carvings date back at least to 2000 B.C., and it is beyond normal belief that Mediterranean boat and ship design could have penetrated so far into the then-unknown world by that date. If it had done so, northern Europe could not possibly have remained unknown to the Greek geographers of 1,800 years later. It would seem perfectly reasonable to assume that the same solutions to the same problems were found in other parts of the world at the same time as in the Mediterranean.

The earliest Scandinavian rock carvings give no indication of the material from which the vessels were made, but it seems most likely that they were constructed of hides stitched across a wooden frame, somewhat in the manner of the modern Irish curragh. The frame is shown in the carvings as extending a little beyond the hull at bow and stern, probably to act as carrying handles for taking the boats across land, for they were longer than a curragh and less handy for carrying on the shoulders of the crew as is still the fashion in Ireland. But many of the later Bronze Age carvings show a sort of keel which projects appreciably beyond bow and stern, curved upwards at the forward end. The general opinion is that what at first looks to be a form of keel was, in fact, a runner, to keep the hull clear of the ground when it was hauled across land. This would imply that boats were by that time

Left: Warriors on their way to Valhalla by ship, on eighth century stone, Gotland, Sweden.
Above right: Late Bronze Age carving showing vessel with projections similar to the Hjortspring boat.
Right: Modern Irish curragh made with hides or canvas.

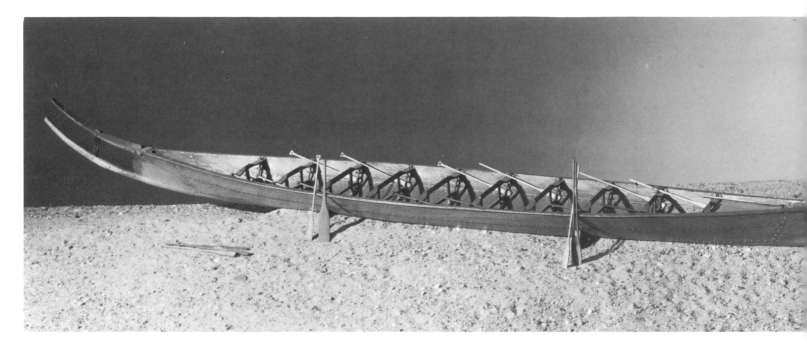

Above: A model of the Hjortspring boat, showing projecting runners at bow and stern.

Above right: Model of the Kvalsund boat, showing keel and overlapping planking.

Right: Crisscross lines on the sail of a ship on one of the Gotland stones may represent strips of leather reinforcing the linen sail.

made with wooden hulls: it would not be possible to haul a hide boat across the ground without damaging it, and it would have to be carried.

This opinion was vindicated when a boat was found buried in a bog on a farm called Hjortspring on the Danish Island of Als in south Jutland. This boat was constructed between A.D. 200 and 300, of wood, and is about 44 ft (13 m) long, with a beam of nearly 7 ft (2 m). Her hull consists of five overlapping planks, 20 in (51 cm) wide and $\frac{5}{8}$ inch thick, forming a rounded shape, with projections left on the inside of the planks to which thin ribs were bound. At the bow and stern these planks are stitched to two shaped endpieces, cut from solid blocks of wood, with the upper parts projecting with a long, gently upward curving sternpiece and stempiece. The most interesting part of the construction is a long piece of wood, which acts as a keel or runner, fixed to the outside of the bottom plank and extended some distance beyond the bow and stern. A short, vertical piece of wood connects each end of this runner to the projecting stempiece and sternpiece, obviously to give added strength to the whole structure. The Hjortspring boat had space for ten thwarts and accommodated twenty paddlers. It was presumably steered by a paddle over the stern as there is no fitting for the usual steering oar. From her long, slim shape, with a length-to-beam ratio of more than 6 to 1, it is unlikely that she was built for trade; more likely she was intended for raiding voyages against neighbouring settlements.

Another form of Scandinavian boat building was based on the dugout. Several hundred have been found, all over the Scandinavian countries, and, though we are apt to look on the dugout as one of the most primitive types of boat, the

Scandinavians used it as a model for larger vessels. Examples of dugouts with outriggers in the form of horizontal bilge-keels, of two or more dugouts joined to form a double hull, of dugouts extended by fixing planks to their sides have all been recovered. One discovered at Bjorke in Sweden is a shallow, hollowed-out trunk, tapering towards each end, to which are fastened two overlapping sides. The shaped bow and sternpiece are attached to the trunk and sides with iron rivets. As in the Hjortspring boat, the inside of the dugout and its sides have been left with natural longitudinal projections to which the ribs of the boat were stitched. This boat, which has been dated around A.D. 100, is nearly 24 ft (7·3 m) long, and the hull takes the form of a shallow curve, not unlike the cross-section of a flat dish.

The shallow cross-section, with a considerable beam in relation to the depth, was a feature of most early Scandinavian types. Apart from the longitudinal runner found in the earliest boats, which may also have acted as a form of keel, the Scandinavian boats were keel-less, though in many cases the bottom plank of the hull, running down the centre of the structure, was thicker than the others. Another universal feature was the overlapping planking, known today as 'clinker' construction; whereas in contemporary Mediterranean vessels – and indeed for many centuries to come in that landlocked sea – the hull planking was invariably set edge to edge ('carvel' construction as we call it today).

The first indication of a true keel as an integral part of the hull construction can be found in one of two boats found at Kvalsund in Norway in 1920. There is the same basic shallow hull section, but the bottom plank has a short, downwards-pointing, vertical extension which would certainly act on the water as a short keel and give a bit more stability to the vessel. For the rest, the hull planking is carried appreciably upwards at bow and stern to form a distinct canoe shape, the earliest example of the actual planking being used to give this pronounced sheer at both ends. This boat is about 60 ft (18·3 m) long, with a length-to-beam ratio of about 6 to 1, and is estimated to date from the sixth century A.D.

Unlike Mediterranean vessels of similar dates, there is no indication of masts and sails in any of the early Scandinavian boats, and it seems clear that this method of propulsion did not come to northern Europe before about the seventh century. Scandinavian craft were all propelled by paddlers until about the fourth century, by which time we begin to get indications of oars pivoted on the gunwale, rowed by men sitting on thwarts and facing aft. Some earlier carvings on rocks and stones show something like a tree growing out of the boat amidships, and this is thought to show that leafy branches were used as temporary sails when the wind served.

Sometime around the seventh or eighth century, if we can believe the evidence of the Gotland pictorial stones, a new type of construction was introduced in Scandinavia, where the bow and stern formed almost a right angle with the keel, the hull planking tapering in to join a distinct stempiece and sternpiece. It would be reasonable to assume that this new hull form coincided with the introduction of a mast and sail, for the longer keel and pointed ends would provide a more efficient and stable sailing form than the shallow, keel-less hulls of earlier boats.

The Gotland stones show a sail set from a short central mast, with a yard at top and bottom and with sheets led to bridles on the lower yard, one each side of the mast. The sail itself, we know, was originally made from a coarse, homespun material which became unduly baggy when wet. For this reason it was usually reinforced with strips of leather, which is why the stone carvings show the sails with a diamond pattern of diagonal lines.

This type of hull was almost certainly designed for trade; the Scandinavian fighting, or raiding, ship was still a long, slim boat, propelled by oars, the rowers becoming the fighting men during an action. At this stage of development this vessel was the forerunner of the fighting longship with which the Scandinavians were later to rampage over most of north-western Europe, though as yet it had no sail and relied entirely on oars for propulsion. The sail trading ship also carried rowers, but few in number, and they can have been used only for short coastal voyages. The merchant ships were completely undecked, carrying their cargo on the boat's floor amidships, clear of the rowing thwarts forward and

Below: The hull lines of a longship, exemplified by the burial ship found at Gokstad, Oslo Fjord.

Bottom: The Oseberg ship showing her excellent state of preservation; note steering oar in the foreground.

aft. They mounted a single steering oar on the starboard quarter of the ship, the helmsman operating it by means of a short tiller set at right angles to the oar.

The Viking era of Norwegian history opens in about A.D. 800 and lasts for about five centuries. It was characterized by the famous longship, and an early example, or prototype, is the ship discovered on Gokstad Farm, near Sandefiord, in 1880. She was found in a 15 ft (4·6 m) burial mound of blue clay and was well preserved. But, although built on longship lines, her overall length of 76 ft (23 m), beam of 16 ft (5 m) and relatively high freeboard of 6 ft (1·8 m) show her to be too small for use as a war or raiding ship. Bows, stern and keel are each fashioned from a solid block of timber, and she has sixteen strakes of clinker planking fixed together with rivets. The caulking is of tarred rope, and the strakes are lashed to the ribs of the vessel by means of cleats, or projections, on the timbers. She carried a 40-ft (12·2 m) pine mast on which was set a square sail with a spread of about 16 ft (5 m). The hull is pierced for sixteen oars a side, and, though there are no built-in thwarts,

the holes for the oars are too low down for the rowers to have stood to their oars. It has been assumed that they sat on their sea chests, or on removable benches. The normal steering oar is fixed to the hull on the starboard quarter, and she exhibits the traditional high bows and stern of the longship.

The Gokstad ship is dated at about A.D. 900,

and when she was unearthed she had thirty-two overlapping shields on each side, the Norse feature beloved of all illustrators of Viking longships. These shields were in fact decorative only, or used in harbour for recognition purposes, and would never have been arrayed along the gunwales at sea. That they were found in the ship buried at Gokstad was almost certainly because she was furnished in full state as a burial ship.

That the ship was seaworthy was proved in 1893 when a replica was sailed across the Atlantic by Captain Magnus Andersen, to be put on show at the Chicago World's Fair held to commemorate the four hundredth anniversary of Columbus's discovery of America. It is strange that this particular ship should be at Chicago to honour Columbus's feat, for it was in a longship of similar construction, though larger, that Leif Ericsson may have made his voyage to the New World nearly 500 years earlier.

An earlier version of the longship – or, like the Gokstad ship, a direct prototype of the longship – is the famous Oseberg ship, discovered on Oseberg Farm, near Tonsberg, Norway, in 1904. Like the Gokstad ship, she was found in a burial mound and is remarkable for the beautiful decorative carving on her bow and stern. Her general constructional details are similar to those of the Gokstad ship and stand as a monument to the skill and precision of Norse shipbuilders of the period. She is reckoned to have been built around a century earlier than the Gokstad ship, around A.D. 800. The decorative carvings may have been added later.

She is smaller than the Gokstad ship, with an overall length of 70 ft (21·3 m), was built of oak and was pierced to row fifteen oars a side, again with the rowers probably sitting on their sea chests. She had a mast, a single square sail, and the usual steering oar operated with a short tiller. Again, she was not a warship but was probably a *karfi*, or *karv*, a vessel built light enough to be used on estuaries and lakes and manhandled along rivers.

That it was not only in Scandinavia, but also in other countries in north-western Europe that the ship was evolving is proved by the discovery of the English royal burial ship unearthed at Sutton Hoo, near Ipswich. She, like her Scandinavian sisters of the same date, was propelled only by oars, although mast and sail had been used in England for some centuries. The Sutton Hoo ship is dated at about A.D. 650. On the other side of the English Channel, in the early ninth century, the Emperor Charlemagne established naval forces at Boulogne and Ghent to check the

Above: The Oseberg ship during excavation of the burial mound in 1904.

Right: Detail of the carving on the stern.

ravages of the piratical Norsemen, who were now using their longships to overrun western Europe in search of women, slaves and plunder.

As has been seen from the construction of the Gokstad and Oseberg ships, Scandinavian shipbuilders were supremely skilled in their trade. As Norse eyes turned more and more seawards, the time came to build larger versions of these ships, able to face the longer voyages and steeper seas associated with more distant targets. The Norsemen invented a form of ship measurement to describe the varying sizes of their longships, based on the *rum*, which was the name given to the space between two adjacent crossbeams. Each *rum* contained one thwart on which sat a pair of rowers, one each side, and the longships varied between the *skuta*, a ship of about 15 *rum* to the *skeid* or *drakkar*, of 32 *rum*. Occasionally larger longships were built: Olaf Tryggvason had his famous *Ormrinn Langi*, which would be translated as *Long Serpent*, built to a size of 34 *rum*; Harald Hardrada's *Buza* was 35 *rum*; and King Haakon's *Kristsuden*, built about 1260, was 37 *rum*. The anglicized form of *rum* is 'room', and when, as frequently occurs in English writings, a longship is described as 'of 32 rooms', it means a 32-*rum* ship.

We know a great deal about these famous ships from the writings of the skalds, who composed the sagas in which so much of Norse history is enshrined. Of the *Long Serpent*, probably the best known of all Norse longships, Snorre, the skald, writes that 'of all the ships in Norway she was the best made and at the greatest cost', and describes how, when she was rowed away after battle, she looked like 'the flutter of an eagle's wings'. She was built by a shipwright named Torberg who introduced a considerable improvement in the fitting of stems and sternposts to the keels. Olaf Tryggvason was one of the great heroes of Norway, finally losing his life at the battle of Svolde in 1000; and his magnificent longship, which was the last of the Norwegian fleet to remain afloat in that decisive battle, is as famous in Scandinavian history as its owner.

By about the year 800, Norse and Danish longships were proving to all western Europe that, as well as being supremely well built and magnificent seaboats, they were a formidable seaborne foe. The Vikings ranged across the North Sea and down the English Channel to the coast of western France and northern Spain, raiding, plundering, and holding to ransom as they went. At first they met no opposition: no other north European country had ships which could match them for speed or manoeuvrability, or indeed possessed any sort of warship at all. But as the years passed, and French, English and Scottish kings realized that the only answer to the intolerable raiding and plundering of their nations was to meet the raiders at sea instead of waiting for them to come ashore and trying to engage them with land forces, some navies were built to oppose them, consisting almost entirely of copies of the existing Norse longships. The raiders' answer was to raise their freeboard a foot or two with additional longitudinal strakes, so as to enable their crews to fire their arrows and throw their darts downwards into any ship that tried to resist them. But it was this increase in freeboard that made possible, and perhaps even inspired, the longer voyages of the longships into the stormy waters of the northern Atlantic. Another development which made this possible was the invention of the *beitass*, a long pole, with one end held inside the ship in a chock abreast the mast and the other end secured to the weather leech of the square sail, holding it boomed out to windward. The use of a *beitass* enabled a ship to sail much closer to the wind, and so for the first time in northern waters a vessel could make way through the water to windward without having to depend on her rowers whenever the wind blew from before the beam.

The northern voyages began in 984 with Eric the Red, who fled to Iceland from Norway to escape trial on a charge of murder. Hearing from another Norse trader that he had sighted land still further to the westward he decided to investigate, verified its existence, and gave it the name of Greenland. Returning to Iceland he persuaded a group of local inhabitants to join him in setting up a colony there, and in the summer of 985 set sail with them to Greenland, rounded Cape Farewell, and landed in Ericsfjord, near the present Julianehaab, where he founded the settlement of Brattahlid.

Eric the Red had a son, Leif Ericsson, who in 999 returned to Norway, visited the Court of Olaf Tryggvason, and obtained from him a commission to proclaim Christianity in Greenland, returning there the following year. According to Norse sagas, and particularly the *Flatey Book*, a trader named Biarni Heriulfsson had been blown off course during a voyage to Greenland and had sighted land to the south-west, but had not investigated it. Leif Ericsson decided to discover whether there was any truth in this report, and in 1001 left Greenland on a voyage to the south-west. He claimed that he discovered the land and went ashore at places he named Helluland (now believed to be Baffin Island), Markland (probably Labrador), and Vinland (thought to be Newfoundland). At Vinland he reported finding self-sown wheat, vines and 'mosur' wood. Recently, these have been tentatively identified by Professor S. E. Morison as lyme grass, the wild red currant or mountain cranberry, and the white, or canoe, birch, all of which grow wild and prolifically in Newfoundland. Nor was this the full extent of longship voyages. Sagas of the same period also describe voyages of Viking fleets to Barcelona, Pisa, Rome, even Constantinople, during the ninth century.

If we can believe the saga of the *Flatey Book* — and most of the sagas have at least a foundation in fact — the first landing on the continent of America took place nearly 500 years before the great voyage of Columbus. But be that as it may, there is no doubt whatever that regular voyages to Iceland and Greenland were well within the compass of Norse ships: a tribute to the skill of their shipwrights and the soundness of their design and construction, for even at this date such ships probably had no continuous deck, but were open craft, or possibly half-decked, superbly built with long, flowing lines and manned by men who were seamen to their fingertips.

Viking longship
(c. A.D. 1000)

Length 150 ft (45·7 m) *Beam* 20 ft (6·1 m)
Complement 180

This longship is based on the famous *Visunden*, or *Ox*, built at Nidaros in Norway in 1026 for King Olaf Haraldsson, later known as Saint Olaf, patron saint of Norway. The largest longships were called *drakkars*. They were battleships of the Viking period, and the *Visunden*, at 30 pairs of oars, was part of the group of 'super-longships' which numbered only sixteen named craft in the period 995–1263. The longship was ideally suited to raiding, with a shallow draught that allowed her to penetrate a long way up estuaries and rivers. Her sailing performance was far superior to Mediterranean galleys and the square sail could be braced to windward so that she could make progress against the wind.

This reconstruction shows some of her oars shipped. At the masthead is one of the gilt wind vanes which have been found among Viking remains. The diagram shows the arrangement of rowers on one side, and an archer firing from a raised platform on the other.

Above: The remains of a Viking merchant ship, or *knorr*, recovered from the bottom of Roskilde Fjord.

The Scandinavian trading ship of the period was the *knorr*, modelled on the traditional long-ship, but bluffer in build with a length-to-beam ratio more like 3 or 4 to 1 than the 5 or 6 to 1 of the longship. An example of a *knorr* was recently excavated in the Roskilde Fjord, Denmark, and her construction closely follows the general pattern of the longship, with the same rounded bow and stern, and with stempiece and sternpiece carried well up above the level of the side planking. *Knorrs* were of course never built as big as a longship, being probably no more than 50 to 60 feet in overall length, and were almost certainly used only for coastal trading. Like the longship, they were undecked.

The development of the ship in Britain is always said to have started with the coracle, a wickerwork frame covered with animal hide. Small, crude vessels of this type were mentioned by Julius Caesar when reporting on his conquest, but he also mentions, though without specifying a type of ship, that there was maritime trade between Britain and Gaul long before his conquest, so it seems certain that something larger and stronger than a coracle was available. During his conquest of Gaul, Caesar records that British ships co-operated with those of the Veneti, and no coracle could have crossed the English Channel and the Bay of Biscay to reach the mouth of the River Loire, around which the Veneti lived. As the British and the Veneti fought together against the Romans, and as there had been mutual trade between them for several years before that, it seems probably that there was at

least a similarity between their respective ship types, particularly as Caesar describes the ships of the Veneti and not those of Britain, perhaps implying that his description covered them both.

In Caesar's words, the ships of the Veneti 'were built and fitted out in this manner. The bottoms were somewhat flatter than those of our vessels, the better to adapt them to the shallows and to enable them to withstand without danger the ebbing of the tide. Their bows, as likewise their sterns, were very lofty and erect, the better to bear the magnitude of the waves and the violence of the tempests. The hull of each vessel was entirely of oak to resist the shocks and assaults of that stormy sea. The benches for the rowers were made of strong beams of about a foot in breadth, and were fastened with iron bolts about an inch thick. They fastened their anchors with iron chains instead of with cables; and they used skins and a sort of thin, pliant leather for sails, either because they lacked canvas and were ignorant of the art of making sailcloth, or more probably because they believed that canvas sails were not so fit to bear the stress of tempests and the rage and fury of the winds, and to drive ships of that bulk and burden. Our fleet and the vessels of such construction compared as follows, with regard to fighting capabilities. In the matter of manoeuvring power and ready command of oars we had an advantage; but in other respects, looking to the situation of the coast and the stormy weather, all ran very much in their favour; for neither could our ships injure theirs with their prows, so great were the strength and solidity of the hostile craft, nor could we easily throw in our darts, because of the loftiness of the foe above us. And this last feature was also a reason why we found it extremely difficult to grapple with him, and bring him to close action. More than all, when the sea began to get up, and when the enemy was obliged to run before it, he, fearing nothing from the rocks and cliffs when the tide should ebb, could, in addition to weathering the storm better, trust himself more confidently among the shallows.' Nevertheless, Caeser's ships gained a decisive victory and the first navy possessed by Britain was completely destroyed.

The interesting point about this description of Caesar's is that it shows that the mast and sail were being fitted and used in English ships during the years before Christ, in contrast to the case in Scandinavia, where they came into use very much later. Not that this is surprising; it would be much more so if they had not been used. Centuries earlier, Phoenician ships had come to Cornwall and the Scilly Islands to barter for tin from the mines there, and, as we have seen, they had a mast and square sail. As trade developed between England and neighbouring France, the Phoenician practice would surely have been noted and followed. And, although the general standard of Roman shipbuilding was certainly far higher than in Britain, there was at least one type of indigenous vessel which impressed the Romans to the extent of their adopting it for their own purposes: this was the ship which the Romans named the *picta*, a long, fast-sailing pinnace, whose hull was smeared with wax to lessen the skin friction, and which carried a square sail on a centrally placed mast and rowed 10 oars on either side. When this type of craft was added to the Roman navy in the Mediterranean, the sail was dyed light blue and the crew clothed in the same colour, presumably to make the *picta* less conspicuous, since its main purpose in the Roman fleet was reconnaissance. (This is, perhaps, the earliest example of a naval uniform.)

Under Roman stimulus and command the Britons were encouraged to build and maintain

Right: A bronze-gilt engraved wind vane from Heggen, probably fitted originally to the prow of a ship.

Below right: Thirteenth century carving from Bergen of the prows of a Norse fleet, some with animal figureheads and some with vanes like the bronze-gilt one shown above.

small squadrons of warships for anti-piracy duties, and such few records as exist show that these were of sufficient strength to discourage any form of piracy in home waters. Since the pure galley design of the Mediterranean was obviously unsuitable for use in British waters, it is fairly certain that these ships must have been based on the longship, though perhaps improved by the use of Roman shipbuilding techniques.

When the Roman occupation came to an end, and Britain reverted to the tribal system, seaborne defence against piracy and invasion was neglected. In this defenceless state Britain was wide open to the ravages of the Vikings. Saxons, Angles, Danes, Jutes and Norwegians, all came and all conquered, and the Scandinavian longship became a common sight around British shores, though some of them had different local names, such as *ceols* (keels), *hulks* and *aescs*. Their size varied, but the largest were built up to about 50 tons.

The Vikings turned the country into petty kingdoms, each ruled by a Viking leader who proclaimed himself a local king. As they squabbled and fought among themselves, some went under; a few flourished. Those that did began to build themselves fleets of warships powerful and numerous enough to meet and defeat any invaders at sea. One such was Offa, King of Mercia, and we know from the Saxon Chronicle that, because of the size and fighting power of his fleet, he was able to treat with even so great a monarch as Charlemagne on equal terms. Unfortunately the Saxon Chronicle is silent about the size and design of Offa's warships but there can be little doubt that they followed the general pattern of the Scandinavian longship. Local English shipwrightry had not yet developed to a point at which it could make advances on the ships of its adversaries.

Alfred, king of the West Saxons, who by the end of the ninth century had extended and unified his kingdom until in effect it became England, built bigger and better longships to guard his ragged dominion against the continual Danish attacks. In the words of the Saxon Chronicle, his ships 'were full twice as long as the others; some had sixty oars and some had more; they were both swifter and steadier, and also higher than the others; they were shaped neither like the Frisian nor the Danish, but so as it seemed to him that they would be most efficient.' Longer and bigger they may have been, but they still embodied the essential longship design.

English warships were still longships at the time of the Norman conquest of Britain in 1066. So, too, were the warships of William of Normandy, if we can accept the evidence of the Bayeux Tapestry. The representation of the *Mora*, William's flagship, clearly shows the longship design, with a tall prow surmounted by a lion's head. The sail has three vertical stripes, red, brown or yellow, red. It has a single sheet, held by the steersman with one hand – unlikely in a ship as big as the *Mora* – while in the other he holds the *clavus*, or steering oar, operating it

with what looks like a yoke of the sort sometimes seen on small boats today. If we can accept the position of the men in the *Mora* as reasonably accurate, then she had a continuous upper deck. On the same evidence, the transports carrying fighting men and horses are undecked. Again, though it is impossible to be certain, the evidence of the tapestry suggests that the majority of the transports were smaller, and of considerably lighter scantling, than the warships.

Like all his forerunners in the history of England since the Roman conquest, William was really little more than a pirate. In fact, all the kings of England during this period, including the rulers of the petty kingdoms, were pirates, dependent on holding their lands by force. Cymbelene, Egbert, Offa, Alfred, Edward the Elder, Edgar, Canute, Harold – all were essentially pirates who happened, in their day, to command the strongest force of ships in the seas around Britain. Power derived from might, and though some of these piratical monarchs proved to be wise statesmen and capable of enlightened thought and action, in the last analysis their power rested on the number of fighting ships that they could muster. William was, perhaps, the last of the pirate kings of England, but he had learned the lesson well and took care to maintain his fighting fleet while he was consolidating his conquest and establishing his dynasty.

Above: Part of the
Bayeux Tapestry showing
the *Mora*, William of
Normandy's flagship.

In one respect, the old records of the time are strangely silent: all through these years fishing was a considerable industry, but there is no description of the craft which fished the North Sea or more distant waters. It is possible to reconstruct, probably fairly accurately, the sort of vessel which fished in waters where herring, mackerel and pilchards abounded. We know that they had surface nets, and any strongly built open boat of around 30 ft (9 m) in overall length could operate a seine net and remain safely at sea for the two or three days required to reach and return from the fishing grounds. But we also know that the whale was being hunted in northern waters round Greenland and in the Arctic Sea. During his reign Alfred sent two Danish seamen, Oddr and Wulfstan, to discover how far to the north the land of Scandinavia stretched. 'So he sailed north as far as whale hunters ever go, and thence north again three days. Then the land bent east and he sailed along it four days till the land bent south, and he sailed also to the south five days till he came to a great river, up which he dared not sail for it was all inhabited.' This must have been the White Sea and the mouth of the River Dwina. But in what sort of ship did he make this voyage? And in what sort of ships did the whale hunters operate? Probably basically the same kind, but it must have been reasonably large to withstand the gales of northern seas and to carry on board enough provisions for a long voyage, and must have been decked, for crews could not live long in those latitudes without shelter and warmth. In some respects, these voyages to the far north are even more remarkable than the Norse voyages to Iceland and Greenland, which were largely island-hopping voyages by way of the Orkneys, Shetland and the Faroe Islands. It is not difficult to imagine a sturdy decked boat of around 15 to 20 tons accomplishing these voyages into the Arctic Ocean, but it is intriguing to guess at its sail plan. It seems unlikely that the normal square sail, even with a *beitass* rigged, would have answered the purpose. Even when the *beitass* was replaced by a bridle on the leech of the sale and a bowline to haul it taut to the wind, the combination would leave much to be desired for a voyage into the White Sea. Perhaps, even by that early date, something like a lugsail was being developed from the normal crossyard and square sail. There is a description of something that might be a sort of lugsail rig as early as about 1050, but the voyage to the White Sea occurred more than 200 years before that date. Yet, so slowly did new ideas, developments and designs travel in those days that it is not entirely impossible that a form of lugsail had been developed as early as 850, especially for whaling.

Seamen would doubtless have experimented with the cut and setting of their sails in the light of their particular needs. A lugsail would have met the needs of the whalemen, while the normal square sail offered so little manoeuvrability that it cannot have been very suitable for whaling.

Meanwhile, development in the Mediterranean had not been standing still. Rome was still the dominant naval power, her fleet divided into thirteen squadrons under the control of the regents of the various districts, which together made up the great empire of Rome. The fleet was needed not so much to fight wars, for, although there were many small ones, there were few of any importance. The battle of Actium and the defeat of Mark Antony had removed the threat to Octavian's assumption of power in Rome, and, with the possible exception of the 30-year war against the Vandals from A.D. 440 to 470, there were only local wars to test the might of Roman sea power. The first serious challenge to Roman mastery of the Mediterranean came in A.D. 825 with the rise of Mussulman power. But the demands of both the war against the Vandals and the Mussulman threat had a considerable impact on the design of warships.

Actium had demonstrated that, for all its ponderous strength, the heavily built, multi-banked galley could be defeated by the versatile tactics of lighter and more mobile galleys. As has been seen, the lighter galleys used at Actium were based on a design evolved in the Adriatic and known to the Romans as *liburnians*, later further developed into *dromons* of two sizes, one pulling two banks of oars, the other single-banked. In the *Tactica* of the Emperor Leo, descriptions of three types of *dromon* are given, but in effect his first two descriptions refer to one type – the larger of the two main ones – merely specifying small differences in weapons and manning. Nevertheless, in spite of Actium, the heavy galley was still being built because it alone was large enough to mount the relatively new weapons of naval warfare – the catapult and the *corvus*, or boarding bridge.

The Roman war against the Vandals was very largely a land war, but Rome was taking no chances of losing her command of the sea through the heavy financial calls of a land war, and continued to devote a reasonable proportion of the national taxes to the building of warships. A new development was the replacement of the relatively small paddling oars, used on galleys for centuries, by longer sweeps, up to 30 ft (9 m) in length or even longer in some cases. The introduction of the longer oar brought with it the necessity of pivoting it further from the rower, and this was solved by the invention of the *apostis*, a strong external timber running parallel to the gunwale and supported on a light longitudinal framework. This external timber carried the thole pins against which the oars were secured. Because, for reasons of strength, the loom of these long oars had to be thicker than that of the paddling oars and probably too thick for a rower to grasp comfortably in his hands, handles, known as *manetti*, were fixed to the loom, enabling three or four men to be employed on each oar. The rowers were arranged in steps, known as *alla scaloccio*, so that each man was at the right height to operate the oar comfortably. The longer oars provided greater leverage and therefore greater speed was attainable, possibly as much as 8 or 9 knots in short bursts, depending on the strength of the rowers.

The rise of Mussulman sea power in the Mediterranean during the ninth century A.D. created new problems for Rome. By 825 they had captured Crete and Sicily, and were consolidating their hold on the north African coast, which formed the southern boundary of the Mediterranean. To counter this Arab threat, Rome needed even faster galleys with better armament. A small increase in speed was achieved by lengthening the oar to 50 ft (15 m) and increasing the number of rowers to as many as seven. There were no radical developments in warship weaponry, beyond an increase in range and efficiency of the catapult and the further development of the *falcas* (a spar with a curved iron head shaped like a sickle to cut through an enemy's rigging). What was a new development was the provision of protective armour, for the Mussulmans were adept at the use of combustibles, including some mixtures which detonated when thrown on the deck of an enemy ship. Some of the Roman galleys were protected against such combustibles by a leather or felt lining on the upper deck, or thick woollen cloth soaked in vinegar.

The Mussulman fleet introduced a new dimension into naval warfare in the Mediterranean by introducing mixed squadrons of galleys and sailing ships. We have no firm date for the appearance of the lateen rig, but it is certain that, although it first appeared in the western world in the Mediterranean (its name is derived from the word 'latin'), it originated many years earlier among the Arab nations. Although in the lateen rig the sail is still set on a yard, the rig is essentially fore-and-aft, enabling a ship to sail about five points off the wind. It is indeed possible that these mixed Mussulman squadrons incorporated sailing ships rigged lateen-style, for Mussulman and Arab worked in very close co-operation. The Romans did, in fact, themselves build some sailing warships, though not as yet to mix with galleys in a fleet, but rather to attempt to contain the wave of Arab pirates.

More dramatic than the development of the Roman warship was that of the Roman merchant vessel, if size and rig is the criterion. Lucian, it will be remembered, gave the size of a Roman corn ship as 180 feet by 45 feet by 44 feet, but as the Roman era approached its end considerably larger cargo ships were built, particularly for the transport of marble and obelisks to Italy. These were the ships which introduced the three-masted rig, which became the standard big sailing ship rig for the next thousand years. They set a square sail on each mast, but on the mainmast an additional topsail, known as a *supparum*, was set, almost certainly a triangular sail with its apex at the masthead. Only the corn ships from

Left: Fourteenth century manuscript illustration of Greek Fire being used from a dromon.

Left: A third century
mosaic from Rome showing
a ship under sail at the
harbour entrance.

Alexandria were allowed to sail into Roman ports with their topsails spread; all other sailing ships had to strike them off the harbour entrance before coming into port. A further feature of these great merchant ships was a platform extending beyond the sternpost, rather in the fashion of the later stern gallery. It was covered with an awning for the comfort of the captain and important passengers.

In these last years of Roman dominance of the Mediterranean, a new sea power was arising in the Adriatic. The independent republic of Venice was becoming richer through trade than Rome herself, and skilled shipwrights were creating a formidable navy both to protect the fast-growing merchant fleet and to further Venetian

interests, particularly in the eastern Mediterranean, through which flowed the great volume of trade brought by the overland caravans from the Far East. And at the same time, on the other side of the Italian mainland, the republic of Genoa was developing on very similar lines. The two were in time certain to fight each other for supremacy at sea. A series of naval campaigns was fought, mainly between galley fleets, although something approaching the galleasse, in which oars were subsidiary to the sail as motive power, began to make its appearance during these wars. This was a big step forward, for in the galley the sail was invariably lowered and the mast unstepped in battle so that the rowers should be unhindered in their task, and the hull design of the galley always reflected this pre-eminence of the rower. As a result, the galley hull had, for the times, an exaggerated length-to-beam ratio, resulting in a vessel that needed a calm sea for maximum efficiency and was virtually useless in a fighting capacity when the waves began to rise. The design of the hull of the galleasse, on the other hand, resembled much more the sailing ship hull, with a length-to-beam ratio of about 4 to 1, sturdy and able to operate even in an angry sea. The fighting galley was essentially a Mediterranean warship, useless in other climates, but even in those usually calm waters storms could blow up with extreme rapidity, rendering the galley temporarily impotent even in its home seas. It was at times such as this that the galleasse proved a notable advance.

Venice has another small claim to shipbuilding skill: the design of the gondola, which dates back at least to the eleventh century and possibly earlier. It is of fairly typical eastern Mediterranean design with ornamental bow and stern pieces, but characterized by the *ferro*, an iron beak, in shape not unlike a halbard projecting upwards from the bow piece. This is a hull design which has not changed through the centuries, although up to the sixteenth century gondolas had a richly coloured awning supported on an arched framework, with both ends open, in place of the usual heavy black cabin of today.

A lack of contemporary illustration makes it difficult to assess the state of ship development in the more distant parts of the world, although it can be taken as certain that a great many far eastern countries were involved in maritime trade. Certainly, by the twelfth century the word *djong*, (meaning ship or large vessel) was an integral part of the Javanese language and spreading to China, Japan and southern India, indicating that ships in those areas had at least reached the large vessel size. The word is the origin of the term 'junk', used in the early days in western countries to describe many different types of eastern ship. The vessel which we now know as a junk (a flat-bottomed, high-sterned ship with square bows overhanging the water) may not necessarily have been anything like the vessels known as junks originally. But in most seafaring countries there is a continuity of design – at least, until some revolutionary advance, such as the invention of gunpowder or the introduction of the steam engine, necessitates radical change – and it is probable that, even in the earliest days, the basic junk design which we know today was found to answer best to the wind and sea conditions of the Pacific and Indian Oceans.

Between Europe and the Far East, particularly among the Arab nations bordering the Indian Ocean and the Persian Gulf, the dhow was deve-

Left: *Venetian galleasse model of the thirteenth century.*

Right: *Arab astronomers at Constantinople and some of the navigational instruments which they developed.*

Below: *Illustrations from* Linschoten's Voyages (1596) *showing the Chinese junk as sixteenth century European explorers saw it.*

loping. The general hull shape followed the Egyptian or Phoenician pattern, probably because both Egyptian and Phoenician ships had traded in those waters since the earliest years of maritime expansion and these had served as a model for local building. The great contribution of the Arabs, however, was the evolution of the lateen rig, which they certainly introduced very early on, though no approximate date has yet been established. It has been suggested that the normal light and steady winds of the area, combined with the tropical heat in which rowers became too quickly exhausted to serve as reliable motive power, provided the impetus for the evolution of a sail plan which was flexible

enough to provide forward motion to a ship even when the wind blew from forward of the beam. The Arabs were experienced seamen – for example, they were considerably quicker off the mark than the men of the West in the invention and practical use of navigational instruments, and they led the West in the use of charts – and the adaptation of a square sail to a lateen sail was a reasonably logical step, requiring no more than the slinging of the yard fore-and-aft, instead of athwartships, and setting it at an angle to the mast, instead of square. Be that as it may, the lateen rig originated among the Arabs, quickly spreading to the Mediterranean upon the realization that it was a highly efficient sail plan for small vessels.

About other types of Eastern vessel, the records are silent. The big outrigger war canoes of the Pacific Islanders certainly have a long history, and were described by the first men from the West to penetrate those waters in the sixteenth century as very much like they are today. Unquestionably, they pre-dated the arrival of western traders and explorers by a long time, possibly centuries. But there are no writings and no contemporary illustrations of the craft used by these peoples. One can only guess that their seagoing vessels developed on lines similar to those of other maritime countries.

The Hanseatic League

It is not possible to give an exact date for the formation of the loose but effective federation of German maritime towns which became known as the Hanseatic League. It was originally formed as a sort of alliance of German towns with a common interest in expansion eastward along the southern coast of the Baltic Sea – a political association, almost, to protect the rights of Germans who settled in the Baltic lands. But this initial loose federation quickly gave way to a stronger organization, based on the Wendish towns of Lübeck, Hamburg, Lüneburg, Wismar, Rostock and Stralsund, whose basic concern was the protection and growth of trade. The first meeting linking these towns was held in 1256, and although the initial objective was to stimulate seaborne trade in the Baltic and concentrate it as much as possible in the hands of the Hanse towns, interest very quickly spread to the growing trade with the west, particularly with Holland and England, and that, too, was brought as far as possible under the control of the league.

The main method of stimulating and attracting trade was to set up 'hansas' in the trading countries and, bargaining from federated strength, extract preferential treatment and, if possible, monopolies in certain classes of goods. As early as 1226 the merchants of Cologne set up a hansa in London, followed in 1266 and 1267 by hansas established by the merchants of Hamburg and Lübeck. Eventually, all three combined in 1282 to form the Gild-hall of the Germans, in order to speak with a single voice. Because of the rich Norwegian trade in iron, copper, timber and fish, a hansa was set up in Bergen in 1343. All these hansas enjoyed special trade facilities, the Gild-hall in London setting up 'counters', or trading settlements, in Lynn, Boston, Hull, York, Norwich, Ipswich, Yarmouth and Bristol, virtually controlling most of the foreign trade in these towns. By 1422 the London hansa had become known as the Steelyard because of the method employed of weighing merchandise by means of a pivoted steel beam, and it claimed right of jurisdiction over all the other counters in England.

Seaborne trade means ships, and under the strong, centralized control of the league, the building of ships in the

various Hanse towns proceeded apace. There was no attempt by the league to dictate to its members the sort of ships that they should build; there was just continual encouragement from the central organization to keep pace with the growth in the volume of trade. But, as the waters of the Baltic, North Sea and English Channel were as frequently rough as smooth, a new type of ship was evolved, designed to sail efficiently whatever the state of the sea. This was known as the 'Hansa cog', and it is pictured on the seals of many of the Hanse towns, those of Elbing, Wismar and Harderwijk being particularly interesting. They show a departure in design from the usual curved bow, which had been such a feature of ship design in those waters, and show instead a straight stem at an angle of about 60 degrees to the horizontal. This was carried down without any curve and fixed to a long, straight keel, which terminated in a sternpiece, also straight, set at an angle of about 75 degrees to the horizontal. The long keel would

obviously give a good grip on the water, ideal for sailing in rough seas, though, if used with a fore-and-aft sail plan, it would make a vessel very hard-headed to steer. But these Hansa cogs still set a single square sail, with braces and bowlines so that the sail could be trimmed to provide forward motion to the ship when the wind was abeam. With this square rig, the straight keel was the best answer in rough water for a deeply laden cargo ship.

It is impossible to estimate the size of a Hansa cog from the town seals, but from other evidence the average deep-water cog apparently had an overall length of about 100 ft (30 m), a beam of about 25 ft (8 m), and a draught of about 10 ft (3 m), which in modern measurement terms would mean a ship of around 280 tons. This was a fairly large size for a merchantman in those early days of the thirteenth century.

Another feature of the Hansa cog were castles built forward and aft, a small one forward and a large one aft. In the earliest seals they appear to have secured with the points. Most sails were tanned with a solution prepared from bark, to prevent rot. Already the cordage used was hemp rope, where formerly it had been made from strips of hide.

Inevitably, the league's monopoly of trade brought national jealousy in its wake. The merchants of England saw no reason why their nation's trade should be dominated by this German federation, and as they grew in political strength they put pressure on their government to bring it to an end. The companies of Merchant Adventurers, set up in England in the sixteenth century to open up new trade routes, commanded sufficient political strength to force the withdrawal of the Hanseatic privileges in England, and, moreover, exacted a concession allowing the formation of an English counter in Hamburg, to compensate for the German retention of the Steelyard in London. Holland,

capturing the bulk of the North Sea fishery, the Baltic grain trade and the French salt trade, broke away from Hanseatic control in the early sixteenth century, and Bergen, in Norway, quickly followed suit.

The league itself lingered on, now completely impotent to enforce trade concessions in foreign countries, and growing less cohesive through the incessant quarrelling among its constituent German towns. In the end, it consisted only of Lübeck, Bremen and Hamburg, charged with upholding the name and inheritance of the league, even though the name now meant nothing in terms of trade and there was no inheritance worth upholding. All that was left were the empty buildings, erected in the foreign cities in the days of the Hanseatic ascendancy. In the end these were sold, the Steelyard in London in 1852, and the counters in Bergen and Antwerp in 1775 and 1863 respectively.

Right: The Hanseatic cog of c.1380 which was unearthed from a Bremen mudflat in 1962, at the Deutsches Schiffahrts Museum.

been appendages added later to the basic hull, probably to provide observation platforms while the ship was under sail, but later seals seem to show them as integral parts of the hull, so they were probably incorporated in the design after they had proved their value. Following the early Egyptian pattern, the ends of the deck beams project through the hull planking, to provide additional strength.

The single square sail had an area of about 2,000 sq ft (185 m^2), and was fitted with reef points, not in the normal fashion of a square sail which is reefed to the yard, but along the bottom so that the foot of the sail was bunched and

Chapter Three
The Development of the Sailing Ship

The most important development in ship design during the three hundred years from 1200 to 1500 was the substitution of a wooden rudder, hung from the sternpost by means of gudgeons and pintles, for the steering oar projecting over the starboard quarter of a ship. The exact date of this innovation is uncertain, but there is a relief carving of a ship on the font in Winchester Cathedral, which looks as though it is meant to depict a stern rudder. It is not easy to date the carving, but it is thought to be a Belgian work of around 1180. There is a school of thought which holds that the hanging rudder was introduced with the cog – probably with the Hansa cog – and so will not accept that the Winchester carving shows a rudder hung from the sternpost. It is true enough that the carving shows the front edge of the rudder – if it is, in fact, a rudder – projecting somewhat in front of the sternpost, but this could well be a vagary of the carver, not knowing how the new rudders worked.

There is a church in Gotland, called Fide Church, which has a picture of a ship carved into the wall plaster, and there is no question that this carving does depict a ship with a rudder hung from the sternpost. The carving is believed, with some degree of certainty, to have been made in the early years of the thirteenth century, perhaps no more than about forty years later than that in Winchester Cathedral. The hanging rudder is worked by a tiller which is curved round the upper part of the sternpost, and there are several other more or less contemporary paintings and carvings which show the same arrangement of the tiller. By making it curved, it was possible to retain the high Norwegian and Danish sternpost which was a standard design feature of all these early north European vessels.

The carving in Fide Church definitely predates the development of the Hansa cog, but it would appear reasonably certain that the initial deve-

lopment of the hanging rudder at the stern took place in the Baltic or in west German waters around the Elbe estuary. And it could just as easily have originated in Hansa ships before the development of the cog. The seal of Dover, one of the most important of the Cinque Ports, is accurately dated 1284, and shows a ship still employing a steering oar, though on the port side of the ship instead of the starboard (unquestionably a mistake on the carver's part).

If we may take the ship in the seal of Dover as typical of the state of English development at this time, the Viking influence on the general lines of the hull is still abundantly evident. But forecastles and aftercastles, which began to come in during the last years of the twelfth century as separate structures built on deck inside the hull, have now become an integral part of the hull and project forward of the stem and aft of the stern. A third castle is shown built on the mast above the yard, and, in a miniature decorating a manuscript produced in 1279 for Queen Eleanore of Castile during the Crusades, fighting men are shown in this mast castle. The Dover seal, however, almost certainly shows a merchant vessel and the mast castle was probably used by a lookout. For the rest, the Dover ship shows the standard square sail on a central mast; however, it has a distinct bowsprit, by no means as highly steeved as in the Mediterranean where the purpose was to set a square spritsail under it, but mounted at a modest angle to the horizontal and obviously meant as an aid to trimming the mainsail. Most likely, the sail had bowlines on each leech which could be rove through a block or hole at the end of the bowsprit to hold the leading edge taut when close to the wind. There are no fittings for the use of oars in the Dover ship, and she was definitely built for use under sail alone, though, no doubt, she carried a few sweeps for temporary use in a flat calm.

Most north European ports of standing during

Left: Thirteenth century Venetian ship with three masts and two oars for steering. (From a mosaic in St Mark's Cathedral, Venice.)

the thirteenth and fourteenth centuries had official seals showing contemporary ships, and from these it is possible to note small design changes as the centuries advanced. A similar source of information is the paintings on walls and ceilings of churches, devotional works calling on the Almighty to safeguard local sailors on their voyages. The most significant change is the gradual growth of the castle forward into a raised forecastle deck fully incorporated into the hull design, with the side planking carried up to the level of the castle floor. Simultaneously, we find the aftercastle expanded so that it terminates a few feet abaft the mast, forming a distinct poop deck fitting snugly onto the gunwale to provide a raised deck aft. The earlier representations of this period still show the Viking influence on hull designs, with the long extended bow and the familiar detachable dragon's head at the top of the sloping stempost, but they have been adapted to modern requirements by the addition of the three castles (the third at the masthead) and the hanging rudder fixed to the sternpost. Their general lines suggest that they were still shallow-draught vessels. Later illustrations, towards the end of the fourteenth century, show a very different kind of ship, approaching the typical medieval vessel in design, with raised forecastle and poop, low waist and obvious deep draught. It was this deepening of the draught, perhaps even more than the invention of the hanging rudder, that really separates the Viking design and the ocean-going ship of later centuries.

There was still only one mast and single square sail on these north European vessels – a surprising slowness in sail plan development in view of the fact that two- and three-masted ships were becoming common in the Mediterranean. After all, by the fourteenth century, a whole series of Crusades had been fought, in which armies from Germany, France and England had been carried to the Levant in Mediterranean ships on which two or three masts were the rule, rather than the exception. There is indeed a record of Richard I attacking a huge Saracen ship with three masts at Acre, so there was no lack of knowledge among north European nations of this extended rig. Richard's own ship, the *Trenchemer*, though sometimes described as a galley, was, in fact, a *dromon* with two masts, although there is no record to say whether she was square-rigged or had the more usual Mediterranean lateen rig of the time. She carried rowers, of course, to drive her along when the wind would not serve.

According to a list compiled during the reign of Richard I (1189–1199), English naval vessels of the period were of the species known as 'galleys', 'gallions', 'busses', 'dromons', 'vissers' or 'ursers', 'barges' and 'snakes'. The English galley was really the galleasse, of basic Mediterranean galley design, but having mast and sail as her primary means of propulsion and rowers who only took over when the wind was foul. The gallion was pure galley, but with only a single bank of oars, small and used only in calm seas. The buss was, with the dromon, the biggest ship in the fleet, of heavy build, deep draught and capacious holds. With single mast and square sail, she was slow and ponderous in the water. She was used in warlike operations as a

Right: Henry I returning to England by ship, possibly an *esnecca*.

transport, and a report made in March 1170 stated that at the foundering of a single buss 400 lives were lost. This statement has been questioned many times, but there seems to be no good reason for doubting its truth. Twelfth-century vessels were a great deal larger than many people imagine, and, as this particular buss was engaged in transport work at the time of her loss, she could well have been carrying as many men again as the number of her crew. And a crew of 200, or even more, was certainly not unusual at this period: Richard of Devizes, writing in about 1195, notes that a large buss could carry, besides her crew, up to eighty knights with their horses, eighty footmen, and twenty-eight servants, and on an expedition carried provisions for a year, as well as a very complete outfit of spare parts for self-refits, including three spare rudders, thirteen anchors, thirty oars, two sails, three sets of all kinds of ropes used on board and duplicates of all her gear, except for the mast and boat.

The dromon could, at this time, be almost any large ship of war. As mentioned in an earlier chapter, she originated in the Mediterranean as a double-banked galley, fast and manoeuvrable (In English her name means 'runner') By the time of the Crusades, there were two distinct types, one of them being a very large, high-sided galley, with both sides flaring outwards at upper deck level. The evidence for this rests in the story of Rognvald's voyage from the Orkneys to the Mediterranean and Palestine. Off Sardinia his six longships sighted two Saracen dromons, and, after taking counsel with his captains, Rognvald decided to attack one of them by running as close alongside as possible. He and one other longship lay alongside the after quarter of the dromon, two more amidships, and the last two forward. The traditional defence against such boarding tactics was to pour brimstone and burning pitch onto the decks of the attackers, but when the dromon tried to do so, it all fell into the sea outside the longships, so great was the overhang of the dromon's sides. So the great dromon was captured, stripped, burned and her crew sold as slaves. The date was 1180.

Above: Relief on the font of Winchester Cathedral, the oldest known representation of a hinged sternpost rudder.

Right: Ships taking
Crusaders to the Holy
Land in the thirteenth
century. Weatherly craft
were needed for the long
voyage from northern
Europe.

The other type of Mediterranean dromon was a two- or three-masted sailing ship, again very large, often used as a transport for troops and with space for horses in the hold. She could be rowed when the wind failed. This was the type used in England, though solely as a fighting ship, not as a transport, and with only a single mast. Her fighting crew were archers and arquebusiers. She too could be rowed in calm weather or to bring her into the position in battle where her bowmen could perform most effectively.

A visser, or urser, was a flat-bottomed craft of shallow draught, used for the transport of horses, again having a single mast and sail. The barge was very similar to the barge of today, a ship of burden, flat-bottomed to take the ground when neaped by the tide. She was the direct ancestor of the barges still to be seen in the coastal waters of Holland and East Anglia today, a remarkable example of a design which has scarcely altered in the 800 years of its existence.

The snake was the English translation of the *esnecca*, a Scandinavian longship of the eighth to eleventh centuries. It first appeared in England as a despatch boat for taking messages from the commander of a fleet to other ships, but it quickly developed into a sort of royal yacht. Henry I and Henry II both had *esneccas* in which they made visits of state, and ambassadors were frequently sent to their stations abroad in them.

There is nothing to indicate that any of these ships had more than a single central mast, though there are some vague suggestions that they may sometimes have spread more than one sail on it. Roger of Wendover, writing in about 1190, mentions three sails set on the single mast, but unfortunately gives no details of how and where they were spread. If it were really so, it would be unusual, as, outside the Mediterranean and Arab waters, shipping generally had not yet progressed beyond the single square sail.

Other types of ship used in English waters were the schuyt, or schuit, and the cog. The name 'shuyt' was applied to any small sailing merchant ship, and was the Dutch word for a flat-bottomed river boat, built with a great breadth of beam and with a square tuck to the sides. The word was

Above: Cogs in battle, from a fourteenth century manuscript.

used of ships in England, not because of any particular similarity to the Dutch *schuyt*, but because the term described small Dutch vessels and it was convenient to apply the Dutch word to any merchant ship that was small.

There has been much argument about what a cog really was. In his uncompleted *History of the Royal Navy*, published in 1847, Sir Nicholas Nicolas said of the English cogs that 'they were short and of great breadth, like a cockle shell, whence they are said to have derived their name'. This might conceivably be true of the early thirteenth-century, as no description or illustration of so early a cog exists, but it was certainly not true of the second half of the thirteenth and the whole of the fourteenth centuries, when the term 'cog' was frequently applied to some of the biggest ships then sailing. Possibly the word came to be used to describe any sort of vessel indiscriminately, much as today we use the word 'ship' to describe a whole variety of seagoing vessels of different sizes and different functions. This might be a later application of the word, but the Issue Rolls for 1210 record that the King hired five ships for his service 'without a cog'.

The English cog was unlike the Hansa cog in that it did not have the straight stem and long keel. It was built with the traditional curved stem that joined the keel considerably further aft than in the Hansa variety. It certainly had the three castles, at bow, stern and masthead, and, while being designed as a sturdy and capacious merchant ship, was liable to be called up for war in an emergency, frequently forming the major constituent of a fleet. Thus, the Cinque Ports fleet employed in the war against Scotland of 1299 to 1300 consisted of fifteen cogs, eight ships, two snakes, and five other vessels whose names are given without any designation of type.

To celebrate his victory over the French at the battle of Sluys in 1340, Edward III had gold nobles struck which showed him standing in a cog. It is difficult to see, as it is in all contemporary seals, coins, etc., whether the ends of the deck beams project through the wooden hull, as they do in the Hansa cog, although there are a number of small circles shown on the strakes which could be taken as a medallist's conception of the ends of deck beams. Although no tiller is shown attached to the rudder, a good example of the noble shows quite clearly the method of attachment to the sternpost by gudgeons and pintles. There was no room on the noble to show any detail of the building of the forecastle and aftercastle, but the aftercastle is large and built forward in the nature of a poop deck.

Various new types of ship are mentioned in the reign of Edward III, but it is difficult today to be sure of what they all exactly were. The most interesting names used, in view of what the words were later to be associated with, were the 'carrack', which started as a description of ships of Spanish or Genoan origin calling at English ports, but later came to be used loosely in England as applying to any ship of large dimensions used as a trader, and the 'dogger', a fishing vessel which took its name from the Dutch word for a cod-fishing boat. Many people believe that this

Right: Gold noble commemorating the Battle of Sluys, showing Henry III standing on board a cog.

vessel took its name from the Dogger Bank, but it is more likely that the bank was named after the vessels which fished it, or the fish that they caught. An Icelandic report of the end of the fourteenth century mentions thirty English *fiski-duggur* fishing in Icelandic waters, and it is clear from many English accounts that this was a yearly custom. So the dogger must have been a fairly large fishing vessel to be able to venture annually into those inhospitable waters.

Among the Rolls at Carlton Ride, in Norfolk, there is a detailed account of the building, at King's Lynn in 1336, of the galley *La Phelipe*. Many of the items listed in this account are familiar to us today, including (to use the modern spellings) a capstan, hawsers, pulleys, stays and backstays, painters, sheets, bolt-ropes, cables, tow ropes, sounding lines, seizings and hatches. Other items with which she was fitted cannot be identified from the old English names (unless a

'david' could mean a davit, which is highly improbable). We know that the galley had one mast, which cost £10, and one bowsprit, costing £3. Her anchor was made from 1,100 lbs (500 kg) of Spanish iron, and she carried five smaller anchors, in addition, at a total cost of £23 10s. 3d. Her sail, dyed red, took 640 ells of cloth and to it were attached 'wyne-wews', dyed black, of 220 ells. Perhaps a 'wyne-wew' was a bonnet (an additional strip of cloth which could be laced to the foot of a square sail to increase its size, in order to take advantage of a following wind). Certainly bonnets were being widely used at that time and a sail might have two or even three bonnets. The galley had no pump, but water that had collected in her bilges could be lifted out by a 'winding-balies', into which the water was put by two 'spojours'. It is difficult to conjecture what this could be, but presumably it enabled the vessel to be kept reasonably dry. Her sides were caulked with 'mosso' and then covered with grease, and her bottom was paid with a mixture of tar, oil, pitch and resin. The accounts record that the master carpenter was paid 6d. a day, ordinary carpenters 5d., 'clinkerers' 4d., 'holderors' 3d. and labourers 2½d.

It is in these Norfolk Rolls that we find the first mention of an English ship with two masts. The date is around 1350, but there can have been very few of them as the largest cogs built – the cog *Thomas*, one of the largest, is recorded as having a tonnage of 240 – had only the single mast. No details of the two masts are given, though one might expect the second to have been a small mizen abaft the mainmast, to help balance the helm. The high forecastle, now fairly standard on larger ships, presented a lot of windage which tended to hold the ship's bows away from the wind, and a small sail aft would have done much to counter this effect. However, this is pure speculation in the light of modern knowledge of aerodynamics; the fourteenth-century navigator may not have appreciated the wind's effect on a built-up bow.

In the Mediterranean, Venice was arising as the chief maritime power, and for his Crusade to the Holy Land in 1268 Louis IX ordered most of his ships to be built in Venice, with rather fewer in Genoa. There are records of these ships and we know that those built in Venice had an overall length of 85 ft (26 m), keel of 57 ft (17·4 m), maximum beam of 21 ft (6·4 m) and depth from rail to keel of 22 ft (6·7 m). Internally they were fitted with two complete decks, upper and lower, and aft they had two short decks in the form of what we would now call a quarter-deck

Right: Detail from a painting by Carpaccio showing a Venetian carrack of the fifteenth century.

well reflect a desire of Mediterranean shipwrights to produce a more robust ship, better able than the current Mediterranean design to hold her own in waters more generally hostile than those of the Mediterranean. This is not to say that the lateen sail was suddenly discarded – it remained the most common sail plan in local use in the Mediterranean – but that, in an era of expanding trade, there was a growing recognition of the fact that, for use in more distant waters, distinct advantages were to be gained from the use of the square sail, mainly because of the difficulty of dipping the long lateen yard round the mast when tacking.

This reversion to the square sail in Mediterranean ships heralded the birth of the ship known as the 'carrack', which in its earliest days was a two-masted ship carrying one large square sail on the mainmast, with a smaller square sail on a mizen stepped well aft, though in some carracks the mizen sail was lateen instead of square. She was fairly bluff in the bows, with a rounded stern ending in a square counter, a fore castle which was so much an integral part of the ship's hull that it was virtually the same as the modern forecastle, and after castle which was unquestionably a quarter-deck. Following the Mediterranean pattern, her hull was carvel-built with the hull planks fixed edge to edge, whereas north European ships still retained clinker construction with overlapping hull strakes.

An important mid-fifteenth-century model of a Spanish ship in the Prins Hendrik Museum at Rotterdam – it originally hung as a votive offering in a church at Mataro, near Barcelona – gives us a good picture of a Spanish ship of the years just before the first great explosion of discoveries began with the Spanish and Portuguese voyages to west and east. The model was originally two-masted, with main and mizen, but although only a single mast remains today, the result of loss or breakage over the centuries, a most significant point about it is that in the early days of its existence someone tried to convert it into a three-masted ship by adding a third mast stepped on the forecastle. The model is described as that of a Spanish não, but as the word is the Spanish for 'ship', it does not get us very far. Today we can say with some certainty that it originally represented a two-masted carrack, and that later on in the fifteenth century someone tried to bring it up to date by adding a third mast.

The carrack design was more or less standard for all large ships in the Mediterranean from about 1400 onwards, the original two masts being increased to three as ships were built bigger. It was during the fifteenth century that, almost worldwide, warships took a great leap forward in size, and, whereas a ship of 250 tons was large

and poop deck. These were added to provide space for cabins for nobles and knights. From mosaics at San Marco in Venice it appears that these ships were three-masted, but it is not possible to be sure as the mosaics are highly stylized. The ships were fitted with a lateen rig and steered with a steering oar on either quarter.

The hanging rudder at the stern came later to the Mediterranean, and its arrival was possibly contemporary with the re-adoption of the square sail in place of the lateen. This gives a date of about 1350, which is to some extent confirmed by a Spanish miniature of that date that shows several ships with square sails and rudders fixed to the sternpost. There was by that time a fairly lively trade between the Mediterranean states and northern Europe, and the northern cog was no stranger in many Mediterranean ports. The ships in this Spanish miniature all bear a distinct resemblance to the northern cog, which could

Left: Contemporary model of a fifteenth century ship from Motaro, Spain.

Right: Late fifteenth century caravel.

So we come to the caravel, one of the most discussed and controversial ships of the period. The word itself is Portuguese and was originally the generic term used in that country to describe small ships used mainly for fishing. This meaning of the term, however, died out quite early, and the word was reborn at the beginning of the fifteenth century and applied to various types of small ship. It earned a place in the history of the sea with the Spanish and Portuguese voyages of discovery of the last decade of the fifteenth century, almost all of which were made in caravels.

All that is positively known about true caravels is that they were relatively small, of sturdy build, with a maximum draught of 6 to 7 feet, and were variously rigged on three masts. One of their early-recognized characteristics was that they were handy ships which could beat to windward, and the early Portuguese voyages of exploration down the west coast of Africa were successful purely because of this. Although always encouraged by Prince Henry the Navigator, who had established himself at Sagres in about 1430, no Portuguese pilot had yet dared to round the Cabo de Não, on the western bulge of Africa, a short distance along the coast from Cape Bojador, because of strongly held superstitious beliefs that (a) a ship could never get back against the prevailing northerly winds, and (b) the sea at the equator boiled and would melt the pitch and tar with which the bottom of a ship was paid. A rough translation of a Spanish couplet of the time, using the English version 'Cape Nun' for Cabo de Não, runs:

When old Cape Nun heaves into sight
Turn back, me lad, or else – goodnight.

However, Gil Eannes, captain of a Portuguese ship and one of Prince Henry's trained pilots, successfully rounded Cabo de Não in 1434 sailing the new caravel which gave him full confidence in his ability to return home by tacking against the northerlies.

This Portuguese caravel used a full lateen sail plan, with a big lateen sail on the mainmast, a smaller one on the mizen, and a very small one on a mast stepped still further aft, which we would today call a 'bonaventure' mast or, perhaps, a 'jigger' mast. The full lateen-rigged caravel, known as a *caravela latina*, while admirable for making to windward in seas no more than moderate, was always labour-intensive, as the spars had to be dipped round the mast on every change of tack. Moreover, they were much more difficult to handle in a rough sea and required a much bigger crew to do so. So, for ocean voyages, the *caravela latina* adopted the main elements of

at the beginning of the century, by the end of it ships of four times that tonnage were being built. Indeed, an official report reached England in 1425 that a Spanish carrack of 1,300 'botts', or tons, was being built at Barcelona, with a second of 1,000 'botts' also under construction. If the report was true, these would be quite exceptional, and a long way in advance of the general run of shipping at that time. But by the end of the century, only seventy-five years later, ships of this size were becoming, if not commonplace, by no means remarkable. Obviously, so large a ship could not be efficiently operated with a two-masted rig, even with the addition of topsails above the large mainsail, and so a third mast, and frequently a fourth in the larger ships, became a necessity.

The early Mediterranean carrack, following the re-adoption of the square sail, appeared first with a smaller square sail set on the mizen, but in a very few years reverted to a small lateen sail on the mizen which was found to provide a better balance for steering the ship on a wind. The lateen mizen then became a standard feature throughout the whole life of the carrack, and, indeed, of its smaller sister the caravel, and was also adopted in north European waters, as soon as the third mast became a regular feature of a ship's rig.

Portuguese caravel
(c.1500)

Length 75 ft (22·9 m) *Keel* 50 ft (15·2 m) *Beam* 25 ft (7·6 m)
Draught 6 ft (1·8 m) *Hold* 9 ft (2·7 m) *Burthen* 65 tons
Complement 30

The caravel is the kind of ship most closely identified with the great voyages of discovery made by Europeans in the fifteenth and sixteenth centuries. Caravels accompanied Diaz, da Gama and Columbus on their expeditions, and Columbus's' favourite ship on his voyage of 1492 was the *Nina*, a caravel similar to the one portrayed here. The qualities that recommended the caravel to explorers were her size, large enough for ocean voyages but small enough to manoeuvre close inshore, her shallow draught, which made it safe for her to enter uncharted rivers and bays, her rig, especially the fore-and-aft rig which was very weatherly, and her general seaworthiness, inherited from her sturdy fishing-boat ancestors. She did not have much space for cargo, but she was light enough to be rowed if there was not enough wind to fill her sails.

The small drawing shows the *caravela latina* rig, while the large drawing shows the same ship as a *caravela redonda* with square sails on the foremast. This transformation might be accomplished by moving the middle mast of the *caravela latina* to the bows and re-rigging it with square sails, and restaying the forward-sloping mainmast in an upright position.

Labels on diagram: GAVIA, VELA MAYOR O PAPAHIGO, PALO MAYOR, PALO MESANA, TRINQUETE, TOLDILLA, BOMBARDA, TOLDA, EL AVE-MARIA, CAMARA DE COLÓN, FALCONETE, FAROL, BONETA, CEBADERA, PALO TRINQUETE, ESCOTILLA DE CARGA SIEMPRE CERRADA, FOGON, BOTALÓN, PETATES, CAJAS DE OFICIALES, AGUJA DE MAREAR, GUINDASTE PARA EL FIRME DE LA DRIZA MAYOR, BOMBA, BODEGA, J. GVILLÉN 1932

Left: Cutaway drawing of Guillen's reconstruction of the *Santa Maria*.

NAVE-LORDANA

PANDORA

the carrack rig and became square-rigged on fore and main masts, a change of rig which gave her the name of *caravela redonda*. It was in a *redonda*-type vessel that Columbus made his voyage to the new world in 1492 and Ferdinand Magellan made the first circumnavigation of the world between 1519 and 1522.

There has been much discussion and argument about Columbus's ship, the *Santa Maria*, and many experts no longer recognize her as a caravel. About the other two ships in the expedition, the *Pinta* and *Niña*, there is no question at all: the *Pinta* was a *caravela redonda*, and the *Niña* started as a *caravela latina*, but was re-rigged in the Canary Islands as a *caravela redonda*, since the *latina* rig was soon found to be unsuitable for Atlantic waters, particularly when the little fleet picked up the north-east trade wind which square sails were able to make the most of.

Columbus himself described the *Santa Maria* as a '*nao*', which means very little. From about 1460 onwards, carracks were turning into large ships with towering stern galleries, with as many as four small decks being superimposed one above the other in the largest, and of one thing we can be certain: that in 1492 the *Santa Maria* was not a carrack. We also know that by the end of the century the large *caravela redonda* was being built up to a size of 110 or 120 tons. Although her tonnage is not known exactly, the *Santa Maria* may have been of as much as 100 tons burthen, though a more likely figure, on the

evidence of Bartolomé de las Casas in his *Historia de las Indias*, would be 80 to 90 tons. Her overall length was about 80 ft (24 m) and she drew about 6½ ft (2 m) of water. According to contemporary accounts, she was 'somewhat' larger than the *Pinta* (about 60 tons) and the *Niña* (about 50 tons). Being a larger vessel, she carried a more extensive sail plan than the others, a small topsail above the main course and a small spritsail below the bowsprit. Apart from those two sails, she carried the normal *caravela redonda* rig. Perhaps, because she was the Admiral's ship, Columbus decided to call her a *nao* to distinguish her from the two caravels which accompanied her. No original building plans exist, and, though many models have been built and life-size reconstructions attempted, no one really knows with certainty what she looked like. The most convincing description is in the work of the distinguished Spanish marine archaeologist Admiral Guillén y Tato, *La Carabela Santa Maria*, on which was based the reconstruction for the Seville Exposition of 1929.

Meanwhile, a small revolution was taking place in England. As has been mentioned, there was virtually no difference here between the merchant ship and the warship, the trading cog being called up for military service in time of war. The task of the ship in war was merely to

Below: Naval engagement in the late fifteenth century, the Battle of Zonchio (1499).

carry the fighting men to battle, and a sea fight was really no more than a land battle fought at sea, with the same weapons and tactics. But by the fifteenth century it was being realised in England that the cog, generically known as a 'roundship' because of her very low length-to-beam ratio, was unsuitable for maritime warfare and that, for the defence of the seas around the kingdom, special ships designed for the purpose needed to be built. As there was no effective central government agency for defence, it fell to the king to build these ships. During Henry V's war with France he built the *Jesus*, a 'great' ship of 1,000 tons, and this was followed by the *Holigost* (760 tons) and the *Trinity Royal* (540 tons). By the end of the war the king owned

seventeen large ships, seven carracks captured from the Spanish, two barges and twelve ballingers, which were barge-type vessels of large build, capable of carrying 100 men or more. Henry's ships had to be sold on his death to pay his debts, but the practice of building his own ships for purposes of war was followed by his successors, though, being generally impecunious, they hired them out to merchants during the years of peace for use in seaborne trade. Within a few years France and Holland had followed the English lead: in France warships were built and owned by the king and in Holland by individual states.

Even more important in warship development was the introduction of gunpowder. It was first used in land warfare in Italy in about 1326, and the first guns were issued to ships in England about fifteen years later. These were mainly hand guns, and, although the store accounts of the *Christopher of the Tower*, a cog belonging to Edward III, include three iron cannon with chambers, which means that they were breechloaders, they were not part of the ship's armament, for she had none. Possibly they were part of the equipment of the fighting men carried on board; they were certainly not mounted in the ship as a weapon to be used against other ships.

Gradually, however, the gun began to establish itself as a real naval weapon, no longer merely an adjunct of the fighting men or soldiers, who up to that time had made up what might be called the 'business end' of a warship. As soon as the gun became an integral part of the ship, it gave a new meaning to the term 'warship': it was the mariners, whose only commitment in naval battle had been to work the ship while the fighting men gave battle, who now became the fighting men as well. The whole art of naval warfare was to change, the land battle at sea giving way to a new type of battle, with an entirely different conception of both strategy and tactics. And it meant, too, that the old interchangeability of merchant ship in peace and warship in war was largely a thing of the past.

As the role of the warship changed, so the ship herself had to change to adapt to her new role. A whole series of interacting developments transformed her completely. The advent of the gun, and its own growth in size from the original small anti-personnel weapon to the first ship's cannon, which weighed about 2 tons and fired a 17-pound ball, dictated a significant increase in size of ship. The fifteenth century, during which these changes were taking place, saw the tonnage of the warship increase fourfold, from about 250 tons at the start of the century to about 1,000 tons at its close, much as merchant ships had grown during the same period. This increase in the size of the ship dictated the adoption of a more powerful and complicated rig, from the single mast of 1400 to the three or four masts of 1500, with topsails and topgallants above the courses. The handling of the new rig called not only for larger crews, but also for a higher degree of seamanship among the men, while the gun called for men trained in its use to be incorporated into the warship's crew. The whole concept of a navy was changed, and in every European country with any pretensions to control of the adjacent seas, a new skilled band of seamen arose to man and work the new warships.

For some years the ship's cannon created as many new difficulties as it solved old ones. The only places on board at which it could be mounted to command an adequate field of fire were in the forecastle and aftercastle, or poop. Smaller anti-personnel guns could be carried in the tops to fire down onto the decks of an enemy ship, and at the break of the forecastle and poop decks for use against anyone attempting to carry the ship by boarding her at the waist, where her freeboard was lowest. But, as naval cannon grew in size, so also did their weight, and it was quickly discovered that any ship's stability at sea was adversely affected by having these heavy objects mounted so high above the waterline. The basic elements of marine architecture demanded that all such heavy weights should be mounted as low as possible in the ship, but it took some years to work out that this could only be done by cutting gunports in the ship's side and making some sort of lid to seal them tightly whenever the sea was rough enough to threaten an entry into the ship

The invention of the gunport, cut in the ship's side and closed with a hinged, close-fitting lid of the same thickness as the side strakes, has been attributed to a French shipwright named Descharges, who worked at Brest. The year of the invention is given as 1500, but there is no doubt whatever that the gunport was incorporated in several warships some years before that date. It is possible that the idea came from Spain, where some of the larger carracks had guns firing through gunports cut in the sides of the forecastle and aftercastle. However, these ports do not seem to have been closed with port-lids, but instead usually with a painted shield in the form of a *pavesse* (the shield-shaped emblem which was used to line the gunwales of warships in the

Left: Fifteenth century warship development: guns project through ports cut in the hull. (Anthony Roll)

fifteenth and sixteenth centuries, ostensibly to provide some protection against balls fired by hand-guns, but more probably to accommodate the contemporary love of colour and display in ships of war).

As we have seen, the growth in size of the warship during the fifteenth century was accompanied by a similar growth in the size of the merchant ship (though not yet to quite the same extent). This was especially marked in the Mediterranean, which was still the only channel of trade with the Far East. Rich merchandise from China, Persia, India and Arabia still came to the Levant by the old overland caravan routes and from there was carried to western Mediterranean ports, particularly Venice, for distribution throughout a Europe hungry for the produce of the East. This was a trade that grew phenomenally during the fifteenth century and brought in its wake the need for larger ships to handle it. But trade was expanding elsewhere, too, and in all maritime countries the merchants and ship-owners were alive to the financial benefits which larger cargoes would bring. Larger cargoes meant larger ships, and, although the merchant ship of the period never quite approached the tonnage of the warship, there were many good businessmen who were prepared to venture their money in ships of 500 and even 600 tons, whereas a century earlier a 250-ton ship was considered to be something of a leviathan.

There was, too, a new art spreading across the sea – an art that was quickly to change the whole face of the maritime world. Ptolemy's geographical treatises, lost from sight for over a thousand years, had come to light again, and a new interest in navigation was being born. Many geographers knew that latitude could be calculated by observation of the sun at noon and the Pole Star at night, but it took many years to pass on the methods to the average pilot at sea, many of whom were uneducated and even illiterate. Much of the application of geographical knowledge to a ship at sea was embodied in the work of Prince Henry the Navigator, who set up an establishment at Sagres in 1430 to encourage ships' pilots to study the art, and the work of his nephew, Don Alfonso V, who took on the task when Prince Henry died in 1460. Catalogues were made of the major stars and constellations; charts were drawn up using degrees of latitude and longitude; and the theory of the precession of the equinoxes, originally the work of Hipparchus and preserved by Ptolemy, was revived and studied. During this same century the first astronomical tables, commissioned from learned

geographers by Alfonso X of Castille and known as the Alfonsine Tables, were published in 1483. With their aid, observation of the altitude of sun or star could be translated into latitude, and over the course of the century the astrolabe and the quadrant were introduced, the first of the navigator's tools to measure altitude. In 1475 Johann Muller published his *Ephemerides*, with tables of the sun's declination calculated for the years from 1475 to 1566. With the *Ephemerides*, the Alfonsine Tables and an astrolabe, a ship's pilot could discover his latitude by means of a very simple calculation.

All this was leading to a growing recognition of the fact that there must be a way by sea to every nation in the world whose shores were lapped by the ocean. For far too long most navigators had been content to accept Homer's idea that the earth was a large land mass or island totally encompassed by an immense river, to which he gave the name Okeanus. It was a convenient theory for the navigator whose longest voyages were still rarely made out of sight of land, even though by now all geographers, and probably some navigators, knew that the earth was a sphere. It needed a German geographer, who joined Prince Henry the Navigator for a time at Sagres, to demonstrate the fact to navigators beyond all question. He was Martin

Above: The Polo brothers setting sail from Venice at the start of their second voyage in 1270

Behaim of Nuremburg, and he is credited with adapting the astrolabe, formerly only used in astronomy, as an instrument of navigation. But of much more importance, and his main claim to remembrance among navigators, is the great globe which he constructed and which showed beyond any doubt that there did indeed exist a route by sea to every country in the world which bordered the ocean. It was the first navigational document to show the existence of antipodes; the first which showed beyond question that there was a sea route to India and China, whose goods were becoming so highly prized in Europe. It is the oldest globe known to exist, and it represents the limit of geographical knowledge in the period which preceded Columbus's first voyage to the west in 1492.

This new navigational knowledge, disseminated from Sagres to the other European nations, was to have an immense impact on ship development, as great indeed as that of the gun. No longer could a merchant shipowner be content to build his ships for coast-hopping voyages; now he had to think of long voyages far out of sight of land, and to design his ships accordingly. Not only did he need a ship stout enough to withstand all that the sea could do to her over the course of a voyage that might last many months, but he had to plan his ship's accommodation to carry enough food, fresh water and essential stores to keep her and her crew in good shape for all that time. He did not yet realize how vast the world's oceans were – Columbus reckoned the distance from the Canary Islands to Japan to be

2,400 miles; in fact it is 10,600 – and when, in a very short space of years, the shipowner was brought face to face with the huge distances involved, he found that he needed still stouter ships, with even more experienced crews, to have some hope of success on these longer trading voyages.

It was not only on the construction and design of the ship's hull that this new concept of world navigation had an effect; it also influenced sails and rigging. It has been noted that even Columbus, Mediterranean-born and trained, had appreciated that the full lateen rig was unsuitable for long ocean voyages and had adopted a modified

Above: Navigation becomes a science: illustration from a sixteenth century treatise, de Vault's *Cosmografia* (1583).

Below: Globes become important aids to navigation because they showed relative distance accurately, without the need for elaborate methods of projection.

Right: A Venetian cog of the sixteenth century, showing the bluff bow and full form amidships.

Below: A near-contemporary seventeenth century print showing Stradanus's ship of the late sixteenth century.

square rig for his ships. This rig (square sail on fore and main masts, and a lateen sail on the mizen) was also adopted in northern Europe, although in those more stormy waters there was little love for the lateen because of the need to dip the yard round the mast every time the ship changed tacks. Nevertheless, it gave a good balance on the helm, the tall lateen sail counteracting the pressure of wind on the high forecastle, and so was accepted until something better should make its appearance. Fortunately, this was already to hand, although it was to be a few years yet before its great advantages over the lateen mizen for the three-masted rig were recognized. This was the sprit, a spar stretched diagonally across a four-sided fore-and-aft sail, with its heel, or forward end, held firmly near the base of the mast. It was not a new idea – Greeks and Romans had used it in small boats, if the evidence of reliefs at Thasos dating from the second century B.C. are to be believed – but it was not introduced into western Europe until the early fifteenth century, almost certainly by the Dutch, as a rig for small coastal craft, for which it proved

much more weatherly than the square sail in the shoal and tidal waters off the Dutch coast.

The sprit rig, where the luff of the sail is held close to the mast and the sail is spread by the spar, can be said to be the first true example of the fore-and-aft rig, more so than a lateen sail spread on a yard. There was nothing to be dipped round the mast when a vessel tacked, and shipowners of the period were quick to see that this led to a distinct saving in the number of men required to handle the ship. Within the space of fifty years, the lateen mizen had virtually disappeared from north European waters.

There can also be no doubt, in spite of some lack of pictorial evidence, that the development of ships in Far Eastern waters was progressing at much the same pace as in the western hemisphere. De Bry, in his many volumes of *Collectiones . . .*, has several illustrations of eastern ships, and they do not differ very greatly in general hull design from their western counter-

Below: A single-masted Javanese *fusta*, from *Linschoten's Voyages*, part of De Bry's *Collectiones*.

parts. In his *Collectiones . . . in Indiam Orientalem* he shows, as an example, a Javanese *fusta*, which is not all that different from a Mediterranean dromon, though shorter and rowed by fewer oarsmen. It has the same raised deck above the rowers to accommodate the fighting men, and the same rounded shelter over the after end of the deck to provide a cabin for the commander. The long pointed ram is mounted at the level of the gunwale, rather higher than in the Mediterranean galleys. A novelty is a stern gallery round the whole of the stern to provide the commander with a private walking place. The *fusta* has two masts, with a single lateen sail on each.

It is difficult to estimate her size from the illustration, because, in common with so many ship artists of the time, De Bry had little sense of perspective or relative sizes, the men pictured on board standing about as tall as one-third of the masts, but from their numbers the vessel could hardly be less than 120 ft (37 m) overall. She has a hanging rudder at the stern and the illustration shows four guns mounted on the gunwale between the rowers, and there was presumably a similar number mounted on the opposite side of the ship.

De Bry's illustration of a trading ship shows a vessel of comparable size, though with a pair of steering oars in place of a rudder. Again, the hull design looks fairly conventional through western eyes, though the whole centre of the ship, from abaft the single mast to the position of the steers-

men, is built up and roofed in, almost certainly to provide protection for the cargo. She carries a single lateen sail and rowers are accommodated in the forward end of the ship, facing forward instead of aft and pushing their oars instead of pulling them. De Bry also illustrates some sailing proas, in outline only, but there are no surrounding objects to permit even the wildest guess at their size. Again there is the single lateen sail, but with a very pronounced curve in the leech, strongly reminiscent of a modern Nile *felucca*, and a large outrigger to provide stability.

This evidence is little enough to go on, but it does offer some indication that in more distant waters the development of the ship was keeping pace, at least in size, with development elsewhere. And this was only to be expected, as seaborne trade in the east was growing in volume, just as it was in the west. There was a lively business, too, in piracy, an activity which has always stimulated the building of fast, weatherly ships, and one can be sure that, in this particular department, the pirates of eastern seas were at least as efficient as those of the west.

With these new ships, and particularly with the new sail plan which their increase in size had dictated, the unknown world was poised like an oyster, ready to be prised open. The century which followed was to witness many voyages of epic proportions, hear many new stories of distant, uncharted waters, and see many new islands and continents drawn in on the map of the world.

Right: An outrigger canoe and other Far Eastern craft. (From *Linschoten's Voyages*)

Henry the Navigator

Henry, Prince of Portugal, and known to history as the Navigator, was the third son of John I of Portugal and, incidentally, a grandson of England's John of Gaunt. He served with distinction in various wars and finally retired from the army to become governor of the Algarve, living at Sagres, near Cape St. Vincent, 'where endeth land and where beginneth sea' as the Portuguese poet Camöens put it. Being an ardent student of geography, he established there a naval 'arsenal' to which he attracted mathematicians and geographers to teach navigation, astronomy and cartography to Portuguese captains and pilots.

In 1455 a papal bull had granted Portugal exclusive jurisdiction over the west African coast of Guinea 'and past that southern shore all the way to the Indians'. Whether Prince Henry consciously accepted the implication in this papal bull that the way to India was round the continent of Africa is uncertain, but he certainly wanted to know what happened beyond the tip of Africa. So he made African exploration one of the aims of his naval 'arsenal' at Sagres, and used the royal revenues to fit out exploring expeditions to push down the African coast, mapping and observing as they went. When these expeditions proved profitable through the discovery of gold in Guinea and the sale of black slaves, as well as increasing knowledge of the globe, Henry found no lack of adventurers ready to sail in his ships into the unknown.

Already the magnetic compass and the chart had made their appearance at sea, though both had severe limitations for purposes of accurate navigation. No navigator, as yet, had any knowledge of the existence of a magnetic pole, to which a magnetic compass pointed, or realised that the north shown by the compass was not the same as that shown on a chart. His chart, if he had one, was a portulan chart drawn on a sheepskin or goatskin, which showed coastal outlines, with the positions of ports and cities and illustrations of their flags and banners, but no details of the hinterland. The sea areas of the charts were covered with compass roses, each with radiating rhumb lines, from which a navigator could read off his course from one place to the next. But since his ship's compass did not correspond accurately to the compass rose on the chart, his reading of the course was likely to be in error.

If he had no chart – and they were still rare and expensive items in the fifteenth century – a navigator may have had a *portolano*, which was a form of pilot guide in notebook form, describing coasts, ports, anchorages, rocks and shoals, and the facilities available for trade at the various ports. A fortunate navigator had both, for the information in the *portolano* supplemented the information given on a portulan chart.

Apart from supplying all his pilots with the latest charts and information for the voyages that he called on them to undertake, Henry's great ambition was to improve the accuracy of the marine chart and the methods of determining a ship's position upon it. His own studies of geography had convinced him that there really was a solution to be found in the position and daily movements of the sun, moon and stars to the problem of establishing a ship's position at sea. He sent invitations to the best known astronomers and mathematicians in the world to come to Sagres, recruiting some of them from as far away as Arabia, whose seamen at that time were leading the world in the knowledge and practice of navigation. At a time of anti-semitism he recruited the greatest Jewish mathematicians, guaranteeing them immunity from persecution in the Algarve.

Amongst other contributions to the relatively new art of navigation, they produced the first accurate tables for the daily declination of the sun, with whose aid a navigator could always determine his latitude by means of a simple observation of altitude. One result of

this work was that, over the years, Portuguese pilots acquired so great a reputation for navigational skill that all organizers of voyages of exploration, whether Spanish, English or French, invariably tried to engage one of them for their ships. Another was that, by 1484 at least, when Henry the Navigator had been succeeded by his nephew Alfonso V, every Portuguese ship carried a chart with an accurate grid of lines of latitude.

No less important to the navigator than the astronomical tables which gave him his latitude was the chart itself, on which he could see where he was, relative to the land. The first great centres of production of portulan charts were Venice and Genoa, as might be expected from their commanding position in Mediterranean seaborne trade. The greatest of the portulan chartmakers was Petrus Vesconte, who, in the fourteenth century, ran a thriving cartographic workshop in Genoa. (Today, five of his original charts are still in existence, highly prized exhibits in museums and libraries.) From Venice and Genoa the art spread to Catalonia, and by the fifteenth century the Catalan school had become supreme in the chartmaking art. One of its greatest exponents was Abraham Cresques, who worked in Majorca, and there are several references in the Spanish royal archives to the King of Aragon ordering a number of special *mappamundi* from him. He died before Henry the Navigator established his naval arsenal in 1420, but one of Henry's first acts was to send for Abraham's son, Jafuda, who was glad to come to Sagres to escape the persecution of the Jews in the kingdom of Aragon. Jafuda founded the school of chartmaking in Sagres which was to make Portuguese charts renowned for their accuracy throughout the seafaring world in the fifteenth and sixteenth centuries.

Simultaneously with the work of preparing astronomical tables for seamen, and charts to plot their voyages, Henry the Navigator turned his attention to the design of nautical instruments with which his pilots could take accurate readings. Some were adapted from navigational instruments used by the Arabs on their long voyages across the Indian Ocean; others were marine versions of measuring instruments used

in land surveys. The first of real importance was the astrolabe, a heavy instrument worked by two men: one to hold it so that it hung vertically; another to sight an arm, pivoted at the centre, at the sun or stars and read off the altitude. It was a difficult instrument to use on the heaving deck of a ship, but useful ashore to calculate the latitude of new lands. For use at sea, the Arabic *kamal* was adapted into the cross-staff, and although it came on the scene a little later than the astrolabe, it arrived in time for all the major voyages of exploration of the sixteenth century.

With these aids to navigation, many of them made available through the interest and encouragement of Henry the Navigator, the Portuguese pilots were admirably equipped for the great surge of world exploration which took place in the sixteenth century. But such secret knowledge as the Portuguese navigators may have enjoyed at first did not remain secret for long. It spread rapidly throughout Europe, and within a very few years was helping the seamen of France, Spain, England and Holland just as much as it had done those of Portugal

Far left: The headland at Sagres in Portugal, home of Prince Henry and point of departure for his navigators.

Above left: Prince Henry the Navigator (1394–1460) in a detail from a triptych attributed to Nuno Goncalves.

Above: An astrolabe made by Arsenio Lovanio, a navigational aid in maritime exploration.

Chapter Four
The Age of Exploration

It has been mentioned earlier how the development of the *caravela latina* with its all-lateen rig, by enabling a vessel to make way to windward, had given Gil Eannes enough confidence to round the Cabo de Não, on the western bulge of the African continent, in 1434, and continue exploring along the coast. It has also been seen how Columbus discovered that the *caravela latina* rig was unsuitable for ocean voyages and put into the Canary Islands on his first voyage to the west, to convert his one *caravela latina*, the *Niña*, to a *caravela redonda*, with square sails on foremast and mainmast and a lateen sail on the mizen. It did not take very long for the Portuguese explorers along the African coast to reach the same conclusion as that reached later by Columbus. Once they had confidence in the caravel's ability to beat to windward, they switched over to the *caravela redonda* rig as one much more suited to long ocean voyages.

At the time when Prince Henry the Navigator died in 1460, his dream of African discovery had been hanging fire. There was so much money to be made out of voyages to the already known African coast, from the discovery of gold or the sale of the black population as slaves, that any urge to venture further towards the equator and beyond was stifled. This lack of incentive was effectively overcome by Alfonso V, nephew of Prince Henry and as interested in exploration as had been his uncle. He granted a Lisbon merchant, Fernão Gomes, a monopoly of all trade on the Guinea coast on the condition that each year he was to explore 100 leagues further. The bargain paid off on both sides. When Gomes's ships swung round the bulge of Africa and sailed east along the coast, they opened up yet richer districts of western Africa, the Gold Coast and Ivory Coast. When his monopoly ended in 1474, Gomes's ships had reached the island of Fernando Po, only three and a half degrees north of the

equator, and had ventured right across the Gulf of Guinea to where the African coast turns to the southward again.

These voyages brought great wealth to Fernão Gomes, but they brought to Alfonso V something of much greater importance. If the earth was a sphere – and no geographer of any repute now disputed the fact – the rounding of the African continent was bound to open a sea route to India. And if Africa could be rounded by Portuguese ships navigated by Portuguese pilots, it would be a Portuguese route by right of prior discovery and India would ostensibly be defensible against all comers. The national prize was immense, and expeditions, financed by the king, pushed further and further south. By 1484 Diogo Cão had reached the mouth of the River Congo, and four years later the great prize was itself achieved. Alfonso did not live long enough to see his greatest ambition realised, but his son, João II of Portugal, who was equally wholehearted and enthusiastic in his patronage of exploration, was in Lisbon in December 1488 when Bartholomew Diaz brought his three caravels home and sailed them proudly up the Tagus. They had rounded

Left: A fanciful impression of the battle between English ships and the Spanish Armada in 1588.
Above right: Portrait of Christopher Columbus.

CALECHVT CELEBERRI: MVM INDIÆ EMPORIVM.

Above: Calicut, where Vasco da Gama landed in India. (From an engraving of 1572)

Right: Illustration of Columbus's discoveries in the 'Indies', from the 1493 edition of his letters to Don Luis de Santangel.

the southernmost cape of Africa, had been driven further south into a wide open sea by a great storm, had steered to the eastward when the storm abated after thirteen days, and on their return to Africa had sailed well up the east coast before a threat of mutiny by his crew had forced Diaz to return to Portugal. The seaway to India was now open, and João and all his navigators knew it. Diaz, remembering the great storm which had arisen off the southernmost cape and driven his ships so far to the south, had named it Cabo Tormentosa, Cape of Storms, but the king soon changed that: it was not Cabo Tormentosa to him but Cabo de Bona Speranza, Cape of Good Hope, for his next expedition would surely reach India, the greatest prize of all. And so it was: in May, 1498, a Portuguese squadron under the command of Vasco da Gama let go their anchors off Calicut on the mainland of India.

In the meantime Spain was chasing the same prize. Christopher Columbus, who had studied charts and globes and was an experienced seaman, had come to the conclusion that the western route to India was much shorter than the eastern route, especially since there was no great continent such as Africa blocking the way. He had a lot of difficulty in selling his navigational ideas to Ferdinand and Isabella of Spain, but in the end they were convinced and agreed to finance an expedition. Columbus's geography was of course, wildly inaccurate, but the world had long forgotten Eratosthenes's calculation of the earth's circumference 1,700 years earlier, and most contemporary geographers reckoned that 'Cipangu', modern Japan and the western gateway to the Far East, lay on about longitude 60°W.

On that reckoning Columbus was not far out when he claimed the western route to India to be shorter than the eastern; it was only the reality of his great voyage that proved contemporary geographers wrong.

His little fleet of three caravels dropped down the Rio Tinto from Palos at daybreak on 3 August 1492, put into Gomera in the Canary Islands for repairs to the *Pinta* and alteration of the *Niña* to the *redonda* rig, and on 6 September set sail for the west, picking up the north-east trade winds.

Above: Part of the world map drawn by Columbus's pilot, de la Cosa, showing Spanish discoveries in the West Indies.

Above right: Spanish caravels similar to Columbus's Pinta and Niña.

At two o'clock in the morning of 12 October the lookout on the *Pinta*, Rodrigo de Triana, sighted a white cliff shining in the moonlight and the cry *'Tierra! Tierra!'* echoed through the ship. Later that morning, with the three ships lying at anchor off a white coral beach, Columbus and the two brothers Pinzón of the *Pinta* and *Niña* went ashore in their longboats flying the royal standard of Castile and the banner of the expedition, a green crowned cross on a white field. 'And, all having rendered thanks to Our Lord, kneeling on the ground, embracing it with tears of joy for the immeasurable mercy of having reached it, the Admiral rose and gave this island the name San Salvador.'

Columbus was convinced that he had reached an outlying island off the mainland of India. As he sailed further west, discovering still more islands, but no land that even began to look like a continent, he underlined his belief that the mainland of India must lie just over the western horizon by naming the islands collectively as 'las Indias' (the Indies) and since India had to lie further to the westward, they became the West Indies, the name by which they are known today. It was not until his third voyage to the west, from 1498 to 1500, that Columbus came to the conclusion that what he had discovered was a new continent hitherto unknown to Europeans. By then he had coasted along the northern shore of the mainland of South America, and he knew by now that it was not India; he knew, too, that it was not China; so it had to be a new and unknown continent, although Columbus would not renounce his belief that India and China must still lie just over the horizon to the west. All the maps and all the globes that he had seen had told him so. They couldn't be all *that* wrong even though they were so obviously wrong over this new continent. How could he justify his assurances to Ferdinand and Isabella that it was *las Indias* which he had discovered in 1492? He was too proud to eat his words; there must be some other explanation that would not discredit the geographical assumptions on which his voyages had been financed. So Columbus decided that this new continent was the Garden of Eden, and that it stood at the top of a large protruberance projecting up from the earth's surface like a woman's breast, in order to bring it nearer to

Heaven than the surrounding land. Only thus could he account for all the miles he had sailed to the west without reaching India. If the earth's curvature had remained normal, he would already have reached India on the mileage that he had sailed; that he had not yet done so was attributable to the fact that his ships had been sailing up the curve of the breast.

Whatever explanation Columbus put forward, the fact remained that he had shown the world that new lands, ripe for commercial exploitation, lay across the ocean to the west. Merchants now had to adjust themselves to the existence of a New World and to design and build ships able to cope with the distances involved.

These great Spanish and Portuguese voyages – Spanish to the westward, Portuguese to the east – were made in small caravels, ranging from a maximum tonnage of 80 or 90 down to a minimum of 30 to 40. This does not by any means indicate that the caravel, in build, design or sail plan, was the 'master' ship of Europe; all it meant was that, for the purposes of discovery and the opening of new trade routes round the world, it was the sort of vessel that the explorers themselves preferred. They wanted, first of all, a ship that drew a minimum of water so that it could

come close into unknown coasts and anchor just offshore, instead of further out in deep water. The average caravel, drawing about 6 ft (2 m), met this requirement admirably. Moreover, the explorers did not come to trade: they only needed a ship with enough room on board to carry a few chests of beads, bells and baubles which they could exchange with the natives for gold, silver, pearls and anything else of sufficient value to indicate to their paymasters that their discoveries were economically significant enough to warrant the financing of further voyages. The little caravel answered this purpose too. Above all, and most important, the explorers did not want large crews. The risk of discontent among the men, of a breakdown in discipline, even of mutiny, was always far greater among a large crew than a small one. The largest caravel carried about ten officers and officials, and about thirty men on the lower deck; the smallest about five officers and sixteen men. It was not too difficult to keep crews of this size in a reasonably good humour through a long voyage, and there was a good chance that morale could be kept up when things were going badly. Columbus himself had managed to do so during his first voyage in 1492, when there were signs of an incipient mutiny that might have forced the abandonment of the venture. A larger ship would obviously entail shipping a larger crew. Columbus recorded

Below: A carrack and two caravels locked in battle near the entrance to the Red Sea. (From Testu's *Cosmographie Universelle*)

in his journal during his first voyage that even the 90-ton *Santa Maria* was larger than he really wanted. Of the three ships in his little fleet, his favourite was the 50-ton *Niña*, the smallest of the three.

The impact on the other maritime nations of Europe of these voyages, to India in the east and to the new continent in the west, was profound. The doctrine of possession by right of prior discovery was accepted throughout Europe, and Spain and Portugal took immediate steps to get their discoveries registered by papal bull. Originally, Pope Alexander VI granted Spain possession of all land lying to the west of a line drawn from north to south 100 leagues west of the Azores, and to Portugal all land lying to the east of it. On a protest from Portugal that this line ran too near the west African coast and would jeopardize further Portuguese discoveries to the south and east, it was moved to 370 leagues west of the Azores. In the event, this paid off well for Portugal, for when, in 1500, Pedro Cabral touched the coast of Brazil during a voyage to India, the new land was found to lie to the east of the line and Portugal's claim to possession was confirmed. But, if Spain and Portugal welcomed the papal bull as providing legitimacy to their claims, the other European maritime nations would have none of it. England and Holland were not bound by papal edict as were Portugal and

Spain, and even France decided that her national interest in the scramble for trade which was bound to follow the new discoveries took precedence over her allegiance to Rome. So far as England, Holland and France were concerned, maritime exploration remained a free-for-all, and the tiny areas of land already visited by Portuguese and Spanish navigators still left a huge undiscovered area, ripe for exploitation under the doctrine of prior discovery.

Holland, at that time a province of Spain – though with an active independence movement backed by England – was at first relatively inactive in the quest for trade, but when she finally rebelled, as the result of a relentless policy of oppression, it was to beyond the Cape of Good Hope that she looked for an empire. France, on the other hand, looked to the west and for a way through the new continent to the Far East, while England tried both east and west. It was in fact Holland who chose the most promising alternative, reaching round the south of India and setting up her empire on the islands of the East Indies. The Frenchman, Jacques Cartier, having landed on the North American coast in 1534, sailed up the St. Lawrence in the belief that, at the centre of the continent, it must join up with another river flowing westwards, thus providing a direct route to China. The west-flowing river did not exist, of course, but the acquisition of

Left: Part of Sebastian Cabot's map of the east coast of North America, produced in 1544.

Above: The *Victoria*, the only ship of Magellan's squadron to complete the voyage around the world.

Right: World map showing the route of Magellan's expedition, dated 1545.

Canada for the French empire and the development of the fur trade paid a handsome dividend.

England's more northerly route across the Atlantic, pioneered by John Cabot's voyage of 1497, brought her the economically disappointing discovery of Newfoundland, though there was a temporary bonus in the form of the great cod fishery of the Newfoundland Banks. But a fishery well off the coast could not be claimed or defended as a national monopoly on the basis of prior discovery, and within two or three years it was the French and Portuguese who were exploiting its wealth far more energetically than the English ever did. English voyages to the east were more successful in establishing 'factories', or trading centres, on newly discovered parts of the coasts of India and the East Indies, though many of them had to be actively defended against Portuguese and Dutch attacks.

Within a few years of the discovery of the New World, as America was known in Europe, its approximate shape and rough limits northwards and southwards were known to geographers and incorporated in their maps and globes. Vasco Nuñez de Balboa had seen the Pacific in 1513, named it the Great South Sea, and claimed possession of it for the King of Spain. Many voyages, and particularly those of Giovanni and Girolama da Verrazzano starting in 1524, had searched the east coast of North and South America for a way through to the Great South Sea, all without success, and it was becoming more and more apparent that the New World was an unbroken land mass placed squarely across the direct sea route to the riches of 'Cathay', as China was then called, and India. The world's geographers showed it as such and the world's navigators reluctantly had to accept that there was no way through it by sea.

Even if there was no way through, there might still be ways round this huge land mass, both to the north and the south. Ferdinand Magellan discovered the southern way round it in his voyage of circumnavigation of 1519–22. Magellan was Portuguese, but having fallen out with the King of Portugal became a naturalized Spaniard and his voyage was made under the flag of Spain. As a navigational feat, it can be said to have been the greatest sea voyage ever made, even though Magellan himself was killed in the process and only one ship out of his original five came home to Spain. (Magellan lost his life in the Philippine Islands at the battle of Mactan in April 1521, but his claim to be the world's first circumnavigator still stands as he had reached that longitude on an earlier voyage to the east when in Portuguese service.)

Magellan did more for the geographers than place the southern route to the Pacific on the map of the world: his voyage made clear the huge

extent of the Pacific Ocean, very much greater than had been thought. Once the surviving ship of his expedition had reached home with her log of the voyage, the true size of the globe became known and far more accurate maps were drawn.

There remained the northern route round America, a heart-breaking search which was to occupy the English for the next 300 years. Martin Frobisher and John Davis both led expeditions in the mid-sixteenth century in search of the North-West Passage; both failed amid the ice of the Polar Sea north of Canada, as did many other expeditions through the centuries, until, in 1850, Vice Admiral McClure found a way.

Left: Ferdinand Magellan, who discovered the southern route around the American continent.

Below left: Martin Frobisher, who tried in vain to find a way round to the north.

Left: A squadron of
Portuguese carracks,
painted in the sixteenth
century.

Below left: *Ark Royal*,
Lord Howard's flagship
at the time of the Armada.

Simultaneously, England was looking to the north-east for a passage to China, around the top of Europe and Asia. The idea that such a passage might exist was first put forward in 1527, in a letter written by Robert Thorne, as the best way of avoiding conflict with the Spaniards and Portuguese, who still claimed the possession of all unknown lands in the world east and west of Pope Alexander's north–south line in mid-Atlantic. English expeditions in search of this North-East Passage were led in mid-century by Sir Hugh Willoughby, Richard Chancellor, Stephen Borough and others, but like the corresponding voyages to the north-west, were all foiled by the polar ice. One thing that they did achieve, however, was a trading contact with Russia, which led to the formation of the Muscovy Company of Merchant Adventurers, to regulate trade between the two countries.

This huge expansion of the known world within the span of twenty to thirty years had a profound effect on the ships of the principal trading nations, for, while the smaller ship might be the ideal vessel in which to discover new worlds, it was the bigger ship that was required to bring home the rich cargoes from the new lands. As the sixteenth century developed, Spain and Portugal made the carrack their 'big ship' for trading purposes as well as war, and expanded her cargo-carrying capacity by building her up to 1,200 tons, and even larger in some cases. In the north European countries the carrack was never popular, even though some were captured from the Spanish and Portuguese and incorporated into the northern fleets. The tendency in England, France and Holland was to expand the cog, by doubling her overall length, adding two more masts to the existing one, and using carvel construction instead of clinker. This enlarged cog was known first as a *hourque* or hulk, and then, when built still bigger, as a *nef* or, in England, as a full-rigged ship. Smaller vessels, with both two- and three-masted rigs, were known as 'pinnaces', or sometimes as 'frigats' (though they should not be confused with later frigates, built by all the world's navies as small, fast and efficient warships).

On navies, too, the effect of the new discoveries was equally profound. Gone for ever were the days when a maritime nation required fighting ships only to uphold the sovereignty of its own territorial waters, to resist invasion by neighbouring powers, to protect its fisheries, to put down piracy in its own patrimonial seas. A national navy now needed the capability to safeguard the country's trade routes to newly discovered countries. Thus Spain needed a large navy, not only to maintain her trade with the West Indian islands and the mainland of America, but also, following Magellan's voyage, to police the Pacific which she claimed as her exclusive possession. Her subsequent lack of success in defending her new territories against freebooters and privateers is a measure of her failure to build a centrally controlled navy and reliance, instead, on hiring and arming privately owned ships. Portugal similarly required an expanded navy to guard her trade route to the east and to hold her African possessions, which she was developing not only as rich colonies in their own right, but also as staging posts for ships on the long voyage to India. So, too, did Holland, with her East Indian empire.

Only in England did this reason for a large navy not apply. She had come badly out of the search for new lands and had virtually no colonies worth protecting. But even in her case a growing navy was needed, partly because of the decision to fight for a share of the trade earmarked by Spain, Portugal and Holland for themselves, partly because the French had become so obsessed with Canada and the St. Lawrence River that they had neglected to occupy and claim that part of the North American continent which lay to the south. There was a wide belt of potentially rich land between the French possessions in Canada and the furthest extent of Spanish penetration of the mainland to the south, and into this gap the English stepped, planting colonies along the coastal strip.

The English navy really began to flower during the reign of Elizabeth I (1558–1603), mainly through her acceptance of the strategic concept that the most effective way to use a navy was to carry the fight to an enemy at sea, rather than to wait at home and fight defensively when the enemy attacked. Her father and grandfather had both built their own warships; Elizabeth added modestly to the number of royal ships, but those built in her reign were greatly superior in quality and endurance. It was during the Elizabethan period that the fight for a trading foothold amid Spain's western possessions began in earnest, not in any way as a national conflict, between the respective navies, but as a series of private struggles in which the crown had a financial interest, usually secured by lending a royal ship, and thus a warship, to the backers of the trading ventures. This was a not unusual course – both Henry VII and Henry VIII had done it – and it had the merit of confining the blame for any possible conflict to private adventurers, relieving the crown of any responsibility for an action which could be held as an act of war if performed openly by the sovereign.

Henry VIII's main contribution to what was the nucleus of a national navy was the *Henry Grace à Dieu*, laid down at Erith in 1512, launched in 1514, rebuilt in 1540, and accidentally destroyed by fire in 1553. She was built to replace the *Regent*, lost in action off Brest in 1512, and like her was a four-masted ship with a fixed topmast on her foremast and mainmast, possibly a fixed topgallant mast above her main topmast, a mizen and a bonaventure mizen. Volpe's famous picture, now at Hampton Court, depicting her at Dover in 1520 does not show her with all sails set, but a contemporary panel, which used to hang in Canterbury Cathedral and was later presented to Admiral Sir John Norris, does. According to this, she set three square sails on foremast and mainmast (course, topsail, topgallant sail), two lateen sails with a small topgallant sail on the mizen and a single lateen with a small topsail on the bonaventure mizen, and she also carried a spritsail on a yard slung from her bowsprit. This mass of sail, certainly unusual for the period, probably represents artistic licence on the part of the painter. Most Tudor warships, even the largest, set only two square sails on the foremast and mainmast, with single lateen sails on the two after masts, and a spritsail on the bowsprit.

The *Henry Grace à Dieu* was built by William Bond, the master shipwright at Erith, under the general directions of Robert Brygandine, Henry's Clerk of the Ships. Many contemporary accounts gave her a tonnage of about 1,500, but this is thought to be an exaggeration and her true tonnage is now given as about 1,000. Even this would make her a very big ship in the context of contemporary English shipbuilding, though by now Spain and Portugal, and possibly France as well, were building as large, if not larger.

Henry's second great contribution to the navy was the replacement of the small anti-personnel gun, of which very large numbers were carried on board, by the cannon, firing a heavy ball or stone shot and, by its nature, an anti-ship weapon. The lower gundeck, and gunports cut in the ship's sides, were natural corollaries of this increase in the size, and therefore the weight, of the cannon. The need to lower the gun's position in the ship for reasons of stability was, in turn, responsible for the pronounced tumble-home, which became such a feature of wooden warships. There is no tumble-home visible in contemporary pictures of the *Henry Grace à Dieu*, for the few cannon she carried were still mounted in the two castles fore and aft; fifty years later it was commonplace. Henry's *Mary Rose* is said to have been the first warship to have gunports cut in her sides; another, sadder, claim to fame is that she was the first ship to be lost by heeling over and having the sea enter her open gunports,

which were only 16 in (41 cm) above her waterline. This tragedy occurred off Spithead in 1545 as she was about to go into action against the French. (In 1982 her well-preserved hull was brought to the surface and has since provided much new data on Tudor naval techniques.)

At the same time, Henry VIII was unable to break away completely from the Mediterranean predilection for the galley as the supreme warship type, even though his introduction of the anti-ship gun was the complete answer to galley warfare and despite the fact that English and Atlantic waters were well recognized as unsuitable for the oared galley. During his reign he built about a dozen, and Queen Elizabeth, right at the end of her reign, had four built to a Mediterranean design. It is difficult to understand why they were built, for they did not incorporate the pointed ram which was always the galley's main weapon of attack, but relied simply on one or two cannon, or demi-cannon, firing ahead. Perhaps the reason for their construction was that neighbouring France had galleys in her fleet and it may have been thought wise to be able to meet like with like. The original square sail on a central mast, which the earlier English galleys inherited from the longship, gave way in the sixteenth century to a single large lateen sail.

If the maritime nations of northern Europe were lukewarm in their appreciation of the galley as a ship of war, the Mediterranean nations still swore by it, and indeed retained it as a warship type right up to the times of the Revolutionary and Napoleonic wars at the start of the nineteenth century, though it was rapidly losing favour by then. One of the greatest and best-known galley actions in naval history was fought at Lepanto, off the western coast of Greece, in 1571 between a combined fleet of Christian nations commanded by Don John of Austria and a Turkish fleet under the command of Ali Pasha. On the outcome of the battle depended the whole future of the Mediterranean, for victory would have assured the Turks not only of complete mastery of the Adriatic and possession of the vast wealth of Venice, but probably also maritime control of the western basin of the Mediterranean. Don John's force consisted of over 200 galleys, rowed by 43,000 oarsmen and manned by 12,000 seamen and 28,000 soldiers, with about thirty other ships attached, six of them huge Venetian galleasses. The Turkish fleet was even larger in numbers, though they had fewer of the large galleys and more of the smaller, and no galleasses. The battle lasted from dawn to midnight and ended in a Christian victory.

Right: Part of Henry VIII's fleet off Dover.

Below right: The Battle of Lepanto in 1571 between the galleys of the Turkish and combined Christian fleets.

We know a lot about the Venetian galley of the sixteenth century. There is a mid-sixteenth century relief of a galley under sail on the tomb of one of the Venetian admirals, Alexander Contarini, in the cathedral of San Antonio in Padua. Even more important are manuscript instructions for the building of galleys written at the same period by Pre Theodoro de Nicolo, one of the best of the galley builders in Venice, and now preserved in the Biblioteca Nazionale in Venice. He gives the dimensions of three types of galley, ranging from the small *fusta*, with a length of 88½ ft (27 m), a maximum beam of 13 ft (4 m) and a depth from deck to keel of 4½ ft (1·4 m), to the large galley, for which the corresponding

Above: Part of the building plans for a Venetian galley.

measurements are 151, 24½ and 10 ft (46, 7·5 and 3 m). He tells us that the *corsia* (the narrow raised bridge between the thwarts, running from stem to stern) was 2¾ ft (84 cm) wide and that the distance between the *corsia* and the *apostis* (the outrigger in the form of a longitudinal beam on which the oars rested) was 14½ ft (4·4 m).

One result of this battle of Lepanto was to prove the value of the galleasse in battle. The Mediterranean galleasse was a very different ship from the north European galleasse, being based on a totally opposite conception. In England the concept of the galleasse was of the normal heavily-built sailing warship, adapted for using oars to provide additional manoeuvrability; the Mediterranean concept was the normal swift oared galley, adapted to sail and given an added robustness of build to permit a powerful all-round gun armament in addition to her ram. The Venetian galleasses used at Lepanto rowed twenty-six oars each side, with four rowers to each oar, had a three-masted lateen rig, mounted eight large guns in the forecastle, two more in the aftercastle and eight broadside guns, four each side, on the upper deck above

the rowers, and, finally, were provided with a powerful ram, reinforced and tipped with iron.

Until 1570 or 1580, the general type of sailing warship did not differ greatly between any of the western nations. Whether it was the enlarged carrack of Spain and Portugal or the expanded cog of England and Holland, it was in either case a so-called 'high-charged' ship, with a built-up castle overhanging the stern, surmounted by another, even higher castle at the after end, and sometimes another and another, so that in extreme cases there might be as many as four built-up decks, rising in steps, one above the other. In fact, only the very largest carracks, of 1,500 to 1,800 tons, were built with four: a big carrack would have three, and an average carrack two. English and Dutch ships were not built nearly as big as Spanish, and the largest of them had no more than two built-up decks aft.

The high-charged ship, standing high out of the water, was very difficult to sail, except directly before the wind. Once she came on to the wind, the large forecastle built out over her stem presented a large surface to the wind which forced her bows down to leeward and gave her a tendency to carry excessive lee helm. The lateen sail on the mizen, which should have counteracted this lee helm, was not large enough, in relation to the amount of canvas carried on the foremast, to do so. So this typical sixteenth century ship was apt to wallow in the waves at sea, her bows being continually pushed down to leeward and making it hard for the helmsman to hold her on course.

Sir John Hawkins realised this drawback in contemporary ship design during the last two of his three 'triangular' voyages, for which Queen Elizabeth hired him one of her ships in return for a share in the profits. The two voyages were made in 1564 and 1567, and the royal ship was the 700-ton *Jesus of Lubeck*, a typical high-charged ship of the period. With her went the *Judith* and *Minion*, two 50-ton vessels described as 'barks'.

The basic plan of all these 'triangular' voyages was to sail first to Sierra Leone with goods to exchange for a cargo of black slaves, carry the slaves across the Middle Sea (that area of the Atlantic lying between the west African coast and the Spanish possessions in the West Indies and Gulf of Mexico), sell the slaves to Spanish planters and load a cargo of sugar or other produce, return to England and sell it. These voyages were not without considerable danger: there was always a risk of meeting a Portuguese warship off the African coast, intent on upholding her country's monopoly of African trade, and Spanish colonists were forbidden by law to trade with any but Spaniards, so it needed a good deal of forceful persuasion to induce them to buy the slaves, even though they were always in great demand. It was the Spaniards' determination to restrict all trade to their own nationals that led to disasters for Hawkins on the third voyage. Stress of weather and a shortage of provisions had forced his little fleet to seek refuge in the anchorage of San Juan de Ulloa, and the Spaniards there agreed to Hawkins's request that his ships be reprovisioned for their voyage home. But on a given signal they were treacherously attacked. The little *Judith* and *Minion* managed to sail clear; the *Jesus of Lubeck*, a slow sailer and unhandy in the water, was unable to win free, and although Hawkins and a handful of seamen were rescued by the *Minion*, the rest of the crew were slaughtered to a man.

The disastrous loss of one of the Queen's ships, brought about in some measure by the deficiencies in sailing ability inherent in her design, made Hawkins consider how the design could be improved. He was a practical seaman and knew a lot about ship construction and the action of the winds on sails and hull. Moreover, the disaster had been precipitated by Spanish treachery and Hawkins, and the captain of the *Judith*, his young cousin, Francis Drake, vowed vengeance. We will see later how Drake fulfilled his vow; Hawkins did so by devoting the rest of his life to the naval service of his country and reshaping Elizabeth's navy with ships of a new design. In 1577 he became Treasurer of the Navy and his practical experience as a seaman brought him

considerable influence on the naval affairs of his day. His views on construction and design were heard with respect, and his ideas for the improvement of the basic ship design were quickly put into effect.

The first of the new breed may have been the *Foresight*, a ship of 300 tons built in 1570, but it is more likely that the *Bull* and *Tiger* were the prototypes. They were both small vessels of 200 tons, both built some years earlier, and both taken in hand in 1570 for rebuilding. It would be a reasonable precaution, in launching a radical new design, to try it out on small, old ships, due in any case for a major refit. Hawkins's notion was to test whether a ship, made to lie lower in the water by cutting down her high sides, could be made more weatherly (that is, able to point higher into the wind when sailing close-hauled) by removing the high forecastle over the stem and replacing it by a lower structure, placed further aft on the foredeck. This gave the new ships a low beakhead with a distinct cutwater, and at the same time removed the large area forward of the bow which caught the wind and forced the bows down to leeward. And, in the course of this process of tidying up, the aftercastle was also reduced in height to make the ship low and snug overall, the length-to-beam ratio was increased from $2\frac{1}{2}$ to 1, to 3 to 1, and the rounded stern was changed to a square one. The new design quickly became known as 'low-charged', to distinguish it from the previous 'high-charged' type.

Above: Sir John Hawkins, who pioneered the new low-charged warship.

Left: The *Jesus of Lubeck*, captured by the Spanish at San Juan de Ulloa.

English galleon
(c.1580)

Length 140 ft (42·6 m) *Keel* 100 ft (30·5 m) *Beam* 37 ft (11·3 m)
Hold 18 ft (5·5 m) *Burthen* 500 tons
Armament 22 culverins, 16 demi-culverins
Complement 320 sailors, 100 soldiers

This is a typical English warship of the new 'low-charged' type introduced during the second half of the sixteenth century. The English fleet which defeated the Spanish Armada in 1588 included many vessels of this type, among them the flagship of Lord Howard, the *Ark Royal*. Being a large ship, she has four masts. Fore and main masts are square-rigged, carrying (in descending order) topgallants, topsails and courses. Her mizen mast and bonaventure mizen, stepped aft, are lateen-rigged, while she carries a square spritsail beneath the bowsprit. Steering in a ship of this kind would have been by means of a whipstaff. As well as having a much lower forecastle than earlier warships, she also has a more streamlined underwater hull shape, both of which would have contributed to her superior sailing performance. Her main armament, of culverins and demi-culverins, comprises guns with longer range and greater accuracy than the traditional cannon, though less sheer destructive power.

She is shown here with bonaventure mizensail, main topsail, fore topgallant and fore topsail set, and her guns run out through open gunports. The small drawing shows her hull profile superimposed, for comparison, on that of a slightly larger ship of the high-charged type. As well as being considerably lower, her forecastle is built further aft than that of the high-charged ship which actually overhangs the stem. The new arrangement presents less wind resistance at the bow, enabling her to sail better to windward, and gives rise to the pronounced 'beak', or cutwater. Her quarter-deck, on the other hand, is a no less lofty structure than that of the other high-charged type of vessel.

Above: An illustration from Matthew Baker's treatise on shipbuilding. Drawn in about 1585, it is the earliest technical drawing of an English ship to survive.

These radical changes made an immense difference to the sailing qualities of the warship, and within a very few years had spread to merchant shipbuilding as well. The new design was given the generic name of 'galleon', a term which never caught on in England even though the design originated there. It was discovered that the low-charged ship could not only hold a better wind than the old high-charged design, but was also faster through the water and much easier to handle, placing less strain on the helmsman. Once these qualities had been demonstrated, Hawkins pressed ahead with building new ships for the Queen, realising that the continual brushes with Spanish ships over the right to trade in the West Indies and the American continent was certain to end in war.

There is a contemporary manuscript on shipbuilding in the Pepysian Library at Magdalene College, Cambridge, unsigned and undated, but reliably believed to have been written by Matthew Baker, the Elizabethan shipwright, in about 1585. It contains several design drawings of the low-charged Elizabethan warship, including a typical sail plan. This shows the now normal four-masted rig, square on foremast and mainmast, with a topsail and topgallant sail set above the course, and single lateen sails on the mizen and bonaventure mizen. In several of Matthew Baker's profile designs he has superimposed a large fish on the underwater part of the hull, evidently a cod, possibly as an indication that the underwater hull design should conform to the shape of a cod's body.

Although the galleon design was introduced in England in the decade 1570 to 1580, it was some time before other maritime nations adopted it. The Dutch appear to have been the first: a model of a Flemish ship of 1593 in the Museo Navale in Madrid is of distinct galleon design. France did not take up the design in her warships until the early years of the seventeenth century, and Spain and Portugal adopted it at about the same time.

It is necessary to return briefly to Francis Drake to see how he achieved his vow of vengeance on Spain following the treachery at San Juan de Ulloa, as it was certainly due in part to his successes that the subsequent war with Spain was fought. He made two inconspicuous voyages to the West Indies in small vessels in 1570 and 1571 to gather information and make plans; then in 1572, sailing in the 70-ton *Pasha* and accompanied by the 25-ton *Swan*, he made his descent on the Spanish Main in search of plunder. He held the town of Nombre de Dios to ransom, crossed the Isthmus of Panama to become the first Englishman to sight the Pacific, and waylaid a mule train bringing treasure across the Isthmus. He returned to England in 1573, a very rich man through the gold and silver that he had captured.

His next venture against Spain was a circumnavigation of the globe between 1577 and 1580. Materially, the voyage was immensely successful owing to the capture of a Spanish treasure ship and the holding of towns to ransom up the length

Right: Francis Drake,
whose exploits were
partly responsible for
bringing about the war
between England and
Spain.

Below right: Model of a
Flemish galleon of 1593 in
the Museo Navale, Madrid.

of the west coast of South America. The moral
value of the expedition was even greater, for it
proved to the English that there was nothing to
fear from Spanish claims to control the Pacific.
When Drake reached the Pacific through the
Straits of Magellan, he had only one ship of
his small squadron left, the 100-ton *Pelican*
which he renamed *Golden Hind*, but he ran her
like a warship. We get a picture of Drake in the
Pacific from a letter written by Don Francisco de
Zarata, owner of a captured Spanish ship, whom
Drake entertained on board the *Golden Hind*:

'The English general is about thirty-five years
of age, short of stature, with a red beard, and one
of the best sailors that sail the seas, both in
respect to boldness and to capacity for command.
His ship is of near 400 tons burden, with a
hundred men on board, all young and of an age
for battle, and all drilled as well as the oldest
veterans of our army of Italy. Each one is bound
to keep his arquebus clean. Drake treats them all
with affection, and they him with respect. He
also has with him nine or ten gentlemen, the
younger sons of great people in England. Some

of them are in his counsels, but he has no favourite. These sit at his table, and he is served on silver plate with a coat of arms engraved on the dishes; and music is played at his dinner and supper. The ship carries about 30 pieces of artillery, and plenty of ammunition and warlike stores.'

On his return to England from this voyage Drake, like Hawkins, devoted himself to naval service. He approved wholeheartedly of the new warship design, and particularly of what might be called the middle order of size, the ship of about 500 tons carrying around forty-five guns of various sizes. Such a ship was the *Revenge*, in which he served as vice-admiral in the battle against the Spanish Armada.

War against Spain was declared in 1585 and Europe watched in wonder as England, still regarded as a ridiculously small naval power, prepared to challenge the maritime might of

Spain. It had to be a naval war, for England had no real army and Spain would have to cross the sea if she was to use her huge army to subdue England. It was Francis Drake who struck the first blow in the war, with his brilliant attack on Cadiz in 1587. His ship was the *Elizabeth Bonaventure*, originally a 600-ton high-charged ship, but rebuilt on galleon lines in 1581. The main naval significance of this Cadiz action lay in demonstrating the complete powerlessness of the typical Mediterranean war galley against the typical north European gunned sailing warship, even in enclosed waters in which the galley should have been at its most dangerous because of its speed and manoeuvrability under oars. Six Spanish galleys attacked Drake's squadron as it sailed into the harbour, but they were scattered by the first broadside and so knocked about that they could take no further part in the battle, nor do anything to stop Drake in his wholesale des-

Below: Contemporary map of Drake's expedition against Spanish possessions in America in 1585.

truction of Spanish ships assembled for the invasion of England.

The Cadiz raid paid one more big dividend to England, in the subsequent capture of the 1,500-ton carrack *San Felipe* off the Azores, homeward bound from the Far East with a rich cargo. The cargo was, of course, always welcome, but of infinitely more importance were the charts and papers captured with her, opening the eyes of English merchants to the huge profits to be made from systematic trade in Indian, East Indian and Chinese waters. It was the *San Felipe's* charts and papers that inspired the creation of the great East India Company, with all that this meant for the development of the ship.

One year later, in 1588, Philip of Spain launched his 'Enterprise of England', in the shape of his Invincible Armada. The running fight up the Channel, the attack by the British fireships off Calais, the subsequent battle of Gravelines, and the pursuit of the Spanish fleet up the North Sea until they were committed to a return to Spain round the north of Scotland – all have their place in maritime history. What is of more importance in the context of ship design is the comparison in performance between English and Spanish ships under battle conditions. For three centuries the general picture presented of the Armada campaign was one of large clumsy Spanish ships harried throughout the long action by smaller faster English ships, which kept their distance and drove the Spaniards on by their superior gunnery. Since then, many historians have tried to change the picture by asserting that, in general, the English ships were as large as the Spanish and that they mounted heavier guns. Neither picture is entirely accurate. Re-

garding the size of the ships, an analysis of the lists of those engaged shows that seven Spanish ships had a tonnage of above 1,000 tons, while of the English fleet two were of 1,000 tons or over. Of ships of 500 tons and over, the Spaniards had sixty-seven, the English thirteen. As to the number and size of guns, the advantage lay with Spain by a ratio of about 5 to 1, but the Spanish artillery was much the less effective because, size by size, the range of most of their guns was a good deal less than that of English guns, and because their gunports were so small as to allow no movement of the gun and, in many cases, even prevented the gunners from sighting their guns before firing them.

However, where the great strategic difference lay was in the actual design of the ships. The Spanish ships, although in some contemporary accounts they are described as 'galleons', were still carracks, high-sided, high-charged ships,

Below: Map showing the route of the Armada around the British Isles.

Bottom: Picturesque view of the Armada battle, seen through the eyes of an unknown contemporary English artist.

slow in the water, very slow in stays when tacking, and incapable of sailing closer than about 7 points off the wind. Their high sides and lofty fore and after castles presented easy targets for the English gunners. Most of the English ships, at least of the thirty-four that belonged to the Queen and formed the backbone of the fleet, had either been built to the galleon design or taken in hand and cut down from their original high-charged form into low-charged. They lay low in the water and thus presented smaller targets to the Spanish gunners, were at least a knot faster through the water and probably slightly more, fast in stays, and able to lay the wind closer than the Spanish ships when sailing close-hauled, to within about 6 to $6\frac{1}{2}$ points. The English guns had longer barrels and thus greater accuracy, while the gunners were better trained and, with the aid of large square gunports, were able to sight their guns before firing.

The defeat of the Spanish Armada has long been considered one of the world's most decisive battles (taking the nine days of fighting as one single battle), because it marks the start of the downfall of Spain as the world's greatest maritime power and the start of the rise of England to the same pinnacle. Although in her own eyes England had been great upon the seas ever since the battle of Sluys in 1340, in the eyes of the rest of Europe she had been something of a minnow in a pond dominated first by the predatory fish of Spain and Portugal, and by Spain alone when she combined the crown of Portugal with her own in 1580. Now the eyes of Europe were opened to a new spectacle: the coming of age of a new navy which had, at its first real blooding, overthrown the greatest fleet that the world had ever seen. For this had been Philip of Spain's boast to Europe: that his armada was so great and so powerful that its victory was assured. To give him his due, it was not Philip who gave it the name of 'Invincible'; he called it *'felicissima'* ('most fortunate'). It was the young officers of the fleet who claimed it was invincible, but in Europe the name stuck.

Although the war with Spain dragged on until James I succeeded Elizabeth on the English throne, there was little naval action worthy of the name beyond periodic attempts by the English to waylay the annual Spanish treasure fleet bringing the gold and silver of America across the Atlantic. But the great trade war, east and west, was now on. The defeat of the Armada had proved that the exclusive commercial policy, which Spain had adopted and tried to enforce in respect of her settlements in the West Indies and on the American mainland, could not be upheld by her sea power, and, where Drake and Hawkins had earlier shown the way by their forceful

trading techniques, a host of merchant adventurers were now ready to follow. And from the capture of the *San Felipe* in 1587 had sprung a new understanding of the rich trade to be found, and if necessary fought for, in Far Eastern waters. All this brought a great new impetus to merchant shipbuilding, almost all of it based on the English galleon design that had proved so successful in war. A much larger number of merchants were now building their own ships for trade than had done so before the Armada battle, arming them with guns, not only for self-defence against the piracy which still flourished in all the oceans, but also to underline their determination to trade wherever they might make a suitable landfall. Merchant shipowners trading to the same areas usually formed their ships into convoys, so that a trading expedition to the east or west might well consist of a dozen or more ships, each belonging to a different owner. Every ship on a long voyage went armed, and few of these joint expeditions returned to England without having had to fight somewhere along the way.

The profits of these joint ventures were so large that they attracted a growing number of merchants who were prepared to invest their money in ships, and by the end of the Elizabethan age the volume of traffic was growing rapidly. This increase was by no means confined to English ships: it was a worldwide movement, taking some advantage of the fact that the original claims to exclusive trade by right of prior discovery had been shattered by the outcome of the Armada battle. It led, too, to the formation in many countries of large trading associations of merchants interested in one particular area, as, for example, the various national East India Companies, which were formed within a very short time of the English victory in 1588. These grew to dominate trade, becoming over the course of years so powerful that they acquired complete monopolies and in the end had to be suppressed. But in their heyday they had a profound influence on the growth and design of merchant shipping all over the world.

This huge expansion in numbers was also reflected in the size of ships. Voyages under sail to India and China, to the Americas and round Cape Horn to the Pacific took a long time and entailed the carriage on board of large quantities of provisions and fresh water to sustain the ship's crew, quite apart from the trade goods for sale in the port of arrival. So ships had to be built larger, and the average merchant ship tonnage of ships employed on the longer trade routes rose to around 1,000 within a very few years. The four-masted rig, popular in the larger ships until near the end of the sixteenth century, quickly gave way to a more efficient, three-masted rig, with a square topsail set above the lateen sail on the mizen to give a better aerodynamic balance.

It is easy, when faced with this huge expansion of merchant shipping, to concentrate on the big, important ships to the exclusion of the smaller ones used on the shorter trade routes. There is an official Dutch estimate, for example, that by the end of the sixteenth century there were no fewer than 10,000 merchant ships in Dutch ownership' While some of these were large ships engaged in the East Indian trade, the great majority were small, trading across the Baltic and the North Sea. This same story was true in England, France, Spain, throughout the Mediterranean and, indeed, across the world. There is no particular design which can be said to be common to all these small trading vessels. In England, for example, the pinnace was probably the most common, a vessel built with a square stern like a miniature warship, three-masted and single decked, generally, though a few of the larger pinnaces were built with two decks. In Holland the commonest small trading ship was the *fluyt*, three-masted like the English pinnace, but with a round stern instead of a square one. In the Mediterranean it was probably the *bergantina* two-masted and lateen-rigged, while in Far Eastern waters the

junk, or local derivatives of it, was the universal coastal carrier.

With the exception of the *bergantina* with its two lateen sails, all these small trading vessels were square-rigged, although it was during the sixteenth century that the fore-and-aft sailing rig was introduced. If we discount certain evidence of Mediterranean rock carvings that the sprit (a long spar spreading a square sail from tack to peak) was used in those waters as early as the second century B.C., the earliest pictorial evidence of the sprit that we have, in Europe at any rate, shows that it was in existence in Sweden as early as 1525, although it is generally believed that it was first developed in Holland a few years earlier. Certainly it was the Dutch who developed the spritsail rig, with its long, heavy spar, into the gaff rig, with a gaff and boom instead of the sprit. For years, the gaff was known as a half-sprit until it acquired its own name.

No doubt, most of those 10,000 merchant ships with which the Dutch credited themselves at the end of the sixteenth century were small gaff-rigged vessels, much handier than the square-rigged fluyts for sailing in the shoal waters off the Dutch coast. It is probable that the upper size limit for the gaff rig in those days was about 50 tons and that these small vessels were used only for very local traffic, up and down the coast and in and out of estuaries and rivers.

Above: Dutch barges at Dordrecht, with their characteristic spritsail rig. (From a painting by Jan van Goyen)

East India Companies

By the end of the sixteenth century it had become common knowledge that the riches of the Far East, spices, silks and precious stones, outweighed those of the Spanish West, in the shape mainly of gold and silver. The Portuguese had been the first Europeans to reach India by ship, a century earlier. The Dutch had followed, to exploit the islands of the East Indies to the south. The British had arrived last of all, probably because they had wasted too much time looking for a new route to the East through the ice-bound seas north of Europe and America. Nevertheless, some English navigators had been employed as pilots on Dutch trading voyages to the East Indies, and they spread the good news when they returned home. This was strongly reinforced when Sir Francis Drake captured the great carrack *San Felipe* in 1587, complete with her valuable cargo of spices and charts of eastern seas. European countries anxious to have a part in this rich East Indian trade set up incorporated companies in order to exploit it to the full, on the realistic grounds that any sort of joint company acting together must be stronger than its individual numbers acting singly.

In all, eight European nations set up East India companies – England, Holland, France, Denmark, Austria, Spain, Sweden and Scotland. Of these, only two became really significant, those of England and Holland, the French company following some way in the rear in importance. The others got nowhere and faded out early.

The English company, known officially as the Honourable East India Company, and colloquially as 'John Company', was founded towards the end of the sixteenth century and was incorporated by royal charter of Queen Elizabeth on 31 December 1600. It had a capital of £72,000 which was subscribed by 125 shareholders interested in trade in far eastern waters. The first trading expeditions, known as 'separate' voyages, were made by the individual shareholders who carried all the cost and took all the profit. But in 1612 a new system was introduced, which became permanent, under which the company as a whole owned the ships and organized the voyages, the profit being shared out among all the shareholders. Already, by 1612, company ships had reached as far as Japan, with whom friendly relations had been established, and had set up two 'factories', or trading centres, on the mainland of India, at Masulipatam and Pettapoli. The company had also, in 1609, constructed its own dockyard at Deptford, on the River Thames, where it built its own ships. These were armed as warships, both to give protection against the chronic piracy at the time and, when necessary, to dispute the right to trade against the similarly armed merchantmen of the Dutch, Spanish and French East India companies.

The Dutch East India Company was incorporated as a company in 1602 by charter from the States-General, to bring together under single control all the existing Dutch trading ventures in the Far East. It was granted a monopoly of all Indian and East Indies trade, was given exemption from all import taxes, and authority to own land, maintain an army and a navy, build and fortify trading centres, to declare local wars and make local peace, to exercise civil and criminal jurisdiction, and to coin its own money. These rights gave the Dutch company immense advantages over its competitors, and the English East India Company took steps to obtain the same privileges. It applied for a revised charter and received from the king the same rights as those exercised by the Dutch.

There was war from the start between the English and Dutch companies, with pitched battles taking place where they came into contact. In 1619 the two companies signed an agreement to stop these disputes, but it lasted less than an hour and renewed fighting broke out, even before the smoke from the guns saluting the signing of the agreement had cleared. This vicious squabbling reached its peak of horror in 1623, when English merchants at Amboyna, while under protection of a flag of truce, were tortured and massacred by the order of the Dutch governor.

At the height of its success, which lasted through most of the seventeenth century, the Dutch East India Company had its main capital in Batavia, with subsidiary stations in Ceylon, Malacca, Java, the Malay archipelago, Ternate and Amboyna. It also maintained a fortified post at the Cape of Good Hope, as a base for the protection and re-provision of its ships, on their way to and from the homeland. It had 150 armed merchantmen, 40 warships, and an army of 10,000 soldiers, and its word was law. But its rigid policy was, in the end, to bring it to disaster. Its aim was always a complete monopoly of trade, maintained by force of arms – an

ambition that was bound to bring it into constant conflict with the English and French East India companies. By the early eighteenth century the Dutch had been driven from the mainland of Asia and from Ceylon by the English and French, and the increase in military costs as the company fought to maintain its monopoly brought it to bankruptcy. It was wound up in 1798 when Holland was invaded by the revolutionary armies of France.

Meanwhile, the English East India Company prospered exceedingly. With the warlike Dutch expelled from the whole of India, an armed neutrality existed between the English, firmly entrenched in their 'presidencies' in Bombay and Bengal, and the French, whose main centre was Madras. But when the Seven Years' War between England and France broke out in 1756, the two East India companies were inevitably brought into the conflict. The end came for the French with the battle of Plassey in 1757, and with that victory the whole of India came under 'John Company's' direct control. This vast accession of power and of territory alarmed the British government at home, and it took steps to assume responsibility for this addition to the empire by making all the top company appointments subject to government approval – a change which eventually brought the financial, military, and political control of all India into the hands of the government in London.

By 1813, the Honourable East India Company was approaching the end of its long history. In that year its

monopoly of trade with India was dissolved, and although Company ships still traded there, competition from other shipowners began to cut it down to size. For another twenty years it was allowed to retain its monopoly of trade to China, but this, too, came to an end in 1833. But, because it was so well established in India, and controlled through its many centres the machinery of government, it was decided in London, as a matter of administrative convenience, to allow it to continue the operation of civil government. This came to an end with the Indian Mutiny of 1857, and particularly with the excessive punishments meted out by the company officers to the mutineers. The government in London was forced to take over complete control, and the Honourable East India Company was officially wound up in 1858.

In the times of their greatness the various East India companies built some of the finest ships the world has ever seen. At the Dutch shipyards at Rotterdam and Amsterdam, the French Biscay port of Lorient (specially constructed and named for this eastern trade), and the English dockyard at Deptford, a succession of magnificent ships slid down the slipways, larger and finer than any others in the world.

Left: An East Indiaman off Hong Kong. (From an 1837 painting by William John Huggins).

Below: East Indiamen under construction on the Thames. These proud, stately ships of any of the national companies were instantly recognisable as ocean aristocrats.

Chapter Five
Command of the Seas

'Whoso commands the seas commands the trade of the world; whoso commands the trade of the world commands the riches of the world.'

The words are those of Sir Walter Raleigh and they were beginning to be understood, if still a little dimly, by most European nations at the beginning of the seventeenth century, particularly by the English and the Dutch. Spain, too, was beginning to recognize this essential truth, though for her they had the opposite significance. She had already seen the command of European waters slip from her grasp with the defeat of her 'Invincible Armada'; now she was seeing her command of American waters and the Pacific continually challenged by English and French expeditions intent on settlement and trade, and was powerless to intervene because she was not prepared to spend money on a fleet of warships to defend the huge territories which she had claimed for herself. Almost her only naval operation during the years which followed the Armada defeat was an annual convoy, in which she deployed her entire fleet to escort the ships carrying the treasure that she had amassed in America and her East Indian possessions home across the Atlantic, and guard them against attack from the French and English squadrons which lay in wait off the Azores. Already she had virtually abandoned the Pacific. Drake, on his voyage round the world, had had no difficulty in capturing the annual treasure ship which brought the wealth, accumulated during a year's trading, from Manila to Acapulco for onward transmission to Spain in the annual convoy; Cavendish, during a similar circumnavigation a year or two later, captured another. These annual treasure ships had to cross the Pacific unescorted. There was no Spanish warship in that ocean to guard them and ensure their safe arrival in Mexico with their rich cargoes intact.

Left: *The Sovereign of the Seas*, a 1st rate launched in 1637. Although bigger than anything yet seen, she was not a success, and was rebuilt twice before being burnt. The portrait is of the co-designer Peter Pett, son of Phineas.

The Dutch, having been materially aided by the English in their struggle to win independence from Spain, took the opportunity offered by that friendship to expand their own trade in Europe and strive for a monopoly of the carrying trade at sea. They built good ships, well suited for trade, in large numbers, and were to be seen in every port in Europe, where they quoted freight rates that local shipowners could not touch. As the century wore on, the other European nations were more or less forced to pass Navigation Laws to safeguard their own shipping, under which a country's exports could only be carried at sea by her own ships. England passed her first important Navigation Act in 1651, and the Dutch were forced into war if they were not to see their pre-eminence in maritime trade wither and die.

The basic Dutch trading ship in European waters was still the *fluyt*, enlarged and modified into a sensible design of ship, incorporating a long, straight keel which gripped the water well when the ship was under sail. She had a straight stem joining the keel at an angle of about 45 degrees, and a vertical sternpost on which the rudder hung, while the stern rounded up into the counter. She had a 'no-nonsense' three-masted rig of courses and topsails, with an upper and lower spritsail set on the bowsprit. As *fluyts* never carried any sort of topgallants – even the largest of them and even in the most settled of weather – they were easy to handle at sea and needed a much smaller crew than ships of similar size belonging to other nations. It was reckoned that a small English ship of around 100 tons required a total crew of about 30 men; a *fluyt* of equivalent tonnage could be handled with a crew of one-third of that number. Because the beam measurement used in the calculation of a ship's tonnage was taken across the upper deck, the sides of Dutch *fluyts* in the first half of the seventeenth century were built with a pronounced tumble-home. This kept the beam measurement down, and with it the ship's calculated tonnage, reducing the harbour and other dues which the owner had to pay. When a new system of measurement was introduced in 1669 which took the ship's beam as the width at its widest point, the *fluyt's* sides were built straight upright instead, to give more width and accommodation on deck. The Dutch pinnace was similar to the *fluyt*, except that she had a flat stern on typical warship lines. Although pinnaces were included in the war fleets to act as fast reconnaissance ships and as convoy escorts, the type was also used for trading purposes. They were generally single-decked vessels, with a comparatively narrow hold, but they were faster through the water than *fluyts* and thus of value in some trades.

The largest Dutch merchant ship of the seventeenth century was the big East Indiaman, built very much along warship lines, though usually to lighter scantlings. These East Indiamen were built up to about 1,200 tons in their largest form, though about 800 tons was a more average size. Like the warships, they had two gundecks, and were three-masted, full-rigged ships, setting topgallants above their topsails. The early Dutch East Indiamen were decorated with much more carving and gingerbread work than the early warships, but by the middle of the century Dutch warships had caught them up in fancy decoration, following the English pattern of embellishing a ship with carvings wherever there was room for them.

For their warships, the Dutch had been quick to appreciate the efficiency of the English galleon introduced by John Hawkins and they took it over as their basic naval design, though only rarely did they build a warship with more than two gundecks. This was probably on account of the generally shoal waters off the Dutch coast, in which vessels of deep draught would be at a

Below: Seventeenth century Dutch East Indiamen entering port. (From a painting by Vroom)

disadvantage. There was also a general lack of cohesion in the Dutch navy, as each of the seven States was completely autonomous in naval affairs. Each built its own navy, manned by its own seamen, and would only agree on an overall commander-in-chief after much bickering with its neighbours. During the First Anglo-Dutch War (1652–54) the largest and best Dutch warship was Marten Tromp's *Brederode*, a ship of about 800 tons mounting 56 guns. The Dutch Navy List of 1654 shows a total fleet of 131 warships, of which only nine mounted 50 guns and upwards. The great majority of their warships carried between 30 and 38 guns mounted on a single gundeck.

It was still the general practice of all maritime nations during a war to hire armed merchant ships to swell the fleet numbers and the Dutch were no exception. But in general these merchantmen were of little value, and many a battle was lost because the captains, having little stomach for fighting, stole away with their ships whenever opportunity offered.

In England, the general run of small merchant vessels was based on the pinnace design, flat-sterned and built up slightly higher aft than the Dutch *fluyt*. Like the *fluyt* they were three-masted, but set topgallants above their topsails, thus needing larger crews to handle them efficiently. They were more like small warships, mounting up to 28 guns on a single gundeck, ostensibly for defence against pirates, but ready to make their presence felt if obstacles were placed in the way of their trade. They had no generic name, being variously described as a 'ship' or a 'bark'.

The large English trading ship of the first half of the seventeenth century was, as in Holland, the East Indiaman, but it was several years before the English version equalled the Dutch in tonnage. A very few English Indiamen were built over about 500 or 600 tons, invariably to the galleon design, and of course armed with a battery of naval cannon, but it was not until nearly the end of the seventeenth century that they approached the Dutch either in numbers or size. One exception to this generality was an East Indiaman called the *Trade's Increase*, in which Sir Henry Middleton commanded a Company voyage in 1610: she was a ship of 1,000 tons.

In warships, on the other hand, England built larger than any other nation. Elizabeth, at her death in 1603, had left a flourishing navy which was held in considerable respect by the other European nations. Her successor, James I, who had brought the war against Spain to a close on his accession, let the navy slide into decay until, in 1607, there were only twenty-seven Royal ships left, of which the Venetian ambassador could report to his government that many were 'old and rotten and barely fit for service'. One year later, perhaps as a warning to other countries that the English navy was not moribund, James ordered the building of the *Prince Royal*, the largest warship yet to be constructed in England. She has been called the navy's first three-decker, in the sense that she carried her guns on three separate decks. While this is true, she could more accurately be described as a two-decker, in the proper sense of the term, since she had only two covered gundecks, the guns mounted on her upper deck not constituting a separate gundeck in the accepted sense of the word. She was built at Woolwich by Phineas Pett and William Bright, with a length of keel of 115 ft (35 m), a maximum beam of 43 ft (13 m) and a depth of 18 ft (5·5 m). According to the contemporary system of ship measurement, her gross tonnage worked out at 1,330, but a more modern figure would be 1,187.

There was tremendous criticism of her design throughout her building, partly because Phineas Pett's ideas were not shared by other well-known naval architects of the day, partly because she was considered a bit of a monstrosity. Pett does seem to have been less than clever in the building of this important ship. His original estimate of 775 loads of timber to build the ship was less than a half of the 1,627 loads actually used, adding £5,908 to her cost. Much of the wood used in her building was green and unseasoned, and in 1621 another £6,000 was required to make her fit for service. Her total initial cost was £20,000. She was built in a dry dock at Woolwich. When the time came to launch her in 1610 she was found to be too wide to pass through the dock opening and it had to be enlarged to allow her to get out.

There were two innovations in the building of the *Prince Royal*. She was the first English warship to be double-planked throughout her hull (built with an inner and outer wood skin) and she was also the first ship to have her bulkheads double bolted with iron. A retrograde step was the decision not to sheathe her bottom. In Elizabeth's time Hawkins had sheathed his ships by double planking below the waterline, with hair impregnated with tar between them which acted both as a preservative for the timber and a deterrent to attacks by marine worms. Some merchant ships had had their bottoms sheathed with lead sheets to prevent attack by the teredo worm, but this practice was discouraged in naval ships, as it was found that in sea water the lead caused the iron of the pintles and rudder to corrode by galvanic action.

Above: The *Prince Royal*, with Charles I on board, at the head of an English fleet.

John Stow, in his *Annales of England*, described the *Prince Royal* thus: 'This year the King builded a most goodly ship for warre, the keel whereof was 114 feet in length, and the cross beam was 44 feet in length; she will carry 64 pieces of ordnance [in fact she eventually mounted 55], and is of the burthen of 1,400 tons. This royal ship is double built, and is most sumptuously adorned, within and without, with all manner of curious carving, painting, and rich gilding.' Indeed, it was this carving and painting which was the most remarkable thing about this first of the great English warships. The Pipe Office accounts in the Public Records Office in London reveal that Sebastian Vicars was paid £441 for the carvings and Robert Beake and Pane Isackson £868 7s. for the painting and gilding – a considerable proportion of the overall building cost of £20,000. Her figurehead was a carving of St. George and the Dragon with, on top of the forerail, a large knight's helmet surmounted by an enormous crown. The three stern galleries were elaborately carved, with the Prince of Wales's feathers on the two lower galleries and the lion and unicorn crest on the upper gallery, all surrounded by gilded ornamental carvings.

Ship decoration was nothing new. Most nations had long embellished their ships with startling colours and decorative carvings. But the *Prince Royal* set a new standard of richness which was copied in their warships by other European nations, and also by private shipowners, notably the East India Companies. Decoration grew to ridiculous proportions later in the century: the *Sovereign of the Seas* when she was launched had more gilded carving on her stern, sides and bulkheads than there was plain timber.

Yet, in spite of her size and prestige, the *Prince Royal* was not a successful ship. She was badly designed and badly built, and showed no real advance on the Elizabethan warships that had preceded her. One of her novel features was three stern galleries, an adaptation of the Spanish carrack design introduced into the English navy for the first time. But in this respect the *Prince Royal* was exceptional. Three stern galleries did not become the rule until much later, when the size of the average first-rate ship of the line rose from around 1,000 tons to more than double.

The *Prince Royal*, though generally unsuccessful as a ship, was important because she marked a distinct step upwards in warship size, a lead which all other navies had to follow. She was followed twenty-five years later by a new warship nearly half as big again, the *Sovereign of the Seas*, built by Charles I for his ship-money fleet. Once again the designer was Phineas Pett, and she was built as something of a showpiece of English naval architecture. Her carving and decoration cost Charles no less than £6,691 out of a total cost of £65,586 16s. 9½d., inclusive of her guns – a fantastic sum even in comparison with the *Prince Royal* – and, as all her carving was covered with gold leaf, she glittered in the sunshine. The Dutch, whom she met frequently in battle, called her the 'Golden Devil'.

The *Sovereign of the Seas* marked a notable step forward in warship rig, for she stepped only three masts, instead of the four which had been more or less standard on all large warships.

Following her lead, all rated warships, and indeed most merchant ships of any size, were to be three-masted for the rest of the sailing era. She was the first true English three-decker in the sense that she had three covered gundecks, and she was also the first warship to carry royals above her topsails. Another important advance in design was the substitution of a round stern in place of the square stern, which was to remain a feature of English warships until the advent of the iron ship in the mid-nineteenth century.

The system of rates, under which warships were graded by the number of guns that they mounted, was brought in during the seventeenth century. By the end of the century, first-rates mounted from 90 to 100 guns, second-rates from 80 to 90, third-rates 60 to 80, fourth-rates 40 to 60, fifth-rates 28 to 40, and sixth-rates below 28. A list of the English Royal Navy (it had been given the prefix 'Royal' by Charles II upon the restoration of the monarchy) of 1660 shows nine first-rates, eleven second-rates, thirty-nine third-rates, forty fourth-rates, two fifth-rates and six sixth-rates. The various other types of ship making up the English navy were bombs, fireships, hoys, hulks, ketches, smacks and yachts, but, with the exception of the hulks, all were small and thought of more as naval auxiliaries than as warships. The hulks were fairly big ships, mostly merchant ships captured from the Dutch. Of the rated warships, no fewer than forty were ships of over 1,000 tons.

This increase in size was general, throughout the warships of all rates: while the first-rate had approximately doubled her tonnage, so had every other rate. It had happened within a span of about thirty years, reflecting experience gained in battle of the fact that a good big ship would always beat a good small ship. It took some time for this simple doctrine to spread to the navies of other countries, but in the end they were forced to follow suit if their maritime ambitions were ever to be achieved. And, as was so

Left: A model of a Dutch 64-gun ship of the seventeenth century. The foremast is raked slightly forward, and the lateen and spritsail topmast are still in evidence.

frequently the case, merchant ships followed the naval lead, doubling their average tonnage, though over a rather longer time span.

It was with fleets such as this, or with fleets very similar, that the three Anglo-Dutch wars of the seventeenth century were fought. They consisted of bitter, hard-fought battles with up to a hundred ships on either side engaged in a gigantic mêlée. The basic cause underlying each of the three wars was the struggle for trading supremacy, not only in European waters, but worldwide. Both countries had realized the truth of Sir Walter Raleigh's words, quoted at the beginning of this chapter, and both were disputing the command of the seas to enable their merchant ships to trade freely and advantageously in every part of the world where trade could be found. After the three wars it was the navy of England which emerged victorious, opening the oceans for unrestricted use by her merchant ships. It was the start of a huge expansion in English merchant shipping. In the course of a relatively few years it was to surpass that of all the other seafaring nations put together.

By the end of the third of these Anglo-Dutch wars in 1674, the sailing warship had attained the general design and rig which she was to retain more or less until the end of her useful life. The only major change still to come was a further increase in size, and even this was limited since there was a maximum size which could be propelled through the water, without raising masts to such a height that they became impossible to stay. There were, of course, minor improvements to be made in general hull design and in the rigging plan, but the basic ship design showed no significant change until new shipbuilding materials, particularly iron and steel, were introduced in the nineteenth century.

Throughout western Europe, both in fighting and merchant navies, the basic hull design remained firmly based on the English galleon. The original low beakhead projecting well beyond the cutwater gave way over the years to a shorter beakhead with a pronounced upward curve. The space inside the beakhead and forward of the forecastle bulkhead was floored with gratings and served as the crew's lavatory. Hopefully the sea would wash up through the gratings when the ship was under way and keep the area reasonably clean. The forecastle itself was built lower as the years progressed, almost disappearing completely in merchant ships in the eighteenth century, but retained in warships to provide a mounting for the chase guns that fired directly ahead at an enemy ship attempting to escape. Abaft the mainmast the largest ships had quarter-deck and poop deck, one above the other, to provide cabins and stern galleries for the officers.

A ship with quarter-deck and poop deck had three stern galleries, on upper, quarter- and poop deck levels; smaller ships, without a poop, had two. In the very largest ships, extra galleries were added on each quarter. These stern and quarter galleries were glazed with lights (windows), and were integral with the more important cabins, providing a private space for recreation for the occupant.

All warships, and a great majority of the larger merchant ships, were built with a pronounced tumble-home. This was to provide enough width on the lower gundecks for the guns to recoil when fired. These were mounted on wooden trucks with wheels and the force of the explosion of the firing charge forced them backwards at high speed across the deck until they were brought to a halt by the rope breeching attached to the ship's side. This width of deck was not required on the upper deck, which normally carried no guns, and so the sides were curved inwards to reduce it to more normal proportions. As most large merchant ships still went armed for self-defence, they too had the tumble-home. And that they still needed their guns is evidenced by an action fought as late as 1804: a convoy of British East Indiamen had to fight its way past a French squadron of one ship of the line and several frigates in the Malacca Straits before being able to continue its voyage home.

The standard rig of all these ships was three-masted, with square sails on all masts except the mizen, which only had square sails above the mizen course. At the start of the seventeenth century the lateen course was giving way to the fore-and-aft sail spread by a long sprit, and after another fifty years this spritsail gave way to a fore-and-aft gaffsail, at first loose-footed, but later with the foot of the sail laced to a boom. Although not technically a course, this gaffsail was generally known as the mizen 'course' until, much later, a square sail was spread as a true mizen course, the gaffsail then becoming known as the 'spanker'. The old bonnet, which used to be laced to the foot of a course to increase its size in a following wind, had completely disappeared, but the same enlargement of the sail area could be obtained by setting studdingsails on the topsail yard by means of studdingsail booms which temporarily prolonged the yards outwards. The old clumsy upper and lower spritsails, set on the bowsprit, gave way during the early eighteenth century to jibs and fore staysails, and additional staysails were set between the masts. Under full sail, with royals set above her topgallants, a full-rigged ship was a magnificent spectacle.

The basic method of shipbuilding had not changed since Phoenician times. The bones of a ship still consisted of a keel, a stempost and stern-

Right: The Texel (1673), last engagement of the Third Anglo-Dutch War.

Below right: Details of a seventeenth century man-of-war, showing the tumble-home (left) and the beakhead (right).

A new Table of all the names of the principal Parts and Rigging of a MAN of WAR Necessary for all sea-faring men and others that desire to be there with acquainted. Also all the Prospects of a Section of a Ship cut thro the Keel, both fore & aft with her Boats, Longboats and Sloops.

Flag Staf Cap
Stern

Stern of the Ship

Stem head

Bulk head of the fore Castle

Stem

Sold by Daniel Midwinter at the three Crowns in St Pauls Church Yard London.

post, scarfed in at either end, and frames or ribs, curved to the shape of the hull, fitted at intervals to the keel to take the side planking and held rigidly in place by the deck beams which ran laterally across the ship between each pair of frames. This general pattern provided a powerful structure which held the ship together longitudinally, laterally and vertically. The strength of the rig was assured by stepping all three lower masts into the keel, so they were held rigidly at deck level, as well as being held firmly in place above deck by shrouds, fixed to the sides of the ship and running up to the mastheads to stop any athwartships movement, and by forestays and backstays to prevent any fore-and-aft movement. Topmasts and topgallant masts were similarly supported by shrouds and stays.

The wooden warship of the seventeenth and eighteenth centuries was a vessel of immense strength. She had massive double-planked sides of oak up to 18 in (46 cm) thick, strengthened longitudinally under the gunports by oaken wales which ran externally along the sides from bow to stern, adding another 6 to 8 in (15 to 20 cm) in thickness. The only real difference between the warships of Britain and those of other European nations was in the shape of the stern, the British retaining the rounded stern and other navies preferring the square stern. This difference lasted into the eighteenth century, when the rounded stern was adopted almost universally.

During most of the seventeenth century the guns with which the world's warships were armed were the cannon firing a 42-lb (19 kg) shot, the demi-cannon (32-lb (14.5 kg)), the culverin (18-lb (8.2 kg)) and smaller guns firing balls varying from 12 to 3 lb (5.4 to 1.4 kg). Later in the century, and throughout the eighteenth, warship guns lost their names of 'cannon', 'demi-cannon',

Left: A sectional drawing of a seventeenth century two-decker (Keltridge).

Far left: Lower gundeck of the salvaged Swedish two-decker *Wasa*. The guns were salved by divers after the sinking.

Below left: Broadside tactics involved close-range cannonading. This is HMS *Brunswick* engaging the French *l'Achille* and *le Vengeur* at the Glorious First of June, 1794.

and so on, and were designated solely by the weight of the shot they fired, as '42-pounder', '32-pounder', etc. It was a formidable armament, particularly at the range at which naval battles were normally fought, colloquially known as 'half pistol shot', or about 100 yards (91 m).

With her massive oaken sides and the batteries of guns on her gundecks, the ship of the line had little to fear in broadside battle, which was almost the only form of action possible under the conditions of the age. There was no means of training the guns to fire at any angle forward or aft. They could only fire at right angles to the centreline, and so could only hit an enemy ship when she was directly abeam. As soon as the naval battle developed, from the disorganized *mêlée* of the First and Second Anglo-Dutch Wars to a more orderly form of combat, this limitation in gunnery obliged warships to fight in line ahead, and so forced them to attack their opponents at their strongest point. It was for this reason that, throughout this period, so few naval engagements ended in a clear-cut victory.

In only two directions did the ship of the line offer any defensive weakness – directly ahead and directly astern. Wooden ships were not built with strong transverse bulkheads, and there was nothing to stop a cannon ball, fired at a ship from one of these two directions, travelling the whole length of the deck. This was particularly true of the broadside fired from directly astern, where the target was large and the only obstructions were the glazed lights of the stern galleries and the relatively flimsy partitions separating the cabins from one another. It was a weakness exploited in battle, particularly by the British, from the second half of the eighteenth century until the end of the sailing warship era.

Royal George
(1756)

Gundeck 178 ft (54·3 m)
Keel 143 ft 5 in (43·7 m)
Beam 51 ft 9 in (15·8 m)
Tonnage 2,041 B.O.M.
Armament twenty-eight 42-pounders,
twenty-eight 24-pounders, twenty-
eight 12-pounders, sixteen 6-pounders
Complement 850

A first-rate ship of the line of 100 guns,
H.M.S. *Royal George* was launched at
Woolwich, on the Thames, on 18
February 1756. Three years later she
took part in the battle of Quiberon Bay
as the flagship of Admiral Hawke. She
was lost, along with 900 lives, in a
notorious accident at Spithead on 29
August 1782. She was being heeled for
purposes of fitting a cock below the
waterline, when water entered through
her gunports and she filled up and sank.

She is seen here with her side cut away to
show (in descending order) the half
deck, middle gundeck, lower gundeck,
orlop deck and hold. The small drawing
shows her under sail. The long mizen
yard served as a spare in case of damage
to another spar.

Right: Cross-section of a fireship. Loaded guns have been piled on deck, to explode and cause even greater destruction.

Below: Fireships in action against the Armada anchored off Gravelines. The danger they presented was enough to disrupt the best-organized formation.

Only warships of the first three rates were true ships of the line. Fourth-rates were described as 'cruisers', although they too fought in the line of battle occasionally (at the battle of the Nile, in 1798, H.M.S. *Leander*, a fourth-rate of 50 guns, stationed herself between two French ships of 74 and 80 guns, and engaged them both with broadsides). Fifth- and sixth-rates were classed as 'frigates' and never fought in the line, and it was an unwritten law no ship of the line would open fire on a frigate unless the frigate fired first.

Apart from what might be described as true fighting ships, that is, ships rated by the number of guns they mounted, all navies included various other types of vessel for use in minor roles or as auxiliaries. Only two need to be considered at this stage: fireships and bombs.

Fireships were relatively old weapons of naval war, having been used in battle in various forms over the centuries. During the seventeenth century, and particularly in the three Anglo-Dutch Wars, they formed an integral part of every fleet that put to sea, to be used whenever the wind served to sail them down upon an enemy. There were no real naval tactics in those days. Ships of each squadron rallied round their admiral and in general fought in a bunch in as close combat as they could manage, thus presenting a good target for a fireship attack. The fireship herself was normally an old vessel, packed with barrels of gunpowder, tar, pitch and anything else that would explode or burn. The fuse was a powder trail that was ignited at the last possible moment. They were sailed by small, picked crews who were encouraged by the promise of a reward for a successful attack. Their method of operation was to sail down so close to an enemy that their grappling irons would inevitably become entangled in her rigging. They towed a longboat astern on a short warp. At the last moment the crew took to their boat, the master fired the gunpowder trail, jumped into the boat himself, and cast it off, and they pulled away as fast as they could, to win clear of the subsequent explosion.

A paragraph in the British *Fighting Instructions* for 1714 reads:

'That if any of His Majesty's Fireships perform the Service expected from them, in such Manner That any of the Enemies Men of War of Forty guns, or more, shall be burnt by them, every Person remaining in the Fireship till the Service be performed, shall receive on board the Admiral, immediately after the Service done, Ten Pounds, as a reward of that Service, over and above his Pay due to him; and in Case any of them shall be killed in that Service, it shall be paid to his Executors, or next Relations: And the Captains of such Fireships shall receive 100l. or a Medal of Gold, with a Chain of the same Value, as he shall make Choice of, to remain as a Token of Honour to him and his Posterity; and shall receive such other Encouragement, by Preferment and Command, or otherwise, as shall be fit to reward him and induce others to perform the like Service. . . .'

Service in fireships was obviously a hazardous occupation in order to command such rewards as this at a time when the normal pay of an able seaman amounted to 19 shillings a month.

The 'bomb' took its name from the missile that it fired, and was a small naval vessel armed with a single heavy mortar which fired a bomb weighing up to 200 lbs (90 kg). It was a weapon used for the systematic bombardment of targets ashore, never against ships. The mortar had been developed as a land weapon towards the end of the sixteenth century. It was first taken to sea a hundred years later, in 1682, when the pirate stronghold of Algiers was systematically bombarded with mortars by a French fleet under the command of Abraham du Quesne. Later, most European navies adopted the bomb as an ingredient of their national fleet.

For the operation of a deliberate bombardment, the mortar was fixed in position in the ship, and the ship herself trained, to give the correct direction of fire. This was achieved by mooring the ship with two anchors and using springs on the cables to swing the ship as required to get the bomb onto the target. It was possible, with springs used thus, to obtain a very high degree of accuracy, which naturally made the bomb an extremely significant weapon in this type of naval operation.

Above: Le Havre under bombardment by British ships during the Seven Years' War.

The heavy mortar was mounted originally on the deck of a three-masted ship, with the foremast removed to provide sufficient space for the weapon. The resulting two-masted rig of mainmast and mizen became widely known in naval circles as a 'ketch' rig, although the only real resemblance to the traditional ketch was in the fact that there was no foremast. Apart from that, the rig and functions of the real ketch and the bomb ketch, were miles apart. Once the foremast of the ship destined to become a bomb had been removed, additional deck beams were added to provide enough structural strength to absorb the very heavy recoil of the mortar. Later, after the new weapon had proved its usefulness, conversions from small three-masted ships by removal of the foremast gave way to two-masted vessels specially built as bombs, with decks designed to take the force of the recoil. Later still, when the bomb ketch had ceased to be a viable naval weapon, they became the most popular type of ship used for polar exploration, their inbuilt strength proving invaluable in resisting the pressures generated by movements of pack ice.

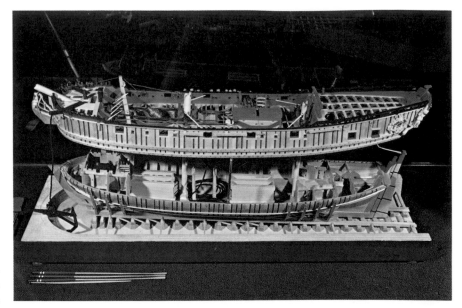

It has been said that the main naval activity of the seventeenth century was the long struggle between the English and the Dutch for a mastery of the seas that would guarantee freedom and expansion of seaborne trade. The three Anglo-Dutch Wars had brought in their train a huge growth of English merchant shipping, and as a result of the wars English ships were able to pass freely and without dispute in waters which had formerly been strictly controlled by the Dutch on almost a monopoly basis. The eighteenth century was to see a similar series of wars fought for basically the same reason, between Britain and a resurgent France.

France was a comparatively late starter in naval shipbuilding in the seventeenth century, in part because the central government held little authority over the coastal provinces. In 1624, when Cardinal Richelieu came to power, he was quick to recognize that power in the world rested on control of the sea and in 1625 he had himself made Grande Maître, Chef, et Surintendant-Général de la Navigation et Commerce de France, a grandiloquent title which nevertheless gave him overall control of all shipbuilding and everything else maritime. One of his first acts was to order five warships from shipyards in Holland, which could be used as models by the naval shipbuilding yards which he was establishing in France. One of these five was the *Saint Louis*, of which the Dutch engraver of maps, Hendrik Hondius, has left us a picture. She was a two-

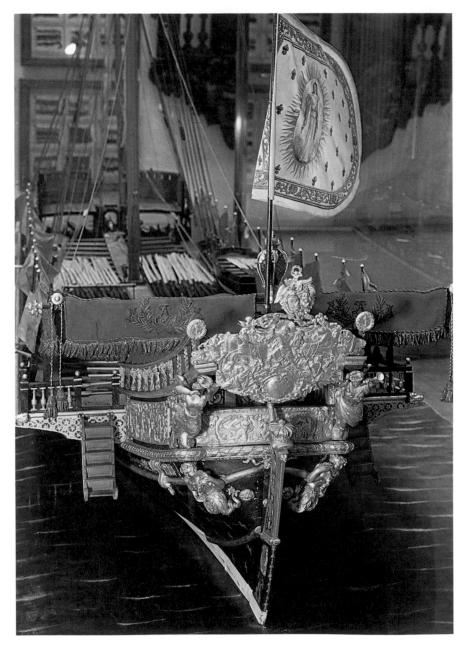

Left: A modern model of the bomb ketch *Granado* of 1742. Note the heavy timbering to withstand the recoil of the 10 inch mortar. (By R. A. Lightley from original plans)

Below left: The ornate stern of a model of the galley *Réale*.

Right: Hoisting the sternpost onto the keel of a ship under construction in the dockyard at Toulon. (From Colbert's *Atlas*)

decker of 56 guns and, according to Léon Guérin's *Histoire Maritime de France*, had a tonnage of 1,200, obviously an overestimate for a ship of her size. Using these Dutch ships as models, Richelieu began to build up a fleet and by the time of his death the French fleet consisted of sixty-three ships and twenty-eight galleys. What was missing, however, were officers and men of experience to command and fight them, for the social order in France made it impossible to appoint a commoner, which most of the experienced sea captains were, to command a fleet, or even a single ship, over the head of a member of the nobility. The French fleet, moreover, was divided geographically between the Mediterranean and the Bay of Biscay, and was woefully mismanaged in both places.

The best known of Richelieu's home-built warships was the *Couronne*, launched in 1638 and possibly the French reply to the English *Sovereign of the Seas*. She was a two-decker of 78 guns and, according to Guérin, a tonnage of 2,000, again an obvious overestimate. A model of her in the Musée de la Marine in Paris shows that she was built with the typical square stern of the Dutch, but an oddity of her design was a small flying poop built up over her stern, giving her the appearance of a carrack almost, abaft the

mizen. She was three-masted, setting topgallants above the topsails on fore and mainmasts, with the typical lateen mizen of the times.

Jean-Baptiste Colbert, Louis XIV's great minister, was the next to take a hand in building up a French fleet. Between Richelieu's death in 1642 and Colbert's ministry of 1663 the navy of France had been in the hands of Cardinal Mazarin, who had no knowledge of, and little interest in, the exercise of sea power. By the time of his death the navy had dwindled to twenty ships and six galleys, some of them dilapidated beyond repair. Colbert virtually had to start again and build a new navy. Nevertheless, at his death in 1683 he left a navy of 117 ships of the line (though included under that designation were some not strong enough to fight in the line of battle) and thirty galleys. To design his ships he imported naval architects from other countries, including the English shipbuilder, Anthony Deane, and one from Naples, Biagio Pangallo, who became famous as a ship-designer throughout France under the name of Maître Blaise. It was he who set a new pattern of French warship building which was to bring French naval architects a reputation for providing the best ships in the world, partly by increasing the beam by a foot or two and reducing the draught, which brought

LE SOLEIL ROYAL.

Above: Stern of the three-decker *Soleil Royal*, pride of the fleet of Louis XIV.

was lateen-rigged on two masts, spreading some 8,000 sq ft (743 m²) of canvas, and carried five large guns, of which the largest was a 36-pounder, under the forecastle, which could only fire directly ahead, and twelve small swivel guns, six each side, on the catwalks which ran the length of the galley outside the oarsmen. The long protruding ram was tipped with an iron replica of a horse's head, with a spike between the ears. The usual narrow *corsia*, or bridge, known in France as the *coursie*, ran the length of the galley amidships between the thwarts, and was patrolled by drivers with long leather whips, to encourage the slaves and the criminals who had been condemned to the galleys in place of a prison sentence. The large poop deck aft was normally shaded by a fine, rich awning supported on a framework of light spars, under which the captain and other officers could take their ease while the rowers sweated below. Although there were a few galleys attached to the Biscay fleet, where they were of little or no use, the majority of them were stationed in the Mediterranean where the era of the galley was not yet over.

The pride of Louis XIV's French fleet was the *Soleil Royal*, a three-decker variously described as of 98, 102 and 106 guns – as big or bigger than any other warship in the world. There is a contemporary drawing of her by A. L. van Kaldenbach which shows her to have been as magnificently decorated, even, as the *Sovereign of the Seas*. The decorations which covered the stern and quarter galleries were carved by Pierre Puget. Her figurehead was a gilded mermaid bearing a golden orb, and the three lanterns on her poop rail were magnificently embellished and surmounted by golden crowns. Eventually she was forced ashore and was burned by the English at the battle of Barfleur in 1692 – a sad end for a ship of much magnificence.

Throughout the seventeenth and eighteenth centuries, the general design of the large ship, whether warship or merchantman, had altered very little. The largest of both had roughly doubled in size from about 1,500 tons to around 3,000 tons. All now had the three-masted rig, carrying royals above topgallants. The typical bluff bow remained virtually unaltered, even though the science of hydrodynamics was beginning to come in for study by some naval architects who realised that a square bow pushing its way through the water caused so much resistance and skin friction that speed was seriously affected. But this was a period of history in which speed was not generally of the first importance.

increased steadiness as a gun platform, and partly by designing a slightly hollower bow and stern, which brought up to an extra knot in speed.

The galleys built for the French fleet were of two types: a smaller version rowing 26 oars on each side, with five men on each oar, and a larger version with up to 33 oars each side, usually with five men on each oar, but with seven on each in the largest galleys. They were known as '*gallées ordinaires*' and '*gallées extraordinaires*'. Among the *extraordinaires* was the galley flagship, traditionally named *La Réale* to indicate that she was the king's galley. The stern of one of these *Réales* is preserved in the Musée de la Marine, complete with the superb decorations carved by Pierre Puget, the leading French sculptor of the day. Her date was 1680, and she was one of the big galleys rowing 31 oars each side with seven men to each oar, giving a total of 434 oarsmen. She

There was no great financial advantage to be gained by bringing in a cargo a week or two before that of a rival shipowner. The demand for the goods of other nations was insatiable and there were not enough ships of any design in the world yet to satisfy it. It was a golden age for trade in a world which was still expanding as new continents became settled and civilized.

Two important innovations, however, should be noticed. During the early eighteenth century, spritsails set above and below the bowsprit were superseded by the much more efficient jibs and fore staysails. Jibs were introduced in the British navy in 1705 for small ships and sloops, and in 1719 for the largest ships of the line. Merchant ships quickly followed the naval lead. It is probable that the jib originated in Holland some forty years earlier on the single-masted *jacht*, built for speed as a naval scout or despatch vessel. The second innovation was the substitution of the steering wheel for the tiller. As ships were built larger, so the tiller had to be made longer to provide enough leverage to move the rudder, and in strong winds it could take five or six men to control it and steer the ship. Another drawback of the tiller on large ships had been that it had to be on the same level as the rudder head, and a helmsman on the tiller found himself below the poop deck and quite unable to see how the sails were drawing. This crucial disadvantage was removed by the invention of the whipstaff (a vertical lever connected to the tiller, enabling the helmsman to move it from side to side through a pivot point below deck). But there was a penalty to be paid for the whipstaff, since it could only move the rudder through a total of about 15 degrees. The steering-wheel, geared to the rudder head by means of ropes or chains, did not necessarily have to be on the same level as the top of the rudder. It was introduced at the end of the seventeenth century and had been adopted for use in all large ships by quite early in the eighteenth. This was the complete answer to the limitations of the whipstaff or the oversize tiller, and when placed on deck at the break of the quarter-deck – its normal position in all sailing vessels – it gave the helmsman a clear view of the sails.

Yet, in spite of the relative lack of progress in the basic hull shape of ships, design changes were in the air. The great Swedish naval architect Frederik Hendrik af Chapman produced his *Architectura Navalis Mercatoria* in 1768, and some of his designs for merchant ships, as well as for small warships, show careful study of the relationship between hull form and speed through the water. He was the first naval architect to build a tank for testing ship models, which were drawn along the tank by a clever

system of drop weights. The results of these studies convinced him, and many others who read his book and studied its superb illustrations and building plans, that the basic shape of existing ships was hydrodynamically unsatisfactory. His studies showed that, to achieve the most efficient shape, a ship's hull needed a fine entry and a clear run aft, qualities which were missing from almost all contemporary designs. In the gun sloops he built for the Swedish navy he adopted these lines to produce fast, stable vessels admir-

ably suited to their purpose. Writing about them, Chapman said, 'When these gun sloops had been built I armed one of them myself [they mounted two 18-pounder guns, one in the bows and one in the stern], took it up to Vartan in Stockholm where the King himself came on board, and then rowed it, fired salvoes, made for land and set out gangplanks, landed with the guns and advanced firing all the time, then retreated still firing until the guns were once more in position in the sloop, all finally coming to an end in that His Majesty made me a lieutenant-colonel.' In addition to gun sloops Chapman also designed and built smaller gun launches mounting a single 18- or 24-pounder. In addition to rowing 7 oars a side, they carried a simple lug rig on two masts.

In 1775 Chapman published his *Tractat om Skepps Byggeriet* (Treatise on Ship Building), a publication which over the next twenty or thirty

Above: A large rigged model of Admiral Balchen's flagship HMS *Victory* (1737). It was built after the ship was lost on the Casquet Rocks in 1744, to demonstrate her characteristics to a Board of Enquiry.

Pl. XLIX

Above: Some of Chapman's plans from his *Architectura Navalis* for yachts and barges. The art of depicting a warship in the form of a drawing advanced rapidly in the seventeenth century, and from 1704 the Royal Navy began to keep plans on a systematic basis.

years was to have a profound effect on ship design in all western countries. Although it took time for naval architects to absorb some of the finer points of Chapman's designs, such as the hollow bow and the tapering run of the hull aft, the days of the tubby ship with a length-to-beam ratio of 3 or $3\frac{1}{2}$ to 1 were now numbered. The longer ship with a more streamlined underwater hull shape was on the way in.

Although the standard design of large ships altered very little, apart from the fact that they approximately doubled in size, there were great advances, as well as a great variety, in the design and rig of smaller vessels during the seventeenth and eighteenth century. The most notable of all the features of small vessels was the gaff rig, which had, in fact, been introduced by the Dutch during the sixteenth century. This was much easier to handle than the square rig, and demanded a much smaller crew. The earliest known example of a vessel setting a full gaff rig on two masts is the two-masted Dutch *jacht*, a small shallow-draught craft used in Dutch inland waters. Because she drew so little water, lee-boards were fitted on each side, the one on the lee side being lowered to prevent leeway.

The two-masted gaff rig was soon found to be unnecessary in so small a vessel, so the foremast was removed to make it a single-masted craft, with a triangular fore staysail to balance the rig and still with leeboards to deepen the draught when sailing on the wind. As the single staysail was insufficient in a strong wind, a running bow-sprit was added from which a jib could be set forward of the staysail. This final version was known as a *bezaan jacht*. At about the same time the Dutch produced the *staten jacht*, which had virtually the same rig, but with a square topsail added. This was built man-of-war fashion with a quarter-deck to accommodate a cabin and was used by important people as a private yacht.

Other European countries copied this fore-and-aft gaff rig, though often with variations. In England the Dutch *bezaan jacht* rig was used on a deeper-draught hull – the coastal waters being less shoal than those off the coast of Holland – to become the English cutter, though a few years later a single square sail was added. The rig was then developed into a larger two-masted craft, with gaff sails on both masts, the cutter's square sail on the foremast, and square topsails on both masts. It could perhaps best be described as a 'schooner' rig, though the term did not come into use until many years later, having been coined in the United States. A similar 'schooner' rig, but without the square sails, can be seen in Dutch marine paintings of around the end of the seventeenth century, and Chapman has similar illustrations in his *Architectura Navalis Mercatoria*.

For coastwise trading and shorter sea voyages, snows, brigs and brigantines were the favoured vessels of the north European nations. They were all two-masted, with variations in rig to suit the particular needs of the trade for which they were built. The origin of the name 'brig' was the much older Mediterranean term 'brigantine'. This denoted a small ship, equipped like a galleasse with sails and oars, built for speed and therefore much in demand by pirates (the Italian *'brigantini'* means 'brigand'). This type of brigantine dates from the early sixteenth century; the trading brigantines of the seventeenth and eighteenth centuries were very different vessels.

At first the trading brig and brigantine were the same ship, 'brig' being merely an abbreviation of 'brigantine', but during the eighteenth century the two descriptions came to signify different rigs. The name 'brig' was given to a ship square-rigged on both masts, with the addition of a fore-and-aft gaff sail on the mainmast; a brigantine was square-rigged on the foremast and fore-and-aft rigged on the main. The snow was almost identical to the brig, except that it had a separate small mast, known in England as

the 'trysail mast', on which the gaff mainsail was hoisted. This mast was stepped immediately abaft the mainmast and brought an advantage in the ease of handling the gaff sail, which could thus be set or furled at will without interfering with the main yard from which the main course was set. Moreover, with a trysail mast, the gaff

Top: The Royal yacht *Mary*, painted by L. de Mann in the early eighteenth century.

Above: The cutter was a popular small man-of-war for inshore work. This is the *Hawke* of 1777.

123

Above right: Model of a Dutch mercantile brigantine at the end of the eighteenth century. The need to save manpower led owners to try simpler rigs.

Below: A snow with her gaff sail furled about the trysail mast, another variant popular among small trading vessels.

could be hoisted higher than the main yard to give a larger sail area and a better balance to the rig. In some snows, the trysail mast was replaced by a horse on the after side of the mainmast which served the same purpose. Brigs, snows and brigantines were built up to a maximum tonnage of around 1,000 and were the main workhorses of the short-sea trade.

Brigs were also widely used in European navies during the eighteenth-century wars, armed with up to 18 guns and known generically as 'gunbrigs'. Many naval officers looked upon them with suspicion, for they were considerably overcanvassed, having on their two masts as much sail as, say, a frigate of similar size carried on three. Being warships, they were often required to make ocean passages with the fleet, long voyages for which their hulls were not designed, and their losses through stress of weather were considerable. During the Revolutionary and Napoleonic Wars a large number of British gun-brigs were sent out to operate against the French in the West Indies, and though some of them performed extremely well in action, a larger number succumbed to shipwreck and foundering in the periodic tropical storms which swept the area. Later, when sailing men-of-war had been supplemented by steam-driven warships, brigs were widely used in most navies as training ships for boy seamen, and in the British navy were retained in this role as late as the first decade of the twentieth century.

Although there were brigs, brigantines and snows operating in the Mediterranean, the more popular types of small merchant ships there were the xebec and the polacre, both of them exclusive to those waters. The true xebec was a development of the pirate's brigantine, with a pronounced overhanging bow and stern, somewhat like a galley. They were built with a narrow floor to give them extra speed through the water, but with a considerable beam in order to provide a base for the extensive sail plan which they

Above: A polacre, with
lateen sails on all three
masts.

carried. They were also built with turtle decks
to make water shipped on deck while sailing run
down into the scuppers, and above these decks
gratings were rigged to allow the crew to work
dry-shod. The distinctive feature of the xebec
was the variable rig which it set according to the
weather and point of sailing. The normal rig was
square on the foremast and lateen on the main
and mizen, but with the wind abaft the beam the
lateen yard on the mainmast was taken in and
very long square yards swayed up from which
immense square sails were spread. When sailing
close-hauled, a lateen rig was spread on all three
masts with outsized yards, and in strong winds
these long yards were replaced by yards of normal length. It was a very complicated rig, which
needed a very large crew to handle it. As Falconer, in his marine dictionary of 1771 puts it,
'By the very complicated and inconvenient
method of working these vessels, it will be

readily believed that one of their captains of
Algiers acquainted the author, viz: That the
crew of every Xebec has at least the labour of
three *square-rigged* ships, wherein the standing
sails are calculated to answer every situation of
the wind.' Nevertheless, there was no other ship
of the times to touch them for speed.

The polacre, also peculiar to the Mediterranean, took two forms, known as 'brig' and 'ship'.
The brig polacre was two-masted, normally
square-rigged on both masts, but occasionally
lateen-rigged on the mizen; the ship polacre had
three masts, lateen-rigged on fore and mizen and
square-rigged on the main, but occasionally
lateen-rigged on all three masts. She was al-
together a bigger ship, being sometimes built up
to a tonnage of around 1,200. They were called
'polacres' because their masts were formed from
a single spar and they had neither tops nor cross-
trees. The yards had no footropes and the crew

stood on the topsail yards to loose or furl the top-gallants, and on the lower yards to loose, furl or reef the topsails.

Of still smaller vessels there was an almost infinite variety. The Baltic nations had the *jagt* and the *galeas* as their main types of small trading or fishing craft, but they were of different hull design and rig in each nation. The Dutch had the *tjalk*, and its many derivatives, the *kof* and the *bezaanschuit* as their main types. In England barges, keels and ketches carried the majority of short passage trade, although in the coal trade down the east coast a type of ship called a 'cat' was used. The best-known of the French small craft was the *chasse-marée*, originally three-masted with square sails on the two forward masts and lateen on the mizen, but later lug-rigged on all three, using very large sails with all three masts raked aft. It proved a weatherly rig which produced a good turn of speed. They were used extensively for smuggling and, in wartime, as privateers. In the Mediterranean there was an equally wide variety of types, of which the best known were the Spanish *felucca*, the Portuguese *fregata*, the Spanish and Italian *tartane*, the Italian *trabaccolo* and the Greek *sacoleva* and

trekandini. None of these was large; in all of them there were local variations in hull design and rig, so that, for example, a *tartane* built in one port would differ slightly from the *tartane* built in the next port along the coast. About the only thing that each type had in common was the number of masts it stepped, and even here there could be local variations.

The rest of the world was equally prolific in the types of ship built and sailed. The Arab nations used the *baghla*, a large ship with a hull design of European parentage, no doubt influenced by the Portuguese, Dutch and English East Indiamen which sailed those waters in the seventeenth and eighteenth centuries. A slightly odder Arabian vessel was the *ghanja*, in which the quarter-deck was extended to overhang the rudder head by a considerable distance. All used full lateen rigs on two or three masts. Farther east, until one comes to the south-western Pacific, the junk is the dominant ship type, both large and small, widely adapted to suit local conditions, in some cases so radically that it might be difficult to establish the junk parentage. One of the geographical features of this part of the world is the wide rivers which provide navigable water far inland, and it is in the river craft that designs have broken away from the junk model. But here again the local variety is enormous.

The junk herself has a history at least as long as, and probably very much longer than, any other type of ship. The earliest description of a junk known in the west – and, with some small modifications, it could be a description of a junk today – is that given by Marco Polo in his account of his voyage to China in 1298. He does not go into any details of the actual hull design – and early European attempts to illustrate a junk usually gave it a European-type hull – but there is no mistaking the authenticity of his description, or that what he saw then is remarkably similar to what he would have seen today. Chinese junks were built to a considerable size even in Marco Polo's time, and carried the trade of China throughout the Pacific and Indian Oceans. They also formed the Chinese war fleet, until the steamship and the long-range gun made their appearance. Today, although most junks are motorized, there are still some sailing junks in use for the local coasting trade.

One of the features of Marco Polo's junk – and one which it took the West centuries to appreciate – was its subdivision into watertight compartments by transverse bulkheads, specifically to prevent the ship from filling and sinking if she were holed by striking a rock or by any other cause (Marco Polo mentions in this respect a hungry whale!). Another was the fact that she had a single rudder, which could mean that the Chinese invented the hanging rudder attached to the sternpost well ahead of Western nations.

Another type associated with China is the *lorcha*, a sailing vessel with a European hull shape surmounted by the Chinese junk rig. It originated at Macao when it was first settled by the Portuguese in 1557. The name, oddly enough, spread to the Mediterranean where the traditional lateen rig was considered to resemble the junk rig, and many small Mediterranean vessels were described, quite wrongly, as *lorchas*.

The south-west Pacific islands remained, by and large, faithful to the canoe design. The Malayan word for boat or ship is *prahu*, and the word *prau* is still widely used to indicate any type of vessel local to those waters. The commonest sail rig was, and is still, the dipping or standing lug, in use around Indonesia and the south-west Pacific for centuries. Vessels designed to carry large cargoes often consisted of platforms constructed on two or three canoe hulls, with a variety of lugsail shapes carried on one or two masts.

Mercator and Harrison

One of the greatest problems facing the first geographers was how to make an accurate representation of a curved surface (the globe) on a flat surface (a chart). No attempt was made to do so in the early portulan charts, which merely set out to show an outline of the land using the positions of known ports and landmarks. Although these portulan charts were of exquisite workmanship and reasonably accurate in what they showed of the general shape of the land, they were of little use for navigation beyond that of a hit-or-miss variety.

Gerardus Mercator, who used the latinized form of his proper name, Gerhard Kremer, founded a geographical establishment in Louvain and began producing his own maps in 1537. His first map of the world, in two hemispheres, was produced in 1538 and showed him to be much influenced by the theories of Ptolemy. A change of religion from Catholicism to Protestantism was followed by a trial for heresy, but he escaped further religious persecution when the University of Duisburg offered him the chair of cosmography, which he eagerly accepted. Here he turned his back on the Ptolemaic theories and introduced his own projection, with parallels of latitude and meridians of longitude cutting each other at right angles. His first work on these principles, the famous world map in eighteen sheets, was published in 1569, and he followed this up with several other maps. In 1585 he issued the first part of his equally famous atlas. Two years later he produced a world map with his projection for inclusion in the atlas, and in the year of his death, 1594, his final world atlas made its appearance.

Mercator's projection proved invaluable to the navigator as it meant that the course that he wished to steer appeared on his chart as a straight line. The shortest route between any two points on the surface of a globe lies along the arc of the great circle passing through those points, but to sail this shortest distance means that a ship must sail a constantly changing course. This cannot be done without great difficulty or inconvenience, and so a navigator making a long ocean passage steers a series of straight courses, along chords of the great circle, which approximate to the shortest route and are much easier for the helmsmen to steer. These straight

Above: Mercator's map of India.

Below: Mercator, whose famous projection altered sixteenth century chart-making.

courses are known as 'rhumb lines', and one will cut all meridians of longitude at the same angle. On a chart produced on the Mercator projection all rhumb lines appear as straight lines, and, since ships normally steer rhumb line courses, such a chart would obviously be of immense navigational value.

Mercator's projection can be imagined as a cylinder encircling the globe, touching it at the equator and prolonged upwards and downwards (i.e. north-wards and southwards) to infinity. The lines of latitude and longitude, together with the features of the globe, are projected outwards onto the cylinder, at right angles to the surface of the globe, and the cylinder, when unrolled, forms a flat chart. Since the sides of the cylinder are parallel to the north-south axis of the globe, it follows that north and south poles can never be shown on Mercator's projection. Moreover, the size and shape of land masses becomes more and more distorted, the nearer they are to the poles, because north-south distances appear progressively greater than east-west distances. For this reason, on a Mercator chart, the land masses of the far north and south, such as Greenland or Tierra del Fuego, appear many times larger.

Nevertheless, for navigational purposes, the fact that a rhumb line always appears as a straight line on a Mercator chart gives it a unique advantage. The distortion does not worry the navigator, because he measures distances by the scale of latitude at the side of the chart.

* * *

How to measure a ship's latitude at sea had been known to navigators for centuries, almost certainly from the times when the Phoenicians were the great navigators of Europe between the eighth and second centuries B.C. A measurement of the sun's altitude at local noon, or that of the Pole Star at night, gave them the answer. But the calculation of longitude, the other co-ordinate of a ship's position at sea, baffled seamen for centuries, and, in fact, was responsible for innumerable shipwrecks simply because navigators did not know how far east or west they were when out of sight of land.

Once it was known that the earth was a globe and that it turned one complete revolution in relation to the sun every 24 hours – which was accepted very early in the history of navigation – navigators realised that they could easily calculate their longitude at sea, if they had a clock which could tell them the time at the prime meridian (longitude 0°). If it took 24 hours for the earth to revolve through 360 degrees, then in one hour it must revolve through 15. Each hour of difference, therefore, between the time of noon on longitude 0° and the time when the sun reached its highest point at the ship's position, must represent 15 degrees of longitude east or west of the prime meridian. It was easy enough to tell when the sun reached its highest point (by observation with an astrolabe, cross-staff or sextant); what was needed was a method of knowing the time on the prime meridian that would remain accurate over the course of a long voyage.

It was to solve this second problem

Right: John Harrison holding a chronometer.

that, in 1714, an Act of Parliament in Britain set up a Board of Commissioners for the Discovery of the Longitude at Sea, which offered a prize of £20,000 for a solution, stipulating accuracy to within 30 miles (48·3 km). The offer attracted the interest of John Harrison, an estate carpenter in Lincolnshire. He and his younger brother James had, as a hobby, already constructed a number of long-case clocks of remarkable accuracy, including one with the first ever bimetallic pendulum, designed to overcome inaccuracy caused by variation in temperature. However, a pendulum clock was useless in a ship, as her motion in a rough sea would be enough to stop the pendulum.

With the £20,000 prize in view, Harrison gave up carpentry to devote all his time to devising new movements which would keep accurate time without a pendulum, and between 1735 and 1760 he constructed four chronometers, all of which proved accurate enough to qualify him for the prize. The first was a massive mechanism made of brass and wood which weighed 72 lb (32·7 kg) – far too large and unwieldy to be carried

about in a ship, although it was taken on a voyage to Portugal and back in 1736 in H.M.S. *Centurion*. But his fourth chronometer was about twice the size of the average pocket watch, ideal for use on board ship, and in two trials at sea in 1762 and 1764 it easily qualified in accuracy for the award. A copy of this watch, made by Larcom Kendall, was taken by Captain Cook on his second voyage round the world, and, when three years later he made his final land-fall at Plymouth, his calculation of his longitude based on the watch's timekeeping proved correct to within 8 miles (13 km).

John Harrison was at first only paid half the £20,000 prize, the Board of Longitude requiring more proof of the accuracy of his chronometer than could be obtained from two voyages. The balance was finally paid in 1773, but the long wait for the full reward embittered Harrison in the last years of his life. He died in 1776, and generations of navigators since then have owed him a vast debt of gratitude for having solved the problem of almost the last of the navigational unknowns.

Chapter Six
Frigates, Sloops, Yachts and Barges

It was noted in the last chapter that, in the days when warships were rated according to the number of guns which they carried, ships of the fifth and sixth rates were known as 'frigates'. But the name is much older than the ship under consideration: its history is a long one, going back to early times in the Mediterranean when the big galleys were equipped with a smaller tender, also oared, called a *'fregata'*. The *fregata* remained in attendance until the demise of the galley, latterly being lightly armed to enable her to intervene in battle when the opportunity presented itself.

In the fifteenth and sixteenth century a frigate could also be a sailing craft, two- or three-masted, usually with lateen sails on every mast. She was built for speed, was generally fairly small, and used mainly as a despatch vessel. It was this version of the frigate that Richard Lovelace had in mind when he wrote in *Lucasta*:

Have you not seen a charact [carrack] lie,
A great cathedral in the sea,
Under whose Babylonian walls,
A small thin frigot almshouse stalls.

Another use of the term, introduced around the end of the sixteenth century, was to denote a medium-sized merchant ship. This practice lasted into the eighteenth century, although, once the naval frigate was firmly established, the merchant version became known as a 'galleon-frigate'. All that this really meant was a merchant ship built frigate fashion (that is, with a forecastle and quarter-deck descending by steps to the waist of the ship).

The naval frigate as such, a rated warship of relatively modest armament, does not appear until the eighteenth century, though the name was used for some warships in the seventeenth. The first English naval frigate, for example, is widely considered to have been the *Constant*

Warwick. She was built in 1646 as a privateer for the Earl of Warwick, but was purchased for the navy three years later. She was a ship of 379 tons, mounting 30 guns when built – which was increased later to 42 – but on this scale of size and armament she can hardly be classed as a true frigate for her day. Perhaps her claim to be the first frigate rests on the fact that she was the prototype of a new trend in English naval architecture towards a longer keel and less freeboard in warships, producing a ship of finer lines, lying lower in the water, and thus slightly faster and stiffer. Although, after the *Constant Warwick*, several more medium-sized warships were built on these improved lines, the tendency to increase the length-to-beam ratio did not become general, and it was not until the eighteenth century that what we now recognise as the true naval frigate emerged – a fast, seaworthy ship, mounting a moderately heavy armament on a single gundeck.

It was during the wars of the first half of the eighteenth century that many navies realised the need for vessels answering to this description. They were required by the battle fleets as reconnaissance ships, and as escorts by mercantile convoys. In the early part of the century the smaller warships of 44 and 40 guns, of which a number had been built, were used for this purpose, but they proved unsatisfactory because they were too slow and, having two gundecks, their accommodation below was terribly cramped. In 1748 the first genuine naval frigates began to be built, mounting 28 guns on a single gundeck. Even they were not quite what was wanted since the largest guns which they could accommodate were 9-pounders, but a few years later a new design of frigate carrying thirty-two 12-pounder guns was produced, and this was much nearer the desired ship. Eventually, certainly by 1757, a 36-gun frigate made her appearance, and she proved to be the ideal vessel for both purposes, with a good turn of speed for fleet reconnaissance and a relatively heavy armament for the defence of convoys.

Left: The Battle of Lissa, fought in the Adriatic on the night of 13–14 March 1811 between four British frigates and ten French and Venetian ships. Captain Hoste won a brilliant victory over the French Commodore Dubourdieu.

131

Each nation had its own design of frigate, and it is interesting to see how the different national naval architects interpreted the requirements for such a vessel in terms of its dimensions. Oddly enough, the French considered British warships to be the best in the world, so far as construction and design were concerned, while the British had almost the exactly opposite opinion, holding that French design, though not construction, was the best. When, in 1758, the French 36-gun frigate *Aurore* was captured by the British, she was put into a dry-dock and carefully measured for comparison with the British 36-gun frigate *Brilliant*. The differences were surprising.

	Brilliant	*Aurore*
Date of launch	1757	1758
Length of gundeck	128 ft 4 in (39·12 m)	144 ft 0 in (43·89 m)
Keel	106 ft 2½ in (32·37 m)	118 ft 9 in (36·2 m)
Beam	35 ft 8 in (10·87 m)	38 ft 8½ in (11·8 m)
Depth	12 ft 4 in (3·76 m)	15 ft 2 in (4·62 m)
Burthen	718 tons	946 tons

It can be seen from this table that the French frigate, though she mounted exactly the same number of guns as the British, was more than a quarter larger in terms of tonnage, and all her other dimensions were also significantly greater.

Later in this same century, when the Americans began to build frigates during the War of Independence, these, too, were considerably larger, gun for gun, than the British. So also were Spanish frigates, but the Dutch approximated much more to British dimensions. One would be hard-pressed to say which was the better design for the frigate's role – the larger ships of the French, Spanish and Americans, or the smaller design of Britain and Holland. Each type had its successes and failures, and in general the quality of the crew probably counted infinitely more than the actual design of the vessel. Nevertheless, there were many British frigate captains who envied the larger size of foreign frigates and would have dearly loved to command one, mainly because they were marginally faster on certain points of sailing.

Right: Original plan for building the Royal Navy frigate *Brilliant* in 1757.

Below right: The French 74-gun *Droits de l'Homme*, is driven ashore by the frigates *Indefatigable* (44-gun) and *Amazon* (36-gun) in January 1797. The *Amazon* was also lost, but the action was Sir Edward Pellew's most famous exploit.

Above: The quarterdeck of the 6th rate *Deal Castle* in 1775. Awnings provided shade, for officers and men, as well as the goats and hens carried on deck.

battle line, if they looked like drifting down onto the enemy line where they could be boarded and captured. Independently, they were the best type of ship for escorting convoys, since they had a fair margin of speed over the merchant ships and could overhaul any ships straying from the convoy and round them up, and also had a fair advantage of firepower over any enemy privateer engaged in the *guerre de course* and looking for the easy capture of a merchant ship. Frigates were admirably suited, too, for use with blockading squadrons, since their speed and manoeuvrability enabled them easily to close the enemy port in order to count the warships inside and see whether they were making any moves to come out, such as crossing their yards or sending up their sails.

They were rigged exactly like a ship of the line, with the standard three masts and square sails on each, but with their finer lines – a length-to-beam ratio of nearly 4 to 1 compared with 3 to 1 in a ship of the line – they could sail as much as half a point closer to the wind than their larger sisters. Towards the end of the eighteenth century their 12-pounder guns were replaced by 18-pounders, and, to provide the extra constructional strength necessary, the scantlings of their bottom planking increased from 3 in (76 mm) to 4 in (102 mm). Towards the end of the century the traditional oak from which all warships had been built (except those built in India where teak was used) began to be replaced by fir in the case of smaller warships, and in Britain seven frigates were constructed of this wood as an experiment. They were found to be excellent ships for use in the West Indies, being very light and airy, but in home waters they were not popular.

Also at this time, a new version of the traditional frigate was introduced, known as a 'donkey-frigate' to distinguish it from the true frigate. Besides the single covered gundeck of the frigate, she had additional guns mounted on the forecastle and quarter-deck. Perhaps a more accurate description of her would have been 'ship-sloop'. The type was not considered a success, and few were built.

As, with succeeding campaigns, the value of the frigate in naval warfare became more and more evident, they were built in larger and larger numbers. Taking Britain as a typical example, in 1750 there were seventy-eight true frigates, that is, fifth- and sixth-rate ships; ten years later their number had risen to 115. By the end of the eighteenth century the number was 159, and this out of a total naval strength of 517 ships, including all the ships of the line and more than 200 smaller vessels, such as sloops, brigs, cutters, etc. Figures for other navies show much the same situation and indicate the importance attached to the frigate by all the navies of the world. They were what might be called all-purpose ships, serving the battle fleets both as scouts and, in action, as repeating ships, lying outside the battle line and repeating the admiral's signals so that all ships could see them without having to peer through the smoke of battle. They were also used to tow disabled ships out of the

The frigate was the favourite warship of the United States, and, although there was no official United States Navy until an Act of Congress of 27 March 1794 authorized six frigates to be built, the revolutionary Congress formed during the War of Independence had, in 1775, authorized the building of thirteen ships. These were small frigates, five of 32 guns each, five of 28, and three of 24. Later in that year, three more frigates were authorized, all of 32 guns. They

Far left: Contemporary model of the *Mermaid*, a 32-gun frigate. She was launched at Sheerness in 1784, having previously been laid down at Woolwich from where the timber frames were transferred in 1782.

Left: The *Constitution* as she is today at Boston. Like HMS *Victory* she is kept in commission as a naval vessel.

Right: The spar deck of the USS *Constitution*, the oldest man-of-war still afloat, as she looked in 1931 before restoration.

Below right: The capture of the 38-gun HMS *Guerrière* by the *Constitution* in August 1812, which created the legend of 'Old Ironsides'.

were all built to the conventional frigate design, the main armament on a single gundeck and chase guns mounted on forecastle and quarter-deck. Later, these frigates were altered by connecting the forecastle and quarter-deck with longitudinal gangways along each side, making the ships appear as though they had a continuous upper deck without a waist. Later still, the Americans mounted guns on these gangways, increasing the number of guns from 32 to 44 in their largest frigates. They were then known as 'double-backed' frigates and proved popular with their captains and crews.

Of these thirteen frigates, the best-known was the 32-gun *Hancock*, built at Newburyport, Massachusetts by Jonathan Greenleaf, Stephen Cross and his brother, Ralph. She was launched in 1776 and was generally considered to be the fastest frigate in the world. Nevertheless, in 1777, she was sighted and captured by the British 44-gun frigate *Rainbow* after a chase which lasted 36 hours. Taken into the British navy and renamed *Iris*, she was repaired and her bottom coppered at Plymouth, and under her new flag she captured another of the thirteen American frigates, the *Trumbull*. Finally, in 1781, she was taken by the French and finished her days as a powder hulk in Toulon, but not before the British had measured her very carefully and taken a draft of her lines as a model for future British frigate building.

As mentioned above, the U.S. Navy came officially into being with the Act of Congress of 27 March 1794 and the order for what were to

become known as the 'six original frigates'. These were the *United States, Constitution* and *President*, all of 44 guns, and the *Chesapeake, Constellation* and *Congress*, originally of 36 guns, although this number was increased during building to 38. They were all good ships, built considerably longer and fuller than most of the frigates of corresponding firepower of other countries. The *Constitution*, built at Boston by Edward, Joseph, and Edmund Hart and launched in 1797, is perhaps the most famous warship in American naval history. She fought and won a notable action against the British 38-gun frigate *Guerrière* in 1812 – an achievement which earned her the nickname 'Old Ironsides' – captured the British *Java* later that year, and followed these victories with another in 1815, against the British *Cyane* and *Levant*. According to the normal American practice she was built very large for her 44-gun rating, with a displacement of 2,200 tons on an overall length of 204 ft (62·18 m), a beam of 43½ ft (13·26 m), and a depth of hold of 14¼ ft (4·34 m). She was restored to her original condition in 1931 and is now berthed as a national memorial at Boston, where she was originally built.

The Americans did not begin to build ships of the line until after 1815, and then they did not enjoy much success with them. But to back up their frigates they built schooners, armed with carronades and long-barrelled 9-pounders and fast enough to overtake pirate vessels or slavers. Even more notably, they built ship-rigged sloops, with hulls based on the Baltimore clipper, endowing them with both speed and good looks. It is these sloops which are said to have marked the transition of the U.S. Navy from the 'frigate theory' to the 'sloop theory'. Certainly they were excellent small warships, and probably the best form of navy for a nation which as yet had very little seaborne trade to protect.

Frigates, sloops and brigs remained the basis of the U.S. Navy until the sailing warship became a thing of the past. By mid-nineteenth century, steam propulsion was being incorporated in sailing warships, existing ships being cut in two and lengthened to accommodate the engine and boilers. They were still wooden ships, with the full ship rig on three masts, but they had an unfamiliar look because of the pair of collapsible funnels amidships. In 1854 the United States ordered five steam frigates and one corvette (normally smaller than a frigate), which proved to be the most remarkable ships yet built. They were of 3,200 tons (3,250 tonnes) – half as big again as the first-rate H.M.S. *Victory* – and mounted twenty-four 9-inch guns, fourteen 8-inch and two 10-inch. The corvette had a dis-

Above: HMS *Galatea* was one of six big wooden steam frigates built in 1857 to match American commerce raiders.

with twenty-four 10-inch guns on the gundeck and two 68-pounder pivot guns on forecastle and quarter-deck. The other four were smaller, of 3,800 tons (3,860 tonnes) displacement, though they, too, mounted 10-inch guns as their main armament. All six proved considerably faster than the American ships (12 to 13 knots as against 8 to 9), and they were the ultimate development of the wooden-hulled frigate.

The sloop (and her French equivalent, the corvette) stood immediately below the frigate in fighting strength. She was originally designed as a counter to the hordes of privateers which roamed the seas in search of merchant shipping in time of war. Any private citizen who owned a ship could become a privateer by obtaining from the naval authority of his country a Letter of Marque. It was a condition of a Letter of Marque that any merchant ship captured had to be brought before the Prize Court to be 'condemned' (a safeguard against outright piracy), and if she was properly condemned by the Court the owner of the privateer took 90 per cent of the value with the other 10 per cent being added to the national Prize Fund. It was an intensely profitable business, and many citizens formed themselves into syndicates to buy and operate

placement of no less than 4,580 tons (4,650 tonnes) – a third as big again as the frigates – and mounted fourteen 11-inch Dahlgren guns.

Faced with this challenge from across the Atlantic, Britain also ordered six steam frigates, in 1857. The two largest, the *Ariadne* and *Galatea*, had a displacement of 4,426 tons (4,497 tonnes) – very nearly as big as the largest first-rate yet built in Britain (H.M.S. *Wellington*) –

ships as privateers. Many of them were not too particular as to which merchant ships they attacked, and it was not unknown for a merchant ship to be captured and ransacked at sea by a privateer of her own country. Some privateers were no more than pirates, attacking every ship they encountered irrespective of her country of origin.

It was to the sloop or her equivalent that most navies looked to check the depredations of hostile privateers. She was smaller than the frigate, usually mounting eighteen guns or less on the upper deck, and was two-masted in contrast to the frigate's three. She was built for speed, with long, fine lines, and after 1796 was often constructed in fir instead of oak, mainly as an economy measure because of the huge wartime building programmes. Since she was not a rated ship, as she did not carry enough guns to qualify, she was usually commanded by a senior lieutenant, who was known as a 'captain', as opposed to a 'post-captain' who commanded a rated ship, and provided valuable command experience for officers on their way up the promotion ladder. Like the frigates, large numbers of sloops were built, and a measure of their usefulness in war can be seen in the fact that the total of forty sloops in the British Navy in 1793, when

the Revolutionary War against France began, grew to 107 by 1800, and this in spite of fairly substantial losses during the course of the war. The corvette was generally built a little smaller than the English sloop, but in just as large numbers. The average sloop ran to about 400 tons displacement, was designed with a length-to-beam ratio of better than 4 to 1, and had a complement of about 120 men.

The word 'yacht', in its meaning of pleasure craft, came to England in 1660 with the restoration of Charles II to the English throne. The word is derived from the Dutch '*jaght*', and it was the gift to the king in 1660 of the jaght *Mary* by the burgomasters of Amsterdam that first introduced sailing for pleasure into England, and the word 'yacht' with it. Yet the original Dutch *jaght* was anything but a pleasure craft. The word in Dutch means 'hunt' or 'chase', and was at first applied to any armed, light sailing vessel with a good turn of speed, and frequently also to any fast pirate vessel. Later, as national navies developed, the small despatch and advice vessels used to serve the Dutch fleet as messengers, etc., which were roughly the equivalent of the English pin-

Above: The yacht *Mary* was one of a number of such craft built after the Restoration of Charles II. The first *Mary* was a gift to the King by the burghers of Amsterdam. (From a painting by van de Velde the Younger, 1677)

Far left: A British gun-brig captures the Spanish slaver *Marinetto* in April 1831. Many brigs were used on anti-slavery patrols but they could be outrun by some of the faster slavers.

Above: 'Dutch Yachts Racing', a painting by van Ertwelt. The Dutch world *jaght* passed into the English language after 1660 to indicate, first a vessel of state, and second any sizeable craft used purely for pleasure.

nace, were called '*jaghts*' or '*jachts*'. Although, before 1660, the term was not used to describe any sort of English vessel, it was not unknown in England as a type of foreign vessel and occurs in English writings as early as 1557, when Stephen Burrough's account of his voyage in search of the North-East Passage mentions meeting three or four Norway 'yeaghes'. Other early English versions of the term were 'yoathe', yaught', 'yolke' and 'zaught'.

In many countries there had for centuries been yachts in the sense of Falconer's *Dictionary of the Marine* definition: 'vessels of state usually employed to convey princes, ambassadors, or other great personages from one kingdom to another.' These were almost invariably highly ornamented varieties of the type of warship then in current use, be it galley, longship, cog, carrack, or whatever. In England the earliest vessel built entirely for pleasure was probably a miniature warship

which James I ordered Phineas Pett to construct for Prince Henry, his eldest son. In his autobiography Pett describes the vessel: 'About January 15th 1604 a letter was sent post-haste . . . commanding me with all possible speed to build a little vessel for the young Prince Henry to disport himself in about London Bridge, and acquaint his Grace with shipping, and the manner of that element; setting me down the proportions and the manner of garnishing, which was to be like the work of the *Ark Royal*, battlementwise. This little ship was in length 25 ft (7·6 m) by the keel, and in breadth 12 ft (3·7 m), garnished with painting and carving, both within board and without, very curiously, according to his Lordship's directions.' She was named *Disdain*, but as Prince Henry died in 1612 he had only a few years in which to enjoy her.

The Dutch *Mary*, Charles II's first real yacht in the sense of a pleasure craft, was a vessel of 100 tons, not unlike the present-day Thames barge, though with a large cabin superimposed on the deck aft. She had the typical Dutch fore-and-aft rig with gaff mainsail and single jib and, another typical Dutch feature, was fitted with leeboards to prevent leeway when sailing close-hauled. Charles was a great lover of the sea and sailing, and in all owned twenty-five yachts, of which the smallest was the *Jamie* of 25 tons and the largest the *Saudadoes* of 180 tons.

Charles's example set a pattern in England that was followed by succeeding monarchs, though none equalled him in the number of yachts that he owned. It was followed, too, by many noblemen and courtiers, and the sport of yachting grew steadily over the years. The first recorded yacht race was sailed in 1661 between Charles's *Katherine* and the Duke of York's *Anne* over a course on the River Thames from Greenwich to Gravesend and back, and this sport, too, prospered over the years. The Dutch took to pleasure sailing with almost equal enthusiasm, but other countries seemed to be less keen.

Most royal yachts were included in their country's national navy, possibly because the cost of their building was paid out of funds voted for the navy or because they were manned by naval personnel. In wartime many of them served in their traditional role as fast despatch vessels, and there are records of some being captured and sold in the Prize Court.

Another small craft was the barge, and it is difficult in the earliest years to distinguish between a barge and a yacht. The essential feature of the barge was that it was always propelled by oars, with a minimum of eight, even in the days of sail, but it was ornamented and decorated with every bit as much splendour as the most regal of the royal yachts. One of the earliest recorded examples is Cleopatra's barge which she used on the Nile and which, in Shakespeare's words,

> '. . . like a burnished throne
> Burnt on the water; the poop was beaten gold,
> Purple her sails; and so perfumed, that
> The winds were love-sick with them. The oars
>   were silver
> Which to the tune of flutes kept stroke, and
>   made
> The water which they beat to follow faster,
> As amorous of their strokes . . .'

Equally famous was the *Bucentaur*, the traditional name of the barge used by the doges of Venice in the annual procession on Ascension Day, commemorating the victory of Doge Pietro

Orseolo II over the Dalmatian pirates in the year 1000 and the subsequent conquest of all Dalmatia. The name *Bucentaur* is an adaptation of '*buzino d'oro*' (barque of gold), an apt enough description as the doge's barge was gilded from the waterline up. The traditional name first occurs in a decree of 1311 as *Bucintoro*, and the barge of this decree remained in commission for over 400 years, until replaced in 1728. She was two-decked like a galley and rowed 42 oars, with four *arsenalotti*,

Above: Contemporary model of a late seventeenth century British royal yacht.

Bucentaur
(1728)

Length 115 ft (35·1 m) *Beam* 22 ft (6·7 m) *Depth* 26 ft (7·9 m)
Complement 168 rowers

This was the last in a line of sumptuous Venetian state barges and surpassed even her predecessors in magnificence. She was the second to bear the name *Bucentaur*, or *Bucintro* (a contraction of *buzino d'oro*, meaning 'barque of gold'). She was designed by Michele Stefano Conti on the lines of a war galley with a ram at the bow, although her function was entirely ceremonial. Four free artisans from the Arsenale, known as *Arsenalotti*, pulled each of her forty-two oars. The rowers occupied the main deck, while the upper deck was a continuous long saloon, adorned with crimson velvet and gold embroidery, and paintings and carvings of mythological characters. At the aft end stood the throne of the doge, surmounted by a canopy in the form of a huge shell supported by two cherubs. The *Bucentaur* was used on state and religious occasions, the most notable of which was the annual Wedding of the Sea ceremony, and there was a special window at the stern through which the doge threw a gold ring into the sea to symbolize the union. This ceremony took place for the last time in 1796. In the following year the doge was overthrown by the French. The *Bucentaur* was beached, stripped of her decoration, and, under the name *Idra*, was turned into a battery and sailors' prison. She was eventually broken up in 1824, nearly a hundred years after her launching.

This reconstruction is based on the model of the *Bucentaur* in the Arsenale museum at Venice. There are two beakheads at the bow, the higher and more prominent of which supports the lion of St. Mark. The tall figure in the group immediately over the stem is that of Justice. Undoubtedly there were alterations made to the decoration at various stages in the vessel's career. The detail from a painting by Canaletto depicts the *Bucentaur* surrounded by an armada of smaller craft on the day of the Wedding of the Sea ceremony commemorating Doge Pietro Orseolo II's victory over Dalmatian pirates in the year 1000.

who were priveleged citizens, manning each oar. The annual procession was led by the *Bucentaur* to the island of Sant'Elena, where the Doge received a bunch of damask roses in a silver vase in exchange for an offering of peeled chestnuts and red wine before throwing a ring into the open sea with the words 'We wed thee, O Sea, in token of our perpetual dominion.'

The next *Bucentaur*, the last of the line, was designed by Michele Stefano Conti and launched in 1728. She was 100 ft (30·5 m) long, 24 ft (7·3 m) high, and like her predecessor was rowed by 21 oars on each side. In 1798, during Napoleon's campaign against the Italian states, she was taken by the French when Venice capitulated. The gold with which she was covered was stripped off and melted down, and she was used as a floating battery, first by the French and then by the Venetians, until she was broken up in 1824. A fine model of this last *Bucentaur* and part of her mast are in the Arsenale Museum in Venice.

In almost every capital in Europe, up to about 1800, the river on which it was built was the main highway for city travel. Individuals could hire skiffs or 'pair-oars' rowed by licensed watermen, to travel up or down river to the nearest landing place to their destination, but important personages travelled on the river by barge which, perhaps inspired by Cleopatra's example, grew increasingly ornate and sumptuous.

In London, for example, the Thames was used not only for the day-to-day travel of citizens, but also for the ceremonial welcome of important visitors, when a procession of decorated barges would provide a spectacular reception. All the London livery companies had their own barge, used on formal occasions and for junketing, as when the liverymen of the Clothworkers Company used to take their ladies to Chelsea to dine (a regular outing which in 1694 led to a restriction to 'a pint of Lisbon' for each liveryman since the earlier 'distribution of wine' had led to 'considerable inconveniences' – perhaps the understatement of the year).

From about 1422 the Lord Mayor's annual procession to Westminster went by water, in decorated barges with musicians on board, a custom which was retained until 1857 when the Lord Mayor and his procession took to the streets. When Anne Boleyn was crowned as Henry VIII's queen in 1533 she was escorted on her voyage up-river from Greenwich by fifty barges, all of which were required to have 'mynstrelsie' on board. Charles II brought Catherine of Braganza by river to London as his queen on 23 August 1662, and John Evelyn, writing in his diary, considered it 'the most magnificent triumph that ever floated on the Thames; considering the innumerable boates and vessels, dress'd and adorned with all

imaginable pomp, but above all the thrones, arches, pageants, and other representations, stately barges of the Lord Mayor and Companies, with various inventions, musiq, and peales of ordnance both from the vessels and the shore, going to meete and conduct the new Queene from Hampton Court to White-hall, at the first time of her coming to towne. In my opinion it far exceeded all the Venetian Bucentoras, etc. on the Ascension, when they go to espouse the Adriatic.' An etching by Theodore Stoop records the gay scene on the Thames that day.

We know some details of these state barges from the records of the livery companies. For example, the Merchant Taylors built their first barge in 1640 at a cost of £120 4s 0d. She was built by Abraham Tue, a shipwright of Southwark, and was manned by a crew of seventeen watermen, sixteen to row and one to steer, who wore sky-coloured plush caps lined with calico. Their fourth barge, built in 1764 by Thomas Searle of Lambeth, rowed nine oars each side and was built of 'white English oak free from Redness, Rot, Sap, and Prejudicial Knotts.' The 'house', or decorated canopy, where the Master and liverymen sat, was 35 ft (10·7 m) long and had sash windows between fluted columns. It was elaborately carved and painted. Their final barge, built in 1800, was 79 ft (24·1 m) long with a beam of 14 ft (4·3 m), and the 'house' was 37 ft (11·3 m) long and 6 ft (1·8 m) high, containing a pantry (no doubt always well stocked to sustain the passengers during their river trips) and – a modern touch – a water-closet. During the 1840s, when her upkeep was becoming too expensive for the Company, she was sold to the Oxford

Left: The water pageant which welcomed Catherine of Braganza, bride of King Charles II, in August 1662.

Below left: The body of Admiral Nelson lay in state at Greenwich after being brought home from Trafalgar. It was then taken in the State Barge to St Paul's Cathedral for the funeral.

University Boat Club.

The last of the great river processions took place in January 1806 when the state barge originally built for Charles II carried the body of Lord Nelson, which had been lying in state at Greenwich, to the Admiralty office in Whitehall, where it was to rest for the night until the burial in St Paul's Cathedral the following day. All the state barges were out on the river, led by the College of Heralds in two barges, with the King's, Admiralty and Navy Board barges following immediately after the state barge bearing the coffin, and all the livery companies' barges bringing up the rear, the whole procession being attended by hundreds of other river boats which lined the route to Whitehall. The state barges 'had all their masts hoisted half-staff-high; the river glittered with the rich assemblage of colours which was displayed, while the innumerable multitude assembled on its banks beheld the pomp with mingled sensations of curiosity and sorrow.' Fortunately the sun shone on this January day to show off the rich decoration of the state barges.

River processions, not only in London, but also in other European capitals, fell into disuse around the middle of the nineteenth century. An entirely new generation of river craft was driving out the graceful barges, and, in the words of Nathaniel Hawthorne, 'the high streets of the metropolis' were now befouled by 'a multitude of smoke-begrimed steamers'.

Ship Models

It seems probable that, in the earliest days of seafaring, the purpose of making small models of ships was almost entirely religious. Models of Nile ships and boats have been found in several of the tombs of the Pharaohs, dating back to around 2500 B.C., and other models of very early Mediterranean vessels have been found in tombs excavated in Cyprus, Crete and other early centres of eastern Mediterranean civilization. That there was some religious significance in burying these models with bodies in tombs is obvious, probably a physical representation of the widely held belief that upon death the spirit embarks upon some form of journey. It would not be surprising if similar models were made as toys for children. But such children's models, if they existed, have not survived the centuries.

The practice of making models for religious purposes continued throughout the ages, and in many churches in ports and fishing villages ship models hang from the beams, often as a thanks-giving for deliverance from shipwreck and drowning, sometimes commemorating great national events. In the church of Notre Dame de la Garde, which over-looks the port of Marseilles, there are many models given as votive offerings, most of them made or carved by sailors who have come safely home after facing perils on the sea. The church of St. Bavo at Haarlem has some beautiful models of

early Dutch ships hanging above the nave, to commemorate the breaking of the boom at Damietta during the Fifth Crusade. Other such votive offerings sometimes take the form of bench-ends and popey-heads in village churches.

During the seventeenth century, when shipbuilding was becoming a more exact science than the rough and ready methods of medieval builders, many naval architects made a model of a ship that they proposed to build, to show their clients before laying down the ship herself. In 1607 Phineas Pett, a master shipwright of the well-known family, wrote in his journal:

'After my settling at Woolwich I began a curious model for the Prince [Henry] my master, most part whereof I wrought with my own hands, which being most fairly garnished with carving and painting, and placed in a frame arched, covered, and curtained with crimson taffety, was, the 10th day of November, by me presented to the Lord High Admiral at his lodging at Whitehall . . . [The King made a] journey from Whitehall to Richmond to see the same model, whither he came in the afternoon about 3 of the clock, accompanied only with the Prince, the Lord Admiral, and one or two attendants.

Above: An Egyptian funerary boat from a tomb in Thebes, now in the British Museum.

Below: The elaborate carving of a model of HMS *Prince* (1670), incorporating in miniature all the decoration which would be found on the finished ship.

Right: A bronze-gilt nef clock attributed to Hans Schlottenheim.

His Majesty was exceedingly delighted with the sight of the model, and spent time in questioning me divers material things concerning the same, and demanding whether I would build the great ship in all points like to the same . . .'

So what started as a model to delight a prince became a new 'great ship' for the navy. She was launched in 1610 as the *Royal Prince*, one of the most famous ships of the Stuart navy.

This started the practice, which was always more pronounced in England than in other countries, of building a model in advance of construction. Charles I's great ship, *Sovereign of the Seas*, the largest warship in the world when she was launched in 1637, was built from a preliminary model 'of exquisite workmanship, curiously painted and gilt with azure and gold. So contrived that every timber in her might be seen, left open and unplanked for that purpose, very neat and delightsome.' Later in the same century, the British Admiralty officially required naval architects to submit scale models of many warships before confirming the building order.

It is from these models, many of them exact records of ships actually built, that we are able to trace advances in design and building techniques from the seventeenth century onwards. Often they were skeletal below the waterline so that details of the ship's framing could be seen by the purchaser before placing a firm order.

Many other ship models were made individually, not necessarily representing any particular named ship, but representative of a type. The best-known are the models made by French prisoners-of-war during the long years of the Revolutionary and Napoleonic Wars, which are made from bone, ivory or boxwood. They were made partly to occupy the long hours of detention in prison hulks, partly for sale to augment the meagre rations. Most of them are inaccurate models of French warships made by the prisoners from memory, and, often enough, given the name of a British ship to increase the chances of a sale, but nevertheless they are very beautiful and command high prices today when they come up for sale.

Another form of ship model, and even more highly prized today than the

French prisoner-of-war models, were the silver and crystal models used on the tables of the nobility in the fifteenth and sixteenth centuries, usually to hold salt (in those days a rare and precious commodity, and thus thought worthy of an ornate receptacle). They were known as 'nefs', as this was the type of ship most usually represented. The work of the finest silversmiths and glassworkers, they were incredibly elaborate, and in many cases had clockwork figures which performed at intervals. One of the most

famous is a bronze-gilt nef clock made by Hans Schlottenheim (1574–1625). The enamelled dial of the clock is under the mainmast, and when the hour struck, a miniature gun on the forecastle was fired and a tune played on a tiny organ. The men standing on deck were dressed as electors and heralds of the Holy Roman Empire, and they moved in procession in time to the organ, filing past the seated figure of the Emperor and each turning towards him and bowing as he passed.

Chapter Seven
The Mechanical Revolution

The desire for some means of mechanical propulsion for ships is nearly as old as the use of sails for propulsion. The sail, particularly in the days before man had learned to brace the yards to the wind when it was ahead, always placed a limitation on the course that a vessel could steer. She could only sail a course which the wind direction allowed, which was not necessarily the most direct, and to reach her destination if the wind headed her might mean sailing three, or even four, times as far as the straight course. And if her course took her across the equator she might lie motionless for days in the doldrums, without a breath of wind to fill her sails.

The Romans are said to have invented a form of paddlewheel, operated manually by means of a crank, but they discovered, not surprisingly, that rowers with oars were more efficient. During the Middle Ages the Chinese are supposed to have built a junk with paddlewheels attached to the keel and driven by slaves on a treadmill, but this, too, appears to have been a failure, since the invention was not followed up. What was needed – and the innovators soon recognized it – was some means of turning the paddlewheel other than by manpower. In 1685 a French inventor put forward the theory that air pressure would force a piston down a cylinder if a vacuum could be created below it, and that the resultant power could be used to turn a paddlewheel. The vacuum was to be formed by condensing steam injected beneath the piston. Twenty-seven years later, in 1712, this idea was, in fact, to be the basis of the first working steam engine, built by Thomas Newcomen, but even this had no application to ships because it proved impossible to generate enough power to drive a paddlewheel.

The first breakthrough came in 1765 when James Watt, in an attempt to eradicate the chronic inefficiencies of Newcomen's engine, invented the condenser and made the cylinder double-acting, by admitting steam both above and below the cylinder. Here, at last, was a steam engine which developed reasonable power and, with the further invention of a centrifugal governor, power at a constant speed. This was what was needed if mechanical power was to replace the sail. In 1768 Watt went into partnership with Matthew Boulton, who had an engineering workshop at Birmingham, and it was Boulton and Watt engines which powered most of the world's first steamships.

Strictly speaking, the world's first steam vessel was the *Pyroscaphe*, a large clinker-built boat with an engine which turned a pair of small paddlewheels. It was invented by the Marquis Claude de Jouffroy d'Abbans, and in 1783 was tried out on the River Saône in France. The engine worked for 15 minutes before breaking down, and during that time the *Pyroscaphe* moved forward through the water under power. It would be equally correct to say that the second steam vessel in the world was the *John Fitch*, a small barge-like hull with an engine which operated, through linking beams, six vertical oars on each side. This vessel, named after its inventor, made a short trip on the River Delaware in the United States in 1786. However, since neither of these two was reliable enough to prove that steam was a viable method of propulsion for ships, it was left to a later vessel to demonstrate the steamship's potential.

The vessel which really inaugurated the era of the steamship was the *Charlotte Dundas*, which made her first voyage in March 1802. She was built on the River Clyde in Scotland to the order of Lord Dundas, a governor of the Forth and Clyde Canal, and he named her after his daughter. She was a wooden vessel 58 ft (17·7 m) long, with a beam of 18 ft (5·5 m) and a draught of 8 ft (2·4 m), with a single tall funnel amidships. Lord Dundas wanted her to replace the horses which towed the barges up and down the canal, and he gave the order for her to William Symington, an engineer with a workshop on the Clyde. She had a single paddlewheel at the stern, driven

Left: The *William Fawcett* (1829) started a mail service across the Irish Sea, thus founding the Peninsular and Oriental Steam Navigation Company, the 'P&O'.

by a single-cylinder steam engine which developed about 12 horsepower. On her first voyage she towed two 70-ton barges up the canal for a distance of 20 miles (32 km) at a speed of over 3 knots, which would have been higher but for a strong headwind. She ran steadily up and down the canal towing barges for three or four weeks, but was then taken out of service as it was feared that the wash from her paddle-wheel would cause the banks to fall in.

With the *Charlotte Dundas* proving that a steam-driven ship was a commercial proposition, the race for steam propulsion was on. Robert Fulton, an American inventor who had lived in Paris, and of whom we shall hear again later in connection with the birth of the submarine, was the next to construct a steam-driven ship. He had been on board the *Charlotte Dundas* during one of her canal trips, and decided to attempt a similar feat on the River Seine in Paris. His first attempts were a failure, as the wooden hull which he constructed was not strong enough to take the weight of the engine and boiler. It broke in two and sank. Undeterred, Fulton built a

stronger hull, recovered his engine from the bottom of the Seine, and in August 1803 gave a demonstration by towing two boats upriver for an hour and a half.

Convinced that the steamship had a commercial future, Fulton returned to the United States and, in co-operation with a financier named Robert Livingston, who lived at Clermont, built a wooden hull, with a length of 133 ft (40·5 m) and a displacement of 100 tons, on the East Hudson River. As there were no engineers in the United States with sufficient experience of building steam engines he sent over to Britain, to Boulton and Watt, for an engine to be shipped across the Atlantic. The engine had a single vertical cylinder, 24 in (60 cm) in diameter, with a stroke of 48 in (120 cm) and, through bell cranks and spur gearing, drove two 15-ft (4·6 m) paddlewheels, one on each side of the hull. She was named *Clermont*, after Livingston's home town, and on her maiden voyage in 1807 she covered approximately 240 miles (390 km) by steaming to Albany and back in 62 hours, at an average speed over the whole distance of 3·9 knots, though her best speed was 4·7 knots. She continued in commercial service on the East Hudson River for two seasons, eventually prov-

Left: Robert Fulton's steamer *Clermont* inaugurated a commercial service on the Hudson River in 1807.

Below left: The *Charlotte Dundas* had a brief career in 1802, towing canal barges. However her wash damaged canal banks.

ing too small for the crowds that thronged the landing stages to take a passage in her. She was so successful commercially that Fulton built a second steam vessel, which he named the *Phoenix* to operate similarly on the Delaware River. Since she was built at Hoboken and had to steam down the coast of New Jersey to reach the Delaware, she can claim to be the first steamship to make a voyage in the open sea, though she hugged the coastline the whole way.

The financial success of the river steamers in the United States inspired a Scottish engineer, Henry Bell, to enter the steamship business. He built the *Comet* at Glasgow in 1812 for a ferry service on the Clyde between Glasgow, Greenock, and Helensburgh, which proved so successful that he extended it up the west coast of Scotland to Oban and Fort William, 200 miles (320 km) away. The *Comet* was smaller than Fulton's *Clermont*, but her engine produced a better average speed of 6·7 knots. Two years later Henry Bell had five similar ferries running services on the River Thames from London as far down as Margate. The biggest ferry of this early steamship period was the *James Watt*, operating a coastal service between London and Leith. She had an overall length of 141 ft 10 in (43·23 m) and

a maximum beam over her paddle-boxes of 47 ft (14·32 m). Each paddlewheel was 18 ft (5·5 m) in diameter.

By 1816 a steamship passenger service was in operation across the English Channel between Brighton and Le Havre, and in 1820 a service between London and Paris was opened with the *Aaron Manby*. She had an engine designed by Henry Bell which gave her an average speed of between eight and nine knots. After a few regular passenger trips she was purchased by a syndicate of French shipowners and used for pleasure trips up and down the River Seine.

All these vessels were, of course, relatively small; all had paddlewheels driven by single cylinder engines (occasionally, as in the *James Watt*, with one cylinder to each paddlewheel); and all were used only for river or coastal passages. But they opened the way to more ambitious steamship operations, across the oceans, with bigger ships and greater horsepower. In fact, by the year in which the *Aaron Manby* made her passage from London to Paris, the Atlantic had already been crossed by a ship with a steam engine, though she did not really rank as a steamship. This was the American *Savannah*, a full-rigged ship with an auxiliary

Below: Henry Bell's *Comet* (1812) ran a ferry service on the Clyde.

Inset: Transverse section of the *Comet* showing the 3 h.p. engine.

engine and detachable paddlewheels. She crossed the Atlantic in 1819 from Savannah to Liverpool in 21 days, but used her engine for only 8 hours during the passage. A similar voyage, and much more noteworthy because steam propulsion was used to a significant extent, was made in 1825 by the *Enterprise*, a ship of 470 tons, which made a passage of 11,450 miles (18,430 km) in 103 days from London to Calcutta. She was still primarily a sailing ship, but used her engine on sixty-four days of the 103.

The great problem still facing marine engineers and designers was the accommodation of sufficient coal on board to feed the boiler throughout a long ocean passage. By the 1830s the steam engine itself, still a single-cylinder reciprocating engine, was reliable enough to be used for ocean passages, but in general the ships themselves were still too small to accommodate the amount of coal required and still to provide sufficient space for passengers or cargo to make the ship commercially viable.

The answer to this particular problem was, of course, one of ship design, and it was finally solved in a somewhat dramatic fashion. The directors of the Great Western Railway Company in Britain decided in 1837 to extend their railway line to Bristol and called in for consultation their company engineer, Isambard Kingdom Brunel. At the meeting one of the directors complained that the line, when extended to Bristol, would be too long, whereupon Brunel said he thought it would be far too short and ought to be extended to New York by building a passenger steamship. The idea was discussed, approved, and as a result Brunel was told to go ahead and build an Atlantic liner, to be named the *Great Western*.

There was at the time a steamship company in existence called the British and American Steam Navigation Company, and as soon as it was learned that the Great Western Railway were building a steamship specially for an Atlantic crossing, they decided that they would beat them to it. It was known that the *Great Western* was to be a ship of 1,340 tons with an engine developing 750 horsepower, and the British and American company placed an order for a larger ship, to be called the *British Queen*.

There were many delays in her building, and before long it became apparent that the *British Queen* would not be ready before the *Great Western*. British and American, therefore, looked round for a ship to charter, and chose the *Sirius*, built for a passenger and cargo service between London and Cork. She was a ship of 700 tons with an engine developing 320 horsepower, and in the race across the Atlantic she was the first away, leaving Cork on 4 April 1838 with 40 passengers on board. Every available space

Far left: The *Savannah* – first steamship to cross the Atlantic. The passage, made in 1819, took 21 days although she only used steam for 8 hours, relying on sail for most of the journey.

Left: The *Great Western* was Brunel's masterpiece, a steamship with ample endurance for crossing the Atlantic. She made the crossing on 23 April 1838.

Below left: To beat the *Great Western* the *Sirius* was chartered by a rival company, but she only made the crossing from Cork to New York by burning all the wood on board.

below decks was packed with coal, and she carried two large heaps of it on the upper deck as well. Out in the Atlantic she ran into a severe storm which slowed her up and entailed the use of more coal than had been planned. As a result she ran out of coal before she could complete her crossing, but, by feeding the furnace with all the cabin furniture, the wooden doors throughout the ship, all her spare yards and one of her masts, she reached New York. She was greeted by an immense throng of cheering people eager to greet the first ship in the world to make an ocean crossing entirely under steam power. She had taken 18 days, 10 hours and her average speed for the whole passage was 6·7 knots.

She was followed into New York a few hours later by the *Great Western*. The latter had left Bristol four days later than the *Sirius*, carrying only seven passengers, and her time across the Atlantic was 15 days, 5 hours, giving her an average speed of 8·8 knots. What was far more important, however, was the fact that when she arrived in New York she still had 200 tons of coal in her bunkers – proof that, with a proper allowance of bunker space in their design, trans-ocean passages were well within the capability of the new steamships.

Although during these early years of development of the marine steam engine the principle of the compound engine was well enough known, it was impossible to incorporate it in a ship because the problem of generating steam at a high enough pressure had not yet been solved. In a compound engine the steam is used twice: first in a high-pressure cylinder and then in a low-pressure cylinder, connected in line on the same shaft. It is a much more efficient and less wasteful engine than the single-cylinder low-pressure engine, but requires steam at a minimum pressure of 60 lb/sq in (4·2 kg/cm^2) to operate it. During the first half of the nineteenth century steam pressure in ships had risen from an initial 2 lb/sq in (0·14 kg/cm^2) to as much as 50 lb/sq in (3·5 kg/cm^2) by 1850, but it was not until the second half of the century that improved boiler design allowed steam to be generated at pressures suitable for the compound engine.

By the middle of the nineteenth century the oden ship had reached her maximum size, with tonnage approaching 7,000 on waterline lengths of about 340 ft (100 m). These huge wooden ships, built only as warships, drew so much water that they could not be used inshore for the classic naval operations of close blockade and bombardment, required immense crews to man them, and were popular only with commanders-in-chief afloat, who found superb personal accommodation in the immense cabins aft. One such ship was the last three-decker of the British navy, H.M.S. *Victoria*, launched in 1859. In her, the wooden hull had been taken to its limit, and there was not enough strength in wood to extend any further, or to support the huge array of masts and yards required to drive so large an object through the water.

Some other shipbuilding material was obviously necessary, if ships were to develop beyond the limitations imposed by wood, and the only obvious alternative was iron. In the late eighteenth century an iron lighter had been constructed on the Thames, and confounded the sceptics when she did not sink. Nonetheless, there were far more doubters than believers, and resistance to the new material was considerable, even in the face of demonstrable success.

The first true ship to be built with an iron hull was the *Aaron Manby*, the first steamship to operate a service between London and Paris. She was a relatively small vessel of 116 tons, and in spite of many gloomy prognostications, she lasted until 1855, when finally she became unsafe through the rusting of her plates. She was followed by a few other iron-hulled vessels,

but they were all small and another twenty years were to pass before reluctant shipowners could be convinced that iron had so many advantages over wood that it was worth adopting for large ships as well as small.

Apart from the obvious fears that iron, because it is heavier than water, was an unsuitable material for shipbuilding, there were other reasons for the delay in its adoption. The science of engineering had yet to perfect a method of bending iron to a desired shape, and the only methods available at the beginning of the nineteenth century were casting in a mould or working when red hot by hammering. These methods frequently led to fractures because of the uneven quality of the iron. There was no knowledge as yet of any means to prevent rusting, which was accelerated by contact with seawater, and it was also quickly discovered that encrustation of the bottom by barnacles and weed occurred considerably faster on an iron hull than on a wooden

Top: HMS *Victoria* was the last three-decker to go to sea, and served until 1867. The ironclads soon replaced these splendid anachronisms.

Above: The *Aaron Manby* began a regular service between England and France in 1820, but was soon relegated to running on the Seine only.

one. And finally there was the effect of the iron hull on the magnetic compass. So great a mass of magnetic material was certain to throw a compass out, and as yet there was insufficient scientific knowledge of the behaviour of compasses to provide an antidote.

Yet the advantages of iron were so obvious that many shipbuilders did not share the conservative views of shipowners, and devised a means of incorporating it in a wooden hull in what was known as 'composite' building. One of the great drawbacks of the standard wooden hull was the massive framing needed to provide adequate longitudinal and athwartships strength. This framing was a great source of unnecessary weight in a ship. The composite ship had an inner framework consisting of iron keelson, frames, knees and deck beams to which the outer wooden planking, keel and decks were secured, thus providing not only a considerable saving in weight, but also a big increase in stowage space through the elimination of the thick wooden framing. It was a compromise that lasted only until shipowners at last overcame their reluctance, and went all-out for the iron ship.

The first sign of a decline in the continued dominance of wood for large ships came in 1838, with the building of the 400-ton iron ship *Rainbow* for trade between London, Ramsgate and Antwerp. Her immediate advantage was that she could stow in her holds nearly twice as much cargo as a wooden-hulled ship of the same size, and she proved herself to be a good ship at sea, safe and easy to handle. And with her iron hull she was not subject to the perpetual small leaks endemic in all wooden vessels due to the working of the hull planking. But the final seal of approval was set in the following year, when

Isambard Brunel persuaded the directors of the Great Western Railway Company to follow up their successful *Great Western* with an even larger ship, to have an iron hull. This was the *Great Britain*, and her keel was laid at Patterson's shipbuilding yard at Bristol in 1838.

With the *Great Britain* Brunel showed all contemporary naval architects how to design their ships in metal and how to use the new material to provide enough hull strength for ships of rapidly increasing size. In the *Great Britain* he stipulated an iron keel of great strength, nearly 1 in (25 mm) thick and 21 in (53·3 cm) wide, and her hull plating varied in thickness between $\frac{3}{8}$ in (9·5 mm) and $\frac{3}{4}$ in (19 mm). The plates were rivetted to frames made of angle iron, and longitudinal hull strength was provided by two fore-and-aft bulkheads carried up to the level of the main deck, and athwartships strength by five bulkheads across the whole width of the ship. These athwartships bulkheads were made watertight so that the hull was divided into six watertight compartments, as an additional safety measure.

Only in warships was the use of iron delayed, for tests carried out at Portsmouth in England had shown that, while a cannon ball fired at short range at iron plating $\frac{3}{4}$ in (19 mm) thick had no difficulty in penetrating it, 8 in (20 cm) of oak would stop it. And, as the average thickness of a wooden warship's hull planking was 18 in (45 cm), the advantages of retaining wood for warships was obvious. Moreover, wrought and cast iron, the only known methods at the time of bending iron to the desired shapes, showed a tendency to crack or shatter under gunfire – a fatal flaw in a warship. Yet, even in these early days of the iron ship, forces were at work which would compel navies to make the change, par-

Above: The iron-hulled *Rainbow* was built in 1838, and proved her worth. She could stow more cargo than a wooden ship and was equally seaworthy.

ticularly the development of the gun from a short-barrelled weapon discharging a solid ball at a relatively short range to a longer-barrelled piece firing an explosive shell over greater distances. But the day for this transition had not yet arrived, and, until it did, the wooden warship remained in many ways just a larger version of the warship of 200 years earlier.

All these early steamships, whether with wooden or iron hulls, were driven through the water by paddlewheels, either a single one at the stern, as in the *Charlotte Dundas*, or by a pair of wheels, one each side of the ship. There were considerable disadvantages in the use of paddlewheels, the principal one being that when a ship rolled in a seaway, each paddle-wheel (if she had two), would alternately be lifted out of the water, putting a tremendous strain on the engine. And, as they projected outside the hull of the ship, they were easily damaged by careless handling or by other accidents. For warships they were largely useless, since a single hit on a paddlewheel would at once cripple the ship. It was these obvious disadvantages which led several inventors to try to devise a means of ship propulsion which would be permanently submerged, and thus capable of driving the ship without putting a varying strain on the engine or providing an easy target for an enemy gun.

The principle of the Archimedes screw was well known, and it was an adaptation of this principle which finally produced the answer. A very early attempt to produce a marine propeller was John Shorter's invention of 1800, but it suffered from a clumsy form of chain drive and a very long shaft which required a buoy at the end to support it in the water. Four engineers are usually credited with the invention of the ship's propeller, the Englishman Robert Wilson, the Frenchman Frederic Sauvage, the Swede John Ericsson, and another Englishman Francis Pettit Smith. They all took out patents for their inventions between 1833 and 1836. It was Francis Smith's propeller which was at first most widely used by shipowners, though an improved design patented by Ericsson in 1838 was the final winner, when he demonstrated its efficiency in a small steamer aptly named the *Archimedes*.

Isambard Brunel, who had laid the keel of his *Great Britain* in 1839, had designed his ship for propulsion by paddlewheels, but he attended the trials of Ericsson's propeller on the *Archimedes* and was quickly convinced of its superiority as a means of ship propulsion. The building of the *Great Britain* was stopped while Brunel prepared new plans and began a series of experi-

Left: Isambard Kingdom Brunel was a far-sighted engineer but he had a fatal knack of inspiring commercial backers to ruin themselves.

Below left: Illustration from a mid nineteenth century *Treatise on the Screw Propeller* by John Bourne showing (above) the Smith propeller and (below) two views of the Ericsson propeller. Several men were working in this field at the time and the parentage of the screw propeller is disputed.

Below: The *Great Britain* lies on the rocks in Dundrum Bay. Only her iron hull saved her from breaking up.

ments on various models of propellers to find the one most suited to his ship. The *Great Britain* was a large ship for her day, displacing 3,620 tons (3,680 tonnes), on an overall length of 322 ft (98·1 m) and a maximum beam of 50 ft 6 in (15·4 m). As a result of his experiments, Brunel gave her four engines, developing 1,500 horse-power, which drove a six-bladed propeller of 16 ft (4·9 m) diameter at 53 revolutions per minute. Steam from the boilers was fed to the engines at a pressure of 15 lb/sq in (1·1 kg/cm^2).

Like all steamships of her time, except for the smallest, the *Great Britain* was fitted with masts and sails. By 1840 the steam engine had proved itself on thousands of voyages, long and short, but in general most shipowners, and almost all passengers, felt less happy than the engineers about trusting their ships and themselves entirely to mechanical propulsion. So sail was carried, mainly as an insurance against break-down. The *Great Britain* could spread 15,000 square feet of canvas on six masts, but although she crossed and recrossed the Atlantic many times during her service as a passenger ship, only once did she have to rely on her sails to complete a passage, when her propeller dropped off in mid-ocean.

If there were still any who doubted the superi-ority of iron over wood as a shipbuilding material, the *Great Britain* put their anxieties to rest. In September 1846 she ran aground on the rocky coast of Ireland at Dundrum Bay, due it is said to excessive deviation of her compass caused by the iron of the hull. She went ashore at the top of spring tides, and it was not until six months later that there was another tide high enough to float her off. All through the winter she lay on the rocks, battered by the winter gales, conditions which would have reduced any wooden ship to matchwood. When she was refloated and docked, it was discovered that her hull was hardly strained at all.

To avoid some of the loss caused by having her off the Atlantic service for so long, the Great Western Railway Company sold the *Great Britain*. Her new owners refitted her with smaller and more economical engines, and until 1886 she operated steadily between Liverpool and Australia. During that year she was damaged in a heavy storm off Cape Horn and was towed to the Falkland Islands and grounded in Port Stanley, to act as a coal hulk. Finally, in 1970, enough money was raised in Britain to salvage her and bring her home to Bristol, where she is preserved as a monument to the genius of her brilliant designer.

Great Britain
(1843)

Length 322 ft (98 m) *Beam* 50 ft 6 in (15·4 m) *Draught* 18 ft (5·5 m)
Displacement 3,443 tons (3,498 tonnes) *Speed* 12½ knots
Sail area 15,000 sq ft (1,400 m²) *Crew* 130
Cargo capacity 600 tons *Passenger capacity* 252 (designed)

The *Great Britain* is chiefly remembered as the first vessel of any real size to be built wholly of iron, but she was also the first screw-driven vessel to cross the Atlantic and was in her day the largest ship afloat. Several features of her construction became the pattern for future shipbuilding in iron, including the division of her hull by watertight bulkheads and the absence of an external keel. The second great shipbuilding project of Isambard Kingdom Brunel, she made her maiden voyage to New York in 1845. The following year she ran aground on the Irish coast and the fact that she had sustained so little damage when she was finally floated off 11 months later did much to promote the use of iron for ship construction. She ended her working career as coal hulk in the Falklands in 1886. In 1970 she was raised to be returned to the same dry dock at Bristol where she was built, as a memorial to Brunel and the days of the first iron ships.

She is seen here as she was when first built. The cross section and cutaway show two of her 88-in (2·1 m) cylinders and the chain drive to the propeller shaft. The small drawing shows her under full sail.

Above: The tug-of-war between the screw-driven *Rattler* (left) and *Alecto* (right) was more of an exhibition to convince public opinion than a scientific test, as the Royal Navy had already ordered seven screw ships by March 1845.

So far as the merchant ship was concerned, the propeller was almost universally recognised as the most efficient means of ship propulsion, but the warship in general remained wedded to sail. This was to some extent understandable, particularly in Britain, which had emerged from the last great war as undisputed mistress of all the oceans. She still maintained the largest fighting fleet in the world, and the officers and men who had manned that navy in war were still serving in it. A radical change from wood and sail to iron and steam meant starting the navy again from scratch, with the present superiority of numbers wiped out at a stroke. But with the invention of the propeller the overriding objection to steam propulsion in warships, the vulnerable paddlewheel, had been removed, and the steam engine at last had to be admitted into naval ships.

But it was not admitted without a struggle by traditionalists, and there was still much argument in naval circles in all countries as to whether the propeller was really superior to the paddlewheel. The argument was finally settled in 1845, when two virtually identical frigates of 880 tons, H.M.S. *Rattler* and H.M.S. *Alecto*, were both fitted with engines of 220 horsepower, that in H.M.S. *Rattler* driving a propeller and that in H.M.S. *Alecto* a pair of paddlewheels. In March of that year the two ships had a race over 100 miles (160 km), which the *Rattler* won by

several miles. In a later test, the two ships, tied together with a towing hawser, set off under full engine power in opposite directions. The *Rattler* with her propeller towed the *Alecto* stern first at a speed of 2·7 knots – conclusive proof that a propeller not only drove a ship faster, but also exerted considerably more power.

So wooden warships, or at least those of Britain, were fitted with steam engines, although they still retained their full complement of masts and sails. The installation was achieved by bringing the ships into drydock, cutting them in half, and lengthening them to accommodate engines and boilers. But, whereas in the merchant ship masts and sails were fitted as an auxiliary source of propulsion, for use if the engine failed, in the warship it was the engine that was an auxiliary source of power, for use if the wind were blowing in the wrong direction. In France, the only other nation with a comparable navy, the adoption of the steam engine, even as an auxiliary source of power, progressed much more slowly. By 1854, only nine years after the *Rattler-Alecto* trials, the entire British fleet sent into the Baltic at the start of the Crimean War was fitted with engines; the entire French fleet in the Baltic still relied entirely on sail.

Although the propeller had emerged as the best means of transforming engine power into motion through the water, one problem remained unsolved. The fitting of a propeller entailed making a hole for the shaft in the ship's sternpost, and technology could not yet ensure watertight fitting. There were cases where ships leaked so badly through their stern gland that they had to be beached to save them from sinking. (Wooden-hulled ships faced an additional hazard. Since the vibration of the propeller could shake the sternpost to such an extent that the seams of the planking near the stern opened up and let the sea in.) It was not until 1854 that this particular problem was solved by John Penn, an engineer whose marine steam engines were widely used in ships. Penn discovered that *lignum vitae*, the hard, smooth wood of the guaiacum tree, which grows in the West Indies and has self-lubricating properties, was ideal for the purpose of lining stern glands. It also suffered very little wear as the propeller shaft revolved inside it. It was used for lining stern glands for the next forty years, until the more modern metallic packings were introduced.

It has been mentioned earlier that, in general, navies were slow to implement the advances in shipbuilding which the first half of the century brought, but this does not mean that no improvements in naval shipbuilding were made. The best wooden warships were still those built

by France, mainly because, with the exception of the United States, she built appreciably larger than other maritime nations. As late as 1845 the British laid down a 74-gun ship of the line on the exact model of a French ship which they had captured in 1794, so great was their belief in the superiority of French design. But in the meantime the Royal Navy had found a naval architect of genius. As a commander, William Symonds had been given permission by the British Admiralty in 1825 to build a corvette to his own design, and the resulting ship, *Columbine*, of 18 guns, was so outstandingly successful that Symonds was promoted. His success as a designer might have ended there had not the Duke of Portland given him a commission to build a yacht. Named *Pantaloon*, she was such a success that she, too, was purchased for the navy and adapted as a 10-gun brig. Symonds was then instructed by the Admiralty to design more ships, including a fourth-rate of 50 guns, and their general excellence resulted in his being knighted and made Surveyor of the Navy, responsible for all warship design. Within the next fifteen years he was responsible for the design of more than 180 warships.

Symonds's designs owed their great success

Below: Captain Sir William Symonds, Surveyor of the Navy, designed many fine sailing warships for the Royal Navy, but could not adapt his skill to cope with steam propulsion.

Bottom: The corvette *Columbine*, designed by Symonds in 1825.

Above: The midships section of the 36-gun frigates *Pique* and *Flora* – sister ships built to the same plan (1832). This is a typical 'Symondite' hull-form.

Although, in general, the fighting navies of the world turned their backs on the revolution in shipping brought about by the introduction of the steam engine, there were some small exceptions. The young United States Navy led the way with the *Demologos*, launched in 1814, but completed too late to take part in the war then being fought against Britain. Designed by Robert Fulton (later she was renamed *Fulton*), she was a queer-looking vessel with two wooden hulls abreast, in one of which was the engine and in the other the boiler, and a paddlewheel mounted between them. She carried an armament of 30 guns designed to fire red-hot shot. She finally blew up in a dockyard explosion.

Britain adopted steam for her navy only reluctantly and, at first, purely for auxiliary services. It was Brunel who at last talked the Lords of the Admiralty out of their ultra-conservative attitude, and in 1822 the *Comet*, a wooden paddle steamer of 238 tons equipped with a Boulton and Watt engine of 90 horse-power, was built by contractors in the dockyard at Deptford. She was joined later by the *Monkey*, a similar paddle steamer of 212 tons, which had been built commercially at Rotherhithe and was purchased into the navy. The two vessels were used solely to tow the sailing men-of-war out of harbour when the direction of the wind made it impossible to sail out. In fact, the British Admiralty carried its disapproval of the steam engine to the extent of refusing to include the names of the engineers in the official Navy List, and requiring the contractors who built the ships to supply engineers with them.

France, Russia and Italy followed the naval lead of Britain by building or acquiring small steam vessels for use with their navies as auxiliaries, but, since in the world strategic situation their navies were of less account than that of Britain, they could afford to experiment. Not that their experiments produced anything revolutionary in the naval sphere; in general they were, like Britain, reluctant to tinker with their capital ships until they knew that they could be sure of the effect. Nevertheless, in Britain, the Surveyor of the Navy was instructed in 1832 to design a steamship, the first to be built in Britain in a naval dockyard by naval personnel. She was the *Gulnare* of 306 tons, mounting three guns, built of wood with paddlewheel propulsion. She was followed by other small steam gunboats, but until 1840 none was built above 1,000 tons, or with anything but a small armament. As they drew very little water, less than 5 ft (1·5 m), they were thought to have a naval use for inshore bombardment purposes, the risk of damage to their paddlewheels by enemy gunfire being accepted.

not only to improved methods of construction, which brought a great increase in structural strength, but also to an improved underwater shape, much less full and heavy than had been previously the case. To some extent he followed the French lead in building large, not so much in overall length as in beam and depth, so that his ships, though shorter than the French, were broader, roomier, and higher between decks. The loss of speed which a shorter overall length might have incurred was more than made up for by the improvement in shape of bottom, which gave his ships a much cleaner run through the water. Another of his improvements was the introduction of a system of standard sizes for masts and yards, so that they became inter-changeable, not only between ships of the same class, but also between ships of different classes, though not of course for the same purpose. Thus, for example, the topsail yards of a second-rate ship of the line were cut to the same size as the main yards of a frigate, and so on. By this means the eighty-eight different sizes of masts and yards maintained for the Royal Navy were reduced to twenty, with no loss of efficiency.

Left: Turner's *Fighting
Temeraire tugged to her
Last Berth to be Broken
Up* is a fitting contrast
between the old and the
new. During the Crimean
War steamers had to stand
by to tow the lumbering
three-deckers in and out
of action.

161

SCREW STEAM SHIP OF WAR, DUKE OF WELLINGTON.

Mizen Mast. *Main Mast.* *Funnel.*

LONGITUDINAL SECTION.

Hammocks in Hammock netting.

Above: Inboard profile of the 131-gun 1st rate *Duke of Wellington* (1852). The addition of a propeller and machinery to a three-decker's hull made for cramped conditions between decks.

Right: Drawings of a typical Paixhans shell gun, showing how the powder-flash ignited the time-fuse of the shell.

Coupe par l'axe de la bouche à feu.

Fig. 1.

Ce Canon à obus aurait le poids d'un Canon ordinaire de 24, ou 5100 livres. Ce qui serait 146 fois son obus chargé.

Coupe par l'axe des tourillons.

Fig. 2.

Détail de la chambre, de la charge, du projectile, du sabot et de la fusée.

Fig. 3.

Not all British naval officers were as reluctant as the Board of Admiralty in London to face the implications of the marine steam engine, and in 1825 Lord Cochrane submitted a memorandum asking for 'six steam vessels, having each two guns in the bow and perhaps two in the stern, not less than 68-pounder long guns'. Such a squadron would have proved a formidable weapon against fleets of sailing men-of-war, and if built might well have speeded up the change-over from the sailing to the steam navy, which in fact took another half century. Only one of the six, the *Perseverance*, was built, and not for the British navy, but for the Greek. She played a useful, if fairly unspectacular, part in the Greek War of Independence against Turkey.

Iron did not enter into the Royal Navy's calculations until 1840, when the Admiralty purchased the iron-hulled steam packet *Dover* for no very clear purpose. No trials were carried out with her, and she was not used with the fleet. In the same year, three small iron gunboats were built, each mounting 2 guns, and with paddle-be designed from the start to incorporate an engine and propeller was the 80-gun second-rate *Agamemnon*, laid down at Woolwich in 1849 and launched in 1852. But in every case, except for that of the smallest vessels, a British warship converted to steam still retained her full complement of masts, yards, and sails as her main means of propulsion. Her engine was a very secondary affair, and elaborate and time-consuming arrangements were made to enable the propeller to be raised out of the water whenever she was to use her sails, in order to eliminate the drag exerted by the screw and retain the ship's sailing performance. It was not until 1861 that the lifting propeller was abandoned in the Royal Navy.

It was no sudden change of heart about the properties of iron that in the end forced every navy in the world to drop the use of wood for warship building; it was the development of a new form of gun and the outcome of its first use in actual conflict that brought the change. The naval gun during the first half of the nineteenth century remained the gun with which Nelson

Below: The troopship *Simoon* was originally an iron-hulled frigate.

wheel propulsion. But they were not followed up with anything larger, even though the way had been shown by John Laird, the Birkenhead shipbuilder, who had designed and built an iron frigate which he offered to the British Admiralty. (On the refusal of the Admiralty even to consider the purchase, she was sold to the Mexican navy.)

Yet the time was coming when the force of public opinion, particularly that of the shipping companies, would drive the Admiralty to begin using iron for warships larger than small gunboats. Orders were placed in 1846 for three iron steam frigates of 1,400 tons, the *Birkenhead*, *Simoon* and *Megaera*, the first fitted with paddlewheels and the other two with propellers. They never made it as warships, for gunnery experiments with an iron hull indicated that iron was still liable to break up and fracture when hit with solid shot, and the three were completed as troopships. (The *Birkenhead*'s tragic end off Danger Point, between Simonstown and Cape Town, in February 1852 is still well remembered.)

So it was back to the wooden hull for the British navy, even though some other navies were persevering with iron, backed with a thick lining of teak or oak to provide additional resistance against damage by solid shot. In Britain, the wooden ships of the line continued to be brought into the dockyards to be lengthened to take an engine and propeller, even the oldest ships being converted to steam. The *Ajax* and *Horatio*, both launched as long ago as 1809 and thus relics of the Napoleonic War, were two of the oldest; another was the *Nelson*, launched in 1814. The first British wooden ship of the line to

had won his battles – big muzzle loading cannon, firing solid round shot. Explosive shells, fired parabolically from mortars, were used solely for bombardment and never considered as a ship-to-ship weapon. But in 1822 a French general of artillery, Henri-Joseph Paixhans, wrote a book called *Nouvelle Force Maritime et Artillerie*, in which he advocated the firing of explosive bombs from the normal naval gun, giving them a flat trajectory instead of a parabolic one, and thus converting the explosive shell into a ship-to-ship weapon. His gun was given its first serious tests in 1824, against the old, moored frigate *Pacificateur*, and proved remarkably successful. In 1853 Paixhans' guns were used for the first time in battle, when a Russian squadron of wooden-hulled ships armed with the new French guns encountered at Sinope, in the Black Sea, a Turkish squadron of wooden-hulled ships armed with conventional naval guns firing solid shot.

It was not just the defeat of the Turkish squadron which opened the eyes of the world's navies, but the fact that the explosive shells fired by the Russian ships set all the Turkish ships on fire and they burned down to the waterline.

The lesson of Sinope was underlined two years later at the bombardment of the Kinburn forts in the Crimea. After Sinope the French constructed a flotilla of floating batteries, protected with iron armour, and at the Kinburn bombardment three of them, the *Devastation*, *Tonnante* and *Lave*, steamed to within 1,000 yards (914 m) of a fort. It turned out that they were relatively impervious to the Russian fire, and they emerged unscathed from a position in which any wooden-hulled warship in the world would have been blown to bits. This demonstration of the advantages of iron construction in modern war conditions could not be ignored, and Britain was the first to put this experience to use by building, in 1856, the first iron-hulled armoured warships in the world – the *Terror*, *Thunderbolt*, *Erebus* and *Aetna*. They were designated 'armoured batteries' and built to a tonnage of 1,950, with an overall length of 108 ft 10 in (33·12 m), a beam of 48 ft 6 in (14·78 m), and a draught of 8 ft 10 in (2·69 m). They mounted 16 smooth-bore muzzle-loading 68-pounder guns, and their 200-horse-power engines gave them a speed of 5·5 knots. It was perhaps a small beginning, but the navies of the world had learned their lesson and began to catch up with merchant navies, which had taken to iron with enthusiasm more than twenty years earlier.

Before leaving the iron warship, mention should be made of the British East India Company, which also built warships to protect and enforce their trade monopoly in India and China. It was in 1839 that the Company first considered using iron for their warship hulls, and in that year they approached the Birkenhead ship-builder John Laird to build iron warships for service in the Far East. One of these was the *Nemesis*, a ship of 660 tons, armed with two 32-pounder pivot guns (at that time an innovation in the mounting of guns, when the normal practice was to mount them on wooden carriages in broadside batteries). Although the *Nemesis* only drew 5 ft (1·5 m) of water she made her way out to India under her own steam via the Cape of Good Hope, and during the First China War (1841–42) was taken over by the British Navy and gave excellent service during the naval operations.

Although during the first half of the nineteenth century the world's trade was expanding fast, it was not yet at a stage where shipowners, except monopoly companies like the East India Companies, could contemplate the building of fleets of ships. It was an event in Britain that first introduced this possibility. Until 1838 the mail

Right: One of the French floating batteries frozen in during the winter of 1855–56 in the Black Sea, after Kinburn.

for overseas had been carried in Post Office 'packets' (small ships built and run by the government solely for the purpose). These were sailing ships, but by this time it was obvious that the steamship was superseding the sailing ship in the commercial sphere and that, in any service where speed and reliability were essential, the day of the sailing vessel was over. Rather than bear the cost of constructing new steamships to carry the mails, the British government decided to put the carriage out to tender by any ship-owner able to guarantee a regular steamship service that would carry the mails to their destination. The value of the contract was enough to provide the shipowner with a sound economic basis for starting a regular ferry service.

The Government offer of the transatlantic mail service attracted two bidders. One was the Great Western Railway Company, which already owned the *Great Western*, on a regular run be-tween Bristol and New York, and had laid down a larger ship, the *Great Britain*, destined for the same service; the second bidder was a Canadian merchant from Halifax, Samuel Cunard, who owned a number of sailing ships. When the terms of the mail contract were advertised, he

crossed to Britain and joined forces with Robert Napier, one of the best known marine engineers of the day, to bid for the contract. His tender for it included a clause that, if successful, he would build four ships and would guarantee to operate a regular service between Liverpool and Boston of two voyages a month, summer and winter. With his tender accepted, Cunard formed a com-pany with the shipowners George Burns, of Glasgow, and David McIver, of Liverpool, and placed orders with Napier for four wooden paddle steamers, each with an overall length of 207 ft (63·1 m) and a tonnage of 1,156, and with an average speed of 8·5 knots. These were the *Acadia*, *Britannia*, *Caledonia* and *Columbia*, and they began their transatlantic service in 1840. It proved so popular and profitable that four years later the company built the *Hibernia* and *Cambria*, both of them larger and faster than the first four. The *Hibernia*, in fact, was the first ship to cross the Atlantic in less than ten days, and was also the first to use the port of New York instead of Boston.

Four years later, with the transatlantic trade still growing, another four ships were built, each of them having a tonnage of 1,820 and a

Above: The Cunard paddle steamer *Britannia*, which began a transatlantic service in 1840. This was beginning of the 'liner'.

Above: The paddle liner *Persia* (1863) gave the Cunard Line mastery of the North Atlantic. She was the biggest ship in the world for a time and also the first liner with an iron hull, but she was one of the last of the big paddle steamers.

service speed of over 10 knots. So much of the trade was now coming to the Cunard Line that the United States decided to encourage their own shipowners to compete by offering their own mail carriage contract. It was given to the Collins Line, which built four new steamers of over 3,000 tons each, the *Arctic*, *Atlantic*, *Baltic* and *Pacific*, all of them with a small margin of speed over that of the Cunard ships. But though they were fine ships, Cunard replied to the challenge by building the *Africa* and *Asia*, both of around 2,000 tons, and now with twelve ships in his shipping line he was able to offer a much more frequent transatlantic service. Moreover, tragedy befell the Collins Line when the *Arctic* collided with the French steamer *Vesta*, and sank with the loss of 323 lives, and when the *Pacific* sailed from Liverpool with 156 people on board and was never seen or heard of again.

In the face of these disasters the Collins Line built the *Adriatic*, larger and faster than the other Collins ships, but so expensive to build that the company went heavily into debt. And it was at this moment that Cunard unveiled his

master stroke, the *Persia*. She was the first transatlantic liner to be built with an iron hull, and at her launch was the biggest ship in the world. Her appearance on the Atlantic killed the Collins Line dead.

It was a government mail contract which gave birth to another of the great shipping lines, the Peninsula & Oriental Steam Navigation Company. It began with Robert Bourne, who had a contract for the carriage of the internal mails in Ireland, which he operated with stage coaches based on Dublin. Bourne bought a small 206-ton steamer, the *William Fawcett*, to carry the mails across the Irish Sea. The company he formed was the City of Dublin Steam Packet Company, and in 1826 he appointed two young men, Brodie Wilcox and Arthur Anderson, who ran a shipping agency, as his London agents. A second small steamer bought by the company was the *Royal Tar*, and she was used to carry cargoes to Spain and Portugal during the Spanish and Portuguese civil wars. Her reliability and regularity so impressed the Spanish government that they asked for a regular steamer service to

Above right: The *Iberia* (1836) was the first ship owned by the Peninsular Steam Navigation Company.

Below: The P&O *Hindustan* leaves Southampton on 24 September 1842 to start the company's mail service to India.

be inaugurated and, with the British Government offering a contract to carry the mails to the Iberian Peninsula in 1837, Wilcox and Anderson formed the Peninsula Steam Navigation Company, whose first ship was the *Iberia*, a paddle steamer of 516 tons with an engine developing 180 horsepower. In 1840 the Peninsula Steam Navigation Company was offered the mail contract to Egypt and India. 'Oriental' was added to the Company's name, and two more steamers, the *Oriental* of 1,674 tons and the *Great Liverpool* of 1,311 tons, were built to carry the mails through the Mediterranean to Egypt. In 1842 the Suez-Calcutta service was inaugurated by the *Hindustan*, of 2,017 tons, and

in the same year the company gained the government mail contract for Australia. With this extension of their Indian route to Singapore, they were now poised to become the most powerful shipping force throughout the Far East.

There were other shipping lines starting to operate to different parts of the world around the same time, for these were the years which saw the beginning of the industrial revolution with its immense upsurge of world trade. It was the start of a golden age for shipping, and the next fifty years were to see more changes and more developments in the size, design, and power of ships than had occurred during the whole of the previous 2,000 years.

The Great Ship

In the early 1850s three brilliant engineers gathered together to air their views about the future of the merchant ship. One of them was Isambard Kingdom Brunel who, with the successful *Great Western* and *Great Britain* already to his credit, was the most influential ship designer in England. He realised that, although there was a limit to the size to which a wooden ship could be built because of the strength, or lack of it, in the building material, this limitation did not apply when a much stronger building material was used. Iron was this stronger material, and with it ships much bigger than the biggest wooden ship ever built could be constructed.

In Brunel's estimation there was, too, a definite need for a very big ship. Emigration was on the increase, the main destinations at this time being the United States and Canada. On the other side of the world, in Australia and New Zealand, there were immense areas of uninhabited land which, it seemed to Brunel, were ready and waiting to receive Europe's dispossessed multitudes. They would need ships to take them there and ships to bring their produce back to Europe after the land had been cultivated. And as the numbers grew, so also would grow the volume of trade with Europe, all of which would have to be carried across the oceans in ships.

The second engineer concerned was John Scott Russell. He had become interested in the maritime side of engineering in 1834 when he was

consulted on the possibilities of introducing steam navigation on the Edinburgh and Glasgow Canal. He owned a shipbuilding yard at Millwall, on the River Thames, but his greatest interest lay in the study of wave-formation. From many experiments, carried out both with models in a tank and with full-sized vessels on a canal, he established that there was a connection between a vessel's wave-making properties and her resistance to forward motion, and that a ship could be driven faster and more economically by designing her underwater hull shape to create the least possible wave disturbance.

The third engineer associated with the new ship, albeit to a lesser extent than the other two, was William Froude, who had been an assistant of Brunel in 1837 when he was principally a railway engineer. After nine years, Froude left the railway to devote himself to the study of ship behaviour and hydro-dynamics, working on very similar lines to Scott Russell.

The new ship was therefore designed with an underwater shape that

Above left: Scott Russell (left) and Brunel (second from right) at the first attempt to launch the *Great Eastern* in 1857.

Above: The incomplete *Great Eastern* awaiting high tide ready for a sideways launching – the final attempt – in 1858.

Right: The *Great Eastern* at sea.

conformed to the principles of Scott Russell and Froude, and an overall size that met Brunel's requirement for accommodation for 4,000 passengers, and space for 6,000 tons of cargo and enough coal for a voyage to Australia or India. The result was an overall length of 692 ft (210·9 m), a beam of 82 ft (25 m) and a loaded draught of 29·3 ft (8·9 m). Her designed measurement tonnage was 18,914, and her displacement tonnage 27,700 (28,145 tonnes). Because of her great size she was to be named *Leviathan*, and an idea of just how revolutionary was the increase in size which Brunel had proposed can be gained from the fact that the biggest ship in the world hitherto had an overall length of 375 ft (114·3 m) and a designed tonnage of 3,300. In tonnage terms, *Leviathan* was to be more than five times as large as any ship yet built.

Brunel persuaded the Eastern Steamship Navigation Company that her construction was a feasible commercial venture, and her keel was laid in Scott Russell's shipyard at Millwall. Because of her great length, it would be impossible to launch her in the normal way, stern first, as the Thames at Millwall was not wide enough, and so she was built broadside on to the river, and would eventually have to be launched sideways.

During building, her name was changed from *Leviathan* to *Great Eastern.* So many difficulties arose during construction that her cost rose enormously. More than one company associated with it was forced into bankruptcy, including Scott Russell's shipyard, and Brunel's own health broke down as a result of the constant worries associated with her building. She was finally ready for launching in 1858, but even this went wrong. After moving a few inches down the slipway, she stuck. Large hydraulic presses had to be built, to push her, and wire cables on winches mounted on the opposite bank of the Thames, to pull her. Finally, weeks

later, she floated off on a very high tide.

Her new owners (the original company having gone bankrupt) decided to use her on the Atlantic run, and her cabins and saloons were fitted out at considerable expense, and with great luxury, for the period. By the time she was ready for her maiden crossing, Brunel himself had died from a heart attack. He was, perhaps, fortunate in not living to see the unhappy fate of his great ship. On her first voyage to America, she attracted no more than thirty-six passengers, instead of the 4,000 for which she had been built, and once at sea she rolled so heavily that prospective passengers refused to travel in her. She was taken out of service after a short period, and found no employment until 1865, when Sir Daniel Gooch chartered her to lay the first electric telegraph cable across the Atlantic. In all, she laid four cables across the Atlantic, and another from Aden to Bombay.

At the end of her cable-laying career, she lay at Milford Haven for twelve years, until she was bought by a firm in Liverpool as a summer attraction for visitors. She was refitted more or less in her original state, her grand saloon was

used as a music hall, and there were side-shows in her cabins and a merry-go-round with a steam organ installed on her upper deck. It was a sad end for a once proud ship, but even in her new guise she did not pay. At the end of the summer she was laid up, and two years later sold for breaking-up.

Yet, commercial failure that she was, the *Great Eastern* marks a very important milestone in the history of ships. She proved Brunel's theory that with iron as a shipbuilding material there was no limit to the size of ship that could be built. Her construction introduced the principle of the cellular double bottom, and she was the first ship to fit a steering engine, at that time a novel means of overcoming the pressure of water on the rudder, but now a universal feature in all ships of any size. And, perhaps most important of all, she was the first large ship whose underwater shape was designed according to the principles of hydrodynamics. It was, at this time, admittedly an inexact science, but after the *Great Eastern* both Scott Russell and William Froude continued their work on the wave-line theory, and it is on this theory that all modern ship design is based.

Chapter Eight
The Growth of the Steamship

It was the improvement of the marine steam engine, through the development of more efficient boilers, that made possible the huge increase in the size of merchant ships during the second half of the nineteenth century. And it was the great expansion of world trade, coupled with a surge of emigration to the New World, which accounted for the simultaneous explosion in their numbers.

The theory of the compound steam engine (in which the steam is used twice in each cycle of the engine, first in a high-pressure cylinder and then again in a low-pressure cylinder, before being drawn off to a condenser to be turned back into boiler feed water) was first propounded in 1783. But to put it into practice demanded a higher pressure than, until later in the nineteenth century, was obtainable with the normal marine boiler. Between 1850 and 1860 new designs of boiler were introduced and steam pressure, which until about 1850 could not be produced at more than about 25 lb/sq in ($1 \cdot 75$ kg/cm^2), rose to between 50 and 60 lb/sq in ($3 \cdot 5$ to $4 \cdot 2$ kg/cm^2). Such pressures made the compound engine a reality for ships, and in 1853 John Elder, a Scottish engineer, took out a patent on a marine version of the engine. Naturally, the new engine aroused keen interest among shipowners, for using the steam twice in a single cycle brought not only a considerable saving in the amount of coal burned, but also a large increase in the power of the engine.

The Cunard Line was the first of the big shipping companies to install compound engines in their ships, and in 1868 the *Parthia* and *Batavia* were both built with compound engines for the transatlantic service. Other big companies followed Cunard's lead, and a great many smaller shipowners, attracted by the saving in fuel costs which could be as much as 30 per cent, installed the compound engine in their new ships and brought in their older ones to have their single-expansion engines removed and the new engine fitted in their place.

Further boiler development followed, and, with the introduction of the Scotch return-tube marine boiler, the next step in engine development became possible. This was a very reliable forced-draught boiler which generated steam at a pressure between 120 and 160 lb/sq in ($8 \cdot 4$ and $11 \cdot 25$ kg/cm^2), and with this amount of pressure it became possible to make the steam work three times in one engine cycle by adding an intermediate-pressure cylinder between the existing high- and low-pressure cylinders. The first engine of this new design to be fitted in a ship was made by Dr A. C. Kirk for the steamer *Propontis* in 1874, but it was not a success because he used the old type of boiler and as a result lacked sufficient steam pressure. But, as soon as the new forced-draught boilers became available, the whole picture was changed: the triple-expansion engine was born – even more economical than the compound engine and developing still more engine power – and it was this combination, the Scotch return-tube boiler allied to the triple-expansion engine, which was to remain the standard power plant for ships, both passenger and cargo, across the world for the remainder of the century. Right at the end of the century, the Germans introduced a quadruple-expansion engine for their four great liners of the *Kaiser Wilhelm der Grosse* class, built between 1897 and 1902. These were the biggest marine reciprocating engines ever built, but even as they were being fitted they were being made obsolete by the next development in marine propulsion.

The big increase in engine power during the second half of the nineteenth century made larger ships possible, and tonnages rocketed. Until 1850 the largest steamship yet built was the *Great Britain*, of 3,270 tons (3,322 tonnes); during the half century which followed, the size

Left: The destroyer HMS *Viper* symbolized the enormous progress marine engineering made in the nineteenth century.

of ships increased nearly tenfold, and, in the case of some passenger liners, more than that. A contributory cause was the introduction of steel in place of iron. The Siemens process of steelmaking was introduced at about the same time as the triple-expansion engine, and as it cut the cost of manufacturing steel dramatically, it made economic sense for shipowners to turn to steel as a building material. With its high tensile strength, steel meant that thinner plates and smaller scantlings could be used in shipbuilding without any diminution of hull strength, producing a saving in weight of up to 25 per cent. This, in its turn, meant lower coal consumption or, in the case of the prestigious liners, an extra knot or two of speed with the same engine power.

The most radical design changes in merchant shipping were to be seen in the big passenger ships. The cargo ship, except in size, did not alter greatly in design, the main consideration remaining the amount of cargo that she could conveniently stow. There was little call for anything beyond a moderate sea speed for a cargo vessel, for in those days of trade expansion on a huge scale there was never a lack of cargoes waiting to be carried. An increase in speed meant an increase in costs, and the successful cargo ship was the one which could quote the lowest freight rates. Gradually, as engines and boilers grew in reliability and power, the merchant ship shed her auxiliary sails, and little was to be seen of the square rig after about 1865, except in the case of passenger ships, which kept their sails, though on a diminishing scale, for another ten years or so, mainly as a reassurance to travellers who had not as yet learned to put their trust in steam.

In 1850 the cargo ship generally still had her sailing ship-type flush deck, except for a central bridge built across the tops of the paddle boxes. When the paddlewheels were replaced by the propeller, the central bridge remained, as it had been found a convenient place from which the captain and watchkeepers could control the ship, even though the steering wheel and the helmsman were still exposed on the upper deck aft. This after steering position was always a place of some danger in a heavy sea, and, since helmsmen were periodically washed overboard, most shipowners began to specify the inclusion of a poop deck in their new ships, to raise helmsman and steering wheel to a safer level. At roughly the same time, a forecastle deck was added to provide living quarters for the crew without having to use valuable cargo space below, while the bridge structure was raised to provide a better command post. Thus the typical flush-decked cargo carrier of the 1850s evolved into the typical well-decked carrier of the 1900s ('wells' being the names given to the two lower deck levels, between forecastle and bridge and between bridge and poop deck). The increase in size of the cargo ship during the second half of the nineteenth century was certainly nothing like as spectacular as that of the passenger liner. But whereas a cargo ship of 2,000 gross tons would have been considered a very big ship in 1850, such tonnages were commonplace fifty years later, and some cargo carriers were being built up to 6,000 gross tons, and in a few cases even larger. The biggest of them were probably the colliers, for the demand for coal was incessant, not only for the growing industrial needs of the world, but also to establish coaling stations around the globe to refuel the world's ships. By the end of the nineteenth century an ocean-going collier could carry as much as 6,000 tons of coal in bulk in her capacious holds, and still the worldwide demand remained unsatisfied.

It was during this half century that the specialized cargo ship, designed to carry one type of cargo only, made her appearance. In 1870 a merchant ship with refrigerated holds sailed from Britain to New Zealand, to return with a cargo of lamb carcases frozen in her holds. The meat arrived in England in excellent condition and thus began a new trade in fresh foods from all parts of the world. In 1886 the *Gluckauf*, built in Britain, became the world's first true oil tanker, with separate tanks for the oil built into her hull. Until her appearance, oil had always been shipped in barrels or drums; now it could be pumped on board directly into the tanks. She, too, started a new trade which was to grow enormously over the years.

The phenomenal growth in passenger liner size was caused mainly by the huge immigration programme of the United States. Her desire for immigrants arose partly from the development of the transcontinental railway from the Atlantic to the Pacific coast, and partly from the rapid growth of the steel industry around Pittsburgh. Both these industries were hungry for cheap labour, and both sent recruiting parties to scour Europe for men to fill the vacancies. What they found in Europe were conditions where emigration often offered the only escape from misery and deprivation. In England, the economics of the industrial revolution had put tens of thousands of men out of work; in Ireland, the periodic failure of the potato crop brought famine to the population; in many countries of Europe, racial or religious persecution had made hundreds of thousands of families destitute. To these millions of people the promise of work on the railways or in the steel mills was a

Above: The collier *Eastwood* and smaller craft in winter ice on the Thames, February 1895.

Right: The *Timaru*, the first refrigerated cargo carrying ship.

Below right: The *Gluckauf* (1886) was the first ship designed to carry oil fuel in bulk.

powerful incentive to emigrate. (Between 1851
and 1905, 4,028,589 emigrants left Ireland alone,
the vast majority going to the United States.)
That the work when they got there was hard,
ill-paid and frequently degrading was discovered
too late; by then the great step had been taken
and they had crossed the ocean, usually accompanied by their families. However, no matter
how mistaken were their reasons for going, there
were literally millions of people eager and waiting to cross the oceans to a new life.

It was a problem which only the big shipowners could tackle – and they only in a somewhat roundabout fashion. Building a new ship is
a long-term proposition: she has to repay her
building cost, as well as her running costs, over
several years of profitable operation. As no shipowner could foretell for how long the surge of
emigration would last, the building of one-class
ships to handle this traffic could well have
proved to turn out a financial disaster. Moreover, the vast majority of the emigrants were the
poorest of the poor, and they could not afford to
pay high enough fares to make a one-class ship
profitable. The only way to handle the traffic
was to build passenger ships in which the revenue
from the first- and second-class passengers alone
was enough to cover the running costs and the
amortisation of the building cost, and to provide
additional space for as many steerage passengers
as possible at a fare which the emigrants could
afford. And that meant big ships.

Brunel had shown the way with his *Great
Eastern*. Although she was a great financial
failure, she proved that with iron as a building
material there was no limit to the size to which
ships could be built, as there was with wood.
And she had proved the soundness of the iron
hull when, in 1865, she grounded on a reef in
Long Island Sound and ripped a hole 75 ft (23 m)

long in the outer skin of her double bottom without sinking. It only remained to find an engine powerful enough before shipowners could build as big as they liked and, as we have seen, the solution of that problem came in the 1870s.

In the meantime, the interior design of passenger liners was changing. The general pattern in most liners had been to have the main passenger lounge and the first-class cabins accommodated in wooden deckhouses built aft on the upper deck, with the less expensive cabins and the steerage accommodation on the deck below. In 1871 the White Star liner *Oceanic*, built in Belfast by Harland and Wolff, made her first crossing of the Atlantic with her first-class accommodation amidships, with larger cabins and scuttles (windows) than ever before. She also had a promenade deck extending the full width of the ship above the cabins and lounges, and thus set a pattern which was to be followed in all future liner design. She was built very long for her beam, 420 ft (128 m) overall with a beam of 41 ft (12·5 m), to give her a speed of over 18 knots.

Another great step forward was made by the Inman Line in 1888, with their two ships *City of Paris* and *City of New York*. By now steel had largely replaced iron as the preferred shipbuilding material, and both ships were built of steel. The triple-expansion engine, also well established by now, was fitted in both ships. But the most impressive novelty in their design was the fact that they had two engines, driving two shafts, with two propellers, one on each quarter. As well as greater efficiency, this arrangement produced considerably less vibration than a single propeller on the centreline of the ship. When the ships came into service they were voted the most comfortable and the most handsome ships on the Atlantic run. They had a displacement tonnage of 14,500 (14,730 tonnes) on an overall length of 560 ft (170·7 m), a beam of 63 ft 2 in (19·25 m), and a draught of 41 ft 11 in (12·78 m). From their maiden voyages they held the speed record across the Atlantic with a passage time of less than 6 days at more than 20 knots until, in 1893, the Cunard Line's *Campania* made the crossing at a slightly higher speed.

Although these and their sister ships were what one would call the 'crack' liners on the Atlantic run, they were by no means the only ones to make regular crossings. There were hosts of other shipping lines, large and small, to carry the growing trade. While they all depended, more or less, on the first- and second-class passengers to cover their costs, none disdained the emigrant traffic, now in full flood, and all had large amounts of steerage accommodation, into which they crammed an astonishing number of men, women and children, eager to begin a new

life in a new country. Even the crack liners, which took the cream of the first- and second-class passengers, could carry as many as 2,000 souls in their steerage compartments at almost no additional cost to the shipping line. While the price of a steerage passage was small – as little as £3 on some ships – all that the shipowner had to provide was a bunk. These were erected in long tiers extending the whole length of the steerage compartment, with a space of about 5 ft (1·5 m) between the tiers. The bunks generally consisted of a wooden frame, with wooden slats or wire netting as a mattress, and there were usually three bunks to a tier. The emigrants provided their own bedding and food, though stoves were erected on the upper deck for the passengers to cook the food that they had brought. Inevitably they were always overcrowded, and in bad weather the lot of the steerage passengers, most of whom had never seen a ship, or even the sea, before, was miserable in the extreme.

The two great ports which handled the bulk of this emigrant traffic were Liverpool, to which the Irish came, and Hamburg, which was the gathering place of the mainland Europeans, and

Top: The liner *Oceanic* set new standards of comfort when completed in 1871.

Above: The Cunarder *Campania* won the Blue Riband in 1893 and ended her days as a seaplane carrier in 1918.

Above right: Steerage passengers aboard the Red Star liner *Pennland* in 1893. Conditions varied, but at best were spartan.

Right: The crack liner *Kaiser Wilhelm der Grosse* won the Blue Riband in 1897. She became an armed merchant cruiser in 1914, and was sunk.

these were, naturally, the terminal ports of most of the transatlantic lines. Cunard, White Star, Inman and many others were based on Liverpool, and the great Hamburg–Amerika and other continental lines on Hamburg.

Although the tonnage of the *Great Eastern* had been surpassed by several liners in the 1880s, it was not until 1897 that a ship with a greater overall length was built. This was the Hamburg–Amerika Line's *Kaiser Wilhelm der Grosse*, the first of four great German liners which were to bring that country into serious competition with the established giants of the transatlantic trade. These were ships of more than 648 ft (197·5 m) overall, and with her huge quadruple-expansion engine the *Kaiser Wilhelm der Grosse* broke the Atlantic speed record with an average of 22·35 knots. They were built mainly with an eye on the European emigrant trade then in full flood, and, although they offered a very high standard of luxury in their first- and second-class accommodation – equal in fact to the best on offer by Cunard, White Star, and the other great lines – they could also carry immense numbers of steerage passengers, who were packed in with the minimum of space between the tiers of bunks. There were two steerage compartments – one for men, the other for women and children.

It was not only to North America that this great European emigration movement was directed, though it was that continent that attracted the greatest proportion of it. Gold had been discovered in Australia, and a gold rush developed. But in this case the distances involved were very much greater, and the problems facing the shipowner entirely different to those presented by the Atlantic trade. At the start of the 1850s, steamships had not yet reached a size at which they could stow on board enough coal for the whole passage, and, although there were coaling stations en route, at St Helena and Cape Town, the last leg of the voyage from South Africa to Australia, where gales and heavy weather were the rule rather than the exception, was still beyond their capacity without refuelling. So this trade, at least until the 1880s, was one of the last strongholds of the big sailing ship, and it was not until the last two decades of the nineteenth century, following the opening of the Suez Canal, that the steamship was able to compete with, and eventually replace, the sailing ship for the emigrant trade.

An unhappy story of a sailing emigrant ship on the Australian run was that of the *Dunbar*, specially built by Duncan Dunbar, a London shipowner, to carry passengers attracted to Australia by the gold rush. She was a ship of over 1,000 tons (big as sailing ships went). On her maiden voyage she left London with her captain making the boast 'Hell or Sydney in eighty days'; for the *Dunbar* was expected to be a flyer among sailing ships because of her high length-to-beam ratio. Seventy-nine days out of London she sighted Sydney Heads, but on the eightieth day, instead of lying at anchor in Sydney Harbour, she was no more than a torn mass of wreckage on the rocks of North Head, her captain having tried to pass them too close in the night. Only one man survived out of nearly 850 carried on board.

The half century 1850 to 1900 saw the beginning of the heyday of ocean travel and trade. Men's horizons were expanding at an unprecedented rate, and with the advent of a reliable marine steam engine and the great reduction in the time taken by an average voyage, a taste for foreign travel was growing fast. This was the foundation on which a number of shipping fortunes were made, backed up by the apparently never-ending emigrant movement of millions of Europe's poor and dispossessed. It was this huge expansion which kept marine engineers and naval architects on their toes, always striving for improvements in the reliability and power of engines, on the one hand, and improvements in hull form on the other.

Below: The immigrant trade to Australia was tougher than on the transatlantic route, because distances were so much greater. Here the Albyn Line *Otago* waits for the tide, her decks crowded with passengers.

John Scott Russell and William Froude, the two engineers who collaborated with Brunel on the design of the *Great Eastern*, were responsible for some highly important research into hull forms, with particular reference to the effects of skin friction and eddy-formation on a ship's forward progress through the water. Froude was the more influential of the two, and in 1870 the British Admiralty gave him a grant to build a tank for testing ship models near his home at Torquay, the prototype of the sophisticated test tanks of today. From his experiments Froude developed the wave line theory, to explain differences in the patterns of waves and eddies caused by bodies as they move through the water. When he applied his theory to the hull of a ship, Froude found that it was the wave pattern produced by the ship, which became more pronounced as the vessel's speed increased, that was responsible for most of the resistance to forward motion. This meant that a naval architect could test the efficiency of a new hull shape, at the planning stage, by measuring the amount of wave disturbance created by a scale model in the tank, and, by finding the shape which created least disturbance, could produce a ship that could be driven faster and more economically.

As the century wore on, the influence of Froude's theories became more and more marked, as evidenced by longer, cleaner runs aft, and a big increase in length-to-beam ratios, in even the humblest cargo-carriers. This increase was one of the main developments in ship design of the period, the old 4 or 5 to 1 ratio being replaced by 8 or 9 to 1 in the case of passenger liners, in which the main consideration was the speed that could be maintained over a long passage. Another important development in ship design at this time was a change in the placing of ships' propellers, again a direct result of Froude's wave-line theory. He had shown in the experiments that, at the stern of a ship moving through the water, there is a partial vacuum, and that a propeller revolving in this partial vacuum loses a proportion of its forward drive. With this knowledge

Below: In 1867 William Froude built two models, the *Swan* and *Raven*, to test his theories.

Bottom: Froude's testing tank, showing the dynamometer carriage at the end of its run.

Inset: William Froude FRS proved that accurate testing of hull-forms could be done with models towed in a tank.

naval architects were able to position their propellers, in relation to the ship's hull, where they avoided this area of partial vacuum and so acted with greater efficiency. All these developments can be summed up by saying that during the fifty years before 1900 the science of hydrodynamics became a live and vital factor in the naval architect's work and that, with the growth of this scientific knowledge, ships improved, both in performance and in the economical transfer of engine power into speed through the water.

One other feature of this period was the development and growth of the steam yacht, a symbol of wealth and leisure that appealed greatly to many rich men of the nineteenth century. In 1827 the members of the Royal Yacht Club at Cowes, Isle of Wight (not yet named the Royal Yacht Squadron) had expressed their opposition to the marine steam engine in a resolution 'that the object of this club is to promote seamanship to which the application of steam is inimical, and any member applying steam to his yacht shall be disqualified hereby and shall cease to be a member.' One of the club's members, Thomas Assheton-Smith, considered the resolution an unwarrantable interference with personal liberty, resigned from the club, and in 1829 built the 400-ton yacht *Menai*, in which he installed an engine driving a pair of paddlewheels. She was the first steam yacht to be built in Britain. A few more British owners followed his lead, all their yachts being paddlers, and fitted with one or two oscillating or walking-beam engines and fire-tube boilers.

With the introduction of the propeller during the decade 1840 to 1850 the power plant changed to the single-stage steam reciprocating engine, still with the fire-tube boiler, to be replaced by the compound engine between 1860 and 1870, and by the triple-expansion engine about ten years later. The new water-tube boiler began to be seen in steam yachts in about 1865, but it was not until Sir Alfred Yarrow designed the three-drum variety of water-tube boiler in 1889 that the older fire-tube boiler finally disappeared.

The first steam yacht built in the United States, which made her appearance in 1853, was the 1,876-ton *North Star* built for Commodore Cornelius Vanderbilt. She set a pattern which caught on rapidly in a country where great fortunes could be made in a very short time. A steam yacht became something of a status symbol, a great many were built, and the desire to display evidence of personal wealth crossed the Atlantic to Europe, where many rich men followed the American fashion.

Above: *La Gloire* was the world's first seagoing ironclad, developed from the floating batteries of the Crimean War.

The great steam yachts, some of them ranging up to 3,000 tons displacement, were always fitted out with extreme luxury. Staterooms were equipped with every conceivable convenience, even to the extent of marble baths and washbasins in some notable yachts; saloons were enriched with gold leaf and massive carvings; and below the upper deck there was thick carpeting to add comfort and help to deaden the sound of the engines. These palatial yachts were symbolic of a period of great and rapidly increasing prosperity for those who were lucky enough to make quick fortunes.

The greatest changes of all, in this half century of change and development in ship design, took place in the world's navies. The lessons of the battle of Sinope in 1853 were quickly learned. It proved that warships could not survive in battle without armour on their sides, to keep out shells fired by the new rifled guns.

The French were the first to act when, in March 1858, they ordered four ironclad warships. Designed by the great naval architect Dupuy de Lôme, three of them were wooden-hulled ships of 5,617 tons (5,707 tonnes), with hulls plated with iron up to the level of the upper deck, $4\frac{1}{3}$ in (110 mm) thick on the upper strakes and $4\frac{2}{3}$ in (120 mm) on the lower. The wooden hull behind the armour was 26 in. (66 cm) thick. The three were the *Gloire*, *Invincible* and *Normandie*. The fourth, designed by Audenet and

and main masts, and fore-and-aft on the mizen only). She was designated a 'frigate', as were the three other ironclads, simply because they carried all their guns on a single gundeck, but by some they were known as 'ironclad frigates' to distinguish them from the sailing frigates, of which there were many still in commission.

The British reply to the *Gloire* was H.M.S. *Warrior*, launched in 1860. She was a ship of 9,210 tons (9,358 tonnes), designed by Isaac Watts, and was armoured with $4\frac{1}{2}$ in (115 mm) iron, backed by 18 in (76 cm) of teak. The armour extended for 213 ft (65 m), and stretched to a height of 21 ft (6·4 m) above the waterline and 6 ft (1·8 m) below it. This covered the length of the gundeck, which was closed at both ends with a $4\frac{1}{2}$ in (115 mm) bulkhead to form an armoured citadel inside which all the guns were mounted. Bow and stern, both projecting 85 ft (25·6 m) beyond the central citadel, were un-armoured. They consisted of plating alone, without any teak backing – a dangerous experi-ment, since there was no transverse watertight bulkheads to prevent the whole stern or bow section flooding, if the ship were hit on or below the waterline.

built at the suggestion of Dupuy de Lôme, was the 6,428-ton (6,531-tonne) *Couronne*. She was an iron-hulled ship, whose sides were composed of 4 in (100 mm) of armour plating, backed by 4 in of teak, then an iron lattice work $1\frac{1}{3}$ in (34 mm) thick and another 11 in (300 mm) of teak, fastened to a $\frac{3}{4}$-in (20 mm) skin of iron. This sandwich construction proved more satisfactory than that of the *Gloire* and her sister ships, and it was adopted by the French for all subsequent naval shipbuilding, until the invention of steel made the iron warship obsolete.

Launched in 1859, the *Gloire* was the first of these vessels to be commissioned. She was rigged initially as a barquentine (square sails on fore-mast and fore-and-aft on main and mizen), but later she was remasted as a full-rigged ship. Later still she became a barque (square sails on fore

Initially, H.M.S. *Warrior*, like the *Gloire*, was designated a 'frigate', again because all her main guns were mounted on a single deck. And, since on completion she had 40 guns, she naturally fell into the fifth rate, even though she was more than a match for any first-rate in the fleet. Eventually, the Admiralty resolved this dilemma by changing the basis of the rating system, from the number of guns mounted to the number of men carried on board. The crew of the *Warrior* numbered 707, and that of the average third-rate ship of the line 705, so the classification of the *Warrior* and her sister ship, H.M.S. *Black Prince*, was changed from 'frigate' – or 'armoured frigate', as some called them – to third-rate ship of the line. Later still, their generic name was altered to 'second-class battleship'.

Left: The British reply to *La Gloire* was HMS *Warrior*. Also an ironclad frigate, she differed in being faster and having a completely iron hull.

Warrior
(1860)

Length 380 ft (115·8 m) *Displacement* 9,210 tons (9,358 tonnes)
Speed 14½ knots *Complement* 707
Armament twenty-six 68-pound muzzle-loaders, ten 110-pound
breech-loaders, four 70-pound breech-loaders

H.M.S. *Warrior* was the first major warship in the world with
an iron hull. (The French warship *Gloire*, launched the year
before, had iron plating on the outside of a wooden hull.)
Designed by Isaac Watts, she was launched at Blackwall, on the
Thames. She was originally classed as a frigate because she had
only one gundeck, but she was larger and more powerful than
any other warship then afloat. Her armour consisted of 4½-in
(115 mm) iron plating backed by 18 in (760 mm) of teak. This
did not extend the whole length of the ship, 85 ft (25·6 m) at
either end being unarmoured, which might have proved a
liability if she had ever seen action. Like all broadside-armed
ships, *Warrior* became obsolete with the advent of the turret-
mounted gun. However, her hull survived and today *Warrior*,
magnificently restored and re-rigged, can be seen in her former
glory.

She is shown here with her armament as it was at the time of
her commissioning. The armoured bulkhead forming the end
of her armoured 'citadel' is visible in the cutaway section. The
diagram shows one of her 110-pound Armstrong breech-
loaders.

The term 'ironclad' was used to describe any armoured warship until the launching of H.M.S. *Dreadnought* in 1906. These first ironclads, apart from their armour, showed few advances in design upon the wooden warships that preceded them. The *Warrior* even had a 15-ft (4·6-m) figurehead, which made her look a handsome ship, but was an expensive concession to tradition, adding 40 tons of useless weight at a point where she could least afford to carry it. (Later she had to have an open shelter deck added aft, to counterbalance the weight of the figurehead and correct her trim.) Moreover, there were still those who mistrusted iron because of its tendency to rust and its surprising proneness to fouling with weed and barnacles, and periodic attempts were made to bring about a return to the good old days of wood and canvas. But, after the events at Sinope in 1853, the superiority of iron could never really be in question. For a moment in 1860 it appeared that the sceptics might win the debate, that immunity from rust and barnacles would be thought more important than strength and size; but the moment passed when, as a result of trials with the *Gloire*, the French government announced a building programme for thirty ironclads and eleven armoured floating batteries. In the face of a French bid to achieve the naval supremacy that had been denied them during the Napoleonic Wars, the opponents of iron in the British navy were overruled. The iron warship had come to stay.

B̲ut an even bigger revolution than the acceptance of iron for warship construction was about to sweep through the world's navies. Already the explosive shell had ousted the older solid shot, and the big gunfounders were introducing the rifled barrel to give the shell a predictable trajectory through the air, greater accuracy and longer range. But the new gun was still mounted on the old wooden carriage, and could still only fire on the broadside. What was now to alter the whole conception of warship design, more, indeed, then all the improvements in the gun itself, was a new gun mounting.

Two men are associated with this revolutionary advance, Captain Cowper Coles of the British Navy and John Ericsson, the Swedish engineer who had been closely associated with the introduction of the propeller and who had become a United States citizen in 1848. It is not possible to say which of the two was first to develop the idea of mounting the naval gun in a revolving turret so that it could fire in whatever direction the turret was trained, and there is a distinct possibility that neither of them was the real

originator and that the credit should go to Prince Albert, the consort of Queen Victoria.

Coles's idea of a gun in a revolving turret, which he called a 'cupola', had its origin in a small armed raft which he designed and built for coastal operations in the Sea of Azov in 1855. This was the *Lady Nancy*, 45 ft (13·7 m) long, by 15 ft (4·6 m) broad, constructed on twenty-nine casks in six rows of cradles, the whole being held together by a framework of spars. On the centre-line was mounted a long 32-pounder. With a draught of only 20 in (50 cm) she could be towed by boats close inshore, and she bombarded the dockyard town of Taganrog with great accuracy. Realising the advantages offered by a very low freeboard and an armament mounted on the centreline, Coles followed up the *Lady Nancy* by designing a larger armoured raft, 150 ft (46 m) long, with an engine and propeller and a single 68-pounder gun, centrally mounted and protected by a fixed hemispherical iron shield that had small gunports dead ahead and on either beam. It was not yet the revolving turret, but to an inventive mind such as Coles's, this was but a short and obvious step. Although the British Admiralty expressed no interest in Coles's armoured raft, which he had intended for attacks on the forts of Sebastopol and Kronstadt, Coles filed his first patent for a revolving turret in 1859. In the same year he submitted to the Admiralty a design for a 'cupola ship' of 9,200 tons (9,350 tonnes), in which twenty of the largest guns of the period were to be mounted in ten cupolas, eight of them on the ship's centre-

Below: Captain Henry Cowper Coles, a gifted but unfortunate designer.

Bottom: In 1855 Cowper Coles designed a gun-raft for use in the Sea of Azov, from which he developed the revolving turret.

line and the other two abreast on a low forecastle deck to provide axial fire on either side of the foremast. Captain Coles, in his description of the ship, admits that Prince Albert gave him 'advice of the greatest benefit . . . for he had previously turned his attention to the same subject and was thoroughly conversant with all the mechanical details involved in the execution of my plan.' In fact, according to Scott Russell, Prince Albert 'had matured an analogous system long before the adoption of the turrets of Coles or of Ericsson.'

Be that as it may, the old broadside gun was now replaced by the gun mounted in a revolving turret, and, as a result, the warship changed her shape again, having already done so when iron took over from wood for hull construction a year or two earlier. In Britain, Coles's ideas were embodied in H.M.S. *Prince Albert*, a coastal defence ship of 3,880 tons (3,940 tonnes) displacement which was laid down in 1862. Her four 9-inch guns each had a centreline turret, which was trained manually by rack-and-pinion gear and by a system of handspikes on the main deck. It took eighteen men about a minute to make one full revolution of the turret, but, as none of the eighteen men, either inside or outside the turret, could see the gunnery control officer, training of the turret was apt to be somewhat haphazard. Nevertheless, it was a start.

More or less simultaneously, the same development was taking place in the United States Navy, though under the more compelling stimulus of actual warfare. In 1861 the American Civil War broke out, and, when the navy yard at Norfolk, Virginia, was abandoned by the North in 1861, all ships which could not be moved away were scuttled. One of them, the wooden frigate *Merrimack*, was raised by the Confederates, given an engine, and a wooden penthouse with sloping sides over her entire deck. This was then covered with iron plates to a total thickness of

4 in (100 mm), with gunports cut in the sides of the penthouse through which her ten guns fired. She was also fitted with a large ram on her bow. Although she was renamed *Virginia* by the Confederates, it is as the *Merrimack* that she is always known and remembered. Two days after her conversion, on 8 March 1862, she went into action against Northern ships blockading the York and James rivers at Hampton Roads, rammed and sank the *Cumberland*, and forced the *Congress* to capitulate by the weight of her gunfire. Although she was heavily engaged by the guns of Federal warships and shore batteries, all the shells which hit her were deflected by the sloping sides of her armoured penthouse, and bounced harmlessly into the sea.

The North, however, had already built a completely new kind of ship, the brainchild of John Ericsson. Named *Monitor*, she was laid down in the Brooklyn yard in October 1861 and was completed in a little over three months. She was an iron ship with a very low freeboard of no more than a few inches, and on her heavily armoured deck she carried two 11-inch Dahlgren guns mounted in a revolving turret 9 in (230 mm) thick.

She reached Hampton Roads on the day after the *Merrimack*'s attack on the *Cumberland* and *Congress*, and for six hours the *Monitor* and *Merrimack* engaged in a gun duel, with neither inflicting much damage on the other. At the end of the day both ships withdrew, and, in fact, never met each other again. In May 1862, when the Confederates were in their turn forced to abandon Norfolk, Virginia, the *Merrimack* was burned and sunk, as she drew too much water to be evacuated up the James River, and in the following December the *Monitor*, which because of her almost non-existent freeboard could never have been considered a sea-going ship, foundered in a gale while on passage up the coast.

Above: HMS *Royal Sovereign* was a 131-gun three-decker cut down and armed with four Cowper Coles turrets. She and the iron-hulled *Prince Albert* were a big step towards the modern battleship, with gun mountings on the centreline.

Left: The Battle of
Hampton Roads between
the *Monitor* and *Merrimack*
was indecisive because the
two ships' guns lacked the
power and accuracy to
inflict heavy damage.

This *Monitor-Merrimack* duel was certainly the first action between ironclad warships, but claims that it was these two ships which ushered in the era of the ironclad are demonstrably false. Several European nations had ironclad warships in their navies well before 1862, and, of American countries, Brazil already had a battleship under construction in a British yard. Nor was the *Monitor* the first of the new turreted ships, for Denmark was experimenting in 1861 with a two-turreted gunboat, the *Rolf Krake*, designed by Cowper Coles and mounting two 68-pounder guns in each turret. The Russian and German navies also ordered turreted ships, again to Coles's design. The real importance of the *Monitor-Merrimack* duel, apart from the interest that it aroused, being the first meeting of ironclads in war, was that it focussed the attention of the world's navies on the need to improve the effectiveness of the naval gun. That two ships could hammer each other for six hours without causing any serious damage pointed not so much to the defensive value of armouring the ships, for that was already well recognized, as to the inefficiency of the gun itself in being unable to penetrate the armour and inflict decisive damage.

Over the next thirty years the gun was developed, in size, range and accuracy, from the short-barrelled muzzle-loader to the long-barrelled breech-loader. The development, in the 1870s, of slow-burning powder made a big increase in muzzle velocities possible, and the adoption of breech-loading removed the need to bring the gun inboard on its mounting every time it had to be reloaded, increasing the rate at which it could fire. But the increase in the efficiency of the gun was answered by an increase in the thickness of armour, to withstand the penetrative power of the new long-barrelled weapons. From 1862, the next two or three decades saw warships mounting guns of ever-increasing calibre – latterly up to 18 in (450 mm) – and protected by iron armour of ever-increasing thickness – as much as 24 in (730 mm) by the end of the period. Eventually, the introduction of hardened steel removed the need for armour of excessive thickness and weight, and improvements in gun design mitigated the need for huge pieces weighing over 100 tons each. By the end of the nineteenth century the calibre of the average battleship big gun had stabilized at around 12 in (300 mm), and the thickness of Krupp steel armour at about the same figure.

It was an odd fact of battleship design during these years that only in Britain, which had pioneered the principle of turret-mounting ships' guns, did the turret fail to find favour. The reason was the British Navy's addiction to masts and sails, and its desire to retain them long after other navies had discarded them. The typical British naval officer was an ultra-conservative who wished to retain the old order at all costs, and there was also a widely held belief that the only efficient sailors were those trained under sail. Although British shipbuilding skill was producing some of the best battleships in the

Right: Sailors relaxing on the *Monitor's* deck, with 11 inch gun turret behind them. Note the dent from one of the *Merrimack's* shells.

Below: The Royal Navy's first seagoing turret ship was HMS *Monarch*. She carried full sailing rig, but her high freeboard gave more seaworthiness than the American *Monitor*.

world, until the late 1870s every British battle-ship was fitted with the heavy masts and extensive sail rig of the old three-decked ship of the line. With masts and rigging it was impossible to provide a clear arc of fire for a gun in a turret, and a compromise was found in what was known as a 'central battery'. This was basically a heavily armoured box, built amidships, from which the guns could fire through ports cut in the sides. Though it did give a reasonable arc of fire on the broadside, it had nothing like the flexibility of the turret.

In the end, though it was not until the beginning of the 1880s, even British naval officers had to accept the fact that their beloved masts and sails could no longer be justified. They were in fact a serious liability, for, apart from interfering with the firing arcs of the main guns, their windage cut down appreciably the ship's speed under steam power, and they concentrated a great weight aloft in the position where a steamship can ill afford it. It was, perhaps, the disaster that befell H.M.S. *Captain* in 1870 which hastened their end. She was a battleship of 7,767 tons, built to a design by Cowper Coles in order to vindicate his faith in turret-mounted guns and low-freeboard ships. On completion H.M.S. *Captain's* freeboard was not more than 6 ft 6 in (2 m). On a relatively small hull (320 ft × 53 ft × 23 ft / 97·5 m × 16·2 m × 7 m) Coles decided for some reason to erect the heaviest masts and spars, and maximum sail area then in use, perhaps as a gesture of his supreme confidence in her stability and her ability to carry as much sail aloft as any other ship in the British navy. She capsized in a gale off the coast of Spain, with the loss of the whole of her crew except seventeen men and a gunner who reached the Spanish coast in one of the ship's boats. Captain Cowper Coles was on board as a privileged observer on this, her first cruise with the fleet, and was among those lost. It was the last experiment with low-freeboard battleships.

As was to be expected during such a rapid revolution in major warship design as was then taking place – from sailing three-decked ship of the line to armoured steel battleship, all within the span of thirty years – the second half of the nineteenth century was a time of experiment. All navies had to face the problems posed by the simultaneous development of guns, armour, engines and boilers, and attempts to reach a satisfactory design of ship that would embody the best of all the technical advances in a single hull. It was extraordinarily difficult, for in each country which boasted a navy there were plenty

of inventors, designers and shipbuilders, 'all with their inventive and constructive powers in the high state of activity, each of them intent on his own point, and none of them under such control as could harmonize their work with that of others.' And at the same time 'there was an immense public opinion clamouring for, and forcing on, the adoption of each nominal advance in offensive and defensive power, and those who clamoured loudest had least thought out the nature of an excessively complex problem.' These words were written by Vice-Admiral Colomb in 1898, and, though he was thinking of the British Navy, they were equally true of all the others. It was through this maze of, often conflicting, advice and experiment, of pet theories and political pressures, that the world's admiralties had to pick their uncertain way. That the occasional white elephant should be produced from time to time in most countries in their search for battleship perfection was probably inevitable. By the end of the century there had evolved a reasonable international consensus on

Above: Cowper Coles was bitterly critical of the *Monarch*, and was allowed to design a turret ship of his own, HMS *Captain*.

Above: The layout of the *Captain* was the same as the *Monarch*, but she had low freeboard amidships as well as a full set of masts and yards.

Left: The immense strength of iron hulls led to a revival of ramming tactics. This is the specially strengthened ram bow of HMS *Minotaur* (1868).

the correct components of an efficient battleship, designed to uphold a nation's power and influence at sea. Obviously there were some differences from nation to nation, since there were differences in the purposes for which battleships were required, and while it is not possible to be specific about size, guns, armour, etc., the average battleship was a steel armoured ship of around 15,000 tons, driven by triple-expansion engines at a speed of about 18 knots, and mounting about four 12-inch guns in turrets and sixteen or more smaller guns.

In only one respect could one say that this average ship was retrograde. With the introduction of the iron ship and mechanical propulsion there had been a revival of belief in the ram as a naval weapon – harking back to the days of the oared galley. Perhaps the idea of the ram as a viable weapon of war in the nineteenth century owed its origin to the theories of Admiral Sartorius, an old sea-dog, born in 1790, who was bewildered by steam propulsion and could think of no use for it other than hurling one ship

against another. His initial plans for the ram concerned no less a ship than Brunel's *Great Eastern*, and involved cutting her down to little above the waterline, covering her with shot-proof iron plates, fitting propellers at each end, installing a heavy gun battery on board, giving her pointed ends and using her hull as a ram. To guard against her being boarded by an enemy, he proposed the construction of towers from which boiling water could be pumped onto the boarders. His proposition was seriously made and, coming from an admiral, was seriously considered, but in the British admiralty it met with the reception which, perhaps, it deserved.

Nevertheless, mainly as a result of Sartorius's advocacy, the ram was brought within the orbit of naval weaponry, and it stayed there for the remainder of the century. It was odd that it attracted so much enthusiasm in naval circles in so many countries, for its record in battle was appalling. It was true that the ironclad *Merrimack* had holed the wooden *Cumberland* with her ram at Hampton Roads, but on the following day

Above: Ramming was used by the Austrian Fleet at the Battle of Lissa, but it only worked because the Italians were badly led and untrained.

both she and the *Monitor* failed to do any damage to each other by continual ramming attacks. At Mobile Bay, the Confederate ironclad *Tennessee*, attempting to ram, missed the *Hartford*, missed the *Brooklyn*, missed the *Lackawanna*, and, when she was herself rammed by the *Monongahala*, received only a glancing blow that did no damage. And when the Northern gunboat *Sassacus* rammed the *Albemarle*, all that she did was smash up her own bow.

The battle of Lissa, fought in 1866, was hailed as a vindication of the ram, though any real analysis would have revealed the opposite. It was a ramming battle if ever there were one, with the Austrian fleet steaming backwards and forwards through the disorganized Italian fleet trying to ram. True, the Austrian flagship, *Erzherzog Ferdinand Maximilian*, struck the Italian ironclad *Re d'Italia* and sank her, but the Italian ship was lying stopped at the time with her rudder damaged. All the other attempts to ram – and there were many of them – missed their targets.

The occasional unfortunate accident, too, was always hailed as a vindication of the ram. With fleets manoeuvring under steam, sometimes at night or in fog, there had inevitably been the occasional collision in which a ship had been sunk. In the ten years between 1869 and 1878 the Russian ironclad *Kreml* had rammed and sunk the frigate *Oleg*, the Russian ironclad *Admiral*

Spiridoff had rammed her sister ship the *Admiral Lazaroff* which was only saved from sinking by being beached in Kronstadt harbour, the Spanish ironclad *Numancia* had rammed and sunk the corvette *Fernando el Catolica*, the French ironclad *Jeanne d'Arc* had rammed and sunk the despatch vessel *Forfait*, the British battleship *Iron Duke* had rammed and sunk her sister ship, H.M.S. *Vanguard*, the French ironclad *Thetis* had rammed the ironclad *Raine Blanche* which managed to beach herself ashore before she sank, and the German ironclad *König Wilhelm* had rammed and sunk the turret ship *Grosser Kürfurst*. All these were hailed as evidence that the ram was an important, if not the most important, weapon of the battleship. The voice of sanity, pointing out that any ship with way upon her could manoeuvre so that a ramming ship would miss, or at best deliver only a glancing blow, remained unheard amid the excited clamour of the rammers. And later in the century, when the gun had been developed into a weapon of real power, those who held that a ship approaching another with the intention of ramming would be blown out of the water were equally ignored. So the ram was built onto the bows of every battleship, making them difficult to steer and reducing their speed.

During the last decades of the nineteenth century, another naval weapon made its appearance. It was to have an immense influence on the

M.T.S. Lightning
Scale 4″–1 Foot.

development of future navies. In 1865 an Austrian artillery captain named Luppis devised a boat-shaped craft, with an explosive charge in the bow, which was driven by clockwork and guided by lines attached to its rudder. He took it to Robert Whitehead, the English manager of a marine engine factory at Fiume, who developed the device into what is now known as the 'loco-motive torpedo', an underwater weapon with a charge of explosive in its head which, by 1877, was capable of a range of 1,000 yards at a speed of 7 knots. Further development increased both range, speed and reliability, making the torpedo an important and powerful naval weapon.

In 1879 the British torpedo boat H.M.S. *Lightning*, originally designed to carry spar torpedoes, was modified by the addition of two above-water tubes for launching the Whitehead torpedo. She was such a success that in 1880 the British Admiralty ordered twelve more like her, and other navies were quick to adopt the type. Between 1881 and 1885 torpedo boats were built in large numbers for the navies of Russia, France, Holland, Italy and Austria, and in 1886 Chile, China, Greece, Spain, Portugal, Sweden and Turkey followed suit.

Having produced the weapon, which in the hands of so many continental navies was now a threat to the naval supremacy of Great Britain, it fell to the same country to devise the antidote. This, it was decided, should take the shape of a larger torpedo boat, carrying a 4-inch gun, with enough speed to catch the smaller torpedo boat and stop her by gunfire before she could make an attack. In 1886 H.M.S. *Rattlesnake*, the first of these new vessels, was launched, but did not have sufficient speed for the job. Finally, in 1893, H.M.S. *Havock* and H.M.S. *Hornet* were launched as torpedo-boat destroyers. With a displacement of 250 tons, a speed of 27 knots, and an armament of four guns and three torpedo tubes, they not only proved more than a match for any existing torpedo boat, but they even usurped their function. Thus was born the destroyer, which by the turn of the century had become an integral part of every navy. Completely unarmoured, she relied on her speed for protection from attack, and this was attained by an increase in the length-to-beam ratio to about 12 to 1, and in some cases even more.

Right at the end of the nineteenth century a new development in marine propulsion made its appearance. This was the steam turbine, invented by the Hon. Charles Parsons. It is a rotary-propulsion engine in which a jet of steam, is directed through a nozzle on to blades set at an angle in a drum, connected either direct or through gearing to the propeller shaft. The action of the steam on the angled blades revolves

Above: The builders' plans of HMS *Lightning*, the first torpedo-boat. These craft were developed from fast steam launches, the only hulls with the right power-weight ratio to give a sea speed of 20 knots.

the drum, and by this means the drive is transmitted to the propeller. After passing through the first set of moving blades, the steam is forced through a set of fixed blades, mounted on the casing of the turbine and angled the other way, to increase its speed before it hits another set of moving blades. And so on, until the steam is exhausted into a condenser to be turned back into boiler feed water.

Parsons introduced his turbine in dramatic fashion, calculated to obtain the maximum amount of publicity for his new engine in a single demonstration. He built a small yacht and installed in her three of his turbines, each driving a shaft on which three propellers were fixed. He selected the naval review, held at Spithead in 1897 to celebrate Queen Victoria's diamond jubilee for his demonstration, knowing well that representatives of all foreign navies would be present in honour of the occasion. On the day of the review he took his yacht, which he had named *Turbinia*, into the review area and steamed her up and down the lines of anchored warships. As the review area was meant to be kept clear for the passage of the Royal Yacht with Queen Victoria on board, the steam picket boats of the fleet were sent in pursuit to warn the *Turbinia* away, but none of them could look at her for

speed. At top speed, she was said to have achieved 34·5 knots – quite unheard of in those days – and her performance so impressed the various naval authorities and shipowners present that the future of the turbine as the new motive power for ships was assured. Its advantages over the reciprocating engine were considerable, not only in occupying much less space in the engine room, but also in the simplicity of construction and an extremely favourable power-to-weight ratio. That the British Admiralty were impressed

Below: The steam yacht *Turbinia*, test-bed for the Parsons steam turbine which made higher speeds possible.

Inset: The Parsons turbine achieved greater power than the triple-expansion engine, with less vibration and wear and tear.

Above: The great Mississippi Steamboat Race in July 1870, with the *Robert E. Lee* beating the *Natchez*.

by these advantages was witnessed by the launch, in 1899, of H.M.S. *Viper*, a destroyer of 325 tons (330 tonnes), with Parsons turbines driving four shafts, on each of which were two propellers. She was the first warship in the world to use this new form of propulsion, and she attained a speed of 36·58 knots on her trials.

Before we leave the nineteenth century, it is of interest to take a look at another type of craft, developed for use on the rivers of the United States. Many of the great rivers, and particularly the Mississippi and Ohio, formed magnificent natural highways for the transport of passengers and goods, and a special type of vessel was built for use on them. The hull form resembled a shallow, elongated dish, giving a draught of water of little more than 4 ft (1·2 m), in even the largest of them. Some of these steamboats were built as large as 5,000 tons gross, with as many as five or six decks rising above the flat-bottomed hull to provide saloons and cabins. All of them were paddle steamers, the larger with two side paddlewheels, the smaller with a single sternwheel.

A remarkable feature of all of them was the engine. With homespun ingenuity, a form of walking beam engine was developed, in which the moving beam and the trusslike structure on which the engine was mounted were built up largely from timber struts and locally wrought iron supports. The moving beam was in full and open view from the top deck, and the engine turned paddlewheels of up to 40 ft. (12 m) in diameter. A pair of tall black funnels was mounted abreast to carry the boiler smoke clear of the top deck and the wheelhouse, and these were decorated with a sort of serrated crown on top, a characteristic feature of these river paddlers. Up to the 1850s wood alone was burned in the boilers; between 1850 and 1880 wood was supplemented by coal; and after 1880 coal alone was burned, owing to the introduction of high-pressure boilers in an attempt to increase speed.

Inevitably, races were organised for these great vessels along certain stretches of river for the title of 'Fastest Boat on the River'. The best remembered of all these races was that held in 1870 between two of the real 'dandies' – the *Natchez*, which held the title, and the *Robert E. Lee*. (The race, won by the *Robert E. Lee*, with a speed of 19 knots on the stretch between Natchez and New Orleans, is depicted in a well known coloured lithograph of Currier and Ives.)

The First Submarines

'And also it is possible to make a ship or boat that may goe under the water unto the bottome, and so come up againe at your pleasure, as this, . . . that anything that sinketh, is heavier than the proportion of so much water, and if it be lighter than the magnitude of so much water, then it swimmeth or appeareth above the water.' The words are those of William Bourne, written in 1578, and they are followed by a description of how such a ship could be constructed. Whether his boat was ever built is not known, but the description is clear enough to show that he was the first to appreciate the principle on which a submarine operates.

To be able to make a ship disappear under water and return to the surface at will was a dream of many inventors, for its advantages for naval war were manifold. But, although Bourne, in his writing, had shown clearly enough how positive buoyancy in a ship might be removed to make it sink and restored to make it rise to the surface again, future inventors concentrated their efforts on an alternative method – that of ballasting a boat until she lay awash, and then forcing her under the surface with oars or other means. Cornelius van Drebbel, a Dutch inventor, used this method in building a 'submarine' in 1620, which was demonstrated on the River Thames in the presence of King James I. It made the journey from Westminster to Greenwich, either just awash or just submerged, but proved nothing beyond the fact that, at the end of the trip, the rowers inside were in poor shape because there was no provision for replacing the oxygen which they had breathed.

Van Drebbel had many imitators. In 1653 a Frenchman named de Son built a submarine at Rotterdam in which forward motion under the sea was to be provided by a paddlewheel revolved by clockwork. He announced his invention in no uncertain terms: 'he doeth undertake in one day to destroy a hondered ships, can goe from Rotterdam to London and back againe in one day, and in 6 weeks to goe to the East Indiens, and to run as swift as a bird can flye, no storme, no bullets, can hinder her, unless it please God.' Unhappily, when the submarine took to the water, the clockwork was not powerful enough to turn the paddle-

wheel and the craft remained motionless.

In 1747 another submersible boat, designed by Symons, was tried out on the Thames, but failed to submerge. In 1773 a ship's carpenter named Day built a boat, ballasted with rocks hanging from her keel, which reached a depth of 30 ft (9 m) in Plymouth Sound, and surfaced safely after Day had released some of the rocks by a mechanism inside the boat. On the second attempt the mechanism failed to work, and Day and his boat were taken to the bottom in 132 ft (40 m) of water, where the pressure of water crushed the boat.

The next steps in submarine development were taken by two Americans, David Bushnell and Robert Fulton, who are generally regarded as the fathers of the modern submarine boat. Though neither man's craft was particularly successful, both were produced under the spur of war, and Bushnell's craft was actually used in action.

David Bushnell graduated from Yale in 1775. Young, ardent and patriotic, Bushnell looked for a new weapon which could break the stranglehold of British sea power, and reckoned that he had found it in the submarine. He constructed an iron hull shaped like an egg, which was held upright in the water by a lead keel of 700 lb (318 kg), of which 200 lb (91 kg) was detachable in an emergency. Two small tanks were fitted in the bottom of the submarine, to which seawater was admitted by a foot-operated push valve and ejected by two hand-operated pumps. The submarine was operated by one man, who produced

vertical movement through the water by means of a small hand-operated propeller mounted on top of the submarine, and horizontal movement by means of a similar propeller mounted laterally. The method of attack was to flood the two tanks, which would make the submarine submerge until the top propeller was awash, then bring the submarine alongside the enemy ship with the aid of the horizontal propeller, and, when alongside, to make the submarine dive under water with the vertical propeller. Once the submarine was underneath the ship, a magazine containing 150 lb (68 kg) of gunpowder was attached to the ship's bottom by a screw, worked from inside the submarine. A clockwork fuse gave a delay of 30 minutes, during which the submarine was to make her escape. The submarine was given the name *Turtle*.

After successful trials in Long Island Sound the first real attack was made, on H.M.S. *Eagle* in 1776, with Sergeant Ezra Lee as the operator of the sub-marine. He reached the ship unobserved and forced the *Turtle* under the vessel's hull, but was unable to screw the charge home, for it had not been realised that the bottoms of British warships serving in foreign waters were covered with copper sheets, as a protection against the Teredo worm. Lee and the *Turtle* managed to escape, and later two more attacks on British warships were attempted, but were foiled by the good lookout maintained on board.

Robert Fulton's submarine, *Nautilus*, was conceived more as a means of making a fortune for her inventor, than for patriotic reasons. He constructed a model of his proposed submarine, offered it to France for use against the British fleet during the Revolutionary War of 1793–1801, and, when turned down by that country, spent the next three years travelling across Europe offering it to various governments, though with no success. By 1800 he was back in France, where Napoleon Bonaparte had now become First Consul. Napoleon, anxious for any new weapon which might break the British naval blockade, gave Fulton 10,000 francs with which to build a full-scale version of his *Nautilus*.

Laid down at the end of 1800, the *Nautilus* was launched in the River Seine in May 1801. Built of copper on an iron frame, in the shape of an imperfect ellipsoid, she was 21 ft 4 in (6·5 m) long and 7 ft (2·1 m) in diameter, with a small hemispherical conning-tower. As did Bushnell's *Turtle*, she submerged by taking seawater into internal ballast tanks, and was propelled under water by a hand-operated propeller. On the surface she carried a mast and sail, hinged and laid flat along the deck when she submerged. She carried a very similar weapon to that used by the *Turtle*, though it was to be attached to the target's hull by a spike instead of a screw.

After successful trials on the Seine, much admired by Napoleon, she was taken to Brest for a full demonstration. An old schooner was anchored in Brest Roads. The *Nautilus* set out to attack her, dived underneath her, attached the charge to her hull underwater, and withdrew. A few minutes later the schooner was blown sky-high. But his very success damned Fulton in France. Napoleon had by then given up his plans for invading England and was marching to new adventures in central Europe, and the French Navy found themselves with a troubled conscience in the contemplation of so terrible a weapon. Without Napoleon to urge him on, the French Minister of Marine washed his hands of the affair.

From France Fulton took his *Nautilus* to England in an attempt to interest the British Navy. He found an enthusiastic ally in William Pitt, the prime minister, who set up a commission of eminent men to examine the project. For a demonstration, the brig *Dorothy* was anchored off Walmer on the coast of Kent, and Fulton was invited to attack her. Again, he was completely successful, and the *Dorothy* was blown in two at the first attempt. But, as in France, his success appalled the commission set up to examine the invention. In spite of Pitt's protest, they refused to have anything to do with this diabolic weapon. Admiral Lord St. Vincent passed the final judgment: 'Pitt', he said, 'was the greatest fool that ever existed to encourage a mode of warfare which those who commanded the seas did not want, and which, if successful, would at once deprive them of it.'

Fulton then returned to America, became a successful steamship operator, and in 1810 managed to interest Congress (to the tune of 5,000 dollars) in a new, steam-driven submarine, 80 ft (24·3 m) long with a beam of 21 ft (6·4 m) and a draught of 14 ft (4·3 m). Fulton himself designed the steam engine, and the submarine was named *Mute* because of the silent way in which the engine worked. Unfortunately, Fulton died during the *Mute's* trials in 1815, and there was no one experienced enough to carry on his work.

I Entrée du sous-marin.
O, O Réservoirs à lest d'eau.
N Soupape d'admission de l'eau.
P, Q Pompes pour chasser l'eau des réservoirs.
E Hélice-vis de traction pour la marche en avant.
F Hélice-vis à axe vertical pour la plongée.
G Gouvernail.
C, D Baromètre à niveau d'eau pour indiquer le degré d'enfoncement.
L, L Tuyaux pour l'aération.
M Ventilateur.
S Torpille.
T Mouvement d'horlogerie pour faire éclater la torpille.
R Vis pour fixer la torpille contre la carène des vaisseaux.
B Lest de sécurité.

Far left, above: Robert Fulton (1765–1815).

Above left: An 1885 representation of Bushnell's *Turtle*. From the inventor's own description it now seems unlikely that the propeller was an Archimedes' screw; it was probably more like a vane in design.

Left: The *Nautilus*, Fulton's submarine.

Wilhelm Bauer, a non-commissioned officer in the Bavarian artillery, was the next man to build a submarine. His design was an advance on those of Bushnell and Fulton in that it dived at at angle, under forward propulsion. Once negative buoyancy had been achieved, by flooding internal ballast tanks with seawater, Bauer gave his craft a bow down attitude by means of a sliding weight which, when moved to the forward end of the submarine, produced a sufficient angle of dive to take the craft down. Forward motion was produced, as in the earlier submarines, by hand-operated propeller.

Bauer had grasped, too, another principle of submarine operation in his recognition of the fact that the pressure of water increases with depth. When, in February 1851, his submarine, *Plongeur-Marin*, with Bauer and two assistants on board, accidentally reached a depth of 60 ft (18 m), during exercises at Kiel, and began to buckle under the pressure, he realised that the only possible way of escape was to flood the submarine until the air inside it was compressed to the same pressure as that of the water outside. Once that was achieved, it would be possible to open the hatch of the conning-tower against the water pressure outside, and rise to the surface in the bubble of air thus released. He managed to persuade his two terrified

assistants that this was their only hope of survival. The hull was gradually flooded until the pressures of air and water were equalized, the hatch was opened, and the three men escaped exactly as Bauer had planned it.

Bauer next interested the Russian Navy in submarine construction and his next model, the *Diable-Marin*, was built at Leningrad in 1855 – an iron submersible with a length of 52 ft (15·8 m). She was a success and it is recorded that Bauer made 134 dives in her, including one in September 1856 during a naval review in honour of the coronation of Czar Alexander II, when he embarked a small orchestra which played the Russian national anthem while submerged. The sound carried through the water, and was clearly heard on board the ships at the review, creating a tremendous impression.

By now the submarine had evolved into something reasonably reliable, far advanced from the haphazard inventions of earlier days which were weighted down with rocks and stones. The use of iron as a building material gave a flexibility of design impossible with wood, and the nineteenth century submarines were beginning to take on the cigar-shaped hull design which promised a better underwater performance. What was still needed before they could be regarded as viable

warships was a weapon less crude than the keg of gunpowder to be attached somehow to the bottoms of ships, and a means of underwater propulsion more efficient than a hand-operated propeller.

The weapon made its appearance during the American Civil War, in the shape of the spar torpedo, a copper case containing 134 lb (60·7 kg) of gunpowder, carried on the end of a 30-ft (9·1 m) wooden spar. With one of these weapons mounted on their bows, submarines began to have an important part to play in naval warfare. It was invented in the Southern States, and in order to exploit it to the maximum they built a series of small submarines, averaging about 50 ft (15 m) in length, which were generically known as Davids, no doubt by way of a comparison to the goliaths of the Federal navy. Most of them had a crew of nine men, eight of them turning a propeller by means of a series of connected cranks and the ninth steering. A few were built with a small steam engine.

The best remembered of the hand-operated Davids is the *H. L. Hunley*, built in Mobile, Alabama, by officers of an Alabama volunteer regiment to plans provided by Horace L. Hunley, James R. McLintock and Baxter Watson. Her midships section was made from a cylindrical iron steam boiler. Tapered ends, containing ballast tanks which could be flooded or pumped dry, were added. On her bows she carried a spar torpedo. On the night of 17 February 1864, she attacked the Federal sloop *Housatonic* which was anchored in about 27 ft (8 m) of water, off the channel entrance to Charleston. When the lookouts on the *Housatonic* saw the *Hunley* coming, they slipped the cable to back away, but the eight men on the crank handles, cheered on by the ninth, redoubled their efforts and the *Hunley's* spar torpedo struck home and exploded, blowing a large hole in the *Housatonic's* side. She sank quickly, and probably took the *Hunley* down with her, for the David never returned.

It was this exploit, the first sinking of a warship in action by a submarine, that really put the submarine on the map. And an ideal submarine weapon, the locomotive torpedo, was already in view in the shape of Captain Luppis's clockwork contraption, which was about to be turned over to Robert Whitehead at Fiume for development as an underwater weapon. The submarine's other requirement, a means of propulsion other than a hand-operated propeller, was also on the horizon, in the shape of the internal combustion engine for surface propulsion and the electric motor, which used none of the precious oxygen in the vessel, for propulsion when submerged.

During the next thirty years there were several inventors in the submarine field, but only four were serious contenders for the prize of designing a submarine which the navies of the world would accept – Holland and Lake,

of the United States, Nordenfelt, of Sweden, and Goubet, of France. It was these four who contributed most to the development of the submarine into a recognised factor in any future naval warfare. In the end, it was the Holland boat which was preferred by the world's navies, although Lake's boat was the greatest advance, in that it had two pairs of hydroplanes, one pair forward and one aft. With these hydroplanes Lake demonstrated that a submerged vessel could remain at a constant depth, even at very slow speed, without the need of constant alteration in her internal ballasting. But Lake failed to win the contract, even though his submarine was of stronger and sounder design than the Holland craft, because he failed to appreciate the true function of the submarine. His idea of the submarine's role in war was sitting on the bottom, and sending out a diver to cut telegraph cables or the mooring wires of mines, or

telephoning back to base the movements of enemy ships. For this reason, he fitted two large external wheels to his submarine, so that she could run along the bottom, and it was this feature which made her unacceptable in naval eyes.

By the end of the century the submarine had established herself as an integral part of every navy in the world, except that of Britain, and Britain, too, was forced to adopt it in 1901.

Far left: Wilhelm Bauer's submarine *Seetaucher* or *Plongeur-Marin*. A bucket dredger raised it 36 years after sinking and it was put on display as an example of early submarine development.

Below: The *Holland*, the US Navy's first submarine, purchased in 1900.

Bottom: The Confederate 'David', *H. L. Hunley*, which sank the Federal *Housatonic* with a spar torpedo in 1864.

Chapter Nine
The End of an Era

It should not be thought that the introduction of steam propulsion during the nineteenth century meant the end of the sailing ship. Steam did, indeed, make prodigious strides throughout that century, not only in terms of the volume of shipping built with engines and boilers, but also in the improvement of the marine steam engine, culminating in the introduction of the turbine – the ultimate in steam propulsion – just before the century ended. But for most of the century the sailing ship still prospered, though on longer routes, and underwent equally dramatic developments in hull design and rigging plans.

For the first thirty or forty years of the century, the introduction of steam made very little impression on the supremacy of the pure sailing ship, both in the passenger and cargo-carrying trades. Where steam was used in ships during these early years it was almost entirely as an auxiliary means of propulsion, to keep a sailing ship moving when there was no wind to fill her sails. Later in the century, when steam propulsion had proved its reliability and efficiency and had ousted sail completely in those vessels in which it had earlier been installed only as an auxiliary, there were still a number of long trade routes beyond the range of the marine steam engine. On these there was no alternative to the sailing ship, and the keen competition for cargoes guaranteed continuing progress towards the ultimate in design and sail power.

The model on which British merchant ships were based at the start of the century was the naval frigate. Built to heavy scantlings, with a blunt and rounded bow, carrying a long bowsprit and jib-boom, a heavy, overhanging stern, very little sheer, and full in the bilge, they were typically sturdy and strong ships, slow through the water, but with a big carrying capacity. The British shipowner was not looking for speed. Often brought up in the tradition of the East

India Company, whose stately ships had enjoyed for two centuries the monopoly of trade to India and China, power, strength and cargo capacity were the qualities most sought after in a merchant ship by the British shipowner. And when the East India Company lost its trade monopoly in India in 1813 and in China in 1833, the owners who stepped in to take advantage of the new free-for-all remained faithful to the old design.

The challenge to the British model came from America. During the War of 1812 against Britain, the United States had built a large number of privateers, mainly schooner- or brig-rigged. Since superior speed was a *sine qua non* for a privateer, they were built with a higher length-to-beam ratio than the British ships on which they preyed, and the hulls were round-bottomed. This hull shape, admirable for speed, was poor in terms of cargo capacity, and when the war ended the Americans found that, though they had an edge over the competition in speed, most traders preferred a big carrying capacity for their goods. But there were two trades in which these American ships (which earned themselves the generic name of 'clipper', because they could 'clip' the time taken on a passage by a packet ship on a regular run) could prosper: one was the so-called 'blackbird' trade, shipping vast numbers of negroes from Africa for sale in the southern states of America, and the other was the Chinese opium trade. In both of these trades speed was essential, and the erstwhile privateers, ranging from 100 to 300 tons displacement, with a shallow draught, but deeper aft than forward, were ideally suited to outrun any ship whose duty it was to prevent this questionable traffic.

As a large number of these American vessels, particularly those constructed after the end of the war, were built in Virginia and Maryland, they were known as 'Baltimore clippers', although they were not true clippers in the sense of the term that eventually came to be accepted. They had the sharply raked stem – the true mark of a clipper – but not yet the hollow bow,

Left: The Boston clipper *Flying Cloud* made a record passage from New York to San Francisco in 1851, averaging 9 knots for the whole journey.

197

a characteristic feature of clipper design. They also had an inclined overhanging counter stern, and they owed their speed to the reduction of wetted surface area at bow and stern.

In 1832 an enlarged Baltimore clipper, the *Ann McKim*, was built at Baltimore and given a square rig, and many have claimed that she was the first of the real clippers, but in fact that honour belongs to the *Rainbow*, designed by John Griffiths, built by Smith and Dimon in New York, and launched in 1849. She had the hollow bow of the true clipper and created such a stir in shipping circles that her unorthodox design was followed by many other builders. Although her hull lines and deep keel were indicative of speed through the water, her length-to-beam

ratio of under 5 to 1 prevented her from reaching the speeds achieved by later clippers.

This first of the true clippers represented a great leap forward in the development of sail. British shipowners, still wedded to the practice of building their trading ships 'frigate-fashion', found themselves losing out to the faster American ships. The competition really began to bite in 1850, when the American clippers discovered the China tea trade, in which the first cargoes to arrive in England each year commanded a substantial premium. In 1849 the British government repealed the deep sea Navigation Act, under which no goods might be imported into Britain and her colonies except in British bottoms or in those of the producing countries, and it was the repeal of this act that opened the China–England tea trade to all comers. The first American clipper to bring tea to England from China was the *Oriental* in 1850, and because of her speed she secured nearly

double the freight rate offered to British tonnage. For the next five years American clippers secured the cream of this lucrative traffic.

The most famous American builder of clipper ships was Donald Mackay, of Boston, whose first clipper was the revolutionary *Staghound*, launched in 1850, and the first of a long line of world-famous Mackay clippers. His *Flying Fish*, *Flying Cloud* and *Sovereign of the Seas*, built for the New York-California run after the discovery in California of gold in large quantities, were all 'flyers', and in 1851 the *Flying Cloud* sailed the 17,597 nautical miles from New York to San Francisco, round Cape Horn, in 89 days, 21 hours, an average speed for the whole passage of something like 9 knots. These ships were built to a length-to-beam ratio of just over 6 to 1, giving them a useful advantage in speed over the shorter, tubbier clippers which had preceded them. But, having to withstand the stormy seas of the South Atlantic and South Pacific, they were very

Left: The *Sovereign of the Seas*, a Mackay clipper.

Below left: The American privateer brigantine *Rambler*, one of a series built to prey on British commerce in the 1812 War.

Bottom: The *Glory of the Seas* ready for launch in 1869 at Boston.

Inset: Detail from a photograph of Donald Mackay, the Boston clipper-owner.

strongly built, and rigged to achieve their maximum speeds in hard winds, and few of these Mackay-built ships were seen on the trade routes where gentler winds prevailed, such as the tea trade from China. And they were not long-lived ships, for they were built with the soft woods which abounded along the American coast, close to the shipbuilding yards. After about five years, particularly in the hands of skippers who were notorious for driving their ships to the utter limit, their hulls became strained and leaky, and the soft wood water-logged and sluggish. But, in comparison to the English practice of building hulls of hard woods such as oak or teak, they were cheap to build, and many enterprising traders found that they could cover the entire

building cost and make a very handsome profit from them during the span of their short lives, sometimes even in one year.

The American competition spurred British owners to try to improve their own designs and rigs. The best of the British ships were those known as 'Blackwall frigates', which got their name because many of them were built at Green and Wigram's yard at Blackwall, and because they were said to be 'frigate-built', though in no way did they resemble the naval frigate design. They were built mainly for the India trade, with a finer run, and therefore faster, than the typical

Above: The Blackwall frigate *True Briton*, an example of ships built on the Thames to meet the challenge of the American clippers.

East Indiaman of Company days, and for many years they dominated this trade after the East India Company had lost its monopoly. The first of the Blackwall frigates was Green and Wigram's *Seringapatam*, of 818 tons, which was launched in 1837, and she set a new record of 85 days from London to Bombay. But these Blackwall frigates were still far removed from the true clipper design, and, if British shipowners wanted to compete with the Americans, they would need to do a great deal better than the Blackwall frigate.

The first British attempt to build a ship to compete with the Americans in speed was the little *Scottish Maid*, built by Alexander Hall at Aberdeen, but, although she once did the Leith–London run in 33 hours – a remarkably fast time – she did not have the essential features of clipper design. The first real English clippers were the *Stornoway* and *Chrysolite*, also built by Hall at Aberdeen, to compete in the China tea trade. Another builder of clippers, and one who was to become in Britain the best known of them all, was Robert Steele, of Greenock. After the decline of American shipbuilding during the American Civil War (1861–65), he was to produce some of the most famous ships of the whole clipper era,

particularly for the China trade.

But as yet, certainly up to 1858, the American clippers reigned supreme. They dominated the New York–California trade, triggered off by the gold discoveries, with magnificent ships driven to their limit by 'hard-case' skippers and 'bucko' mates, who drove their crews as hard as they drove their ships. Inevitably some were lost in the fierce storms of Cape Horn simply because skippers and mates refused to shorten sail and literally drove their ships under, but it was an immensely profitable trade and the occasional ship loss was quickly recouped from the profits of the others. Everything had to go by sea, the gold miners themselves, their tools and machinery, their food, drink and building materials, even the girls specially imported to separate the miners from their earnings in the saloons. There was as yet no transcontinental railway, and a covered wagon from the eastern states to California would take very much longer than a clipper round Cape Horn. There was really no alternative to the clipper, and the entire trade, down to the last nut and bolt, was in their hands. This shipping boom lasted until 1857, when a railway built across the Isthmus of Panama, with steamship connections at its east and west terminal points, so shortened the time from New York to San Francisco that the clipper could no longer compete. One of the oddities of this clipper traffic was the huge quantity of port and sherry shipped for the voyage round Cape Horn and back. There was a theory prevalent among the wealthy New York wine-drinkers that these fortified wines were much improved by a good shaking up, and what better way to shake them up than in the holds of a clipper ship as she battled her way around Cape Horn.

The largest of the American clippers built for the New York–San Francisco trade was Mackay's *Great Republic*, a four-masted barque with an overall length of 325 ft (99.1 m) and a beam of 53 ft (16.2 m). She never had a chance of showing her paces, for after a fire on board while she was fitting out for her maiden voyage her hull and rig were both cut down to more modest proportions, removing her original promise.

In 1848 gold was discovered at Ballarat in Australia, and another gold rush developed across the world. The Australian trade was very largely in the hands of James Baines's Black Ball Line, of Liverpool, who hitherto had been content to use the slower Blackwall frigates for this traffic. But, with a new gold rush developing, speed was essential. Baines had a new ship, the *Marco Polo*, built on clipper lines at St John's, New Brunswick, and she broke all records for passages to and from Australia in 1852–53. In 1853 he chartered Donald Mackay's *Sovereign of the Seas* for the Australian run and in the following year ordered four more big clippers from Mackay – the *Lightning*, *Champion of the Seas*, *James Baines* and *Donald Mackay*. The *Lightning* and *James Baines* were considerably larger than the average clipper, of over 2,500 register tons, and were among the fastest vessels in the world at that time. In 1854, the *James Baines*, on her first voyage to Australia, sailed the 14,034 nautical miles from London to Melbourne in $63\frac{1}{2}$ days, carrying 700 passengers, 1,400 tons of cargo and 350 mail bags. She did the return trip, loaded with cargo, in $69\frac{1}{2}$ days. Some of the speeds credited to these Baines clippers were phenomenal: the *Sovereign of the Seas* was said to have achieved 22 knots at times during her record passage from New York to Liverpool of 13 days, 14 hours; in 1856 the *James Baines* recorded in her deck log 'ship going 21 knots with main skysail set'; the *Lightning's* log during her passage from Boston to Liverpool records that from noon on 28 February to noon on 1 March she ran 436 nautical miles, 'lee rail under water and rigging slack', giving her an average speed throughout the 24 hours of over 18 knots. And this was surpassed later that year when the *Champion of the Seas*, on her maiden voyage to

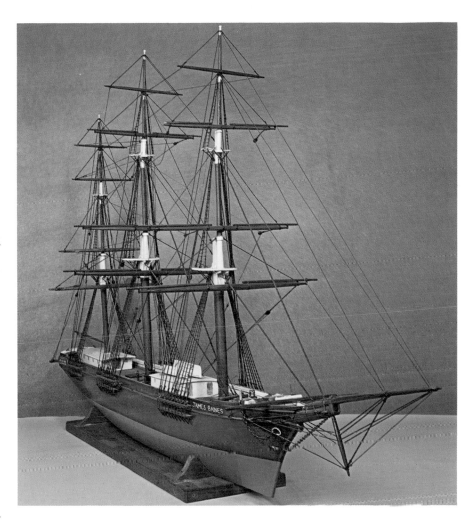

Melbourne for the Black Ball Line, logged 465 nautical miles in 24 hours while running her easting down. As she was sailing east, the difference in longitude cut her noon-to-noon period from 24 hours to 23 hours 17 minutes, to give her an average speed over the whole period of just on 20 knots. It is speeds and endurances such as these which testify to the supreme skill of Donald Mackay as a designer and to the sturdiness of his ships.

The Civil War gave Americans preoccupations other than the building of large clipper ships, and by the time it was over they had lost their superiority, never to regain it. It was now the turn of British shipbuilders to produce sailing vessels which were the wonder of the world. They retained the essential clipper features of raked stem, hollow bow and overhanging counter stern, but their ships had finer and more delicate lines, and an improved sail plan that enabled them to 'ghost' in light airs, yet was still marvellously efficient in a gale. These ships were a distinct type of their own, not just copies of the American clippers, and, although they never

Above: Model of the Mackay clipper *James Baines*, which once logged a speed of 21 knots under full sail. In 1854 she sailed 14,000 miles from London to Melbourne in $69\frac{1}{2}$ days.

quite managed the amazing bursts of speed of the Americans, they had a better all-round performance in that they were as much at home in light weather as in heavy. In general, they were smaller than the Americans, with a gross tonnage of around 1,000 to 1,200. Their high average length-to-beam ratio of between 7 and 8 to 1, with the raked stem rabbeted on to a long, straight keel, gave these clippers a very good grip of the water when sailing on the wind. They were wet ships in a head sea, but then so were the Americans, and indeed any ship with so fine a bow would be.

These British ships were built specifically for the China tea trade, and the best of them were built by Robert Steele, by now in his prime as a designer. During the 1860s he produced a number of very fine ships, of which the *Taeping*, *Ariel*, *Sir Lancelot* and *Serica* were world-famous for their speed and beauty. His ships were mainly of composite construction, the wooden hull planking being bolted to frames, deck beams and stringers of iron. The hull was sheathed with copper below the waterline to provide extra protection against marine growth and wood-boring worms.

By 1865 the China tea trade, which had earlier threatened to become an American monopoly through the speed of their ships, was firmly back in the hands of the British. British clippers, better designed and better rigged for the particular conditions to be expected during the 16,000 nautical miles between China and London Docks around the Cape of Good Hope, could put up considerably better passage times than the fastest of the American clippers. Each year the English ships raced home from China with their holds stuffed with cases of the new crop of tea, and it was a race well worth winning, for the premium paid by merchants for the first cargo to arrive was considerable. The most famous of these annual races was that of 1866 when five clippers were engaged. The *Fiery Cross* left Foochow on 29 May, the *Ariel*, *Taeping* and *Serica* on 30 May, and the *Taitsing* on 31 May. The first to arrive in London Docks was the *Taeping*, at 8.45 p.m. on 6 September. The *Ariel* arrived half an hour later and the *Serica* at 11.45 p.m., after a voyage halfway around the world that took just 99 days. The other two clippers docked in London two days later. It is remarkable that the first three were all Robert Steel ships and that they were of such equal excellence that only three hours separated them after 16,000 miles of sailing. (The average time for the clipper passage from China to London was around 110 to 112 days.)

The competition to build still faster clippers continued until about 1870. In 1868 Walter

Hood of Aberdeen built the *Thermopylae* of 991 gross tons to a design by Bernard Waymouth. She was claimed to be the fastest sailing clipper in the world, and her owner gave her a golden cock to be secured to her mainmasthead as evidence of her supremacy. On her maiden voyage she sailed with passengers and cargo from London to Melbourne in 59 days – a record for a sailing ship that has never been beaten – then sailed in ballast to Foochow to load tea, and brought her cargo home from Foochow to London in 101 days. It was specifically to challenge the *Thermopylae* that, in 1869, John Willis commissioned the Dumbarton firm of Scott & Linton to build him a clipper of 963 tons gross, to be named *Cutty Sark*. She made her first voyage with tea from China in 1870, taking 109 days from Shanghai to Beachy Head – no very remarkable passage. But in fact both she and the *Thermopylae* came too late for the 'Flying Fish

Top: The clipper *Fiery Cross*, one of five tea clippers to take part in the famous race in 1866.

Above: The clippers *Serica* and *Lahloo* at Foochow in 1868. The clipper, with her small cargo-capacity, depended on high-value cargoes like opium and tea for her profit, and her brief reign ended as soon as steamships could match her speed by better timekeeping.

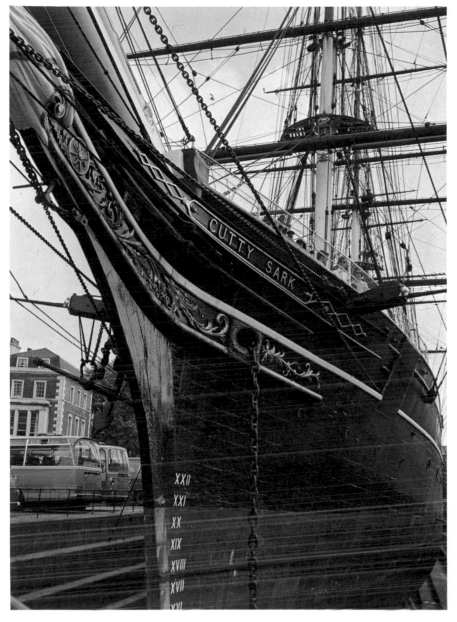

Above: The *Cutty Sark* was one of the greatest of all clippers, but arrived when the tea-trade was dying. Like other clippers she survived by going into the Australian wool trade.

on board for the long voyages; but, as the century wore on, more and more coaling stations were established at strategically placed ports around the world, and this obstacle was gradually removed.

The biggest of the British composite clippers, and in some ways the most remarkable, was the 2,131-ton *Sobraon*, which was built by Hall of Aberdeen in 1866 for the firm of Lowther, Maxton & Company, trading to Australia. She was remarkable in that she was designed as a steamship but completed as a clipper. Her maiden voyage was made as a passenger ship in 1867, and until 1891 she made regular voyages between London and Sydney – a very popular ship with all who sailed in her. In 1891 she was taken over by the New South Wales government, as a reformatory ship in Sydney Harbour. She was surveyed in 1911 for recommissioning as a training ship and was found to be sound throughout after forty-five years of service. She was paid off as a training ship in 1916 and became the floating clubhouse of an Australian charity. In 1937 she was again surveyed, and once again her hull was found to be sound throughout – a remarkable tribute to the excellence of British shipbuilding during the second half of the nineteenth century.

By the early 1870s, the composite-built clipper was giving way to the iron clipper, the introduction of an anti-fouling composition for bottom painting having overcome shipowners' opposition to a building material which attracted more marine growth than wood. The first tea clipper of wholly iron construction was the *Lord of the Isles*, built by Scott of Greenock, and notwithstanding the longevity of the composite-built *Sobraon*, mentioned above, the iron clipper hull was undoubtedly stronger and more durable than the composite. Half way through the twentieth century, there were many iron clipper hulls still trading vigorously, shorn, alas, of masts and sails and fitted with engines instead.

It is not easy to estimate the effect of the opening of the Suez Canal on the decline of the sail trading ship, for the steam-driven passenger and cargo ships were at that time already proving their reliability and regularity, and were fast becoming an automatic choice for enterprising shipping companies anxious to increase their profits. Up to 1870, the clipper was a certain money-spinner, mainly because the marine steam engine was still in the early stages of its development, and the compound engine had not yet made its appearance on the oceans. The profits which a good clipper could make were enormous: Donald Mackay's *Staghound* not only repaid her entire building cost in her first year's trading, from New York to San Francisco, Canton

Trade', as the China run was known to seamen, for in 1869 the Suez Canal was opened and the steamships took over. With a much shorter route through the canal and more regular sailings, they could well afford to undercut the sailing ships, bringing tea to London in less than half the time taken by a clipper.

Yet as the tea trade ceased to be viable for the clippers, another trade presented itself. This was the wool trade from Australia, which involved an outward passage round the Cape of Good Hope and a homeward passage round Cape Horn, to take advantage of the prevailing westerly winds on both legs. The wool trade lasted until about the end of the century, though with returns steadily diminishing as, once again, the steamship companies stepped in and undercut the clipper rates. That it remained profitable for sailing ships as long as it did is attributable to the difficulty for a steamer of carrying enough coal and back, but showed a profit of over $80,000 over and above that. Similarly, the *Sovereign of the Seas* earned more than $84,000 in freight rates on her maiden voyage, and the average earnings of a single clipper voyage from New York to San Francisco during the gold rush were estimated at $78,000. The Suez Canal was opened to traffic in 1869 and, as has been seen, almost at once took the China tea trade out of the clipper's hands. But the Canal made little difference to the Australian trade, and it was simply the development of the steamship herself over the next twenty years which was to take that trade, too, away from the sailing ships. By 1880, steamships were making the London–Sydney run in around 50 days, compared with about 65 for the fastest of the sailing vessels.

Some figures of the period show that in 1868, the year before the canal was opened, world tonnage of sailing ships was 4,691,820; that of steamships was 824,614. In 1873, four years after the opening of the canal, sail tonnage had dropped to 4,067,564, while that of steam had more than doubled to 1,680,950. Within ten years, steam tonnage had overtaken that of sail, due to the development, first, of the compound, and then of the triple-expansion steam engine.

In the natural course of ship development, steel took over from iron as the prime shipbuilding material from about 1885 onwards, and this applied to sailing ship construction just as much as to steamships. The higher tensile strength of steel enabled shipbuilders to build larger, and so to introduce the final stage of the development of the sailing ship and the epitome of grace and power – the big four- and five-masted barques and schooners with which the age of commercial sail came to an end. Steel was used for more than just the hull: masts and yards were also made of steel, saving much weight aloft, and wire rope replaced the cordage of the standing rigging, saving yet more weight and reducing windage.

There were still some profits to be made by sailing ships. It is recorded, for example, that in the late autumn of 1891, there were 77 big sailing ships loading wool in Sydney Harbour for the London wool sales which were held in the first three months of every year. They carried immense cargoes, for screwjacks were used to compress the bales into the holds until the ship was almost bursting at the seams. The medium-sized clipper *Mermerus* once screwed 10,000 bales worth £132,000 into her holds, and in 1894 the smaller *Cutty Sark*, loading at Brisbane, carried 5,304 bales screwed home until the wool was almost solid.

Another good trade was wheat, barley and corn from the west coast of Canada and the United States to European ports – a long passage around Cape Horn. In 1882 one and a quarter million tons of wheat and barley were shipped in 550 sailing vessels from California and Oregon alone. This, too, lasted until about the turn of the century, before the steamship took over.

There was one other profitable trade remaining open: coal and manufactured goods round Cape Horn to the south Pacific coast of South America, and hides, nitrates and guano from there back to Europe. No steamship owner could even consider the Cape Horn run yet, mainly because of the lack of coaling stations along this long and distant route, but partly also because they lacked the flexibility and steadying influence of sail in the tumultuous seas that prevailed in those waters. While it lasted, it was a good trade for the big sailing ships, but some of the smaller ones, though Cape Horn weather held no fears for them, found cargoes progressively more difficult to obtain. This was because, being about the only employment now left for sailing vessels, the trade attracted almost every sailing ship available, and most shippers preferred to use the ship with the largest capacity.

Whereas the clipper had made her fortune by her speed, accepting a diminished cargo capacity because of the fine lines of her hull, the new generation of sail trading ship, always faced with

Above: Hands reefing sails aboard the *Garthsnaid*. Another reason for the decline of the big sailing ship was the number of men needed to man her.

Right: The five-masted barque *France II* was built in 1911, the largest sail merchantman ever.

growing competition from steam, had to shift the emphasis from speed to capacity, and so had to adopt the more or less square cross-section of the steamship in order to provide the large square holds in which a maximum of cargo could be stowed. This sometimes made them a bit slab-sided. Gone were the graceful lines of the clipper hull, but the beauty of the barque and schooner rig made up, to some extent, for the ugliness of the hull. However, not all this last generation of sailing ships were ugly in their hull design: some builders managed to combine the large holds and a beautiful hull, but there were many more built like elongated boxes with a raked bow and counter stern tacked on at either end.

These last trade sailing ships were much bigger than the clippers which preceded them. Two thousand five hundred tons was big for a clipper, the great majority being considerably smaller, but if the new sailing ships were to be able to earn their keep in competition with steamers, they needed to carry very much larger cargoes. In 1890, Henderson of Glasgow built the *France*, a five-masted steel barque, for the A. D. Bordes Line, with a deadweight tonnage of 5,900 (3,784 tons gross). At that time she was the largest trade sailing ship ever built, and also one

of the fastest, once returning from Chile round Cape Horn to France with a cargo of nitrates in 63 days. In March 1901 she was struck by a pampero off South America, took on a list of 45 degrees as a result of her cargo shifting, and sprang a serious leak. She staggered on for two months, but in the end had to be abandoned, her crew being rescued by a German barque.

Even larger was her successor, *France II*, built in 1911 by Chantiers de la Gironde, Bordeaux, for the Société des Navires Mixtres. A five-masted barque, she had a deadweight tonnage of 8,000, and was the largest sail trading vessel ever built, just exceeding in size the German *Preussen*, which had been built nine years earlier. She, too, came to a sad end, drifting in July 1922 onto a coral reef in the Pacific near Noumea because of lack of wind. Although it would have been possible to salvage and refit her, the depressed state of the freight market made it an unprofitable proposition and her hull was sold for £2,000 for breaking up. The days of the sail trader were fast coming to an end.

Two events hastened this end. The first came in 1897 when Lloyd's, the world centre for shipping insurance, introduced a big increase in insurance rates for sail tonnage. Some owners,

Preussen
(1902)

Length 438 ft (134·5 m) *Waterline* 407 ft (124 m)
Beam 54 ft (16·5 m) *Registered tonnage* 5,081
Sail area 54,000 sq ft (5,000 m²)
Cargo capacity 8,000 tons

The *Preussen* was the largest full-rigged ship ever built and the only one ever to have five masts. These, like her hull, were made of steel. There were two steam engines on deck providing power for winches, pumps, anchor handling, etc. She was built for the nitrate trade and once made a run of 370 miles (595·5 km) in 24 hours (an average speed of $15\frac{1}{2}$ knots). In October 1910 she was run down by a Newhaven-Dieppe steamer, who underestimated her speed, and went ashore on the Kent coast.

The diagram below shows two of the brace winches, situated behind the mast, which swung the three lowest yards simultaneously when the ship tacked or altered course. (Only the port side braces are shown.)

unable to pay the new rates and still make a profit in a declining freight market, sold some of their ships; others tried to economize on running costs by undermanning, or by taking apprentices on board in place of paid crew. This racket began to give these hips a bad name, for there were some captains who did nothing to teach their apprentices the seaman's trade, but used them purely as unpaid ordinary seamen.

The second event to hasten the end was the opening of the Panama Canal in 1914. Just as the opening of the Suez Canal in 1869 had taken the China tea trade out of the hands of the clippers and given it to the steamships, so the opening of the Panama Canal did the same to the South American nitrate trade, the last stronghold of sail. Some other cargoes were still available to the sailing ships, non-perishable bulk cargoes such

as steel rails, timber, coal and grain, but they were growing progressively fewer and less remunerative for sailing ships, as the numbers of steamships continued to mount. There were far too many sailing ships competing for a dwindling share of the market, and many owners were forced to pay off their crews, strip their ships down to the last gantline, and leave them where they lay. Many harbours of the world had a collection of sailing ship hulls, left by their owners to decay.

But the steam come up and the sail went down,
And them tall ships of high renown,
Was scrapped, or wrecked, or sold away.

A few owners, still in love with their graceful ships, tried to sail against the tide, by tramping. By taking cadets, who paid a premium to the

Above: Despite fierce competition a large number of sailing ships survived into the twentieth century. This is Port Blakely, Washington, in 1905.

Above right: The deck of the *Passat*, one of the famous 'Flying P' Line.

Right: The *Pamir*, which sank during a hurricane in the Atlantic in September 1957, with a loss of 80 lives.

owners to learn the seaman's trade, and the occasional enthusiast, who would even pay for the privilege of working a passage in a tall ship, they just about covered the costs of a voyage, or even made a small profit. But all the time freight rates were being undermined by the ubiquitous steamship, and as the years went by the going got harder.

The last British windjammer in active commission was the four-masted barque *Garthpool*, built in 1891 as the *Juteopolis* by W. B. Thompson of Dundee. She was bought in 1912 by Sir William Garthwaite, who ran her until 1928 in the Australian grain trade. He felt a deep love for the old, square-rigged ships of the last days of sail, and it was more through sentiment than the profit motive that he kept her running. When she was wrecked on Ponta Reef, in the Cape Verde Islands, in November 1929, it was the end of Britain's participation in commercial sail.

There were one or two others who kept it going. In Germany, Ferdinand Laeisz of Hamburg, who in the 1870s founded the famous 'Flying P' line of sail trading ships, kept his flag flying until the outbreak of World War II, though with a greatly depleted fleet. His ships, *Preussen*, *Penang*, *Pamir*, *Passat*, *Potosi*, *Pommern*, *Padua*, *Priwall* and others, were among the queens of commercial sail during the last forty years of its existence. In the eyes of many people, the *Potosi* was the finest sailing vessel in the world. She was built in 1895, a five-masted barque big enough to carry 6,000 tons of cargo in her holds, and she was one of the fastest sailing ships engaged in the nitrate trade and never made a bad passage. The biggest ship of the Flying P line was the *Preussen*, built in 1902, with an overall length of 407 ft (124 m) and beam of 54 ft (16·5 m). With a registered tonnage of 5,081 tons, she had room in her holds for just on 8,000 tons of cargo. She was remarkable for being square-rigged on all of her five masts – the only ship in the world ever to carry such a rig. Under full sail she spread 54,000 sq ft (5,000 m²) of canvas.

Another owner who kept his flag flying on sailing ships to the end was Captain Gustaf Erikson, of Mariehamn, Finland. His connection with the sea started when he was a boy serving on a North Sea timber barque at the age of nine, was a sea-cook at thirteen, then able seaman, bosun, and finally mate of a timber ship at the age of eighteen. After two years as a captain (aged nineteen), he decided that the North Sea and Baltic runs were not for him and went deep sea, as mate of big square-riggers for five years and as master for eleven, his final command being the Finnish 1,753-ton barque *Lochee*. He then came ashore to become an owner and began to build up a fleet. Perhaps the best-known of his many ships was the lovely *Herzogin Cecilie*, a four-masted barque of 3,111 gross tons built in 1902, tragically lost in 1936 when she went ashore on Bolt Head, Devon.

Today, sailing ships still exist as training vessels, and many maritime countries have one or two in commission to give their young people a taste of the seafaring life. Others have been taken in hand as permanent memorials of the last and greatest days of the sail trading ships, so that men and women can still see and wonder at the beauty that has had its day.

The demise of the great sail traders coincided with the end of two other, very different, types of sailing vessel. One of these was the Banks schooner, a type of small schooner evolved purely for line fishing for cod on the Grand Banks off Newfoundland. They were built almost entirely in the fishing ports along the Massachussetts coast, particularly at Gloucester, which became the headquarters of the cod fishing industry in the United States. The type was originally based on the Baltimore clipper, and was inaugurated in 1847 with the small schooner *Romp*, built with a clipper bow and overhanging counter

Above: J-class yachts racing between the two World Wars.

Above left: The beautiful four-masted barque *Herzogin Cecilie*, which ran aground on the Devon coast in 1936.

Left: The fishing schooner *Elsie*, racing in 1921. Like the clippers, these Banks schooners needed speed to get the best price for their catch, and they were among the best-looking of all sailing craft.

stern. But, as in other occupations, speed was at a premium, for the first vessels home with the catch commanded the best prices in the fish markets. The 'plumb stern' schooner, setting two jibs, a staysail and jackyard topsails above the foresail and mainsail was the next development, but in 1910 Thomas McManus, the best known of all the fishing schooner designers, launched the 98-ton schooner *Elsie*, which was hailed as one of the most beautiful small vessels ever to sail the seas. She had the rounded bow and long, sloping entry of the modern yacht, ending in a long keel drawing more water aft than forward. Her length-to-beam ratio of just over 4 to 1, allied to a hull shape with its maximum beam forward of the mainmast, was indicative of speed and power, and with jackyard topsails and a main topmast staysail set above the conventional gaff schooner rig, she was very quick through the water. These Gloucester-built Banks schooners were the ultimate sail fishing vessels, with beautiful yacht-like lines, complemented by a powerful, balanced sail plan. When they, in their turn, were overtaken by technological progress – not so much by steam in this case as by the internal combustion engine – some of the loveliest of all small working sailing ships vanished from the oceans.

The other type of sailing vessel which succumbed at about the same time was the victim not of steam or the internal combustion engine, but of excessive specialization. Big racing yachts had a well-established place in history running back to the early years of the nineteenth century, but the visit of the schooner *America* of 170 tons measurement from the United States to sail in English regattas in 1851 gave the sport a great fillip in Britain. In a race at Cowes sailed on 22 August of that year, she finished first out of a fleet of fifteen yachts to win the 'one hundred guinea cup' presented by the Royal Yacht Squadron, later to become an international challenge trophy as the America's Cup, and it was these races that stimulated competition among yacht designers to produce huge racing machines which could move faster through the water than any of their contemporaries. It would not be correct to lay the blame for this extreme development wholly on the America's Cup races, for the national competition between individual owners was also intense, but the effect of the glamour and publicity which surrounded the periodic races for the America's Cup certainly did work back to the drawing boards of the great designers and spur them on to greater lengths in the search for speed.

The final developments of this international competition for speed in big racing yachts were the J-class yachts of the 1920s and 1930s, each one being more extreme in design than her predecessors. They were all, of course, the toys of extremely rich men, but they nevertheless set an unhealthy trend in the yacht design world that did no service to yachting as a whole. It was forgotten that a yacht, even a racing yacht, is basically a small ship, and needs to have some of the sturdy seaworthiness that characterises a ship. Of these ultimate in racing yachts, with their slim hulls and immensely tall masts, it used to be said, perhaps rather unkindly, that before turning in for the night owners would set a lighted candle on the main boom, and that if it was still burning in the morning they would agree that there was not enough wind for racing, and, that if it had gone out, that there was too much wind to race. This may be an exaggeration, but they were always essentially light-weather craft and could not stand up to winds of force 5 and above. They ceased to exist as a racing class in 1936, though some of them were converted into useful cruising yachts, with their extreme rig cut down to a handier size. By that time the rising costs of construction, maintenance, professional crews and endless new ideas in equipment intended to give them another fraction of speed, had combined to price them out even of the very exclusive market they had hitherto catered for.

211

The Dreadnought Battleships

By the opening year of the twentieth century the battleship had evolved into a more or less stereotyped form that was common to all navies – a steel ship of around 17,000 tons, mounting four big guns (usually of about 12-in (300-mm) calibre) in two turrets, and up to forty smaller guns, ranging from about 9-in (230-mm) to small quick-firing 3-pounders, protected along her sides and around her turrets by about 12 in (300 mm) of case-hardened steel, and propelled by two triple-expansion engines which produced a maximum speed of 18 to 19 knots. There were, of course, local variations, but these figures are a fair approximation for the average battleship. They were known generically as 'mixed-armament' ships, because of the variety of gun sizes they mounted.

With so little difference in gunpower, speed and armour protection between the battleships of the various maritime nations, sea power depended largely upon numbers, and the country which had the most could be said to dominate the oceans. In 1900 this happy condition was enjoyed by Great Britain, whose policy was to maintain a 'two-power standard' of naval strength (i.e. her navy was equal in numbers to the combined fleets of any two other nations). Britain had good reason for wanting a navy of such proportions, for she had dominions and colonies all over the world, and the British empire depended for its survival on command of the sea routes which linked them together. In this situation she was fortunate in having a shipbuilding

capacity unexcelled throughout the world, being able to build better and faster than any other country, and well able to maintain her lead in numbers over all other navies.

In the early years of the new century the serene calm of British naval supremacy was ruffled by a chill breeze, which was to be felt all round the world. It began with an article in the 1903 edition of Jane's *Fighting Ships*, by Vittorio Cuniberti, the foremost Italian warship designer of the day. Under the title 'An Ideal Battleship for the British Navy', he outlined a design for a battle-ship of about 17,000 tons, carrying twelve 12-inch guns, protected by 12-in (300 mm) armour, and capable of steaming at 24 knots. The basis of his argument for such a radical departure in battleship design was that her twelve 12-inch guns could bring a devastating volume of fire into action at long range.

The one great disadvantage – more so in the case of the British navy than any other – was that the introduction of this powerful new battleship design would make all the mixed-armament battleships in the world obsolete. British naval supremacy, which was based on numbers, would be removed at a stroke, and she would have to start rebuilding her battle fleet from scratch, on a par with other countries.

Yet, even before Cuniberti's article, Britain was already beginning to move towards this new conception of battle-ship design, though with different reasoning. In 1903 the fighting range of battleships was still only 3,000 yards

(2,750 m), though Admiral Sir John Fisher, when Commander-in-Chief in the Mediterranean, had experimented with much longer ranges. Improvements in gun control were coming in, and Fisher's experiments were suggesting that the battleship's fighting range should be more like 6,000 yards (5,500 m) than 3,000, and even that a good proportion of hits could be achieved at 8,000 yards (7,300 m).

At this range, the only reasonable method of achieving accurate gun control was by firing salvoes, and, since it was impossible to distinguish between the splashes made by 12-inch and 9·2-inch shells, corrections to range and direction were made for the salvo as a whole. If some of the shells fell short and some fell beyond the target, it was likely that at least one would hit it. But if all the guns were of the same calibre, the likelihood of one shell hitting the target was increased, and exactly the same corrections to the elevation of the gun would apply to all.

Thus, for its own reasons, the British navy was coming round to Cuniberti's point of view.

In 1904 Fisher, one of whose major preoccupations was gunnery efficiency at long ranges, was appointed to the Admiralty as First Sea Lord, and thus principal naval adviser to the government. He had made up his mind that the new type of battleship was essential if Britain was to retain her naval supremacy, simply because other navies would build them if Britain did not. If Britain were to get in first, her proven shipbuilding capacity would ensure victory in any numerical race that might follow.

Fisher wasted no time, and the keel of H.M.S. *Dreadnought* was laid at Portsmouth dockyard on 2 October 1905. She was launched just four months later, on 10 February 1906, and was ready for trials on 3 October 1906. She joined the fleet in December of that year. She had ten 12-inch guns in five turrets, 12-in (305 mm) armour, a displacement of 17,250 tons (17,527 tonnes), and a speed of 21 knots.

She was greeted with a chorus of abuse, from naval officers, designers and publicists who were advocates of the mixed-armament ship and could not conceive of a naval battle fought at a range of more than 3,000 yards (2,750 m). They were also aghast at her price, £1,783,883, even though it was not much more than her mixed-armament predecessor, the *Lord Nelson*, still not completed, would cost. It was not until a paper was published in the United States, written by Lieutenant-Commander W. S. Sims (later Admiral Sims), drawing attention to the overwhelming advantages which a fleet of *Dreadnoughts* would enjoy over a fleet of mixed-armament ships, particularly in the concentration of heavy fire against an enemy battle line, that criticism of the *Dreadnought* in Britain finally died away.

Fisher's gamble paid off. Because the *Dreadnought* was built in great secrecy and record time, it was not until she made her public appearance when she joined the British fleet that the rest of the world's navies knew what they were up against. In appearance, she was awe-inspiring, with an impression of uncompromising efficiency and colossal power, overshadowing every other battleship afloat. All other navies had to stop their battleship building programmes and take stock of this new phenomenon. For Germany, already emerging as the principal challenger to British naval supremacy, it was a particularly severe blow. She had already embarked upon building a series of 'Deutschland' class battleships, 18-knot mixed-armament ships of 13,400 tons (13,615 tonnes), but it would be obvious folly to complete them, in view of the British *Dreadnought*. But to build large enough to carry an armament comparable to *Dreadnought's* meant enlarging the Kiel Canal, only recently completed, but unable to take ships above 16,000 tons. It also meant enlarging their naval dockyards and rebuilding their dry-docks.

While Germany and the other maritime nations pondered the problems, Britain went ahead with her building programme, and so kept herself well ahead of the competition.

H.M.S. *Dreadnought* marked the beginning of a worldwide revolution in naval design and building. Fisher was cock-a-hoop at the stroke which he had dealt to the rest of the naval world. In a official paper which he prepared for the Admiralty he proclaimed 'We shall have ten "Dreadnoughts" at sea before a single foreign "Dreadnought" is launched.' And his paper was headed:

New Name for the Dreadnought: 'The Hard-Boiled Egg' Why? Because she can't be beaten.

Far left: The launch of the *Dreadnought* at Portsmouth in February 1906.

Left: Stern view of the *Dreadnought*.

Chapter Ten
Big is Beautiful

During the early years of the twentieth century there was a great revolution in marine engineering caused by the introduction of the steam turbine, demonstrated so dramatically by Charles Parsons at the Spithead Naval Review of 1897. It had so many advantages over the reciprocating steam engine – a considerable saving of space and weight, greater efficiency, less maintenance, virtually no vibration when running – that it received general acceptance remarkably quickly for such a radical invention.

The turbine was first used on British destroyers, but its usefulness was by no means restricted to naval ships, and merchant shipowners were quick to grasp its advantages for commercial purposes. As early as 1904 the Cunard Line ordered two new passenger ships, with a gross tonnage of 38,000 each, to be powered by four steam turbines, driving four propellers and producing a total of 70,000 horsepower. The ships were the *Mauretania* and *Lusitania*, both launched in 1906. On her maiden voyage the *Mauretania* crossed the Atlantic at an average speed of 27·4 knots, beating the previous record set up in 1897 by the *Kaiser Wilhelm der Grosse*.

The *Mauretania* was, perhaps, the most successful transatlantic liner ever built, and a favourite with passengers for over thirty years. With an overall length of 790 ft (240·8 m), a maximum beam of 88 ft (26·8 m), and drawing 36·2 ft (11 m) of water, on seven decks she could accommodate 560 first-class passengers, 475 second, and 1,300 third, all in reasonable

Left: The *Mauretania* and her sister *Lusitania* were the first liners to use the Parsons turbine. The former is shown here with the *Turbinia* alongside.
Below: The *Mauretania*'s dining saloon.

comfort, and the 560 in the first class in extreme luxury. Fifteen transverse bulkheads divided her into 175 watertight compartments, giving her a wide safety margin should she be holed.

The comfort and luxury of the passenger accommodation was one of the major attractions of ocean travel, and they reached a peak on the great liners of this period. The first was the *Oceanic* in 1871, which had an extra deck built above the upper deck to provide lounges across the whole width of the ship. The *City of Paris* and *City of New York* of 1880 had gone a bit further in this direction, and also proved especially popular because their twin screw installation provided a smoother passage. Now the *Mauretania* improved on the *City of Paris* and *City of New York* by having two passenger decks above the upper deck, providing space for more and bigger passenger lounges and larger cabins and staterooms, with scuttles and port-holes open to the outside air. In addition to the luxury of staterooms and lounges, the *chefs de cuisine* produced meals equal to those served in the world's finest hotels, and there was a small army of stewards and stewardesses to look after the comfort of the passengers. Every big liner had an orchestra to provide music during meals and for dancing. There was almost no limit to the luxury and, it seemed, no limit to the number of passengers who, wishing to cross the oceans, were prepared to pay a substantial premium to do so in style. It was the start of a golden age of ocean travel and the beginning of tourism, though as yet it was restricted to the very wealthy, who were ready and indeed eager to travel, regardless of the cost.

This valuable trade attracted shipowners of many countries, and almost every nation with a tradition of maritime trade had at least one, and often several, major steamship lines, operating across the Atlantic and other oceans of the world. Those who wanted a major share of this business had to have at least one of these palatial liners, if they were to stand a chance in the competition for the cream of the traffic. The design of the big ocean liner was now becoming more or less standard, and she was a ship with at least two passenger decks above the upper deck, a cabin and steerage capacity of around 2,500 to 3,000 passengers, turbine propulsion to eliminate the vibration associated with the reciprocating engine, and a speed of more than 25 knots. This meant a ship of about 40,000 tons to provide the passenger accommodation, and an installation of four turbines geared to four propellers, in order to drive a ship of this tonnage fast enough to attract the high fares (in the first class) required to cover overheads. To run a ship of this sort on a regular

schedule required a very large crew on deck, in the engine and boiler rooms, in the kitchens, and in the cabins and lounges, and it required also a large and efficient back-up organization of dockworkers, office staff, and a miscellany of officials to ensure a rapid turn-round at the ship's terminal ports. All this, in a way, was an extension of the ship herself, the means by which she could justify her existence and the faith of her owners in putting up the money to cover the costs of building and fitting-out. In the *Mauretania*, for example, the shipboard crew totalled 812.

What was true of the Atlantic was as true of the other oceans, and there were similar, though usually slightly smaller, liners operating regular services to India, China, Australia, South Africa, South America, and across the Pacific from the west coast of Canada and the United States. They were just as luxuriously fitted to attract the passengers who could afford to pay for comfort, and, in fact, the major steamship line serving India and China, P & O, charged a premium on the already high fare to those who wanted a cabin or stateroom on the shady side of the ship while crossing the Indian Ocean. The glare of the sun on the water was something to be avoided if possible, and a cabin on the port side of the ship on the outward voyage and the starboard side on the homeward voyage avoided the worst of it. Those passengers who could afford to pay a bit extra for this particular comfort had the letters 'POSH' (Port Outwards Starboard Homewards) printed on their tickets, adding a new word to the English language.

These great liners, wherever they operated, were the queens of the ocean passenger trade, majestic ships designed to carry very large numbers of passengers across the oceans, at great speeds and in a maximum of comfort. Resplendent in their company livery, they sailed proudly across the seas – moving symbols of grace and power. It was to the invention of the turbine that they owed their ever-increasing size, for, with the four big German liners of the *Kaiser Wilhelm der Grosse* class, the steam reciprocating engine had reached its ultimate development. Each of these four liners had two immense quadruple-expansion engines, standing 40 ft (12 m) high, each with eight cylinders, two for each stage of expansion. An impression of their immense size can be gained from the fact that each low-pressure cylinder was no less than 9 ft 4 in (2·85 m) in diameter. They were the largest marine reciprocating engines ever built, and to accommodate their huge bulk and weight in the

Right: The launch of the *Lusitania*. Her sinking in 1915 has been hotly debated ever since.

Below right: The liner *Olympic* was much luckier than her sister *Titanic* and survived until 1936. The White Star Line emphasized comfort rather than speed in its ships.

ships' engine rooms created many problems of design. The total output of each pair of engines was 42,500 horsepower, sufficient to drive these 20,000-tonners at 22 knots. That was in 1897; but only ten years later the biggest liners had added nearly another 20,000 tons to their gross tonnage and 5 or 6 knots to their speed, needing another 30,000 or so horsepower; and no reciprocating engine which could produce that range of power would fit inside an acceptably sized engine room of a ship. In some of the big liners, designed before the turbine had fully proved itself, but still on the stocks when it was generally accepted, a compromise had been reached: the existing big triple-expansion engines drove the outer propellers and turbines drove the inner ones, or in some cases there was a single turbine driving an additional centreline propeller. This was the machinery layout in the two new White Star Atlantic liners *Olympic* and *Titanic*. They had been designed originally as 21-knot ships with two reciprocating engines only, but a central turbine had been added while they were still on the stocks.

In one respect, all these great liners were very much less than perfect. Most maritime nations exercised control over their national shipping through the provisions of a Merchant Shipping Act, or its equivalent, which laid down certain conditions, concerning safe levels of loading, etc., with which their ships had to comply before being given a certificate allowing them to operate. One of the provisions of the British Merchant Shipping Act – and those of other countries were similar – was that ships of over 10,000 tons had to carry a minimum of sixteen lifeboats on davits. As the largest ship's lifeboat could accommodate about sixty-five passengers, the total capacity of the life-saving equipment of a big liner was somewhere around 1,000, while she probably carried on board a total of some 3,000 or more passengers and crew. It was to take a great disaster to get the safety regulations tightened up.

This came in 1912. In 1907 the White Star Line decided to build two new ships for the Atlantic trade, to be followed by a third if the first two proved profitable. They were to be the biggest ships yet built, with an overall length of $852\frac{1}{2}$ ft (259·8 m) and a beam of $92\frac{1}{2}$ ft (28·2 m), giving them a gross tonnage of 46,328 tons. In accordance with White Star policy of sparing no expense in the building and fitting out of their liners, these ships were to be the epitome of comfort and elegance. White Star had never competed with other transatlantic steamship lines in the quest for speed, placing the comfort of their passengers first, and 21 knots had been put down as the specification for the service speed required. The addition, during building, of a centreline turbine undoubtedly gave them a speed well in excess of 21 knots if required, but these ships were not built with an eye on breaking records across the Atlantic. Like her sister ship the *Olympic*, the *Titanic* was built with three passenger decks above the upper deck and seven decks in all. Below the upper deck there was a transverse watertight bulkhead approximately every 60 ft (18 m) along her length.

The *Titanic* sailed on her maiden voyage from Queenstown, Ireland, for New York on 10 April 1912 amid a great fanfare of praise and excitement ov   the world's newest and largest ship and, as suc   , an example and advertisement of British shipbuilding skills. There was speculation when she sailed as to whether she would be trying to make a record crossing, and later, indeed, a belief that she was trying to do so, when it was revealed that she had been taking an extreme northerly course, as near as possible to a great circle, and therefore the shortest route between Britain and the United States. But, in fact, she maintained a steady speed of about 22 knots throughout her passage. Fortunately, cabins were not filled to capacity: she had on board 1,318 passengers, out of a total capacity of 2,435, and a crew numbering 885.

Shortly before midnight on her fourth day out, in the vicinity of the Grand Banks off the Newfoundland coast, she struck an iceberg which tore a hole 300 ft (90 m) long in her starboard side some 30 ft (9 m) below the water-line. Just over two and a half hours later she sank, leaving 916 passengers and 673 of the crew to die in the icy water. The results of the disaster were far-reaching, the most important being that new regulations were enacted requiring ships to carry sufficient lifeboats to accommodate everyone carried on board. Other effects were the institution of a more southerly track for liners crossing the Atlantic, and an ice patrol which continues to this day.

This tightening up of lifesaving requirements for all ships was, of course, long overdue, but the original requirements had been framed with a view to improving the structural design of large ships. Because the average-sized freighter of the times was of necessity built with large cargo holds and, as a result, could not be split up internally into a large number of watertight compartments, the lifesaving regulations required her to carry enough lifeboats on each side of the ship to accommodate the entire crew – in other words, twice the capacity to embark everyone on board. The less stringent regulations for passenger liners were designed to encourage owners to build additional watertight bulkheads into their big ships, on the argument that if they were made virtually unsinkable, large numbers of lifeboats would never be needed. It was certainly an odd way of encouraging improvements in the structural design of ships, and it took a disaster on the scale of the *Titanic* to show that this was not the right way of achieving the best and safest in ship design.

Beneath the exalted level of the big prestige liners, there existed an enormous variety of smaller commercial ships. The massive emigration movement of the second half of the nineteenth

Above: The *Titanic* suffered terrible damage when she collided with an iceberg on her maiden voyage. Despite rumours to the contrary, her design ensured that she sank slowly and on an even keel. This kept the loss of life lower than it might have been.

Right: The Hamburg-Amerika Line's *Cleveland* was one of the first cargo-liners, carrying a mixture of luxury passengers, emigrants and refrigerated cargo.

century was still in progress and, if anything, more extensive than ever, as the masses of underprivileged in Europe struggled towards a new life in the wide-open spaces. As a still very profitable trade, it attracted some shipowners who built one-class ships specifically for emigrants but with space in their holds for a substantial cargo in addition. Examples of these special emigrant ships were the 4,900-ton *Gerania*, built specially for the Austria-United States run with a cargo capacity of 8,000 tons and space for 1,000 emigrants, and the 8,000-ton *Ancona*, built for the Italian emigrant trade, able to carry 8,200 tons of cargo and 2,500 emigrants. Germany, though she did build ships expressly for the emigrant trade, did not exclude passengers of other classes as well, those travelling in the steerage being kept more or less out of view of those who paid higher fares. A ship of this nature was the Hamburg-Amerika Line's 17,000-ton *Cleveland*, which was built with accommodation for 250 first-class passengers, 392 second-class, 494 third-class, and steerage space for 2,064 emigrants.

These were the good ships, with a good standard of accommodation and safety, but unhappily there were others, old ships which had had their day, but had been bought cheaply and patched up to operate for a few more years. Into these ships men, women and children were packed like animals and carried to their dream world overseas in conditions of utter squalor. It was still a period of social irresponsibility whenever there were quick profits to be made, and few national shipping authorities bothered

to inquire too deeply into the seamier side of the emigrant traffic. Perhaps fortunately, in this age of marine steam propulsion, voyages did not take long to complete, and even in the worst emigrant ships the state of destitution on board was, in many cases, no worse than the destitution these people had left behind them in their homes. It was to take a world war to eliminate these undesirable and worn-out ships, partly because during the war years they rusted away or were broken up, partly because after the war, when emigration was again in full spate, new worldwide regulations were in force, laying down minimum standards of safety and accommodation.

During the first twenty years of the twentieth century the great trade expansion, generated by the industrial revolution of the nineteenth, continued, and the world tonnage of merchant shipping grew in proportion. Ignoring all warships and ships of less than 100 tons gross, the registration figures for 1900 amounted to a worldwide total of 29,093,728 tons; ten years later it had grown to 41,914,765 tons, an increase of close on seventy per cent. A breakdown of these figures by nationality of ownership showed that in 1910 forty-five per cent of the world tonnage was registered in Great Britain, twelve per cent in the United States, ten per cent in Germany, with smaller proportions owned by Norway, France, Italy, Japan, Holland, Sweden, Russia, Austria, Spain and Denmark, in that order.

It was during the first decade of the twentieth century that the movement towards designing ships specially for a particular trade accelerated. The first ship built specifically to carry oil in bulk was the S.S. *Gluckauf*, built in Britain in 1886; a ship fully refrigerated to carry frozen meat began to operate in 1870. As world trade expanded, so bigger cargoes, particularly of food and raw materials, were needed, and shipowners quickly realised that a bigger bulk cargo of any one given commodity could be stowed in a ship specially designed for it. Ships were designed and built especially to transport mineral ores (mainly iron and copper), grain, fruit, oil, and indeed any similar cargo suitable for transport in bulk.

As a generalization, it would be correct to say that the normal merchant ship of this period, even one specially designed for a particular trade, was of what was known as the 'three-island' type. Unless she was very small or very big, she would be built with four cargo holds, two forward of the central bridge structure and two aft. The masts were placed between the two forward and between the two after holds, to the heels of which derricks were fixed to load or unload the cargo in each hold. The 'islands' of the three-island freighter were the forecastle deck, the bridge structure and the poop deck, all rising some feet above the upper deck level so that, of a ship hull down on the horizon, the only parts visible were the three islands. About the only notable variations on this design were the big ore and grain ships on the Great Lakes, where the bridge was usually constructed well forward on the forecastle, thus removing the need for the centre island and providing space for additional cargo holds. This design, which would be considered unseaworthy on the open ocean, is acceptable on inland waters, even those as vast as the Great Lakes, and the additional cargo space is an economic bonus.

The American Lake steamers, in waters more placid than the open sea, were remarkable ships during this period, having a length-to-beam ratio of 10 to 1 to accommodate six large holds and a whole series of cargo hatches along the length of the upper deck. They were built with a short forecastle deck to provide quarters for the crew and a deckhouse aft for the officers. Below the deckhouse were the engine room, boiler room and coal bunkers. All the rest of the ship was taken up by holds. A typical Great Lakes ore carrier of the period had an overall length of up to 600 ft (180 m), a maximum beam of 60 ft (18 m), would draw 19 ft (6 m) of water, and have a cargo capacity of 11,000 tons. She was virtually no more than a long rectangular steel box, pointed at bow and stern.

No less interesting in design were the passenger ships on the Great Lakes and on some rivers. A typical example was the *Hendrick Hudson*, built in 1906. On a hull 380 ft (116 m) long, a beam of 45 ft (14 m), and drawing 8 ft (2·4 m) of water, the passenger decks were built out from the hull to the full width of the paddle boxes, 82 ft (25 m), supported beyond the ship's side by steel struts. With five passenger decks above the level of the upper deck, she could carry no less than 5,000 passengers – a phenomenal load for a hull of such modest size. Her feathering paddlewheels, 24 ft (7·3 m) in diameter and 16 ft 6 in (5 m) wide, gave her a speed of 22 knots.

Small passenger ships abounded in all parts of the world, some for short sea passages, more as ferries. Before World War I, road bridges were not considered an essential way of saving time when the water to be crossed was navigable. The world still moved at a relatively slow pace, and a ferry across a river or estuary served well enough to keep the traffic moving. Many of them, particularly at river crossings in the United States, were relatively large ships, carrying up to 2,000 passengers in saloons built out beyond the hull, with the midships part of the main deck reserved for horses and carts or the occasional motor car. Most of them were double-ended with a wheelhouse at each end, a simple enough arrangement with paddle-wheels, when a simple reversal in the direction of rotation would enable the vessel to proceed equally efficiently in the opposite direction, but rather more complicated with screw propulsion. An example of the latter type was the *Guanabacoa,* built by Cammell Laird in Britain for service in Havana Bay. She was 140 ft (42·7 m) long, 38 ft (11·6 m) in beam, with a moulded depth of 13 ft 3 in (4 m) from deck to keel, and had two engines with screw propellers at each end driving the ship at a speed of 11 knots. Saloons along the sides of the vessel gave accommodation for 1,000 passengers, and between them was space for forty carts and horses. She made the passage from Britain to Havana under her own steam and ran successfully there for many years.

Another type of passenger ship, as yet not replaced by the motor car, was the excursion steamer, immensely popular among city dwellers who had few other means of transport for a day out. Typical of such ships was the Thames paddle steamer *Royal Sovereign*, which ran day

Dreadnought
(1906)

Length 526 ft (160 m) *Beam* 82 ft (25 m) *Draught* 26 ft 11 in (8·2 m)
Displacement 17,900 tons (18,187 tonnes) *Speed* 21 knots
Armament ten 12-inch, twenty-four 12-pounders, five Maxims,
five 18-inch torpedo tubes *Complement* 729

The launching of H.M.S. *Dreadnought* made existing battleships obsolete, including those of the British navy, and she immediately became the model for all future battleship development. As well as being the first battleship to have a main armament all of one calibre, she was the first to have steam turbine propulsion, which made her the fastest battleship afloat. She served through World War I, in 1915 ramming and sinking a German submarine in the North Sea. She was sold for scrap in 1920.

She is seen here with her torpedo nets rigged. The diagram gives a section through one of the wing turrets. These could only fire on their own broadside. Later Dreadnoughts often had four turrets on centreline as they were built at different levels.

trips from London to Margate and back. Her length overall was 300 ft (91·4 m), her beam 33 ft (10·1 m), and her draught 6 ft 6 in (2 m), giving her a gross tonnage of 891 tons. She could carry 2,320 passengers at a speed of 21 knots. She was typical of thousands of others, up and down coasts and along the rivers of the world, invariably well patronized by a public ready to pay a modest fare for a day trip on the water.

The first train ferry had appeared before 1900, on Lake Constance, but the majority that were built in the nineteenth century were for services between the Danish mainland and the outlying islands. The early ones had a single railway track along the deck, but, as they began to prove their value, larger ferries with double tracks were built. As the service expanded, still larger train ferries were built to operate between Denmark and Germany, and the *Drottning Victoria*, of 3,050 gross tons, carried trains on two tracks between Trelleborg and Sassnitz, a distance of 65 nautical miles. She had to be specially strengthened in the bows to act simultaneously, at times, as an icebreaker and train ferry.

One of the more difficult orders for a train ferry came from Russia to the firm of Armstrong Whitworth in Britain, for a ferry with four tracks for service on the River Volga. The Volga itself presented great problems, for the difference in water level between spring and summer is as much as 45 ft (14 m), owing to the huge additional volume of water in spring from melting snow. This particular problem was solved by fitting hydraulic hoists in the bows of the train ferry, which could lift the wagons 25 ft (7·6 m) above deck level, and by having the railway lines at the landing places built on two levels. Another problem was the thickness of the ice on the river in winter, rarely less than 2 ft (60 cm), and in some winters as much as 3 ft (0·9 m). This

could only be solved by building two ships – one an icebreaker to precede the ferry up and down the river in winter. But the biggest problem of all was caused by the Marinsky Canal system, through which both ships had to pass to reach the river at all. The locks were not wide enough to allow either ship to pass through, so the icebreaker (147 ft × 37 ft 6 in × 16 ft 6 in) (44·8 × 11·4 × 5 m) was built with an amidships longitudinal bulkhead from bow to stern, and on arrival at the canal system was divided longitudinally into two halves, each of which went through the locks on their own, to be joined up again when they reached the Volga. The train ferry (252 ft × 55 ft 6 in × 14 ft 6 in) (76·8 × 16·9 × 4·4 m) had to be built with a similar longitudinal bulkhead to allow division into two halves, and, in addition, an amidships transverse bulkhead to allow each half to be divided again. She went through the canals a quarter at a time, and was joined up again at the end of her passage to the Volga. Such a thing could never have been done before the days of the iron or steel ship – an example of the great flexibility of the new shipbuilding material.

Steam propulsion also came to small fishing

Top: The Swedish train ferry *Drottning Victoria* was built in 1909, and lasted until the 1970s.

Above: The two halves of the Russian icebreaker *Saratovski Ledokzl* which preceded the train ferry *Saratovskaia Pereprava*. Both were built by Armstrong Whitworth for use on the Volga, and launched in 1895.

Top: The Hull trawler *Asia* on the Dogger Bank in 1912. The sail on the mizen was hoisted to steady her while trawling.

Above: One of the first British submarines *Holland No. 3* in September 1902, with HMS *Victory* in the background.

To take figures for Britain again, there were three petrol-driven lifeboats employed around British coasts in 1910, compared with four steam-driven lifeboats. Of the total of 281 in service, all the remainder relied on oars to reach the scene of disaster.

Only in one type of vessel had the internal combustion engine proved a real break-through: this was the submarine, which needed some alternative form of propulsion on the surface to the battery-driven electric motor used when submerged. This was provided first by the petrol engine and later by the heavy-oil engine, which removed the fire hazard. An electric motor, the only form of propulsion which did not consume valuable oxygen, was essential for underwater use; when used on the surface it ran down the batteries, considerably reducing the submarine's radius of action. The internal combustion engine changed all this. It produced a positive drive on the surface when the conningtower hatch was open and oxygen freely available, thereby conserving the batteries, and it could also be used to drive the electric motors as dynamos and recharge the batteries without recourse to an external power supply. The introduction of the internal combustion engine, particularly in its heavy-oil form, made the submarine into a viable weapon of war.

In the world of warships, development during this period was stimulated largely by national rivalry. In Europe, until about 1898, the main competitors were Great Britain, on the one hand, and France and Russia, on the other, with Italy playing a significant part in the Mediterranean. Every European nation kept a keen eye on the naval developments of the others, particularly in the spheres of gun development and armour protection, and each new move in one of these directions by any of the main naval powers was either copied by the others or the balance was redressed by some compensatory design improvement. Outside Europe, the principal naval powers were the United States and Japan, and while they naturally kept an eye on all European warship developments, the need for them to compete was much less pressing.

In 1898 a new protagonist appeared on the European scene. Until that year Britain's 'two-power standard' of naval strength had been balanced against the combined navies of France and Russia, which were bound together by a treaty of alliance. In 1898 Germany passed the first of her Naval Laws, giving notice to the world that she was entering the naval world by building a modern navy that would, within ten

vessels around this period, both trawlers and drifters. It had started when some enterprising trawler-owners had purchased some old paddle tugs and fitted them out with nets. In spite of their age, they proved remarkably profitable, encouraging other owners to change over entirely to steam fishing, building new vessels with steam engines especially for the purpose. In comparison with the distant water trawlers of today, they were very small craft, averaging about 50 tons net, but, even at that size, very much larger than the fishing boats that still used sail. A British census of fishing vessels held in 1910 found that there were 3,000 steam fishing craft totalling 150,000 tons, compared with 23,000 sail fishing boats with a total tonnage of 200,000.

The internal combustion engine, using either petrol or naptha gas, was beginning to make its appearance on the seas, though as yet in a very small way and in very small vessels. The fire risk inherent in a petrol engine in those early days of development was considerable, and only in very few types of ship, such as small yachts, lifeboats, and occasionally as an auxiliary engine in a big sail trading ship, were they used.

or twelve years, bring her up to the status of the second naval power in Europe. This decision was to start a naval armaments race among the European nations, not only in numbers of warships built, but also in their design and development, each advance in this sphere being calculated to frustrate the naval aspirations of the other nations. The German decision had less effect on the navies of the United States and Japan, as they were still reasonably remote from the European scene, but some ripples from the European arms race did reach them across the oceans. This was particularly true of Japan, when Russian aspirations for naval bases on the eastern coast of Siberia brought her into direct contact with the European power struggle.

The closing years of the nineteenth century and opening years of the twentieth saw a complete change in the whole philosophy of warship design. In the days of the wooden warship, and the iron ship which succeeded her, the objective of the naval architect had been to design a ship of whatever size was required and stuff her as full of guns as was possible in the deck space available. She then fought her battles at a range of about 100 yards (90 m) hoping to succeed by the intensity of her gunfire at almost point-blank range. The development of the gun during the second half of the nineteenth century, particularly in the type of missile fired (explosive shell instead of solid shot), put an end to that conception of battle, and all naval tacticians accepted that future battles at sea would have to be fought at greater ranges — about 1,000 yards (900 m) by 1860, 2,000 (1,800 m) by 1880, 6,000 yards

(5,500 m) by 1900, and up to 18,000 yards (16,500 m) by 1914. In the face of this progress in weaponry, naval architects realised that it was now necessary to design and build the warship around the weapon, rather than adapt the weapon to the ship. And by 1900 the gun was not the only form of armament to be considered; the torpedo and the mine had both been developed by then into significant naval weapons.

As has been noted, the naval big gun at the end of the nineteenth century was of 12-in (305-mm) calibre, but it was mounted in battleships in conjunction with big guns of slightly smaller size — 10-in (254-mm), 9-in (229-mm), and so on — and the basic design of battleships was arranged to accommodate these big guns of different sizes in the best positions for producing the maximum intensity of fire on various bearings — ahead, on the bow, abeam, on the quarter and astern. Admiral Fisher revolutionized battleship design when, at the end of 1906, H.M.S. *Dreadnought* was launched with an all-big-gun armament of ten 12-inch guns and nothing between them and small quick-firing 12-pounders carried as anti-torpedo boat weapons. The *Dreadnought* was designed wholly around her 12-inch guns, primarily to provide a steady gun platform for them at sea, with masts, funnels and bridge structure placed so as to produce the minimum interference with their arcs of fire. Even her turbine propulsion was designed to increase the effectiveness of her armament, by making her fast enough to overhaul other ships and bring them within range of her big guns.

Below: Although Admiral Fisher did little more than provide political backing for the *Dreadnought* his dynamic energy ensured that she was built in only fourteen months, and thereby stole a march on the Royal Navy's rivals.

Bottom: The revolutionary battleship *Dreadnought*. Many of her features were merely extensions of ideas tried in preceding ships, but the adoption of the Parsons turbine was a great improvement.

Development of the naval gun over the next eight years increased calibres, in Britain, from 12 in to 13·5 in (343 mm), and finally to 15 in (381 mm), and in other navies by a similar amount. Battleship design reacted accordingly. The main effect was on tonnage, for as guns and their mountings increased in size they also increased in weight, and so required a bigger and heavier hull to support them. It was realized, too, that the small quick-firing guns with which the *Dreadnought* had been equipped, as an anti-torpedo boat weapon, were no longer big enough to deal with the new destroyers, and so a bigger secondary armament, usually of guns of a calibre around 6 in (150 mm), was now required. The big 15-inch turrets of the later battleships posed further problems for the naval architect, for to get a maximum concentration of all-round fire the turrets needed to be mounted on the ship's centreline, and to provide enough space along the centreline to enable them to be trained across wide arcs on either side of the ship called for very long ships indeed, adding to cost, displacement and engine power needed to maintain speed. This particular problem was solved in the United States with the battleships *Michigan* and *South Carolina* where the forward and after turrets were super-imposed, saving an appreciable amount on the overall length of the ships. This arrangement was quickly followed by other navies, the advantages being considerable, without any loss of efficiency. These two ships, the first American all-big-gun battleships, were, in fact, better designed than the *Dreadnought*, but did not come into service until September 1909.

The development of the locomotive torpedo also had an effect on battleship design. During the thirty-odd years since its introduction, it had developed from a small underwater weapon, with a range of 1,000 yards (900 m) at 7 knots or 300 yards (275 m) at $12\frac{1}{4}$ knots, to a big underwater weapon, with a range of 4,000 yards (3,700 m) at 44 knots or 10,000 yards (9,000 m) at 28 knots. One hit with a torpedo in a vulnerable position could well be lethal to a battleship. Many ways were tried of minimizing the danger from underwater explosions against the hulls of battleships, the first of them being to build ships with their coal bunkers lining the insides of the hull, on the assumption that the coal in the bunkers would be the equivalent of an extra 2 or 3 in (63 mm) of armour plate. A test of this assumption was made in Britain in 1904, when an 18-inch torpedo was fired at the old battleship *Belleisle*. The coal in the bunkers was found to provide no protection, the force of the explosion blowing a 12-ft (3·7-m) hole in the side of the *Belleisle*, bursting the upper deck, and scattering 400 tons of coal all over the ship. The problem was never fully solved, but underwater vulnerability was mitigated by the introduction of longitudinal armoured screens inside the armoured hull plating, by more internal watertight subdivisions, by the provision of an extra 2 or 3 knots of speed to enable the ship to turn away from torpedoes and outrun them, and by the provision of steel anti-torpedo nets rigged round the ship at a distance of a few yards and held in position by booms projecting from the ship's side. This latter precaution, however, was mainly for harbour use.

Below: Had the US Congress been less dilatory, the USS *South Carolina* might have had the same impact as the *Dreadnought*. However she appeared two years later, and did not have turbine propulsion.

Left: Aerial view of HMS *Queen Elizabeth* in 1918. She introduced oil fuel and the 15 inch gun, in one of the most balanced and successful designs ever produced.

Below left: The French 2nd class cruiser *Du Chayla* was built in 1895 for scouting and commerce-raiding.

With the increase in gun size from 12 in (305 m) to 15 in (381 mm), battleship displacement increased from the 18,000 tons of the *Dreadnought* in 1906 to the 28,000 tons of the German *Baden*, laid down in 1913 – an enormous increase in so short a time. Main engine horsepower similarly increased from 23,000 *(Dreadnought)* to 53,000 *(Baden)*, though in the British *Queen Elizabeth* class, laid down a year before the *Baden*, it reached 75,000. The increases in speed were less dramatic, from about 18 knots in 1900 to 24 or 25 knots in 1914 (a reflection of the scientific fact that to raise a vessel's speed by 1 knot requires a very much larger increase in engine power at 20 knots than it does at, say, 10 knots).

Many people, not only in Britain, would agree that probably the ultimate in battleship design and grandeur during this period was the British *Queen Elizabeth* class. They were designed in 1912 by Sir Philip Watts as a new class of fast battleship, and when they made their first appearance at sea in 1915 they stood out by virtue of their majestic appearance and exceptional fighting qualities. The five *Queen Elizabeths* were the first battleships to mount 15-inch guns, the first big ships to be completely oil-fired, and the first to be given the then high battleship speed of 25 knots. Their 15-inch guns could each fire a shell weighing 1,920 lb (860 kg) over a range of 23,400 yards (21 km) at the rate of 2 a minute. Many regarded them when they first went to sea as the most perfect example of the naval constructor's art yet seen afloat, and without any question they were most handsome and powerful fighting ships. Moreover, while their speed meant that they could fulfil the role of the battle-cruiser (fleet reconnaissance to within sight of the enemy battle fleet), they lacked the great drawback of that hybrid warship, and could take their place in the line of battle as fully protected by armour as any other battleship in existence.

The cruiser came next below the battleship in importance, approximating roughly to the fourth-rate ship of the line in sailing navies, battleships), with a wide radius of action and medium-sized guns which packed a good punch. France inaugurated her cruiser programme with armoured ships carrying 7·5-inch guns, unique as cruisers at that time, and continued to develop these powerful ships, both in size and armament. Until 1898 the British had no answer to them, but during that year the new Krupp process of making case-hardened steel made possible the introduction of modest side armour in British cruisers, sufficiently strong to keep out a 6-inch shell. And from this was developed a new generation of big cruisers carrying 9·2-inch guns, all designed to counter the French armoured cruisers on the trade routes.

Apart from reconnaissance before, during, and after battle, the cruiser really had no place in the battle fleet. Yet battle fleets surrounded themselves with them, mainly because they were now carrying such big guns that they were assumed to have real value in battle. So much so, that by about 1910 the biggest armoured cruisers had been renamed 'battle-cruisers', a description that had no basis in fact and was probably responsible for their wide-spread misuse in battle. Apart from her commerce raiding and commerce protection, another role for which the armoured cruiser had been developed – and for which eventually she carried guns of the same calibre as battleships – was to serve as a reconnaissance unit, able by the power of her guns to sweep aside the outlying forces with which a battle fleet screened itself at sea, and by her superior speed escape before she could be brought to action and annihilated by the superior firepower of battleships. In terms of modern naval warfare this was a reasonable enough proposition during the early years of the twentieth century, but the change in generic name from 'armoured cruisers' to 'battle-cruisers' led many admirals to believe that they had a place in the actual line of battle. The battle of Jutland, fought between modern navies in 1916, was tragic proof of the fallacy of this argument.

In all the larger cruisers, it was the gun which was the dominant weapon; in the smaller light cruisers, the gun had to share its pre-eminence with the torpedo, discharged above water from tubes mounted on the upper deck. There was therefore very little difference between this small cruiser and a destroyer, and in many navies flotillas of destroyers were led by a cruiser.

In displacement tonnage, the armoured cruiser grew from the 13,000 tons of the *Duke of Edinburgh* (1906) to the 26,500 tons of the *Renown* (1916), in gun size from the six 9·2-inch guns of the former to the six 15-inch of the latter, and in propulsion from 23,000 horsepower and

Above: Admiral Fisher wholeheartedly supported the 'dreadnought armoured cruiser', later known as the battle-cruiser. He believed that it could replace the battleship but heavy losses in battle showed how wrong this was. HMS *Inflexible* was one of the first of the type.

smaller than the first three rates which were designed to lie in the line of battle, but larger than the frigates. Of all classes of warship, it was this one which was most diverse, ranging from big armoured cruisers carrying a battleship's armament to unarmoured light cruisers that were little more than glorified destroyers. Originally, the cruiser was a class of ship developed for trade protection and for general policing work at sea, largely unarmoured except for the main deck and applicable at first mainly to nations that maintained large overseas empires or depended economically on a large volume of overseas trade. But, particularly in France, where Admiral Aube was preaching a new doctrine of war, backed by an enthusiastic chorus of young naval officers who christened themselves the *'Jeune Ecole'*, it was becoming widely held that wars at sea could be won by the destruction of merchant shipping and the paralysis of a nation's trade, without the need ever to fight a major naval battle. And the best means of destroying commerce was by cruisers (which could be built far more economically than

229

23 knots to 126,000 horsepower and $32\frac{1}{2}$ knots. The light cruiser eventually stabilized at around 4,000 tons, with 6-inch guns and above-water torpedo tubes. A very similar advance was to be seen in destroyer development, with a growth in tonnage from around 350 to 1,000, in speed from 30 to 36 knots, and in armament from the 12-pounder to the 4-inch gun. The destroyer's main armament, however, was the torpedo, with triple-tube mountings on the upper deck.

Perhaps the most significant warship development of the period was in the submarine, where the successful solution of problems attendant on the heavy-oil engine completely revolutionized its role in naval warfare. The early submarines of the twentieth century, relying on the petrol engine for surface propulsion, had a role limited to coastal defence, as they were small boats with a very limited radius of action, and, with the risk of fire always present with the petrol engine, were obviously unsuited for distant-water operation. The heavy-oil engine changed all that. It was reliable and economical in its use of fuel, and with a relatively small increase in size to accommodate the necessary fuel tanks, changed the submarine from a short-range, tactical weapon into a long-range, strategic weapon, with great endurance and a wide radius of operation. This particular development was more or less simultaneous in all the navies of the world, but no one as yet could appreciate the devastating effect which this new weapon was to have upon all the carefully planned navies of maritime nations, or indeed upon the whole nature and philosophy of naval warfare. What was, within fifty years, to become the queen of the oceans was not yet even a small princess.

One other naval weapon was also emerging during these years, though it was not to reach real operational status by the time of the conflict which then lay only just beyond the horizon. This was the naval aircraft, with which the first experiments were beginning in 1910. By the end of 1911 an American, Eugene Ely, had demonstrated the possibility of flying off and landing an aeroplane on a platform erected on the deck of a cruiser, and in Great Britain the same feat was achieved by Lieutenant Samson using a platform over the bows of the battleship *Africa*. These feats led to the development of seaplanes, and from there to the development of seaplane carriers (old warships or merchant ships with a flight deck built above the forecastle from which seaplanes, mounted on trollies, could take off directly into the air, landing on the sea alongside the carrier ready to be hoisted aboard when their flight was over). These seaplane carriers, ready for use very shortly after war was declared, were direct ancestors of the aircraft carrier.

There is one more major revolution in ship development in the early part of the twentieth century to be described – the substituion of oil for coal as fuel for the marine steam engine. At first it was used only in warships, and then only in conjunction with coal, for the oil industry was not yet geared to a large enough scale of production for a complete transition to be possible. There was still a lot of ignorance in the world as to the extent of oil deposits, and, in his comment on a British Admiralty paper of 1906 pointing to the advantages of oil fuel for naval ships, a First Lord of the Admiralty could write: 'The substitution of oil for coal is impossible because the oil does not exist in the world in sufficient quantities.' Yet by 1914, in almost all the world's navies, virtually every ship up to and including battleships burned oil, at least in conjunction with coal, in their boilers, while many smaller warships, such as destroyers, gunboats, etc., carried no coal at all.

Above: Eugene Ely showed by 1911 that he could fly an aircraft off a wooden platform on board the cruiser *Pennsylvania*. When he landed as well, the foundations of naval aviation had been laid.

Thus, the first decade or so of the twentieth century saw a procession of new warships make their way down the slipway. The race had been started by the announcement of the German naval building programme in the Naval Law of 1898, which had galvanized every shipyard in the world into non-stop production. With the utmost ingenuity, naval constructors and architects were able to progress a step or two further with each successive design that came from their drawing boards, so that every year something new, something faster, something more powerful than the last, slid down into the sea. The world had never before seen fleets so big, so powerful, so widely dispersed across the oceans. And, so keen was the competition, internationally, for naval supremacy that very little was needed to set them all in motion.

It was, in a way, an irony that these immense fleets, representing an investment of thousands of millions of pounds, had been built without any experience of modern naval war, with no practical guidance as to how these expensive monsters would stand up to actual armed combat. The two small wars which had been fought at sea since the coming of the armoured ship taught very few worthwhile lessons. During the Sino-Japanese War (1894–95), a naval battle had been fought at the mouth of the Yalu, but all that it demonstrated was that a well-led superior modern fleet would always have the advantage over a poorly led, inferior, out-of-date fleet, even when the latter possessed a few larger ships. Perhaps the battle proved that a good margin of speed over an enemy allowed tactical flexibility, and that the offensive role was more likely to be successful than the defensive, but it offered no conclusions about warship construction and design.

The second small war, the Russo-Japanese War

231

(1904–05), provided two naval actions for the world's navies to study, one off Port Arthur and one in the Tsushima Straits. The first, off Port Arthur, indicated the ranges at which modern naval battles were likely to be fought, the Russian battleships opening fire at 20,000 yards (18,280 m) and dropping their shells 200 yards (180 m) beyond the Japanese ships. A little later in the action the Japanese flagship *Mikasa* was hit by a 12-inch shell at a range of 14,000 yards (12,800 m). A second notable lesson – and this lent support to the radical design of the British *Dreadnought* – was that in naval battle only the big gun counted. Both Russian and Japanese ships carried secondary batteries of 8-inch and 6-inch guns, as well as main batteries of 12-inch and 10-inch, and an eyewitness opinion expressed after the battle was that 'for all the respect they instill, 8-inch or 6-inch guns might just as well be pea-shooters.' The result at Tsushima, like that on the Yalu, again proved that the course of a naval battle, and its result, could be dictated by the admiral commanding the faster fleet, though there were other features of this battle which suggested that the Japanese success was not entirely attributable to this factor. In any case Tsushima had no real effect on battleship design, because, by the day it was fought (28 May 1905) the British Committee on Warship Design had long since reached its decisions and their new battleship, H.M.S. *Dreadnought*, was already in frame on her building slip in Portsmouth Dockyard. And she, with her all-big-gun armament of 12-inch guns and speed of 21 knots, already anticipated any of the lessons which could be learned from the actions of the Sino-Japanese and Russo-Japanese Wars, even though in fact her radical departure from previous battleship design owed nothing in its conception to either of them.

The conflict which was to set these vast fleets of warships in motion came in 1914, and the four years of war provided an acid test of the validity or otherwise of developments in warship design, construction and armament which had occurred throughout the previous years. Perhaps the hardest of the lessons which this new war had to teach was the proof that the big armoured cruiser was already an anachronism, less than twenty years from her original conception. So much had been hoped from her, so many dreams of naval glory embodied in her design, that her failure was a sad blow to the thousands who had believed that she held in her hands the keys to naval victory. What had happened was that in her short life she had already been overtaken by the new 'fast battleship' design and she had no fleet function to fulfil.

Another lesson that this war was to teach – a tremendously frustrating lesson to almost everyone who had anything to do with navies – was that so much money and power was locked up in each individual battleship that they had become too valuable to risk unduly in battle. The one extended naval battle of the war, that of Jutland on 31 May 1916, had seen the battleships of both sides turn away from the battle line whenever they were seriously threatened.

A third lesson, which took a lot more time to learn than it should have done, was that the big naval gun was no longer the dominant weapon at sea: it had been overtaken by the torpedo and the mine. They, and new weapons still to come, were strong factors in the eventual elimination of the battleship as a viable warship. But, until that lesson was learned, there were still some years of life ahead for this type of ship.

The last important lesson to be demonstrated in World War I was the power of the submarine, far beyond anything that had been predicted. Thanks to the heavy-oil engine it had been able to make its influence felt far out in the world's oceans, and its powers of destruction appeared to be virtually unlimited. It was still among the smallest of the world's warships, but by far the most lethal, and its effect upon the overall shape of the world's navies had already been immense, and through the next three or four decades was to become greater. During World War I, it was responsible for several new designs of ships, some whose sole purpose was to hunt and destroy this one type of vessel, others whose purpose was to screen and protect ships from underwater attack. Its huge depredations, particularly in attacks against merchant vessels, filled the world's shipbuilding and repair yards with orders and led also to a search for new shipbuilding materials as the call for steel, particularly for warship building, began to outrun the supply. A number of small merchant ships, required quickly to replace the many coasters which had fallen victim to the submarine, were built of concrete, reinforced with steel rods, but although useful temporarily to fill the gap, concrete proved to be too inflexible and too heavy a material with which to build a satisfactory ship. As yet, there was nothing to replace steel.

When the war ended, the exhausted combatants stood back to count the cost and to replan their shipping future. The first and most obvious task was to replace the immense tonnage of commercial shipping that had been lost in the war, for it was certain that, although the war had restricted the operation of seaborne

Above: The Russian battleship *Tsarevitch* was interned at the German port of Tsingtao after sustaining damage in the Battle of the Yellow Sea in August 1904.

Above: Artist's impression of Admiral Beatty's flagship, the battle-cruiser *Lion*, in action at Jutland. She escaped destruction from a cordite fire in one of her turrets, but her sister *Queen Mary* was lost with nearly all hands.

could foresee that one result of the experience of war was a coming boom in the transportation of oil. Uses were also being developed for new raw materials, and for these new ships would need to be specially designed and built. If the first decades of the century had seen the introduction of many types of specialist ships, the following ones would see even more.

In warship development there were to be just as many changes. Right at the end of the war the first real aircraft carrier had emerged, taking the place of the seaplane carriers with which navies had been equipped when the war started. There was no one as yet who could foresee all the directions in which this new weapon would affect the traditional warship but that it would do so profoundly was accepted worldwide without question. The first aircraft carriers were no more than adaptations of existing ships, with a flat flight deck built over their entire length, but it was certain, even on the limited experience gained from these conversions, that purpose-built ships would inevitably be needed in due course.

However, in spite of all the lessons which had been learned, it was to be some time before the experiences of war were translated into warship development. The chief obstacle was a general lack of enthusiasm for military projects, not surprising in a world that had just endured four years of war, but the delay was going to cost the nations dear when another war loomed over the horizon.

trade, there was still no alternative to the oceans as the main highway along which international trade could pass. And as the smoke cleared, it became equally certain that the volume of trade would grow at least as fast as it had done during the years before the war, and probably much faster, for the whole world was now hungry for the commodities which the war had denied it. But, though new ships were required in great numbers, they would not necessarily be the same ships as ten years earlier. Shipowners

Freak Ships

The old wooden sailing ship did not lend herself to experiment. Being entirely dependent on the wind for her motive power, she had to have a more or less conventional hull shape in order to make forward progress, and a more or less conventional sail plan in order to harness the power of the wind and convert it to forward propulsion. There were, of course, certain limits within which a ship designer was free to try and improve her performance – by altering the shape of her hull underwater, increasing the length-to-beam ratio, or changing the cut or arrangement of her sails – but basically she was always the same ship. However, with the introduction of the steam engine, which was able to impart motion to a ship in any direction, regardless of the wind, and iron construction, which gave much more flexibility to designers, there was almost no end to the possibilities for experiment with the design of special ships for special purposes. Not all of them were successful, and many were extremely odd.

One of the oddities was a collier, designed to bring coal down the east coast of England, from Newcastle to London, and built on the Thames at Blackwall in 1863. She was named the *Connector*, and her owners were registered as the Jointed Ship Company. The inventor's ingenious idea was to produce a ship somewhat like a railway train with an engine and two trucks, so that when fully loaded with coal she could detach a 'truck' at any port requiring coal, as she passed. It was an

idea with great possibilities, if it could be made to work, for the *Connector* could be loaded with coal for three different destinations, and deliver it with the minimum loss of time through the ship having to enter port and wait until the coal was unloaded before proceeding to the next port. The empty 'trucks' would be collected on the return voyage to Newcastle, and connected up again.

The ship was built with three separate hull sections, joined together by huge metal hinges, so that in a seaway each hull could pitch independently of the others. The engine was in the aftermost hull, which pushed the other two ahead of it. The latter were fitted with masts and sails, so that when they had been detached they could sail independently to their port of destination.

The *Connector* was tried out on the Thames, but on the day of the trial there was no wind, and so the sailing part of the experiment could not take place. Nevertheless, the ship proceeded up the river, detaching her two forward hulls *en route*, one by one, which, because it was windless, were secured to buoys, while the stern section carried on upriver. When she turned and came back, she picked up the two hulls which were secured to buoys, connected them up successfully, and returned to her starting point.

However, what was possible on a windless day, on the flat calm surface of the Thames, was not necessarily possible in a rough sea. The ship might have managed to survive intact if motion in a

rough sea involved only fore-and-aft pitching, though even this would have put a very severe strain on the connecting hinges. But sideways rolling – and it was inconceivable that all three parts would roll as one – would shear the connecting hinges as though they were made of matchwood, no matter how massively they were built. Even the inventor realised that his ship would never be able to stand the strain, and, in fact, the *Connector* never ventured out to sea at all.

A very weird ship was a battleship of completely circular design, built in Russia in 1875. She was designed by Vice Admiral Popov, with the idea of providing a steady platform for her big guns, whatever the state of the sea. She was an iron ship of 3,553 tons with a diameter of 101 ft (31 m). She was built at Nicolaev, on the Black Sea, and being as long as she was broad, could neither pitch nor roll in the heaviest of seas. Her armament consisted of two 11-inch guns mounted in a central circular armoured barbette, and she was powered by eight steam engines driving six propellers. Her guns were aimed by revolving the ship, using the outer propellers to provide the turning movement. She was given the name *Admiral Popov*, after her designer, and was considered so successful that a second battleship, named *Novgorod*, was later built to the same design. These two battleships were known in naval circles in many countries as 'popoffkas'.

At this stage in the development of control of the big naval gun, a steady platform was a considerable asset, and in this respect these two ships had considerable advantages over the conventional battleship design. They were reasonably robust, but in anything of a sea they proceeded with their circular deck awash, as they had no more than a foot or two of freeboard. This meant that they were apt to pound, sometimes quite badly, in a rough sea, and the stresses involved placed a severe strain on their plating. It was also discovered that, although when used in rivers they handled quite well when going upstream, they were completely unmanageable when coming downstream, the rudders failing to grip the water so that they revolved continuously.

The *Admiral Popov* was inspected on her trials by Czar Nicholas II, who was deeply impressed by the absence of roll and pitch, even in a seaway. As he suffered badly from seasickness, though fond of the pleasures of yachting, he gave Admiral Popov instructions to design him a royal yacht on the same principle, though it was to look like a yacht and not like a floating dinner plate. In conjunction with the builders, Popov solved the problem by designing a more or less circular, or turbot-shaped, underwater hull and constructing a conventional yacht's upperworks on top of it, so that only the upperworks were visible above the water. The yacht was named *Livadia* and was built in Scotland by John Elder and Company, being completed in 1880. Three engines installed in the submerged part of the hull drove three propellers, each 16 ft (4·9 m) in diameter, to give her a speed of 17 knots, while the royal cabins and staterooms occupied the part of the hull above water. The *Livadia* had a tonnage of 3,900, and was 235 ft (71·6 m) long, with a maximum underwater beam of 153 ft (46·6 m), and proved to be a very comfortable and successful yacht, being broken up in 1926 after forty-six years service. She had an odd arrangement of masts and funnels, her five masts being placed in pairs athwartships, like goalposts, with the fifth on the centreline halfway between the pairs, and her three funnels were placed abreast.

The avoidance of seasickness was the basis for the design of another ship – this one by Sir Henry Bessemer, more famous perhaps as the inventor of the Bessemer process in the manufacture of steel than as a naval architect. She was built in 1875 as a cross-Channel steamer and named the *Bessemer*, after her designer. She had a perfectly normal hull and engines, but the passenger saloon was mounted on metal guides and could be manipulated by hydraulic machinery so that it would always remain level, no matter what the angle of roll or pitch of the ship herself. This hydraulic machinery was controlled by an engineer, and was regulated by reference to a large spirit-level set in the deck of the saloon. The idea worked reasonably well on its first trial, as the sea was smooth and the roll was very small and slow. On her second trip from Dover to Calais, the sea was rougher, and the engineer on duty found that he could not produce counteracting movements from the hydraulic machinery fast enough to match the amount of roll. No more ships were built to this design, as it was at that time impossible to get a quick enough response from machinery to meet, or anticipate, the movements of a ship in a seaway. But it could be said that the seed of Bessemer's idea took root through the years, and eventually blossomed into the automatic ship stabilizers of today.

Far left: The articulated *Connector*.

Above left and left: The circular Russian *Novgorod*, and the *Bessemer*.

Chapter Eleven
The Legacy of War

When World War I ended, the nations which had fought in it, particularly the maritime nations, had to pause and take stock. The losses in terms of ships, both mercantile and naval, on both sides had been prodigious, but much more so in the case of the Allies (Britain, France, Italy, the United States) and neutral countries than in that of the central powers (Germany, Austria, Turkey). This was natural and to be expected, for the sea blockade, imposed by the Allies at the start of the war and maintained throughout it, virtually closed the oceans to any shipping but their own.

The enormous losses were mainly due to the new weapons, the mine and torpedo. Mines, it is true, had been first introduced as a naval weapon during the Crimean War (1854–56), but that particular mining operation had been on so small a scale that it had not called for any changes in ship construction to meet the danger, and indeed the mines themselves were too small to be the lethal destroyers that they had become sixty years later. But even more devastating, to warships as much as merchant ships, was the torpedo, especially when discharged from a submarine. It was this weapon which was responsible for the biggest proportion of the losses.

When, at the end of the war, a final count was made of allied merchant ships lost through enemy action, the total came to 5,531 vessels totalling 12,850,814 gross tons. To that figure must be added the tonnage lost during the war years through 'natural' causes, such as shipwreck, collision, stress of weather, etc., and the final loss figure comes to just over 15,000,000 gross tons. Against that figure should be set the tonnage of ships built during the war – and a massive effort was made, worldwide, to try to keep pace with the rate of wartime loss – so that

the net loss of allied shipping amounted to 1,811,000 gross tons. British shipping had fared more disastrously. At the beginning of the war she owned and operated about 45 per cent of the world total. During the war she lost through enemy action 2,480 ships, totalling 7,759,090 gross tons, and her net loss, allowing for new ships built, amounted to 3,084,000 gross tons, or approximately 16 per cent of her pre-war total.

It was very much the same story with regard to warship losses. Great Britain, having borne the brunt of the naval war throughout the four years of its duration, had lost proportionately more than any other naval power, so that, both in terms of warship and merchant ship tonnage, she emerged from the conflict relatively worse off than any other nation. And if this were true of her shipping, it was equally true of her economy. Being more impoverished than most other combatants, owing to the magnitude of her war effort, the trident of sea power was about to leave her hands, not entirely because she could no longer afford the financial burden of retaining it, but in part also because of the deep revulsion of the British nation against warlike projects, caused by the massive slaughter of young men on the Western Front.

The normal course of events after a major naval war would have been to analyze and assess the performance of the various types of ships engaged, before dashing into placing repeat orders to make good the war losses. And one might expect this to be particularly the case after a major war in which new and untried types of warships had been engaged. The two previous wars fought between fleets of armoured ships, the Sino-Japanese and Russo-Japanese Wars, had been too small and localized, and between fleets too unequal in quality and training, for valid lessons to be learned; but when World War I ended in 1918, there existed an extensive fund of experience of large-scale naval conflict, detailed analysis of which would certainly have produced new lines for warship development in the future.

Left: Two American battleships lead a squadron of heavy cruisers into Lingayen Gulf in the Philippines, October 1944, to begin the bombardment before an amphibious assault against the Japanese.

Even as the war ended, two of the main maritime nations were already engaged on big warship building programmes, likely to perpetuate the existing types of capital ship. European eyes had, of course, been focussed on the North Sea and the Atlantic Ocean throughout the war, but other eyes were now looking at the Pacific. A gigantic building programme was getting under way in the United States with the authorization by Congress of the building of six new battleships of 43,200 tons, each carrying twelve 16-inch guns, and six new battle-cruisers of 43,000 tons, each carrying eight 16-inch guns. Japan had already built two 33,800-ton battleships carrying eight 16-inch guns, was building two more of 39,900 tons to carry ten 16-inch guns each and two battle-cruisers of 43,000 tons to carry eight 16-inch guns each, and had plans for building two or three 45,000-tonners, each with eight 16-inch guns, in the next year or two. Faced with this threat to her naval supremacy, Great Britain in 1921 ordered four 48,000-ton battle-cruisers mounting nine 16-inch guns each, to be followed by an unspecified number (probably four or five) of 48,500-ton battleships, also with a main armament of 16-inch guns and a designed speed of 32 knots.

Although the United States was the first in the field in ordering these immense new ships, the fact that Japan immediately followed suit, and later Great Britain, caused the Americans to pause in their plans. The estimated cost of these huge warships was the then astronomical

sum of £252 million. And that was only the start, for such ships would need to be supported by large numbers of cruisers and destroyers if they were to form a balanced fighting fleet. Appalled by the shipbuilding snowball which they had set in motion, and by the danger of a Pacific war if a naval race were to develop between America and Japan, politicians in the United States decided to try to stop it by calling a disarmament conference in Washington, in the hope of reaching an international agreement on the limitation of naval armaments. It was held in 1921–22, with the main naval nations, France, Great Britain, Italy, Japan and the United States taking part.

After a great deal of argument and bargaining, the Washington Conference resulted in the following agreements:

(i) The British and American battlefleets to be limited to 580,450 and 500,650 tons respectively, with the Japanese to 301,320, the French 221,170 and Italian 182,800.

(ii) Capital ships to be limited to 35,000 tons displacement, and guns to a maximum of 16-in. (301-mm) calibre.

(iii) Existing capital ships not to be replaced less than twenty years from their date of completion, and no new construction to take place in the meantime.

(iv) Reconstruction of existing capital ships not to add more than 3,000 tons, and to be restricted purely to defence against submarine and air attack.

There were a few small variations to allow for

the two completed Japanese battleships, Great Britain being allowed to build two new ones and the United States being allowed to retain three of the four already on the stocks, while scrapping the fourth. Nevertheless, the Washington Treaty hit the British Navy harder than any other, as it involved scrapping 657 warships, totalling 1,500,000 tons.

As a means of halting the threatened arms race the agreement reached at Washington succeeded admirably, but at the same time it removed much of the incentive for experiments in new types of warship better suited for modern warfare. The treaty merely ensured the survival of the existing type of battle fleet, and, in a way, set the seal of international approval on the continued organization of the world's navies as they had been constituted in 1914. Few nations were prepared to expend much energy in this field of research and development, if they were not permitted to put the results into practice in the building of new ships. But, more important, it appeared to substantiate, by its endorsement of the battleship and her big guns, the claim of the gun still to be the dominant weapon at sea. All the experience of the four years of war between 1914 and 1918 went to show that the importance of the big gun had been exaggerated in relation to that of the torpedo and the mine, which had, between them, claimed so many more ships than had the gun.

Nevertheless, the war had taught one or two unmistakable lessons, one of which was the vulnerability of the big armoured cruiser, on which so many navies had spent millions of pounds in the years leading up to the war. No more were built. Their place had been taken more efficiently and safely by the fast battleship, and although some nations continued to build what they called battle-cruisers, they were that in name only for they carried the same thickness of armoured protection as did the battleship.

Another unmistakable lesson was the lethality of an underwater torpedo hit, even upon heavily armoured ships. The British battleship *Formidable* was sunk in the English Channel by a single torpedo hit; the armoured cruisers *Aboukir*, *Cressy*, and *Hogue* were all sunk in the course of one morning by torpedo hits from a single German submarine off the Belgian coast. A partial answer to this danger was to increase the speed of ships, on the grounds that it was more difficult for a submarine to hit a fast-moving ship than a slow one, and this was reflected in the increase of battleship speed over the next twenty years from an average of about 19 or 20 knots in 1918 to

around 29 or 30 knots in 1940. Another was to build outward bulges on the underwater hull, so that when a torpedo hit the ship the main force of the explosion would be taken on the plating of the bulge, leaving the inner hull, it was hoped, more or less undamaged. This was the solution chosen by many navies for existing battleships, under the clause in the Washington Treaty allowing reconstruction up to a limit of 3,000 tons. But, in cases of new construction, the practice of adding an outer bulge sometimes produced serious problems. Great Britain, for example, was permitted to build two new battleships, as mentioned above, and naturally designed them to the full 35,000-tons maximum. The effect of adding anti-torpedo bulges outside the armoured hull would have been to make them too wide to enter most of the existing dry-docks in the country. The difficulty was overcome by retaining the planned hull dimensions, but sloping the main armoured belt inwards, so that a space was created between the outer skin and the armour – in effect an inwards bulge instead of an outwards one. These changes in design, with some local variations, became a feature of battleship design throughout the world. Although it could not remove all the danger from a torpedo hit, it did make it more difficult to sink a battleship by a single torpedo, or even a salvo of torpedoes unless, by a lucky chance, two torpedoes hit consecutively in exactly the same place along the hull, or the flash of a torpedo explosion found its way into a cordite magazine.

Defence against the mine was much more

Above: The cruiser HMS *Endymion* and her three sisters were specially 'bulged' against torpedo-attack to allow them to provide fire support off the Gallipoli beaches in 1915.

difficult. The conventional double bottom, a feature of all shipbuilding for the previous seventy years, offered virtually no protection. The new battleship *Audacious*, only completed in 1913, struck a mine off the north coast of Ireland in 1914 and sank before she could be towed to the shore and beached, in spite of her extensive division into watertight compartments and double bottom. A countermeasure to the moored mine was achieved later in the war with the invention of the paravane, but, even as it was being introduced, a new design of mine, against which the paravane was useless, was being produced. This was the magnetic mine, first used operationally in 1918, which was to pose an immense threat to shipping twenty years later. The mine remained a menace against which no measures of defence in the design or construction of ships was adequate. It called instead for a new type of warship to be developed, in the shape of the minesweeper.

World War I ended before the full potential of aircraft in a fighting role at sea could be developed, although enough was by then known to indicate that they were certain to have a very profound effect indeed. Already, aircraft had flown off and landed on the flying decks of converted ships under way at sea; a ship at sea had been sunk by a torpedo dropped from a seaplane; a seaplane had been launched from a carrier for reconnaissance duties (during the early stages of the battle of Jutland in May 1916). When all these were considered in the light of the limited evolution which the flying machine had undergone in the few years since the Wright brothers had demonstrated the possibilities of heavier-than-air flight, it was quite clear that, as the aeroplane evolved further, its influence on naval warfare was bound to be enormous.

The first essential step along this new road was to design and produce a ship capable of stowing and handling its own aircraft, with hangars below deck for stowing and servicing them, and a flight deck for flying off and landing on. As has been seen, the first ships designed to handle aircraft were the seaplane carriers developed at the beginning of World War I, each operating up to a dozen seaplanes, used purely for fleet reconnaissance duties. These were all ships converted for the purpose, for the most part small liners or cross-Channel ferries, with the speed required to keep up with a battle fleet at sea. As the war progressed, some larger naval ships were similarly converted, not for seaplanes, whose value for many naval duties was restricted by the large floats that they had to carry, but for aircraft with conventional wheeled undercarriages, whose radius of action was always greater than that of a seaplane. All these early

carriers had a large flight deck forward of the bridge structure, quite suitable for an aircraft to fly off, but almost impossible for one to land on. It was occasionally done – one was successfully landed on the flight deck of H.M.S. *Furious* in 1917 – but it was an operation fraught with danger, and most pilots who attempted it finished up over the side and in the sea.

Part of the problem was solved when the *Furious* was taken into the dockyard and an after flight deck constructed abaft the bridge structure, giving her in effect two separate flying decks, one forward and one aft, the after deck being used for landing. But this again was unsatisfactory, as there was not enough length of deck to bring the aircraft to a stop before it hit the bridge structure. The next obvious step was to bring in another ship and give her an unobstructed deck over her whole length. This

Top: The dreadnought battleship *Audacious* sinking after running into a German minefield.

Above: The answer to mines was the paravane, a cutting device which could be towed on either side of a ship. Here sailors hoist the port paravane out on a boom.

Top: The aircraft carrier *Argus* was converted from a liner, and commissioned late in 1918. She was the first flush-decked carrier and proved successful.

Above: Squadron Commander Dunning made the first deck-landing on the deck of HMS *Furious*, but on his second attempt the aircraft skidded overboard and he was drowned.

was realised in H.M.S. *Argus,* but not without the need for a great deal of ingenuity to achieve the desired result. Her navigating bridge, an obvious necessity in every ship, was linked to a hydraulic system whereby it was raised or lowered as required, providing the flush deck while aircraft were being operated. Her funnels were replaced by a system of trunking which discharged the boiler smoke and hot gases over the stern.

This arrangement of bridge and funnels was moderately successful, but the retractable bridge was plainly not ideal, while the hot boiler gases discharged over the stern affected the stability of the aircraft just at the moment that they were coming in to land. So another carrier, H.M.S. *Eagle,* was brought in for reconversion. She had started life as a battleship, the *Almirante Cochrane,* being built in Britain for the Chilean

navy, but had been taken over during the war while still on the stocks and completed as a carrier. She was now reconverted, with a flight deck running the whole length of the ship, but with her bridge superstructure, mast and funnels as a permanent structure on the starboard side. Although this narrowed the flight deck amidships, it was not so much that aircraft met with any interference. She emerged in her new shape in 1920, and this design was endorsed in 1923 when H.M.S. *Hermes,* the first ship to be built from the keel up as an aircraft carrier, also emerged with her bridge and funnels offset to starboard. These two ships were known as 'island' carriers, the island being the bridge superstructure, and it was this that became standard carrier design in all the world's navies.

The American and Japanese navies both commissioned their first small aircraft carriers, the *Langley* and *Hosho* respectively, in 1922. Both were flush-decked, with funnels offset to one side and lowered to deck level when flying operations were in progress. No more aircraft carriers were built until after the signing of the Washington Treaty, when Britain, the United States and Japan each converted two more ships (battleships or battle-cruisers) which would otherwise have been scrapped under the terms of the Treaty. All of them were converted to the island design.

The Washington Naval Treaty was due to expire at the end of 1936, and although there had been comparatively little naval building around the world, except of the smaller classes of warship, most navies had their plans ready for quick expansion once the treaty limitations were removed. Little that was radically new in design or development had emerged during the treaty years, except perhaps in the case of the destroyer where there was a fairly large increase in overall size, while, in Britain, the memory of the mine warfare of 1914–18 had produced a minelayer of radical design. In World War I minelaying had been undertaken by fast liners converted for the task, or by destroyers similarly converted, and Germany had adapted some of her submarines to lay mines while submerged. The essence of surface minelaying was speed, for if a minefield in enemy waters was to be effective it had to be laid under the cover of darkness, with the ships engaged well clear of the area both before and after the actual lay. Great Britain built H.M.S. *Adventure* in 1926 as a cruiser-minelayer, a new type of ship, but instead of being fitted with steam turbines which could have provided the speed essential for the task, she was given instead heavy-oil diesel engines which could not. She was a failure. Britain also built minelaying submarines, but they, too, turned out to be a doubtful investment, for by the time the next war came to be fought most minelaying in enemy waters was better and more expeditiously done by aircraft.

During the years of the Washington Treaty, with virtually no new building of capital ships taking place, a protracted argument raged about the vulnerability of the battleship to bombs. There were some who held that the advent of the aeroplane made the battleship obsolete, since so large a ship was a sitting target to an aeroplane with a bomb. The other side of the argument was that a bomb dropped from 12,000 ft (3,660 m) takes 28 seconds to fall, that a battleship at 21 knots moves 1,000 ft (300 m) during that time, that she would therefore be very difficult to hit even if she held a straight course, and that if she were steering a zigzag course it would be virtually impossible. So an old battleship, the *Agamemnon,* had her guns and other valuable gear removed, and was fitted with radio-control for her steering gear, worked from an attendant destroyer. A series of exercises were held in which aircraft attacked her with bombs, in varying conditions of wind and sea and at heights of from 12,000 to 5,000 ft (1,520 m). During these exercises, 114 bombs were dropped, but not a single one hit the ship. Similar results were obtained in bombing trials carried out by other navies. Nevertheless, the threat of attack from the air was taken seriously, and an anti-aircraft armament was added to the gun establishment of all large warships.

By the beginning of 1937, when the limitations of the Treaty were lifted and the world's navies again began to build big warships, there was again, as in the years before World War I, a threat to the naval balance of power, and again it was Germany. As a result of her defeat in 1918, her navy had been limited to six old battleships, with an age limit of twenty years, and no replacement was allowed to exceed 10,000 tons (10,160 tonnes) displacement. In 1929 she laid down the first of three heavy cruisers, and as the details gradually became known, it was clear that she was of a novel and most provocative design. Although declared as being within the tonnage limit of 10,000, she was actually of 12,000 tons (12,200 tonnes), the first of a long list of deliberate underdeclarations by which Germany consistently built larger ships than permitted by the treaty. She mounted a heavy armament of six 11-inch guns, eight 5-inch, and six 4·1-inch, and she was powered by three sets of diesel engines which gave her a maximum speed of 28 knots, and a radius of action of 10,000 nautical miles at 20 knots. It was obvious from her armament and range that she was designed purely for commerce raiding, and with her 11-inch guns she could out-shoot any other cruiser in the world. Even her construction was novel, for in order to save the weight of rivetting her hull plates, bulkheads and decks were welded.

Although officially described as a 'cruiser', the rest of the world coined a new name for her, describing her as a 'pocket-battleship'. She was the *Deutschland,* later renamed *Lützow,* and in 1931 and 1932 she was followed by two larger sisters, the *Graf Spee* and *Scheer,* of the same design, but with thicker armour protection, bringing their displacement tonnage up to 12,500 tons (12,700 tonnes).

More was to follow. In 1934, with Hitler established as German chancellor, two fast battleships, the *Scharnhorst* and *Gneisenau,* were laid down. They were declared at 26,000 tons (26,400 tonnes) displacement, but were in fact 32,000 tons (32,500 tonnes), and, with a maximum speed of 32 knots and a radius of action of 10,000 miles, they were immensely versatile and powerful. In the same year, Hitler denounced the Treaty of Versailles, under which the naval limitations had been imposed, and announced the building of two more fast battleships to the maximum tonnage agreed around the world, 35,000 tons. These were the *Bismarck* and *Tirpitz,* which eventually emerged as 31-knot battleships of 42,000 tons (42,800 tonnes) displacement each. Since, at the same time, it became known that Germany had secretly built twenty submarines in contravention of the Treaty, it was obvious that she was already deeply engaged in rapid naval rearmament and thereby threatening the naval balance round the world, so painstakingly engineered at Washington. By 1939 she was also building heavy cruisers, declared at the agreed world maximum of 10,000 tons, which, in fact, when completed had a displacement of 15,000 tons (15,200 tonnes). All these ships were part of what was known in Germany as the 'Z' plan, designed to create a navy by 1945, consisting of 13 modern battleships, 4 aircraft carriers, 33 cruisers, 250 submarines, and a large force of destroyers. In 1939 two more 'Z' plan battleships were laid down at Hamburg, to be named *Friedrich der Grosse* and *Gross Deutschland.* They were to be monsters of 50,000 tons (50,800 tonnes) displacement, but with diesel engines instead of the steam turbines of the *Bismarck* and *Tirpitz.* The remaining battleships of the 'Z' plan, which never got beyond the drawing board, were even more extreme in conception, ranging from 84,000 tons (85,300 tonnes) to 120,000 tons (121,900 tonnes). It was perhaps fortunate for the Allies that World War II broke out in 1939 and not in 1945, when the 'Z' programme of naval building might have been complete. Another fortunate event occurred on 31 December 1942, when an escort group of British destroyers drove off a superior German force, including the pocket battleship *Lützow,* which was trying to attack a convoy of merchant ships. This action completely destroyed Hitler's faith in the battleship. All building work on the 50,000-ton leviathans at Hamburg was stopped, and the remainder of the 'Z' plan building cancelled.

The main interest in these German battleships, actual and projected, lies in the fact that, unlike all other battleships in the world, they were not designed for battle, but for commerce raiding. That was the reason for fitting them with diesel

Below: The Japanese battleship *Mutsu*.

Bottom: The *Bismarck* in a Norwegian fjord. Her destruction in 1941 marked a turning point in the naval war.

propulsion which, being a more economical user of fuel than a steam boiler, almost doubled their radius of action. The impact of these monsters, had they ever been loosed on the world's trade routes, defies imagination, especially in the light of the fact that it needed forty-eight surface warships to hunt down and destroy the *Bismarck* in 1941.

On the other side of the world Japan was also entering the monster battleship stakes. Two ships of 65,000 tons (66,000 tonnes) displacement, each mounting nine 18·1-inch guns, were laid down in 1936 under conditions of great secrecy, being both concealed from the public gaze behind a mile of sisal matting. Contrary to the German philosophy of battleship warfare, these two, the *Musashi* and *Yamato,* were designed for battle against other battleships, and it was ironic that both of them were sunk by air attack before they could fire a single shell from their immense guns at another ship of their own breed.

Right at the other end of the scale of naval developments was the landing craft, a box-like vessel with a hinged ramp in place of the conventional bow. Propulsion was by internal combustion engine and the small craft drew so little water that they could reach a shelving shore and land their occupants dryshod, or through only a few inches of water, when the ramp was lowered. These military landing craft were first developed by Japan for war in Manchuria, although the germ of the idea had been formed in 1915 with the Anzac landings on the Gallipoli beaches in the eastern Mediterranean. The Japanese craft were seen in action in Manchuria by several foreign observers who were so impressed by their obvious value in amphibious assaults on an enemy-held coast that they persuaded their own governments to introduce similar craft. Until 1939 this was done on only a tiny scale, both in Britain and in the United States, but by 1941, after two years of war, the original small landing craft, with its capacity for landing perhaps one platoon of men, had been developed into a whole complex of ships designed for this one purpose. They ranged from big infantry and tank landing ships, for carrying troops and all their fighting equipment in bulk, to small assault craft, slung from davits on the landing ship, to put them ashore with their varied assault weapons. The smaller craft were of simple construction to allow for rapid production – steel, box-sided craft with a diesel or petrol engine, designed to ground themselves bows-on to a shelving shore-line and discharge their burden, human or mechanical, directly on to the shore over the lowered bow ramp. Many of the big infantry landing ships were converted liners, their role in an assault landing being to lie offshore and land their troops in their own assault craft.

So, under the stimulus of war, a completely new species of ship was developed, and, although the initial design was concerned entirely with the requirements of amphibious warfare, it was found after the war was over that there were a number of peacetime operations where they could prove of enduring value. The wartime tank assault craft made an admirable short-haul car ferry for access to small island communities, and adaptations of these craft served well for the carriage of supplies and for inter-island trade where the use of a larger conventional merchant vessel would prove uneconomic.

Before leaving naval development, a word needs to be said about the submarine problem, in relation to the defence of trade in wartime. As has been mentioned, the losses of merchant shipping during World War I to submarine attack were prodigious and the answer to it was only produced towards the end of the war, in the shape of the convoy system. The greatest sufferer in terms of merchant ship losses during that war had been Britain, and if a second similar war were to take place, she would again, by reason of her geographical position and dependence on overseas trade, be worst hit. During the years of peace a means of underwater detection of submarines, known as 'Asdic', had been developed, and so great was the faith put by Britain in this new invention that she felt able to neglect the building of destroyer-type ships suitable as escorts for convoys. But, as the war clouds gathered over Europe in 1937 and 1938, and a period of feverish naval rearmament began, it became obvious that, once again, merchant shipping would need to be organized into convoys, if it were to have any defence at all against attack by submarine or surface raiders. It was a problem that affected Britain more than any other nation, and in 1937 and 1938 she found herself remarkably unprepared to meet it. Her faith in the Asdic submarine detectors was waning as a result of the experience of many fleet exercises, and she had to face the stark reality

Below: US infantrymen wade ashore from a Landing Craft Medium (LCM). Thousands of these ungainly but vital craft were used in amphibious operations.

of a repetition of her World War I experience of unrestricted submarine warfare directed against merchant shipping. A new type of small warship was therefore developed during the last years of peace, designed especially for this type of warfare and known generically as an 'escort vessel'. She was something less sophisticated than a destroyer, but larger and more robust than the trawlers which, fitted with Asdic and anti-submarine weapons, were adequate escorts for coastal and short-range convoys. Under this one generic name, three new types of escort were developed during the next four or five years – the frigate, the sloop and the corvette. Of these, the largest was the frigate, first put in hand in 1940, a ship of around 1,500 tons displacement with a good speed, fairly long endurance, and an impressive array of anti-submarine weapons in the shape of 4-inch guns and depth-charges. The sloop, smaller and slower, did not have the range required for full ocean convoy duty, but was a valuable ship in anti-submarine warfare, particularly when it became possible to form support groups to reinforce the escort group of a convoy coming under actual submarine attack as required. The last of the trio was the corvette, a small vessel of 860 to 900 tons based on the design of the whalecatcher, sturdy little ships of great endurance and able to stand up to the stormiest weather. They were simple, easy to build, and were produced quickly in very large numbers. With a maximum speed of only 16 knots, they were too slow to catch a submarine escaping on the surface, but nevertheless did yeoman service in escort work until the larger and more powerful frigates and sloops were built. Being based on the whale-catcher design with its rounded hull sections, they rolled horribly in a seaway, and were very uncomfortable ships in rough weather, but at least they helped to hold the fort until the bigger escorts came along.

Just as warships were changing rapidly, so was merchant shipping. The pattern of world trade had much to do with the change, for the manufacturing industry was turning even more quickly to new methods of mass production to satisfy the needs of an increasingly affluent

Below: Over 300 'Flower' class corvettes were built in British and Canadian shipyards as cheap convoy escorts. The design was based on a large whalecatcher.

world, and this higher level of production meant that ships were urgently needed for its distribution. The first task was to replace the tonnage sunk during the war, which was done mainly with fewer ships of larger individual tonnage, the majority being mixed cargo carriers and passenger liners of the type which had borne the brunt of the sinkings. At the same time, new specialist ships had to be built on a large scale to serve new industries. An example is provided by the motor car. Under the spur of war the internal combustion engine underwent rapid and extensive development, for application to aircraft as well as motor vehicles, and when the war ended it was possible to mass-produce cheap motor cars, bringing them within the price range of a huge new public. Although as yet its transport from maker to market did not call for a specialized design of ship, the petrol that it consumed necessitated a very large increase in tanker tonnage. With the main oil producers concentrated in the Middle East and the main consumers concentrated in the West, the overall size of tankers was generally limited by the maximum that could use the Suez Canal. In the third and fourth decades of the twentieth

Above: Fifty elderly destroyers were handed over to the Royal Navy by the US Navy in September 1940. They served with distinction until 1945, when the survivors were returned.

century, when the oil boom was growing almost daily to keep abreast of soaring car production, a tanker of around 25,000 tons was a big one. Oil was not the only trade affected by the car boom: rubber, for tyres, from Malaya and Borneo was another commodity that shared in the boom and required ships to transport it.

Tankers were built with longitudinal, as well as transverse, bulkheads, to provide a large number of separate tanks for the oil – a precaution to minimize the escape of oil in the case of the

vessel being holed. Transverse cofferdams were built right across the ship both forward of and abaft the tanks to isolate the oil from the dry cargo space forward and the engine room aft, as a safety measure. Steam pump rooms, also built transversely across the ship between every section of tanks (usually containing about twelve), acted as additional cofferdams. The majority of tankers had dry cargo space under the forecastle deck, and the engine room below the poop deck, crew accommodation being in the poop with, officers' cabins in the bridge structure. In most tankers built between the wars, the bridge structure was amidships, with a longitudinal monkey bridge connecting the forecastle, bridge and poop deck.

Probably the most important single development in merchant shipping during the years between the wars was the changeover from coal to oil as the main bunker fuel for ships. It was a cleaner fuel than coal, with a distinctly greater thermal efficiency, and, at the same time, much easier to handle, being pumped into fuel tanks on board instead of manhandled from a collier or coaling wharf across the deck into coal bunkers, where sweating stokers had to trim it to fill all the corners. At the same time, a great many shipowners adopted the heavy-oil diesel engine as the propulsion unit on board their ships, again because it was more economical to run, especially in manpower, doing away with the need for boilers and the stokers to fire them. Here again, this was largely a legacy from World War I, for it was the needs of the submarine which had stimulated research into the production of powerful and reliable diesel engines.

But the biggest of the post-war revolutions in shipping was in the passenger trade, particularly the luxury liner, which was to grow to an unparalleled size. The huge rush of emigration which had had such an influence on the passenger trade in the late nineteenth and early twentieth century had eased off considerably. There were many people still eager to start a new life in another part of the world, but whereas in earlier years they had been counted in millions, now they were counted only in hundreds of thousands. And the days of crowded steerage spaces were passing; would-be emigrants were richer, or were helped by subsidized passages to countries needing immigrants. Passenger ships were now built with cabins for all they carried. A few shipping lines, in particular some of those of Mediterranean nations operating to South America, still ran a few elderly passenger ships with the old-fashioned steerage accommodation, because of local poverty and the inability of some emigrants to afford cabin accommodation. As the world grew richer, even these few ships quickly became obsolescent, and were withdrawn, either for scrapping, or conversion to all-cabin accommodation, or for sale to another shipping line further down the social scale.

At the top end of the passenger liner business, the most important attractions were still luxury and speed, as they had been in the years before the war. Several of the pre-war luxury liners had been sunk, either in action against other ships, after they had been converted into armed merchant cruisers, or by torpedo from a submarine. One of the best-known to suffer the latter fate was the *Lusitania*, sister-ship of the *Mauretania*, which was sunk off southern Ireland in 1915 by the German submarine U.20. Replacement tonnage was quickly built after the war, still with the same degree of luxury as before, but with more modern machinery capable of producing higher speeds.

Although fine, luxurious, and fast liners were built for all the main passenger trade routes, to South Africa, India, China, Australia, and South America, and across the Pacific from the west coast of America to Far Eastern and Australian ports, it was still the North Atlantic route which carried the most prestige and attracted the most competition. The race for the largest and most prestigious liner was begun by France when, in 1932, the mighty *Normandie* was launched. She was the first ship over 1,000 ft long, and her dimensions of 1,029 ft (313·6 m) overall, 117·8 ft (35·9 m) beam, and 36·6 ft (11·2 m) draught gave her a gross tonnage of 86,496 tons. To drive this huge bulk through the water at a record average speed of 31·3 knots eastbound, with which for a short time she held the Blue Riband of the Atlantic, required an engine horsepower of 160,000. She was built with a total of eleven decks and had cabin accommodation in three classes for 2,170 passengers, who required a crew of 1,320 to look after them.

Two years later, in 1934, the Cunard Line launched their reply, in the shape of the *Queen Mary*. She was slightly smaller than the *Normandie*, her dimensions of 1,019·5 ft. × 118·7 ft × 39·6 ft (310·7 m × 36·2 m × 12·1 m) giving her a gross tonnage of 81,237 tons. With engines of the same horsepower as the *Normandie* she proved fractionally faster, with an average maximum speed of 31·69 knots eastbound. She had twelve decks, with a passenger capacity of 776 in the first class, 784 in the tourist class, and 579 in the third class – a total of 1,939.

The *Queen Mary* was followed four years later by the *Queen Elizabeth*. Of similar design,

but slightly larger, she had an overall length of 1,031 ft (314·2 m) and a gross tonnage of 82,998 tons. Although launched in 1938, her fitting-out was overtaken by the outbreak of war in 1939, and it was not until October 1946, when the war had been over for a year and a half, that she made her first appearance on the Atlantic as a passenger liner operating between Southampton and New York.

Other maritime nations joined in the race for size, speed and luxury, the United States, Italy and Germany all building transatlantic giants in their desire to capture the cream of the passenger traffic. As yet there was no competition except from other liners, and, if a liner had a slight edge in the comfort of her cabins, the quality and variety of her cuisine, a fraction of a knot in speed, or a faithful following of passengers who would prefer her to any other ship, she would never sail empty. But already the writing was on the wall. Alcock and Brown, Lindbergh,

Left: The giant hull of the liner *Queen Mary* under construction on the Clyde.

Below: The *Queen Elizabeth* serving as a troopship during wartime.

Bottom: The *Queen Mary* in her peacetime livery.

Amelia Earhart, and one or two others had piloted flimsy aircraft across the Atlantic; Cobham, Mollison and Amy Johnson had pioneered the way by air to South Africa and Australia. After another world war, with its intensification of research and development, these isolated achievements would turn into a new era of mass air travel, in which the mighty ocean liners could not survive.

Before leaving these magnificent ships it is of interest to see what happened to them during the war which engulfed the world in 1939. Some were unfortunate, the *Normandie,* lying in New York harbour when France was overrun by the Germans in 1940, was taken over by the United States for conversion into a troop transport, being renamed the *Lafayette.* In 1942 she caught fire alongside her fitting-out wharf, and capsized under the weight of water pumped into her to extinguish the fire. She lay on her

side where she capsized for four years, being then sold for a small sum to be broken up for scrap. The German *Bremen,* flagship of the German Norddeutscher-Lloyd Line, escaped from New York at the outbreak of war, evaded the British fleet, and eventually reached Germany safely by sailing a northerly course and sheltering for a few weeks in the Russian port of Murmansk. However, when she reached Germany there was no useful employment for her, and she finally had her back broken when she was hit by bombs during an air raid.

The British *Queen Mary* and *Queen Elizabeth* were converted into troop transports at the beginning of the war, with a carrying capacity of 8,200 each, and until 1943 were based in Sydney Australia, and employed continuously world-wide in the carriage of troops. In April 1943 they were both brought into the Atlantic, their troop-carrying capacity increased to over 15,000 during the summer months and 12,000–13,000 in the winter, and were used for the build-up of American and Canadian troops prior to the invasion of Europe in 1944. Of the 865,000 American and Canadian troops brought to the United Kingdom across the Atlantic, 320,000 were carried in these two ships alone. Other liners, American, Belgian, Canadian, Dutch and Norwegian, as well as British, were converted for this type of war service, and because of their great speed they made their passages across the Atlantic unescorted, because of the virtual impossibility of a submarine, restricted in her movements by her slow underwater speed, reaching an attacking position before the liner had disappeared over the horizon.

Other liners were taken into navies for

Normandie
(1932)

Length 1,029 ft (313·6 m) *Beam* 117·8 ft (35·9 m)
Draught 36·6 ft (11·2 m) *Gross tonnage* 86,496
Speed 32 knots *Crew* 1,320 *Passenger capacity* 2,170

The *Normandie*, the first ship ever to exceed 1,000 ft in length, was for a time the largest ship in the world and the holder of the Blue Riband of the Atlantic with an average speed of 31·3 knots. Although she soon lost both titles, the first to the *Queen Elizabeth* by a mere 2 ft (60 cm) in 1938 and the second to the *Queen Mary* in 1936, she was virtually the ultimate development in size of the ocean liner. She was built for the Compagnie Générale Transatlantique and had turbo-electric propulsion. She operated on the Atlantic run until France fell in 1940. Renamed the *Lafayette*, she underwent conversion to a troop ship in New York in 1942 but caught fire, capsized and then was sold for scrap.

She is shown here with her side cut away to reveal her machinery, cabins and the first-class dining room. The six ships in profile are the *Sirius*, *Great Eastern*, *Kaiser Wilhelm der Grosse*, *Normandie*, *United States* and *Queen Elizabeth II*, showing the changing scale and appearance of ships on the Atlantic run.

conversion to armed merchant cruisers, which helped to enforce the blockade of the enemy's trade, into command ships for amphibious operations, into landing ships for infantry and tanks, and for a variety of other auxiliary naval purposes. Some were sunk in action, others survived to be reconverted to their original use when the war ended.

In modern maritime warfare the merchant navy of a belligerent nation is often no less important than its fighting navy. The general modern practice is for a nation at war to assume responsibility for the operation of its merchant navy as a whole, fitting it into a co-ordinated war effort, so that every ship is used in the best national interest. More often than not, the experience of war produces new ideas for application in peacetime, new short cuts to

maximum efficiency, and new operating techniques, which, in turn, lead to new developments in ship design. Moreover, the need for urgency in replacing ships lost and repairing ships damaged through enemy action brings in its train new, faster, and more efficient methods of shipbuilding and ship repair. War can bring dividends for peacetime, and this was particularly so in the case of some of the smaller ships, especially ocean-going tugs which had a major role to play during the war, and an equally important one in the years of peace which followed.

It is not within the scope of this book to follow the various events of World War II, except in so far as they affected the development of existing ships or the design of new ones. After the invasion of Poland at the outset of war in September 1939, there was not much fighting on land for the first six months, but the war at sea began at once. On the very day war was declared, a British liner was sunk in the North Atlantic by a German submarine, giving notice that submarine warfare against merchant shipping was to be as much a feature of this war as it had been of the previous one. This was a crushing blow to Britain, for it meant that all her shipping had to be organized at once into convoys, in spite of the severe shortage of escorts and the non-existence of any escort with sufficient endurance to

Below: Albacore torpedo bombers taking off from HMS *Indomitable* during the 'Pedestal' convoy to relieve Malta in August 1942.

remain with a convoy for the whole duration of a transatlantic passage. It therefore entailed the start of an intensive emergency building programme for corvettes, sloops and frigates, and an intensive programme of research into new and more powerful anti-submarine weapons, a better means of illuminating an area of sea at night than with the old-fashioned starshell, the most efficient convoy formation for defence purposes, and similar problems. This lack of preparedness was, in part, a legacy of the Washington Treaty, in part a lack of understanding of the lessons taught by World War I, and in part caused by diversion of so large a part of the money voted for naval rearmament to the building of big battleships. It was to be 1943 before the emergency building programmes had produced enough escorts for the job, but by the time the goal was reached the actual ships produced, particularly the frigates, were fine sturdy vessels with all the weapons and equipment required to carry the war to the submarine and defeat her utterly.

The Norwegian campaign of 1940 highlighted another problem, one that had been guessed at, but not fully appreciated in any of the world's navies. This was that a warship could not survive in waters within range of enemy aircraft unless she was accompanied by fighter aircraft to cover her during operations. The answer was to hand, of course, in the aircraft carrier, introduced in most navies during the years between the wars, but development had been slow, and they were still very thin on the ground. Being a very big ship, the building of a new carrier was a long-term project, hardly suitable for a wartime emergency building programme. An answer to the problem for the Allies did not appear until the United States was drawn into the war in 1941, and, with her immense industrial potential, was able to initiate a crash programme of carrier construction, using modern methods of prefabrication to speed up output. These were small carriers of two main types,

known as 'light fleet carriers' and 'escort carriers', and what they lacked in aircraft capacity they more than made up for in numbers. They began to become operational in 1942 – an incredibly short building time for ships of that size – and by 1943 they were appearing in a steady stream. Inevitably, they became known as 'Woolworth' carriers. The simultaneous application of new fast building techniques and a large measure of prefabrication which produced the aircraft carriers required also held immense promise for rapid ship production in the years to come.

In 1940 and 1941, before the small American carriers arrived on the scene, the British had produced a partial solution to the problem by the adaptation of merchant ships. Their solution was aimed entirely at convoy protection. In 1940 convoys were being attacked by German long-range aircraft, as well as by submarines, and to protect them some merchant ships were fitted with a small launching platform and a catapult, and carried a fighter aircraft on board. They sailed in convoy in the normal way, and on the appearance of an enemy aircraft the fighter was catapulted into the air. On completion of its task, and being unable to land on deck, it ditched itself alongside the nearest ship and the pilot was picked up. They were known as 'camships' (Catapult Aircraft Merchant Ships). A more sophisticated conversion was the 'macship' (Merchant Aircraft Carrier). These ships, usually tankers or grain ships because they were longer and had an uncluttered deck, were fitted with a temporary flight deck above the superstructure, where fighter aircraft could be flown off and land. When, as a result of these measures, attacks by German aircraft ceased, macships were used with naval Swordfish aircraft, adapted to carry depth-charges instead of a torpedo, and used in an anti-submarine role. They lasted until the American escort carriers arrived to take over the task, and, although they were only makeshift and temporary substitutes for the real thing, they filled the gap.

Just as World War I had demonstrated the weaknesses of the battle-cruiser, so World War II demonstrated the deficiencies of the battleship in fleet action. Very occasionally there was a meeting of battleship with battleship, but in the major actions fought between fleets of which battleships formed a part, the two sides never came within 100 nautical miles of each other. These major fleet actions, all fought in the Pacific, were long-range affairs between carrier air groups, showing that the capital ship of the period was now the big aircraft carrier and no longer the battleship. Indeed, the battleship's main role in a fleet action was to serve as an

Below: CAM-ships were merchantmen equipped to launch a single Hurricane fighter from a catapult on the forecastle. The pilot had to 'ditch', but the measure provided a much-needed antidote to air attacks on Gibraltar convoys.

Above: A mixed battery of anti-aircraft guns aboard the battleship USS *Arkansas* in 1944. Long after the battleship had ceased to be the main striking unit, the big guns made her useful for shore bombardment, while her AA guns gave cover to other ships.

anti-aircraft support to the carriers – a sad descent from their previous position of pre-eminence. True, they had a subsidiary role, for bombardment in support of amphibious assaults, in which they proved themselves to be still a potent weapon, but this was hardly a justification of the huge cost of building them. And, as the war progressed, they increasingly fell prey to concentrated attack from the air. The loss of the British *Prince of Wales* and *Repulse* to Japanese air attack, and of the Japanese giants *Musashi* and *Yamato* to American air attack, spelled the end of these big ships. Since the end of World War II, apart from those already too far advanced on the building stocks to be cancelled, no maritime nation has built a battleship and, with the exception of one or two preserved in mothballs in the United States, all have been broken up for scrap.

Alongside the aircraft-carrier, it was the submarine which emerged as the other most significant weapon in naval warfare. Apart from an increase in size and more sophisticated methods of torpedo fire control, there had been little basic development between the wars. The submarine of 1939 was still limited when submerged by the capacity of its electric batteries for propulsion, and when the batteries were exhausted she had no alternative but to come to the surface and recharge them with her diesel engines, driving her electric motors as dynamos. And a submarine on the surface is highly vulnerable to attack, for being low in the water her range of visibility is restricted, and it is difficult to identify enemy craft and evade them. What was recognized as the true submarine, a vessel completely independent of the surface of the sea at all times, had been dreamed of for years, but in the current state of research and development there appeared to be no way of supplying energy without burning up oxygen.

During the war, German scientists came near to it. They had a piece of good fortune, when Holland was overrun in 1940, in coming across a Dutch invention, a long breathing tube which, fitted to a submarine, enabled the diesel engines to be run while the submarine was submerged. Development was completed by 1944, and the first operational submarines using it put to sea in that year. This was still not the ultimate submarine, but it was a step in the right direction as it enabled the submarine to recharge her batteries without having to come to the surface, and even enabled her to use the diesel engines for propulsion when submerged. The depth at which this could be done was limited by the length of the tube, or 'schnorkel' as it was named. It had a disadvantage, too, in that the exhaust fumes of the diesels also had to be discharged up the schnorkel, and more than one submarine was sunk because its diesel smoke, betrayed its presence near the surface.

Although the schnorkel was not the final answer, it went some way towards making the submarine invisible for longer periods, particularly at night – the normal time for surfacing and recharging – when radar was sweeping the darkness. Having developed the schnorkel, German scientists went a step further in the evolution of the submarine by providing oxygen for the diesel engines while submerged, without using the oxygen in the submarine's atmosphere, all of which the crew needed to breathe and keep alive. They did this by designing a closed-circuit diesel installation, using a catalyst with liquid hydrogen-peroxide to provide the gaseous oxygen to mix with the diesel fuel, thus making combustion possible without using the boat's atmosphere. Later, this was changed to a closed-circuit gas-turbine installation, which was more efficient and produced a very high underwater speed. They were known as Walther boats, from the name of their designer Dr. Walther. It was, perhaps, fortunate for the Allies that the war came to an end before this new design of submarine became operational, for it would have posed tremendous problems for the anti-submarine units.

The German submarine offensive, directed against trade, was even more devastating in World War II than in World War I. It sank 2,828 merchant ships, totalling 14,687,231 tons. To this figure must be added the tonnage sunk by raiders, mines and aircraft. These huge losses were far beyond the capacity of the Allied shipyards, using normal shipbuilding methods, to replace, and for four years the final outcome of the war hung in the balance, with the submarine seeming gradually to gain the upper hand. But even when the U-boat was finally defeated in 1943, there was still the tremendous loss of merchant tonnage to be made good, and indeed more was needed than before to carry across the oceans all the weapons and supplies needed for the final assault.

The answer was a vessel with the generic name of 'Liberty ship'. She was the brainchild

Above: A 'Liberty ship' bound for Murmansk wallows in heavy seas. Heavy losses were sustained when the Allies undertook to send convoys to Russia.

of Henry Kaiser, a businessman who had never run a shipyard before. In 1941, he reorganized a number of shipyards in the United States to undertake the construction of a standard merchant ship with a deadweight tonnage of 10,500 and a service speed of 11 knots. They were built to spartan standards, without frills, and by laying down a procedure for quantity production on a massive scale, Kaiser arranged for the continuous provision of these ships throughout the remaining four years of the war.

The chosen design had been produced as long ago as 1879 by the Sunderland Company of Newcastle-upon-Tyne, England, and Kaiser adopted it because the plans incorporated simplicity of construction and operation, rapidity of building, large cargo-carrying capacity, and a remarkable ability to withstand damage. To these qualities Kaiser added prefabrication, which was undertaken in factories away from the shipyards, and welding together instead of rivetting the prefabricated parts. Because the entire production of turbines and diesel engines in the United States was earmarked for naval and other essential construction, these Liberty ships were powered with triple-expansion engines and steam-driven auxiliary machinery.

During the four years between 1941 and 1945, no fewer than 2,770 Liberty ships, of a total deadweight tonnage of 29,292,000, were produced, of which twenty-four were equipped as colliers, eight as tank carrier ships, thirty-six as aircraft transports, and sixty-two as tankers. They proved to be sturdy, reliable ships, perhaps unglamourous in their complete lack of frills and their uncompromising design for the humbler tasks of war, but they helped turn the tide for the Allies and proved to be a remarkably successful experiment in rapid, large-scale shipbuilding.

Electronics and the Navigator

World War II saw many developments and new inventions of great value to ships. Without doubt, two of the most important and far-reaching were radar, which makes it possible to see the objects around a ship at a comparatively long range, in darkness or fog, and hyperbolic navigation systems, by which a navigator knows exactly where he is, without having to perform the long calculations and observations involved in the older processes of navigation. Both these modern aids can have dangers if used to the complete exclusion of older, and usually more laborious, methods: radar because it cannot predict the future course and speed of a ship depicted on the radar plot; hyperbolic navigation because of what is known as the occasional 'crumb in the set'. The wise navigator uses both radar and, if his ship is fitted with the equipment, hyperbolic navigation, but he also keeps a continuous check on his ship's position by the older and more primitive methods of determining his position.

Radar (RAdio Direction And Range) was known in its earliest days as RDF (Radio Direction Finding), but the name was changed in 1941 to 'radar', to avoid confusion with high-frequency direction finding (H/F D/F), an entirely different system in which a bearing is taken on the source of a high-frequency radio signal. The conception of radar is very nearly as old as the invention of wireless telegraphy itself, and the first experiment in reflecting radio pulses off a solid object was made by Christian Hülsmeyer of Dusseldorf in 1903. His idea, which is, in fact, the whole basis of radar, was that, knowing the speed at which radio waves travel, it would be possible to calculate the distance of an object by measuring the time which elapsed between transmitting a signal and receiving its echo, while its direction, or bearing, could be obtained by noting the direction in which the transmitting aerial was pointing at the time of the echo. Herr Hülsmeyer's experiments were inconclusive, but in 1922 Senator Marconi suggested that further experiments along these lines should be performed, as the science of radio telegraphy had by then advanced considerably further.

Serious development was started in Britain, France and Germany during the decade 1930–1940, and the first ship-

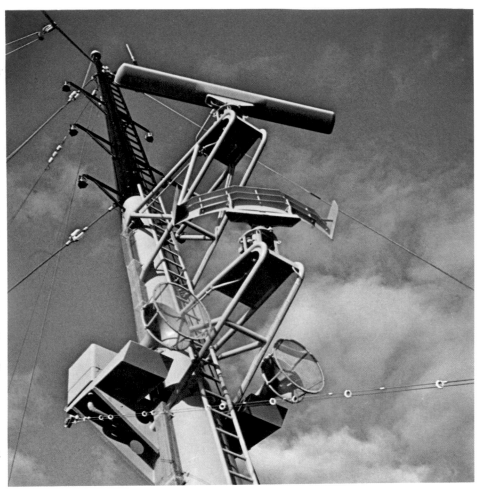

borne radar aerials, forerunners of the modern ship arrays, were fitted in the British battle-cruiser *Repulse* and the German pocket-battleship *Admiral Graf Spee* in 1936. But they proved to have a very short range, were not very accurate, and were cumbersome in operation and appearance. In 1937 a radar set was installed in the French transatlantic liner *Normandie*, but its maximum range was no more than 5 miles (8 km) – still too short to be of use for navigation. Nevertheless, progress continued to be made, and during the first years of the war reasonably accurate sets were used in warships for shadowing enemy ships and for gun aiming. The first time these were used in actual naval operations was during the pursuit of the German battleship *Bismarck* in 1941, when the British cruiser *Suffolk* used radar to shadow the *Bismarck* while keeping out of sight and range. The *Bismarck* also used her radar, to find the range of the British battle cruiser *Hood*.

The great breakthrough came in 1940 with the invention, in Britain, of the magnetron, by means of which very short wavelengths could be produced – a great step forward in range, accuracy and definition. By 1941 the wavelength had been reduced to 10 cm, and by 1943 to 1·9 cm, which enabled a radar set to obtain a definable echo from as small an object as the periscope of a submarine.

Radar sets were installed in merchant ships after the war, as aids to navigation, and they became standard equipment after 1950. The maximum range of a radar set depends on the height of the aerial above sea level, but would hardly be less than 25 nautical miles in a modern merchant ship.

It was assumed at first that radar would enable ships to use full speed even in poor visibility. It took a series of what became known as 'radar-assisted' collisions to prove that radar alone is not enough to tell the course and speed of another vessel even if it is visible on the radar screen.

Hyperbolic navigation originated from systems evolved during World War II, by which bombers flying over enemy-held territory could fix their positions accurately and keep to a pre-determined flight path to their target. The British system, introduced in 1940, was known as 'Gee', and in 1942 the United States introduced a similar system known as 'Loran'. These were then developed for application to ships, and one of the resulting systems known as 'QM', which later became Decca Navigator, was used in 1944 during the Allied invasion of north-west Europe, which called for extremely accurate navigation in the difficult tidal conditions of the English Channel.

After the war an international maritime conference was held in Great Britain where it was agreed to develop four hyperbolic navigational systems eventually to cover the whole world. The four systems selected were Consol, Decca Navigator, Loran and Omega, each varying slightly in operation and in the frequencies used. Very high frequencies give great accuracy up to a distance of about 50 miles (80 km), and are therefore used for coastal systems where a ship's need to fix her position continuously and accurately is greater. Very low frequencies give rather less accuracy, but have a very long range, and cover the mid-ocean areas, where pinpoint navigational accuracy is less vital.

Hyperbolic navigation is so-called because a ship's position is expressed in terms of two co-ordinates that are hyperbolic (i.e. curved) lines, not straight ones. A typical system consists of four transmitter stations, one 'master' and three 'slaves', at different locations on shore. By measuring the interval between the arrival of radio signals transmitted simultaneously by master and one slave station, a co-ordinate of the ship's position is obtained, which appears on the chart as a curved line passing through the gap between the two stations. By repeating the process, using a transmission from another of the slave stations, again in conjunction with the master, the vessel's position can be fixed precisely at the intersection of the two curves. (The transmitters are located so that there is always a good 'angle of cut' at the point of intersection.)

In practice the two co-ordinates are displayed automatically and continuously by the shipborne receiving apparatus, and all that remains for the navigator to do is to read off his position on an overprinted lattice chart.

Far left: Foremast of a modern ferry, showing the navigation radars.

Below: Decca chart of the English Channel with red and green 'decometers' (inset) that give co-ordinates of ships' positions.

red decometer   green decometer

Chapter Twelve
Ships and Technology

When, in 1945, World War II came to an end both in Europe and the Far East, there was as much work to be done by planners, naval architects, shipowners and shipbuilders as there had been at the end of World War I, although in some respects the maritime nations were better prepared for it. One factor was the great advance in ship construction techniques which the impetus of war had encouraged; another was the emergence of the United States from her years of isolationism, ready now to play a greater and more influential part in world affairs.

So far as merchant shipping was concerned the immediate problem, as after 1918, was to get seaborne trade moving again. Because of the early successes of the U-boats in the battle of the Atlantic and the heavy losses of the Mediterranean and Russian convoys, the Allied merchant navies were all very short of ships. Many that had survived the war were damaged, or worn out by six years of continual hard work without the chance of a refit. There was a fairly simple answer to this particular problem in the mass-production methods evolved for the Liberty ships, and an immediate programme was put in hand to build a new series known as 'Victory ships', standardized merchant vessels of substantial cargo-carrying capacity. They followed much the same design as the Liberty ships, though built more strongly with a longer hull and a forecastle deck added. They were less austere than the wartime Liberty ships, and steam turbines replaced the latter's triple-expansion engines. They had, like their predecessors, an all-welded hull and were built to a gross tonnage of 7,607 (about 12,000 tons deadweight), their turbines giving them a top speed of 16 knots. Like most standardized products they had their drawbacks, especially in so varied a business as the carriage of cargo at sea, but they served well to tide over the immediate shortage of tonnage until individual shipowners could design and build ships better adapted to their particular trade requirements.

By 1946 most of the surviving passenger liners, taken over during the war for conversion into troop transports, armed merchant cruisers and so on, had been reconverted to their original role and were reappearing as luxury liners on the oceans. Because of the loss of the French *Normandie* during the war, the British *Queen Mary* and *Queen Elizabeth* were the largest passenger liners still in commission, although France was already planning another transatlantic giant and Holland, Sweden, Norway, Italy, Greece, Canada and the United States were again competing in the passenger business. Their ships were not comparable in size to the new French liner *France* and the two British *Queens*, but were very big ships nevertheless. The shipyards in Britain, too, were busy building new passenger liners to replace the many that had been sunk or damaged on wartime service.

For the next ten years this passenger trade was booming, for the world was opening up more rapidly than it had ever done before and there was a growing demand for travel, as much for holidays and recreation as for practical and business purposes. With the steady expansion of trade to keep pace with the opening up of new markets all round the world, there was no lack of revenue to pay for luxury in the new ships, and at this level of the passenger trade the new liners were fitted out in a style to match their older sisters. There was generally little increase in speed beyond the 30 to 31 knots of the *Queen Mary* and *Queen Elizabeth* until 1952 when the new American liner *United States* crossed the Atlantic at a record average speed of 35.59 knots. However, this was generally regarded among the shipping fraternity as an expensive stunt (the *United States* cost $74 million to build, a colossal price in those pre-inflation days) in order to acquire a mark of prestige that in fact carried little weight among the *élite* passenger ships; the extra 4 knots in speed made no apparent impression on the ability of the other big transatlantic liners to attract passengers in profitable numbers. Indeed, the very high initial cost of achieving this fast service speed did little more than make the *United States* commercially uneconomic, even though

Left: The *Queen Elizabeth II*, the first liner built to combine the tasks of transatlantic passenger liner and holiday cruise ship. During the Falkland Islands operations of 1982 she was used by the Ministry of Defence as a fast troopship to ferry an entire brigade 8,000 miles (12,875 km) non-stop to the fighting front.

her alternative wartime role as a fast troopship had made her eligible for a sizeable government subsidy towards her cost of construction. But in one respect she was notable, being the first really big ship to have her superstructure fabricated in aluminium alloy in order to save weight above the waterline, an innovation quickly followed by other ship designers and builders and still being put to use nowadays.

But already the competition from the air was building up and shipowners were not slow to recognize the writing on the wall. The war had seen the development of the big four-engined bomber and had provided a substantial fund of experience in their operation. With their considerable payload they were the natural prototype for the long-distance airliner, and by 1952 the big national airlines were already operating many long-distance air routes, of which the Atlantic was the most profitable and promised the greatest growth potential. The jet engine, developed for military purposes shortly before the end of World War II, had also become a reality in the world of civil aircraft, and as it increased the speed of aircraft by well over fifty per cent at a single stroke, it meant that would-be transatlantic passengers now had the choice of crossing the Atlantic at 600 knots in an aircraft in six to eight hours or at 30 knots in a liner in four to five days. And exactly the same choice was being offered on all the other main passenger routes – to South Africa and South America, to India and the Far East, to Australia and New Zealand, and across the Pacific Ocean – which until then had been the monopoly of ships. Shipowners, taking the long view, knew that their days of reliance on passenger traffic alone to produce profits were numbered.

One or two of the big shipping companies looked for a way out by buying a controlling interest in an existing airline and trying to run the two together as a complementary service. Actual operating experience proved that this was not really an answer as it did nothing to help the ships to hold their own against the aircraft and most of the companies engaged in this dual role discovered that it did not pay. What did emerge as an answer was the conversion, or building from new, of ships designed for a dual purpose – passenger transport and holiday cruising. On the transport side, no matter how many millions of passengers may prefer to save time on their journeys by flying, there has always been a hard core, recently estimated at about six per cent of the whole market, who accept the longer travelling time because they prefer to go by ship, a more

leisurely and relaxing method of ocean travel. On the other hand, holiday cruising is a boom industry, and the combination in one ship of the two distinct roles has given the liners a new lease of life.

During the 1960s all the very big liners built between the two world wars and immediately after the second, such as the *France*, found the competition from the airlines too fierce for them and they were gradually withdrawn from service – the *Queen Mary* in 1967, the *Queen Elizabeth* and *United States* in 1969, and the *France*, subsidized for some years by the French government until the cost became prohibitive, in 1975. They no longer had any role to play at sea, being too large and of too deep a draught to serve as cruise liners. The *Queen Mary* still exists at Long Beach, California, as a tourist museum and hotel, and the *Queen Elizabeth* was to have served as a university at Hong Kong until she was set on fire and sank in harbour. No decision has as yet been taken on the future, if any, of the *France*.

A good example of a dual-purpose ship is the Cunard Line's *Queen Elizabeth II*, launched in

Right: The *United States* was not only the largest American liner ever built but also the fastest in the world, crossing the Atlantic at an average speed of over 35 knots.

Below: The *France* was the last liner built purely for the transatlantic trade but like all the others found the competition from the airlines too fierce for economic operation. She was withdrawn from the Atlantic in 1975.

Above: An aerial view of merchant ships being fitted out in a shipyard in Genoa, Italy. After their launch, the hulls of new ships are towed to the fitting-out yard for the installation of engines and all other internal and deck gear.

Right: The *Queen Mary*, after the end of her career as a transatlantic liner, was sold for conversion to a floating hotel and conference centre. She now lies alongside a wharf in Long Beach, California.

times of war as her sisters during World War II, operating as a fast troop carrier. Adopting the naval techniques of refuelling at sea, she carried a brigade of troops, 3,000 men, and delivered them to the seat of war, 8,000 miles (12,900 km) away, in a non-stop voyage and at a speed considerably faster than any other ship could have maintained. She was not the only one with a different role to play in times of conflict; other cruise liners were taken up as troop carriers and hospital ships, civilian ferries, container ships, tankers, and other general types were quickly adapted to a wartime role, to speed supplies of all varieties required by the troops fighting in the Falkland Islands. As in all previous wars, the versatility of merchant shipping to adapt quickly to different requirements and different roles was again proved beyond question.

The *Queen Elizabeth II*, as well as providing an economic answer to the competition of the transatlantic airlines, is also an excellent example of the technical engineering and shipbuilding advances of the last thirty years. She has a very refined hull design and, like the *United States* before her, all her superstructure above the upper deck is constructed in light alloy. Her engine room shows even more startling advances. The *Queen Mary*, launched in 1934, had twenty-four Yarrow boilers delivering steam at 400 lb/sq in (28 kg/cm²) to drive her four sets of Parsons turbines at 180,000 horsepower. Four years later the *Queen Elizabeth* had twelve Yarrow boilers delivering steam at 450 lb/sq in (32 kg/cm²) to drive similar machinery at the same speed and horsepower. The *France*, which made her maiden voyage in 1962, had eight boilers delivering steam at 910 lb/sq in (64 kg/cm²) which drove four sets of turbines geared to two propellers to give a comparable speed. The *Queen Elizabeth II*, launched in 1970, produces about the same speed with only three Foster-Wheeler boilers which deliver steam at 650 lb/sq in (46 kg/cm²) to two of the most powerful sets of turbines ever constructed for a ship. They had been made possible by new advances in metallurgy, particularly in the development of nickel-chrome steel with its better heat-resisting qualities.

1970 as a replacement for the *Queen Mary* and *Queen Elizabeth*. Although smaller than her two predecessors, she is still a very big ship at 65,000 tons gross. A great deal of preliminary planning went into her design, largely to produce a draught of less than 32 ft (9·75 m) so that, in her cruising role, she would be able to enter some of the more exotic foreign harbours which had insufficient depth of water for a normal ship of her tonnage. During the summer months she makes up to a dozen or so direct crossings of the Atlantic as a passenger liner, and for the remainder of the year operates as a luxury cruise liner. And, as we have seen in the recent turmoil in the South Atlantic, she still has the same role to play in

As, in the face of competition from air travel, the liner has become progressively smaller, so the average merchant ship has become progressively larger. They have had to primarily because of the great increase in the volume of world trade since the end of World War II, the great majority of which is still carried in ships because there is virtually no competition from

Above: Until 1976 the ULCC *Globtik Tokyo* was, at 484,000 tons, the largest oil tanker in the world but has since been overtaken in size. The present slump in the world's oil demands has raised some questions of the economic viability of these huge tankers.

the airlines in bulk transport. Another important reason for this growth in size is that it makes more economic sense to carry large cargoes in fewer ships than small cargoes in a large number of ships.

The biggest growth in size has been in oil tankers, due very largely to extraneous reasons. These were the two periods of closure of the Suez Canal, the first in 1956 after the Suez Crisis, the second in 1967 after the Six Day War between Israel and Egypt. Until the first closure the normal route for tankers bringing oil from the Middle Eastern oilfields to the Western industrial nations was through the Suez Canal, which put a physical limitation on the size of any tanker using this route as the Canal was not wide enough, or dredged to a suitable depth, to take very big ships. The maximum size of a tanker using the Suez Canal was about 30,000 tons gross. After the Canal was closed in 1956, all oil brought from that source to the Western countries had to be carried by the very much longer route round South Africa. With so much further to steam, the existing size of the average tanker made the longer voyage uneconomic in terms of the cargo able to

be carried, and was the cue for the introduction of what became known as the 'supertanker'.

The growth in size of the average tanker during these years can perhaps best be illustrated by taking actual examples. Although there was the occasional tanker up to about 24,000 tons deadweight built between the two world wars, the average size of the large tanker was from 10,000 to 15,000 tons deadweight. In 1950 a tanker named the *Velutina* of 28,000 tons deadweight was launched, and in 1953 she was followed by the *Tina Onassis* with a deadweight tonnage of 45,750. Six years later, after the first closure of the Suez Canal, a tanker with a deadweight tonnage of 68,840, the *W. Alton Jones*, was built in the United States.

The second closure of the Suez Canal in 1967 was a much longer affair and occurred at a time when there was an unprecedented world demand for oil, partly because world trade, and therefore manufacture, was buoyant and partly because of the huge explosion in numbers of the motor car and aeroplane, both completely dependent on oil for their motive power. The combination of these two – the closure of the shorter route to the West and the great surge in demand – gave an enormous boost to the design and construction of new and bigger tankers which made the earlier supertankers look almost like midgets. Thus a new generation of tankers was born, to be known as VLCCs (Very Large Crude Carriers) ranging up to between 250,000 to 275,000 tons deadweight. There were at first some doubts whether so huge a ship could be built strong enough to withstand the strains, especially of hogging and sagging, which all ships undergo when steaming in a rough sea. But the experience of actual operation of such large ships proved that they were viable both in terms of economic transport and of safety at sea. And as the proof of their strength and viability was recognized, so the next generation took its place on the building slips. They were known as ULCCs (Ultra Large Crude Carriers) and were first built up to a deadweight tonnage of around 400,000. With the world demand for oil still increasing at a large rate, it was not long before even larger tankers were deemed to be necessary, and designs of ships of up to 800,000 tons deadweight were on the drawing board. With the success of the VLCCs and the first of the ULCCs as far as hull strength was concerned, it seemed that there could be no limit to the size to which a ship could be built using the modern methods of construction and modern metals. While this is no doubt a fact of modern ship design and building, the imagination shudders at the size of the disaster if one of these ultra large tankers should break up in mid-ocean or run ashore when approaching the coast. The extent of the damage caused by the stranding of the smaller tankers *Torrey Canyon* off Land's End in 1967 and *Amoco Cadiz* off the coast of Brittany in 1978 was severe enough to be still remembered.

By 1976 the largest of the ULCCs in commission was the *Globtik Tokyo* of 483,664 tons deadweight, although since then several larger tankers have been completed, including in 1981 the *Seawise Giant* of 564,763 tons deadweight. Converted by Nippon Kokan of Japan from another tanker (to which an extra midship section was added), the *Seawise Giant* is at present the largest ship in the world with a length of 1,504 ft (458·5 m), a beam of 226 ft (68·8 m) and a draught of 98 ft (29·8 m). Whether she will prove to be an expensive white elephant or an economic unit of the oil-carrying trade only the future will reveal. But even before she began her career as a tanker, things in the oil market had begun to change. In the mid-1970s the oil-producing countries raised the price of their oil to four times what it had been previously, and a year or two later doubled it again. This huge increase in price started a chain reaction throughout the world, with consumer nations adopting policies of energy conservation to reduce their consumption of expensive oil – policies which helped to lead the world into a trade depression which still further reduced the oil consumption. Consequently, shipowners around the world found themselves with an excess of tanker tonnage, leading to a cancellation of building orders and the laying-up of a large number of existing tankers, particularly the biggest ones. One result of this decrease in consumption, which looks as though it could well become permanent as the nations of the world become more conservation-conscious, is that the average size of the modern tanker, particularly in the case of new vessels being built, has gone into reverse and is dropping to more modest dimensions.

Below: An aerial view of the oil tanker *Torrey Canyon* broken in two after running aground on the Seven Stones rocks off Land's End, England, in 1967 as a result of faulty navigation. The resultant pollution around the neighbouring coasts was a local disaster.

Right: A merchant ship unloading in Hong Kong harbour. She is lying at a mooring buoy and discharging her cargo into barges secured alongside, which will then ferry it to the shore.

Below: The oil tanker *Tactic* labouring in a heavy sea. It had been thought that the stresses set up in the hull under such conditions would have proved critical in such large ships but modern methods of construction have overcome this problem.

Another factor which is influencing this reduction in size has been the worldwide exploration for new sources of oil. Large deposits have been found in Africa, under the North Sea, in Alaska and in many other parts of the world. So geography now has to come into the calculations of the oil companies when working out the requirements for transporting their crude oil to the world's refineries. The days of almost total dependence on the Middle East, with long voyages round the south of Africa to the west, are no longer the prime consideration in the determination of tanker size. The two great canals in the world, Suez, which has been widened and deepened, and Panama, which can take ships of up to 100,000 tons, are again exerting an influence in tanker design and size. The possibility, for example, of being able to transport Alaskan oil from the Pacific to the Atlantic through the Panama Canal is obviously a more attractive project than doing so around Cape Horn. A tanker of up to 100,000 tons can make such a passage

through the Canal; bigger tankers are forced into a voyage three times as long with the added cost of more fuel consumed on the voyage, a larger wage bill for the crew, and all the additional costs of ship maintenance and wear and tear.

All large tankers are steam driven with turbines, although some of the smaller ones are fitted with diesel engines. Steam propulsion in tankers has an added advantage as a ready producer of inert gas, mainly carbon dioxide, which all tankers need in order to minimize the risk of explosion, particularly from the mixture of air and petroleum gas which is present when the oil cargo is being discharged or has recently been discharged. Inert gas is readily available in steam-driven tankers from the boiler uptakes and, when amalgamated with the air and petroleum gas mixture in the empty tanks, makes them safe from explosion. Steam in tankers is also required for heating the crude oil cargo to make it fluid enough to be pumped, and to drive the pumps, capstan, and winches on board, as electric motors are too dangerous to be used in a tanker for fear of sparking and setting off an explosion. Tankers which are diesel driven are always fitted with a steam boiler, which may be fired from the diesel exhaust gases, partly to provide the inert gas required and partly to generate steam, to drive the auxiliary machinery on board.

Surprisingly for such large vessels, all of them are single screw ships, unlike liners, most of which have twin screws. The quadruple screw ships of the years between the wars are now past history and are never likely to return, for modern technology in the shape of new propeller designs (including the variable-pitch propeller), high-pressure steam and turbines of increased power, has enabled the single propeller to drive even the largest ship at a reasonable speed with, at the same time, a considerable increase in overall efficiency.

Tankers do not necessarily all transport oil. Some are designed to carry water, some small ones are used for the transport of wine, others carry molasses, liquefied gas, or liquid chemicals. But whatever their cargo, the basic tanker design is the same, the cargo being carried in insulated tanks, or compartments, within the main tank which forms the largest part of the hull.

The post-war development of the cargo ship has followed a similar pattern of growth in size, due not so much to the two closures of the Suez Canal as to the phenomenal growth in world trade throughout the years following World War II. Modern technology allied to intensive research has resulted in vast increases of production in almost every sphere of man's endeavour, from agriculture to manufacturing, and virtually the whole of the export and import of this greatly increased production has to be handled by cargo ships. The general post-war trend has been to build large ships to handle imports and exports in bulk to world centres of distribution and to use smaller cargo vessels to act as feeders to and from these centres. The general increase in size has not been nearly so dramatic as in the case of oil tankers, and a cargo ship today of 60,000 to 80,000 tons is a very big ship. Developments in the method of cargo carrying, rather than in the cargo ship itself, have dictated most of the changes in merchant ship design during the last twenty or thirty years. There were ships built specifically to carry one type of cargo – coal, wheat, mineral ores, etc. – from the last century onwards, and virtually the only change to be seen in today's ships of this type is in their size, now very much larger to compete economically with the growth in demand. There have also, of course, been some changes to adapt to more modern methods of loading and unloading these bulk cargoes, but the basic essentials of the ship engaged in this trade have not changed overmuch. There are new standards of crew accommodation, more efficient installations for ship propulsion and better handling methods on board, but these are the normal improvements which are to be found in virtually every modern ship operating on the seas today.

The most radical new method of cargo handling today is that of containerization, and this has

Below: A multi-user container terminal at Tilbury Docks, London. The containers are picked up by travelling gantries using a spreader which locks onto the four top corners. They are then lowered into the hold or onto the deck stowage of the ship.

brought about one big change in cargo ship design since the end of the war. The use of metal containers of standard size throughout the world has revolutionized the stowage of cargo on board ship and has also changed the overall shape of the ship from the typical cargo carrier of forty years ago. In those days the average cargo ship was what was known as the 'three island type' – a forecastle where the crew had their accommodation, a forward well-deck for the forward holds, a midships bridge structure, an after well-deck for the after holds, and a poop, below which was the boiler and engineroom; the forecastle, bridge

and poop formed the three islands. The growth of containerization has changed all that.

Most dry cargo, except of course those carried as bulk cargoes such as grain, coal, sugar, etc. can be packed, or 'stuffed', into standard-size containers in depots ashore and easily transported by rail or road to the nearest container-loading port. There they are picked up by travelling gantries or special container cranes equipped with a 'spreader' which fits on top of the container to be lifted and, by remote control from the crane driver, engages in twist locks on each corner of the container so that it can be hoisted and

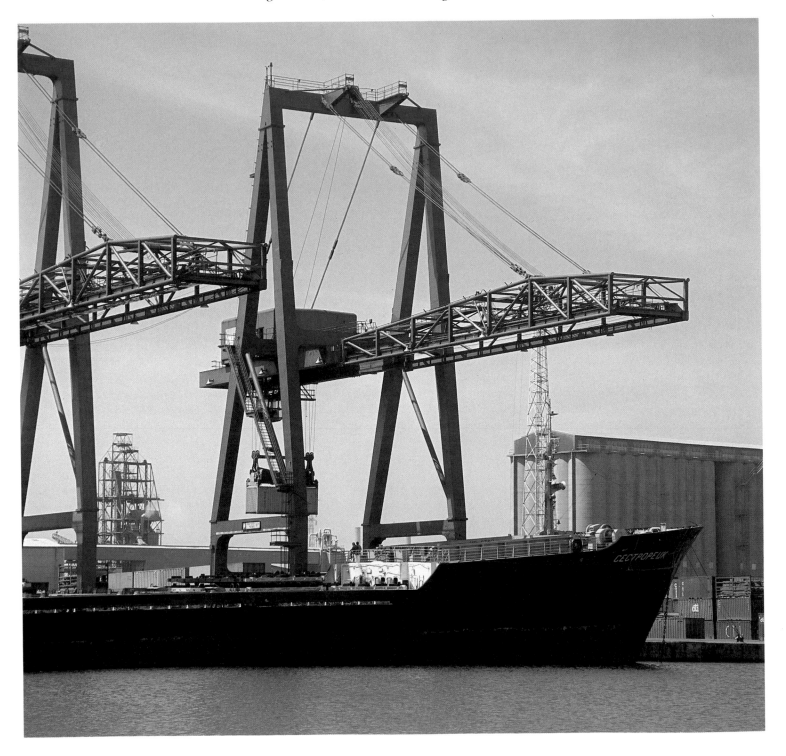

lowered without fear of it being dropped. Knowing the exact size of the container, the naval architect can design his cargo-carrying ship with holds of the right size needed to take the containers, and with a clear deck space of the right size to take an additional deck cargo of containers. The holds have wide hatchways, and the sides are lined with angled steel guides into which the containers are lowered vertically so that they are unable to move. Deck cargoes, stacked two, three, or even four deep, are held solid by the four corner twist locks on each container. With the steel guides in the holds and the twist locks on deck, there can be no danger of the cargo shifting in a rough sea (so often the cause of disasters at sea in past years) and of course no problems, as also in the past, of fitting items of different size and shape in the holds so that they are not damaged in transit. In order to create unobstructed space on deck for the containers, the central island of the conventional 'three island' ship containing the bridge structure has been removed to the poop deck aft, and the forecastle as such has disappeared, with the crew quarters also moved aft to the poop. The new deck layout makes for an efficient ship, even if not a handsome one, generally somewhat slab-sided and with a bulbous bow (see p.303) which does not add to good looks. These ships are officially described as cellular container ships, are driven either by steam or diesel and are normally fast ships with a service speed (average speed when fully loaded) of over 20 knots.

The stowage of cargo containers on deck sometimes causes problems of stability through the reduction of the ship's metacentric height, at times to as little as a few inches. A ship's metacentric height, which is the vertical distance between her centre of gravity and a theoretical point above it known as the 'transverse metacentre', is an important element in determining the righting movement which is exerted to bring a ship back on an even keel when she rolls under the influence of the sea or the wind. The greater the metacentric height, the greater the righting movement, and stowing cargo on deck obviously raises the position of a ship's centre of gravity and thus reduces her metacentric height. In the case of container ships fully loaded with a heavy deck cargo of containers, this problem is accentuated during the course of her voyage by the consumption of fuel and other stores, which reduces the weight normally carried low down in the ship and thus raises further the centre of gravity. This possible danger is only lessened at the first port of call where the top layers of containers forming the deck cargo are unloaded, thus lowering the centre of gravity and increasing the metacentric height. This is a problem which is

well recognized by naval architects and allowed for in their initial calculations, so that there is no real danger of such a ship actually capsizing under the weight of her deck cargo. The main effect on a ship of a small metacentric height is that she will probably have a very slow period of roll in a seaway.

Although in its essentials the merchant ship of today does not vary greatly from her sisters of yesterday except in the case of overall size, there has been a considerable revolution in what one might describe as the infrastructure of the shipping world. The navigational work of a ship has been considerably eased by the introduction of both long-range and short-range hyperbolic navigation systems (see pp. 256–7), by the adoption of separation zones in restricted areas carrying heavy traffic such as the English Channel, equivalent perhaps to a motorway on land, and to the compulsory fitting of radar in all ships of any size. Automation on board has also greatly eased the amount of manual work in a ship normally carried out by the crew. The effect of this can be seen in the average size of a modern ship's crew as compared with a similar-sized ship of the

Above: The container ship *Kowloon Bay* at sea with her cargo of containers. Computerized loading ensures that containers are stowed on board in the correct order for unloading when the ship reaches her destination.

years between the two world wars. Today, even the big tankers of a quarter of a million tons are operated by a crew of between thirty and forty men. If one could imagine a similar ship of that size between the wars, she would have needed a crew running into hundreds of men. Today, boilers can be automatically stoked, engines can be automatically operated, and ships steered on a pre-set course, all electronically monitored.

It is the same story in cargo handling. Forty years ago ships were loaded and unloaded by cranes on the dockside which hoisted items of cargo into the air, usually in a net, and swung them over the ship's side to be lowered into the hold where a swarm of dockers manhandled them into position, wedging them in so that they would not move about during the ship's passage. In some ports, where dockside cranes were not available, this was done by the ship's own derricks. Today, many merchant ships are built on the roll-on, roll-off (Ro-Ro) loading principle so that cargo does not have to be hoisted and lowered by cranes or derricks to reach the hold. This kind of loading is usually done by pre-packing the cargo onto pallets, which are then

lifted by fork-lift trucks to a large loading port in the ship's side or bow, from where they are taken by an inboard fork-lift truck direct to the hold.

Modern port installations also play a large part in this infrastructure. New commercial ports have been built, older ones expanded and modernized, and all designed to provide a quicker turn-round of the ship in harbour – faster unloading and faster loading – so that she spends as little time as possible lying in port and more time at sea earning her keep. The organization of a modern port is a complex affair, all computer-based, so that there is a constant supply of essential information of when ships are due, what stores they will need to take on board, what cargo is due to be loaded and unloaded, the order in which it is to be loaded according to destination and the ship's planned voyages, and so on. Work goes on day and night so that the ship, the main essential factor in the whole operation of sea transport, is not needlessly held up in her task of distributing the world's agricultural and manufacturing produce from its points of production to the points of its consumption.

One other small design change is the attention

Above: An aerial view of the Northfleet Hope container terminal at Tilbury Docks, London. Containerization has revolutionized the transport of mixed cargoes.

now paid in all new shipbuilding to the accommodation of the crew on board. The reduction in the size of crews in modern ships allied to the general move of crew accommodation from the old-fashioned forecastle to the new poop structure, has resulted in widespread improvements both in comfort and in the general standard of living. Instead of the crowded bunk space under the forecastle deck in which the crew slept, ate and spent their time off watch in the old days, the men now have cabins, single in the big ships and perhaps two-berth or four-berth in the smaller ones. The modern seaman's food is good, served in a general mess-room and usually on a cafeteria basis in the larger ships; he has a library; a games room; and even perhaps a swimming pool. He can expect mail and newspapers not only at the ports of call during the ship's voyage but also, on some big ships with built-in helipads, delivered by helicopter from ports close to the ship's route. In many large ships he can also expect his quarters to be air-conditioned. It is all a part of the new look of today's shipping industry.

Left: The control console in the engine-room of a modern merchant ship. The visual display of information allows remote control of all engine-room operations by a single engineer.

Below: The roll-on, roll off ferry *Seaspeed Arabia* seen at anchor at Suez.

The speed with which ships can reflect in their design the public moods and requirements of the immediate present is quite remarkable, particularly since World War II when this change has been more rapid than ever before. As has been seen, the explosion in oil tanker building followed quickly on the first closure of the Suez Canal, grew even greater after the second, and almost as quickly faded out again as the price of oil shot up and the main consuming nations became conservation-minded. A similar example was the case of the big whale-factory ships which made their appearance in the South Atlantic and North Pacific during the years after the end of World War II. There had in fact been whale-factory ships in the Atlantic in the 1920s, but they were relatively small and not particularly well adapted to their task. It took the world shortage of food during the years immediately following the end of World War II to transform them into large ships of up to 26,000 tons, specially designed and built to process whales on almost a production-line basis. This was made possible by their open stern with a sloping ramp up which the whales could be hauled directly onto the flensing deck. The huge post-war demand for whalemeat, both for human consumption and the production of pet foods, and for other whale products such as candles, soap, margarine and cosmetics, led to a great increase in the design and building of whale-factory ships and smaller whale catchers, with many nations attracted to this very profitable trade. After a very few years the resultant overfishing almost led to the extinction of this gentle mammal, to an extent where the conscience of the world became revolted by the slaughter. An International Whaling Com-

mission was set up to agree on measures of conservation, together with some national decisions to ban the use of whale products, both of which steps have brought the overfishing to an end. The main result has been that the whale-factory ship is a dying breed, only just kept alive by Russia and Japan who still send annual expeditions to the whaling grounds. The other nations, including Britain, who used to take part in this trade, have broken up their whale-factory ships and adapted their whale catchers for other purposes.

But the general efficiency of the design has not been lost, and is seen today in some of the new fishing trawlers. The traditional trawler, known as the 'beam trawler', worked its trawls from the vessel's sides, using a single trawl which was brought up alongside, hoisted over the fish well with a derrick, emptied of its catch, and then shot (let out) again for another catch. The more modern development is the stern trawler, not unlike a miniature whale-factory ship, which works two trawls through a square opening in the stern, one trawl being shot as the other is hauled, so that no time is lost between trawls while she is on the fishing grounds. Distant water trawlers are relatively large vessels of up to about 3,000 tons and are equipped to stay as long as five weeks on the fishing grounds, often with a fish-factory processing ship in attendance.

One area of phenomenal post-war growth is in ferries. There have, of course, always been ferries, ranging from quite small boats carrying passengers across rivers to large, long-distance ferries carrying passengers, cars and cargo. The earliest large development, before the days of cars and lorries, were train ferries, normally with a single train deck with from one to four rail tracks and usually converging to one track at the bow and three at the stern. The early train ferries

Above left: The carcass of a slaughtered whale is winched up the stern ramp of a whale-factory ship.

Above: A modern type of deep-sea motor trawler, the *Norina*, built at Goole in Britain, with a stern ramp for the more efficient shooting and hauling of trawls.

Above right: Nets (trawls) being handled on the stern of a trawler after being hauled.

Below right: A Russian fish carrier off Dakar, on the west coast of Africa. These ships either accompany their own trawler fleet or purchase the catches of local fishing vessels for bulk transport to Russia.

loaded and discharged over the stern, but more modern ones are double-ended with an opening bow door and stern ramp. As rail cars have to be loaded over a comparatively level track, the rise and fall of the tide necessitates the use of a link span at train ferry terminals with facilities for elevation and depression. Ships which carry trains, and some car ferries, are fitted with equalizing tanks with automatic flooding and pumping to correct any angles of heel which may be caused when loading or off-loading heavy railway vehicles or cars and coaches.

The fastest area of growth, however, has been in passenger/car ferries, mainly due to the roll-on, roll-off system of loading developed since the war. In the older car ferries cars were slung on board with a four-point chain bridle, one leg to each wheel, and lifted into the ferry's hold by a dockside crane. The immense worldwide explosion in car ownership and the resultant demand for touring holidays in foreign countries called for a much more efficient method of loading and off-loading, and this problem was quickly solved using wartime experience of tank and infantry landing craft. Initially, the roll-on, roll-off facility was embodied in the introduction of a stern door opening onto a ramp along which cars could be driven directly onto the ship's car deck. It was only a short step from this to the introduction of a hinged, lifting bow section in addition to the stern doors so that cars could be driven into the ferry and off again without having to turn round – the full, modern, roll-on, roll-off facility. Some car ferries, which operate from ports which have no modern car terminals so that they have to lie alongside a jetty, load and off-load through large doors cut in the ship's side, from which a ramp leads down to the jetty. They are mostly to be found in the Mediterranean and Baltic seas, where the very small rise and fall of the tide does not affect the level of the side door in relation to the level of the jetty.

Most ferries are powered today by the medium-speed, V-form diesel engine driving

Above: The car and passenger ferry *Finnjet* photographed at Helsinki, Finland. She is the largest and fastest car ferry in the world and is powered by two gas turbines.

twin variable-pitch propellers which can be controlled directly from the bridge. In medium-sized ferries, up to about 5,000–6,000 tons gross, this machinery will give a service speed of about 20–24 knots. In the earlier post-war car ferries steam turbines were the most popular form of propulsion, but they are now being gradually withdrawn. A typical car ferry, such as those which cross the English Channel, would have a capacity of around 1,250 passengers, 200–250 cars, and about 50–60 commercial vehicles.

The largest car ferry yet built is the Finnish *Finnjet*, which operates between Helsinki and Travemünde in West Germany, a passage of 600 nautical miles which she covers in 22 hours. She can carry 1,532 passengers, all accommodated in two-berth and four-berth cabins, and 350 cars. She is a monster ferry at 24,605 tons gross, and is remarkable by being powered by two Pratt and Whitney gas turbines which give her a speed of over 27 knots. Her consumption of fuel on each round trip is over 600 tons, an indication of the great thirst of gas turbines. With the aid of

powerful bow thrusters (see p. 303) she can turn in her own length without the assistance of tugs. Today she is the ultimate development in car ferries; whether she can remain profitable depends on her being able to maintain an economic level of passengers and cars.

Given the flexibility and strength of modern shipbuilding materials and the versatility of modern engineering methods, there are few demands that a good naval architect allied to a good shipbuilder cannot meet. Not all the craft which they produce fall into the conventional categories of warships and merchant ships; exploitation of the sea's resources has called upon the shipbuilder to adapt to the new demands of specialist constructions. Exploitation of the seabed, and particularly the search for offshore oilfields, has produced specially designed drilling ships and production platforms (see pp. 295–301); the new demand for specialist oceanographical surveys has stimulated the design and building of the bathyscaphe, a sophisticated development of the bathysphere, which is in its essentials a small free-moving submarine constructed and armoured to withstand tremendous pressures as it explores the ultimate depths of the sea. In 1960 a bathyscaphe descended to a depth of 36,000 ft (11,000 m) in the Guam Deep Trench. The pressure of the water on the hull at this depth is over 8 tons per square inch, which gives some impression of the strength of her construction. These are but one or two examples of the versatility of the modern shipbuilder; given the particular problems to be faced, he can more often than not produce a solution.

There are, naturally, still some limitations which restrict the naval architect and shipbuilder, of which the most important is probably initial cost in relation to the market which the ship is designed to serve. Every shipowner, for example, would like his ships to be fast in order to cut down the length of time spent on their voyages, but the cost of additional speed, in the shape of fuel consumption and engines of greater power, rises astronomically for every extra knot achieved above a ship's economical speed. Additionally, if cost were no criterion in construction, aluminium alloy would almost certainly replace steel as the prime shipbuilding material, for it has the strength to bear the normal strains imposed on a ship in a seaway, is much lighter in weight than steel, thereby achieving a saving in fuel consumption, and is also much more resistant than steel to corrosion. It can be welded as easily as can steel, which makes it an attractive material for shipbuilders. All steel ship construction is now welded and the sound of the rivetting hammer, so long the noisy accompaniment of work in the shipyards, is no longer heard in the land. Welded construction, as strong if not stronger than rivetted, has the advantage of saving weight through the elimination of rivets and of providing a more streamlined hull with no overlapping plates. Aluminium alloy is used for the construction of some small warships, where economy in initial cost is not the prime consideration, and for the superstructure of liners and some other large ships where the saving of weight is an important asset. But it is still too expensive a material to be used for most merchant ships where the initial cost is very much a factor of their economic life. Similarly, if the cost were not

to be counted, most merchant ships would be propelled by gas turbines, as their power-to-weight ratio is so much greater than any other form of marine propulsion. Their great drawback lies in their inordinate thirst for fuel, which makes them very expensive to operate.

Another restriction on the naval architect and shipbuilder lies in the limiting strength of metals and their liability to fracture under pressure. The most economical means of ship propulsion today, in terms of fuel consumption and running costs, is the diesel engine and many shipowners prefer it above all others for that reason. In theory there

Below: A merchant ship under construction on a building slip on the River Tyne, England, towers above the houses in an adjacent street.

Above: A VLCC oil tanker under construction in a Japanese shipyard. In many such large ships the deck crew are issued with bicycles.

Above right: The hovercraft is the first really radical innovation in sea transportation since the introduction of steam.

Right: The hydrofoil is another quite recent innovation. As it picks up speed the angled foils raise the hull clear of the water, thus reducing drag and making high speeds possible.

The post-World War II years also saw the development of the hydrofoil as a very fast short-haul passenger carrier. The basic idea of a boat's hull lifting itself clear of the water onto planes, or foils, when driven fast is not new; the first experiment along these lines dates back to 1891, and in 1906, in trials on Lake Maggiore in Italy, Enrico Forlanini demonstrated a small craft fitted with ladder foils which reached a speed of 38 knots. Until 1927 these craft operated with their foils submerged, but in that year German engineers evolved what became known as the surface-piercing foil, in which the foils rise completely to the surface and the craft skids across the top of the water. By lifting the hull in this way completely out of the water, all drag and skin friction is eliminated, enabling very high speeds to be achieved. It was not until 1956 that this new revolutionary method of marine propulsion was put to commercial use with the establishment of a fast passenger ferry service operating between Sicily and Italy. This was quickly followed a year later by Russian passenger-carrying hydrofoils built at the Krasnoye Sormovo shipyard for use on the Russian rivers. Since then hydrofoils have been introduced as fast ferries on a number of relatively short sea crossings. They have also been tested for possible naval use, mainly in the fields of anti-submarine warfare and minesweeping.

There are two basic types of hydrofoil, those fitted with the *canard* type foil in which thirty per cent of the vessel's weight is supported on the forward foils and seventy per cent on the after foils, and the conventional type in which the percentages are reversed. In the *canard* type the foils are surface-piercing so that the whole vessel and its foils ride on the surface; in the conventional type, the foils remain submerged although the hull of the vessel is lifted clear of the water. The *canard* type produces a very high speed but less control, the conventional type less speed but greater stability. Powered by gas turbine engines, many hydrofoils can attain speeds of over 60 knots.

Both types of hydrofoil burn fuel at a very high rate, which limits them to comparatively small size and short range. Some visionaries have produced designs for ocean liners built on the hydrofoil principle to carry up to 500 passengers at 60 knots, but a realistic examination of such ships' plans indicates that they would probably need to carry additional fuel tanks to the exclusion of all passenger accommodation in order to reach their destinations.

Exactly the same considerations limit the uses to which the hovercraft can be adapted, for here

was no reason why it could not be developed in size and power to drive even the largest ships, but its limitation lies in the size of the crankshaft required to stand up to the enormous pressures generated when the engine is a very big one. This has restricted the engine to a power output of around 16,000 to 17,000 shaft horsepower, suitable for a ship of around 18,000 to 20,000 tons. Recent engineering advances, coupled with variable-pitch propellers, now make the diesel engine a possibility for larger ships, and it may well be that its use in the future will be extended in the field of marine propulsion. Nevertheless, the larger merchant ships still rely on the steam turbine, almost always with single or double reduction (a form of gearing), as the main source of motive power, with a few using turbo-electric drive in which the turbines are used to drive dynamos which, in turn, produce current to drive electric motors geared to the propeller shaft. Some diesel-engined ships do the same thing in a diesel-electric drive.

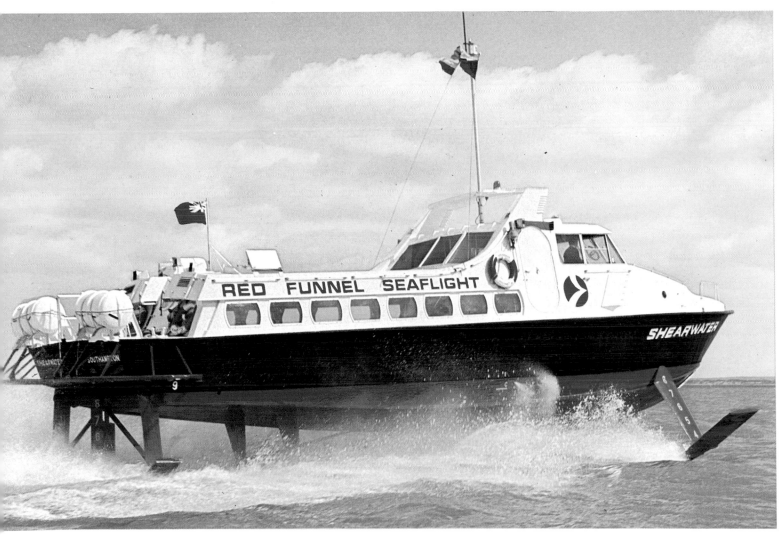

again the fuel consumption is too high to permit long-distance operation. Like the hydrofoil the idea of the hovercraft is not new, for the principles on which it operates were first investigated in Holland in 1875. Constructional difficulties prevented its development then and it was not until 1950 that these were overcome, when a practicable design was produced by the British engineer Christopher Cockerell. It took another eight years to get official sponsorship and funds to develop it.

The hovercraft is a vehicle (there is still argument as to whether it should be ranked as a ship or an aircraft, although as it has to obey the International Navigational Rules of the Road at Sea it must surely be nearer a ship than an aircraft) which rides on a cushion of air between it and the surface over which it is travelling. The largest hovercraft at present in commercial operation as a passenger/car ferry is the SRN-4, a vessel of 165 gross registered tons with an overall length of 130 ft (39·6 m) and a beam of 77 ft (23·5 m). As a car/passenger ferry it has a capacity of 256 passengers and 30 cars, or as a passenger-only ferry 610 passengers. Its power unit consists of four gas turbine engines which drive four variable-pitch aircraft propellers to provide forward movement and four 12-bladed centrifugal fans to provide the cushion of air on which the vessel rides. This cushion of air is prevented from escaping sideways by a neoprene skirt which hangs down to the water all round the vessel. The SRN-4 has a cruising speed of 55 knots and a maximum speed of 65 knots. It has two considerable advantages over the conventional car ferry. With its high speed it can make many more passages a day and it does not need any car terminal facilities since it can ride ashore for loading and off-loading on any hard area of beach. Smaller versions of the SRN-4 have been evaluated for military purposes, particularly in the field of amphibious warfare. US hovercraft were used operationally in Vietnam, and proved especially useful in transporting troops across boggy ground.

While steel remains the major, and virtually the only, building material for the hulls of ships of any size, there has been a revolution since World War II in the construction of smaller craft by the introduction of completely new building materials. The most widely used of these is glass reinforced plastic (GRP), more commonly called 'fibreglass'. This has almost completely revolutionized small boat construction, replacing the original individual wooden hulls of earlier days by mass production in modern plastics.

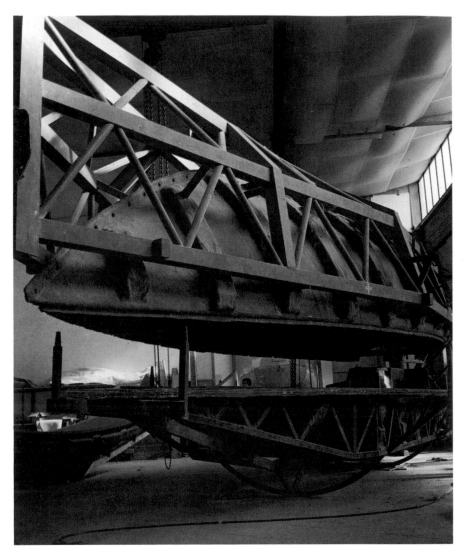

Glass reinforced plastic consists of a mat of very fine fibres of glass saturated with a liquid polyester resin and laid in a pre-formed mould. A catalyst, such as methyl-ethyl ketone peroxide, together with a hardener, is then applied as a liquid and causes the resin to set rock hard. The outside of the hull has an extra layer or skin, known as a 'gel coat', which contains the colour pigment and gives an exceptionally hard, smooth and shiny surface. One of the many advantages of this method of hull construction is that it lends itself to the mass production of small craft of all varieties, from dinghies to sailing and motor yachts, by the use of moulds onto which the GRP is applied. Other advantages of GRP are its lightness in relation to its strength, its complete freedom from rust, corrosion, and rot, and its resistance to all the marine organisms which attack wood and to knocks and minor collisions. All these advantages are such that today something approaching ninety per cent of all dinghies, yachts, and other craft up to about 75 ft (23 m) in length are constructed of it. Some of the modern life-saving craft are also made of GRP, and because of its non-magnetic properties several

Above: Hulls of smaller vessels can be moulded in glass reinforced plastic (GRP or fibreglass). This material does not decay or corrode and for minesweepers it has the added attraction of being non-magnetic.

navies have adopted it for the construction of minehunters, as minesweepers are called today.

Another new material developed for small craft production is ferrocement. Ships made of cement are not new; during World War I some small merchant ships were constructed in Britain of this material as quick replacements for some of the horrifying losses caused by the German U-boat attacks, and it was also used during those years, though in small numbers, for the building of dumb lighters for use in loading and unloading ships lying out at anchor in the stream. The modern method of cement construction, however, is much more refined than the crude methods of World War I. Several layers of wire mesh, usually of the welded type, are wired to the intersections of steel rods and tubes to form a close-knit framework for the vessel's hull. This is then made waterproof by the application of a semi-liquid mortar mix, applied simultaneously from both inside and outside the hull structure. The mortar is made with cement, very fine sand and *possolano* or volcanic ash to make it more

workable. When this has set and cured over a period of about a week, it produces a very hard, smooth, and resilient hull. Ferrocement can be used for hulls of up to about 80 ft (24 m) in length, and in addition to thousands of harbour launches, yachts, and other small craft most modern Chinese sampans are mass-produced in ferrocement, replacing the traditional wooden sampans of earlier days. The same material is widely used for building ashore; the roof of the Sydney Opera House is constructed of ferro-cement, for example.

There has been a revival, too, in the multi-hull theory of construction, almost exclusively in the yachting world. A multi-hull is a type of vessel with two or more hulls, or floats, propelled by paddles, sails, or mechanical power. The inspiration for the modern multi-hull was undoubtedly provided by the outrigger canoes of the Indian and Pacific Oceans which date back hundreds of years, but its appearance in European waters is of more recent date. With a view to eliminating rolling in choppy seas, a twin-hulled ferry of

Below: Second World War experience gave birth to the design of the frigate, mainly for anti-submarine warfare but also armed with a gun and/or anti-ship and anti-aircraft missiles. The design of this Mark 10 frigate, capable of 30 knots, dates from 1962.

Nautilus
(1954)

Length 324 ft (99 m) *Beam* 28 ft (8·5 m)
Standard displacement 3,530 tons *Speed* 25 knots (submerged)
Armament six 21-inch torpedo tubes *Complement* 105

The launching of the U.S. submarine *Nautilus* marked the beginning of a new era not only for submarines but for ships in general, since she was the first vessel of any kind to have nuclear propulsion. Her nuclear reactor powers two steam turbines giving 15,000 h.p. She also has conventional diesel and electric propulsion units. Because the nuclear reactor consumes no oxygen, the only effective limitation on her ability to remain submerged is the endurance of her crew and their oxygen requirements. On one occasion without refuelling she covered 91,324 nautical miles, 78,885 of them under water. She can dive to a depth of 720 ft (219·5 m). On 3 August 1958 the *Nautilus* passed under the North Pole on her way to becoming the first submarine to travel from the Pacific to the Atlantic beneath the ice-cap, succeeding where the earlier submarine of the same name had failed in 1931.

This reconstruction of the *Nautilus* is based on the information that is available. The cutaway section shows (from bow to stern) the torpedo room, crew's quarters, officers' quarters, operations and control rooms, radiation shield, nuclear reactor and engine room. The diagram gives a cross section through the hull amidships, showing operations room (above) and control room, and the cylindrical pressure hull. The photograph shows the *Nautilus* under way on the surface.

Above: The ferrocement yacht *Petralis* under construction at St Katharine's Dock, London. The work of amateur shipbuilders, she is the largest ferrocement yacht to be built in Britain. The photograph shows the projecting mesh webs for bulkhead attachments and as supports for the cabin floors.

1,533 gross tons, named the *Castalia*, was built in 1874 for crossing the English Channel from Dover to Calais, and she was followed a few years later by a similar but larger ferry, the *Calais-Douvres*, of 1,820 gross tons. Both consisted of two identical hulls joined at deck level by a platform carrying the bridge and upperworks. They were propelled by a paddlewheel working between the hulls. The twin hulls provided extra stability and reduced the rolling in rough seas, but added quite considerably to the fuel consumption as the resistance to two hulls was considerably more than to one.

The experiment was not a commercial success and the multi-hull concept remained in abeyance until after World War II when it was revived for sailing yachts. The main advantage is that with lightweight sailing boats there is a smaller area of wetted hull surface when under sail, and this will produce a considerably greater speed for any given sail area. There is also an added stability, and these two factors have made them very popular as leisure craft. Large numbers of catamarans (two identical hulls connected by a central platform) and trimarans (one central hull with two outrigger-type floats) have been built. In heavy seas the structural stresses on catamarans and trimarans are considerable, but many long voyages, including circumnavigations of the world, have been successfully accomplished by multi-hulls.

In Europe World War II came to an end in the traditional and long-established pattern, with sea power, in this particular case allied to air power, providing the conditions in which armies could establish themselves on the battlefield for the decisive thrust. The same pattern heralded the end of the war in the Pacific a few months later, even though the final surrender was perhaps hastened a little by the explosion of atomic bombs at Hiroshima and Nagasaki. But even before these bombs were dropped, Allied sea power had already opened the way for armies to establish themselves on the final battleground. No doubt the two atomic bombs saved the lives of thousands of American and Japanese soldiers which would otherwise have been lost in the subsequent land campaign, but they had little or no effect on the inevitability of Japanese defeat which sea power had brought about. That the cost in civilian lives was horrific must remain on the conscience of us all.

The normal reaction at the end of any war is for those involved to relax through national exhaustion, to disarm and to indulge in a period of little or no progress in the development of new armaments. The lessons of the war are largely forgotten in the euphoria of victory or the bitterness of defeat, for the urgency of war is no longer operative. But at the end of World War II this normal pattern was reversed as the world split into two mutually antagonistic ideological camps, forcing the nations into a fairly large-scale arms race instead of the expected post-war disarmament. There was also the revelation, during the very last hours of the war, that an entirely new weapon had made its appearance on the military field, a weapon of incalculable power with an application to navies, armies and air forces alike. It was not something to be left in limbo while nations relaxed.

With hindsight, it is interesting to pick out the features of World War II which were truly indicative of the changes to come. The small rocket carrying an explosive was used operationally both by aircraft and by warships, and was developed by Germany into a big medium-range missile called the V2. With the achievement of atomic fission in the shape of the two atomic bombs dropped in Japan, scientists could not only see the way ahead to nuclear fusion, which would produce explosions beside which those in Japan in 1945 would seem almost like pinpricks, but could also see a marriage between the nuclear explosion and a development of the V2 rocket. Naval architects could perhaps see a little further: yet another marriage between this new weapon and the submarine. The application of these new weapons to ships would be purely as a purpose of carriage and delivery, for such a huge and instantaneous release of energy in an explosion had no application as an anti-ship weapon. There was, however, one intermediate step to be taken before the two could come together in a virtually foolproof weapon of immense strategic power.

The fission of uranium atoms was accompanied by intense heat, and if this fission could be slowed down and controlled, the heat produced could be harnessed to the production of steam for normal ship propulsion. The great advantage of such a form of steam production was that it would be achieved in a reactor without the need of oxygen from the surrounding air. This at once made it particularly attractive as a means of propulsion for submarines, giving them for the first time the ability to proceed indefinitely underwater without the need to come periodically to the surface in order to recharge their batteries.

The decision to go ahead with the harnessing of nuclear fission for ship propulsion was taken by the United States in 1948 when the U.S. Atomic Energy Commission awarded a contract to the Westinghouse Electrical Company to develop a nuclear propulsion plant suitable for use in a submarine. Progress was rapid, and the keel of what was to be the world's first nuclear-powered submarine, the U.S.S. Nautilus, was laid on 14 June 1952. She was launched in January 1954

and commissioned in September of the same year. Built by the General Dynamics (Electric Boat) Corporation, she was a large submarine as submarines went at that time, with a length of 324 ft (98·8 m), a beam of 28 ft (8·5 m) and a surface displacement of 3,530 tons (3,586 tonnes).

The controlled nuclear reaction in a reactor takes the place of a marine boiler in a conventional ship's steam propulsion unit, and the heat produced is used through heat transformers to generate steam for the turbines which either drive the propellers direct or through electric motors. The reactor has to be totally encased in a heavy safety shield to prevent the escape of radiation. The Nautilus at first used Uranium 235 as fuel, but was refuelled two years later with enriched uranium, now the standard fuel for all nuclear propulsion units.

One of the immense advantages of nuclear propulsion for ships is the length of time it takes to use up one charge of uranium fuel and the consequent ability to run a ship at full speed for a vast distance before it is necessary to refuel her. On a single fuelling of her reactor, the Nautilus was able to cover a distance of 91,300 nautical miles, of which nearly 80,000 were submerged.

The advantages of nuclear propulsion for

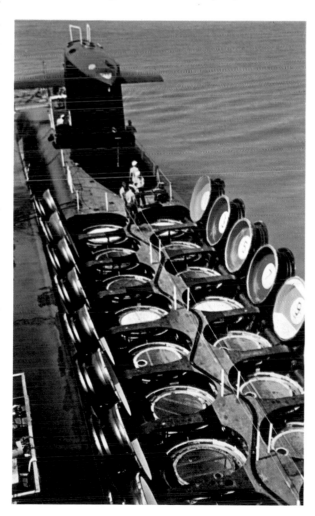

Left: The hinged caps over the vertical tubes of a Polaris sea-launched ballistic missile submarine. These missiles are propelled by a two-stage solid-fuel rocket motor and are effective at ranges up to 2,500 miles (4,000 km).

submarines are incalculable. The conventional submarine, using its diesel engine for surface propulsion and its electric batteries for operating when submerged, has many limitations. It is dependent on its oil fuel capacity both for its radius of operation and for the length of time it can stay out at sea on operations. It is limited in speeds to the power of its diesel engine on the surface – perhaps 16 to 18 knots – and on its batteries for submerged speed – perhaps 10 or 11 knots for a very short time or a much slower speed for a longer period of dive. Submerged propulsion exhausts the capacity of its batteries quickly, and to recharge them using its diesel engine, the submarine has to come to the surface, or else lie submerged just below the surface and obtain oxygen for the engine through its schnorkel breathing tube. In either case she is very vulnerable to discovery and attack as modern radar can obtain a reflection from the top of a schnorkel tube as easily as it can from the above-water hull. Nuclear propulsion changes all this. In the case of the *Nautilus,* one charge of nuclear fuel in the reactor lasts, on average, about two years, giving the submarine a virtually unlimited radius of operation. Without the need of oxygen for combustion, she can use her steam turbines for propulsion both on the surface and submerged and, with these turbines producing 15,000 horsepower, she has been able to maintain a submerged speed of over 25 knots.

The success of the *Nautilus* opened the way to a wide expansion in nuclear propulsion, mainly in submarines where it has revolutionized the practice of submarine warfare, and also in some surface warships. As far as submarines are concerned, development has concentrated largely on obtaining increased underwater speed by streamlining the hull and adopting a teardrop hull shape, which has produced underwater speeds of up to 35 knots, greatly in excess of anything previously obtained.

Nuclear-propelled submarines normally fall into two distinct categories. There are those whose weapon is still the torpedo, though a much more sophisticated torpedo than that used in World War II. Modern torpedoes have a considerably greater range of up to around 20 miles (32 km) and are guided towards their target until their own guidance system can take over and lock itself onto the target so that it cannot miss. The other category is an alliance between the nuclear-propelled submarine and the long-range guided missile carrying one or more nuclear warheads. These are much larger, normally over 7,000 tons, so that they can accommodate a battery of large missiles of the Polaris and Poseidon type, giving reality to the post-war vision of a combination of submarines and long-range

rockets. Although Polaris and Poseidon are classed within the intermediate range of rockets, they are nevertheless effective up to 2,500 miles (4,000 km). Following the remarkable feat of engineering by the U.S. in solving the problems of firing the missiles while the submarine remains submerged, large missile-firing submarines of this type have also been built by Britain, France and Russia.

No weapon, however efficient it may be, and the Polaris/Poseidon weapon is remarkably efficient, is immune from refinement and further development. Today a new submarine-launched weapon in this family is under development; it is larger so that each rocket can carry several warheads which can be targeted individually on different objectives, and range is increased to 4,000 miles (6,400 km). This is the Trident missile, and its considerably larger size will call for a

Above: The Polaris submarine-launched missile has been one of the most effective elements in the defence armoury of the West. Although superseded by the Trident system it is likely to remain in service for some time.

revolution in submarine building. Submarines of around 14,000 to 16,000 tons or even more will be necessary to carry these new weapons, far larger than anything envisaged in the past. With their increased range allied to the vast expanse of ocean available in which to operate, no target on earth will be beyond their reach.

The cost of this new weapon, mainly in its requirement of new and very large submarines, is of course, very heavy, but it has strategic advantages. Unlike a similar land-based missile, its firing position from somewhere in the vast expanse of ocean is mobile and unknown, and, being submerged, is invisible. It is, therefore, essentially a second-strike weapon, always available for use if a sudden enemy attack should be made on the land-based missiles whose firing positions are known. The strategic argument used to justify its existence is that fear of the vast scale of destruction which would be caused by unlimited nuclear war has kept the world free from nuclear war for the last thirty-eight years and that an efficient and reliable second-strike weapon is a sufficient deterrent to any would-be opponent to keep it so. It must of course be realized that these missile-carrying submarines are not really warships in the accepted sense of that term; the weapons they carry have no role to play in naval warfare. Their missiles are essentially land weapons fired in the last extremity at a shore target. The submarine which carries them is no more than a submersible and mobile launching pad for nuclear weapons intended to make all-out war unthinkable.

Below: USS *Bremerton*, one of a recent class of large nuclear-powered submarines designed mainly to operate against enemy submarines. She carries Subroc and anti-submarine torpedoes and tube-launched Harpoon missiles.

285

Nimitz
(1975)

Length 1,092 ft (332 m) *Beam* 134 ft (40·8 m)
Draught 37 ft (11·3 m) *Flight deck width* 252 ft (76·8 m)
Standard displacement 81,600 tons; 91,487 tons deep load
Speed 30 + knots *Complement* 3,300 + 3,000 assigned to air wing

U.S.S. *Nimitz* is the world's second nuclear-powered aircraft carrier, following U.S.S. *Enterprise* which was commissioned fourteen years earlier. She has two pressurized water-cooled reactors compared with the eight fitted in the earlier *Enterprise* but the nuclear cores for her reactors are designed to provide enough energy to keep the ship operational for at least thirteen years, with the ability to steam up to one million nautical miles between each refuelling. The *Enterprise*'s reactors needed refuelling every two to three years, providing energy to steam up to about 300,000 miles, though after her last extensive refit the endurance of the new nuclear cores for her reactors is expected to be longer, probably from ten to twelve years.

The *Nimitz* carries an air wing of over ninety aircraft capable of all normal carrier duties of attack, defence, reconnaissance and early warning. The wing is divided into two squadrons of fighters, two light attack squadrons, one medium attack squadron, two anti-submarine squadrons of which one is of Sea King helicopters, and detachments of reconnaissance aircraft, electronic warfare aircraft, early warning/control aircraft and tanker aircraft for inflight refuelling. The illustration above right is of a Grumman F.14A Tomcat fighter. The *Nimitz* is fitted with over thirty radar sets to cover a variety of purposes, and also with satellite communications antennae. Her deck armament consists of three multiple launchers for Sea Sparrow missiles.

Nuclear propulsion, so successfully developed for the submarine, has many obvious advantages for the warship, most notably in the long life of the fuel element which obviates the necessity of frequent refuelling and provides an almost unlimited radius of action at continuous high speed. The United States uses it to power their new and large aircraft carriers and some of their larger cruisers. It has some disadvantages, in its high initial cost and in the extra weight of the reactor's heavy shielding, necessary as a safeguard against radiation leaks. All modern warships have to be extremely weight-conscious because of the heavy installations of modern weaponry and ancillary services, such as radar and essential counter-measures, mounted on and above the upper deck. The overall weight of a nuclear propulsion unit can therefore become a critical factor in warship design, particularly in the case of smaller ships.

Another naval lesson of World War II was the influence of the large aircraft carrier both on tactics and strategy. Misreading the lessons of World War I, which indicated that the torpedo and the mine were more destructive weapons than the gun, all the maritime nations entered World War II still pinning their faith to the battleship armed with the big naval gun. Their vulnerability to attack from carrier-borne aircraft made them virtually useless in naval battles at sea and they were soon relegated to the sidelines of sea warfare. Only in one aspect of naval warfare could they still prove their value, when their support fire in amphibious assault landings proved devastatingly effective, but this relatively minor role was not enough to justify their retention in the post-war naval world. No country has built a new battleship since the war ended, although a few of them have been preserved in care and maintenance status by the United States. It seems that, in the face of modern airborne and shipborne weapons, they will never again find a fighting role at sea.

The aircraft carrier, developed after the war to a size undreamed of by wartime naval architects, has had a chequered career over the years that followed. With the development of new weapons, and particularly of the smaller guided missiles carried in ships and aircraft, many navies came to the conclusion that the big carrier was too vulnerable a target to roam the oceans and that her aircraft, too, might well be excessively vulnerable to the target-seeking anti-aircraft weapons mounted in ships. These navies gradually phased out their carriers, relying on the helicopter to do some of the tasks of the carrier-borne fixed-wing aircraft and deciding to dispense with the others.

Only the United States Navy differed from this policy. Instead of phasing out their carriers they have developed them to more than twice their original size. Their latest ships in this category are nuclear-propelled and, with a displacement of around 95,000 tons (96,500 tonnes), are capable of operating up to about 100 aircraft each. In recent years Russia, too, has built carriers of about 40,000 tons (40,640 tonnes) and, even more recently, Britain has re-entered the carrier field. Her new ones, however, are comparatively small ships of around 20,000 tons (20,300 tonnes) and capable of operating only helicopters and vertical take-off aircraft in small numbers. While these are extremely versatile aircraft, they are comparatively slow and lack the range of normal fixed-wing aircraft.

It is the technological advance in weapon development during recent years which appears to have given the conventional aircraft carrier a new lease of life. For some years missiles have had guidance systems which virtually ensure them hitting their target, initially discharged along a radar bearing until they approach near enough for their own guidance system to take over and lock onto the target. This final guidance system is frequently visual in the form of television pictures sent back from the missile to an operator on the launching vessel. It was this threat of an almost certain hit which caused the temporary lack of confidence in the carrier by so many navies, a very big and expensive target whose loss might well be a naval disaster. But the development of the missile has in more recent years been matched

by the development of the anti-missile-missile, which can track and intercept an incoming missile, destroying it before it can reach and hit its target.

In a somewhat roundabout way the anti-missile-missile has again justified the large aircraft carrier operating fixed-wing aircraft. The maximum range at which the anti-ship missile can be fired is about 20 miles (32 km), because it can only start its run on a radar contact and a radar beam cannot be bent round the curved surface of the earth. But these missiles, most of which skim the surface of the sea, travel so fast that there is not sufficient reaction time to bring an anti-missile-missile to bear if the original discharge has not been detected. It is here that the carrier with fixed-wing aircraft earns part of her keep, for she can fly air patrols out to a range of about 200 miles (320 km) and detect the incoming enemy long before he comes within his firing range. The fixed-wing aircraft can also use their own missile armament to attack enemy ships and aircraft while they are still far distant unless the enemy fleet also has an aircraft carrier which is flying air patrols.

For some years after the ending of World War II it was possible in very general terms to say that the main effect of modern weapon development on warship design was a reduction in the size of the ship, in spite of the obviously contrary experience in the case of carriers and submarines. The post-war years saw the end of the battleship and the big cruiser, and the general run of naval shipbuilding was concentrated on the smaller warships such as destroyers, frigates, fast patrol craft and minehunters. In those days the general pattern was to build the ship, place her weapons on board and give her a good radar installation, and that was that. Technology has today advanced far beyond that. Although many warships still carry a gun, it is a far more sophisticated weapon than it was even a few years ago, being fully automated with a very rapid rate of fire and not even requiring a gun crew to operate it. Modern warships are also armed with anti-air and anti-ship missiles, and the most modern ones with anti-missile-missiles. Radio and radar decoys and counter-measures are also accommodated on board, so that in recent years the actual sizes of frigates and destroyers have had to be increased to carry the new weapons and their associated electronics. Thus the destroyer, which during World War II averaged perhaps 1,800 tons (1,830 tonnes) is now a ship of approaching 5,000 tons (5,080 tonnes), with the frigate a ship of perhaps half that size or a little more.

The big amphibious assaults which were such a feature of World War II are now operations of the past; any assault on such a scale on an enemy-held coast would today almost certainly draw a nuclear response. But, on a smaller scale, such as in the Falklands, an amphibious capability is too valuable a weapon to throw away and it calls for a ship of special design to combine all the elements of amphibious warfare on a smaller scale. The British solution is perhaps typical of the skill of the naval architects when faced with such a problem. Basically it takes the form of a small streamlined floating dock within the hull of a ship, used to carry landing craft which can put a full commando unit ashore. To launch the landing craft, water ballast is taken on board to lower the ship in the water until the dock is flooded and the landing craft can be floated out. They are re-embarked in the same way, with the water ballast pumped out when the landing craft have been floated into the dock, allowing the ship to rise and the dock to drain. Smaller landing craft are carried additionally on davits to add to the troop-carrying capacity, and the ship has a small flight deck capable of operating large helicopters. All this is contained in a ship of 20,000 tons (20,320 tonnes) with twin turbines giving her a speed of over 20 knots.

Apart from weapons, the greatest advances of these post-war years have been in the field of ship propulsion and naval engineering. As has been seen, nuclear propulsion is a huge if expensive step forward, particularly in the case of submarines, transforming them into a particularly lethal weapon of naval warfare. Advances in metallurgy have also played a large part in the development of the modern submarine, by

Far left above: The loss of British ships to the missiles and bombs of the Argentine air force during the Falklands War of 1982 was mainly due to the lack of extensive air cover. Here a Royal Navy Sea King helicopter hovers over liferafts from the blazing landing ship *Sir Galahad* after the devastating Argentine air attack during the landing at Bluff Cove.

Far left below: The destroyer HMS *Sheffield*, armed with a gun, Sea Dart missiles and helicopter-launched anti-submarine missiles. During the Falkland Islands operations she was hit and sunk by an Argentine air-launched Exocet missile.

Above: A Rolls Royce Olympus gas turbine being hoisted aboard the Thai frigate *Makut Rajakumarn.* Although gas turbines have a shorter life than steam turbines, the ease with which they can be replaced means less time in harbour for repairs.

Above right: Radar is probably the greatest gift which modern technology has given to seamen. It is an invaluable aid to navigation, particularly in darkness and fog, but is also vital in modern sea warfare.

producing steels whose strength enables submarines to dive to depths of up to 1,000 ft (305 m) where they are well below the reach of surface-borne sonar detecting devices. (It has recently been claimed that by using additional titanium in the steelmaking process a steel has now been produced that is strong and flexible enough to enable a submarine to operate at 3,000 ft (915 m). If this steel has in fact been produced, there is no reason why submarines built with it should not dive to this depth.) In the larger steam-driven warships, advances in engineering have produced vastly more efficient marine boilers and engines, considerably reducing the number of boilers needed to produce the required steam output, and at the same time increasing the power output of the engines.

More important than the modern steam installation, particularly for warships such as destroyers and frigates, and, indeed, for all but the largest ships, is the gas turbine. All the experimental work on it was done by the aircraft industry, the marine version being an adaptation of the aircraft engine. It was first used at sea in conjunction with the steam turbine, originally to give an additional boost to the engines when a sudden burst of speed was required for tactical reasons. With its reliability proven at sea it became the sole propulsion installation for many of the smaller ships until, with extended experience of its operational value, it was adopted in the British Navy for all major warships; even the new 20,000-ton carriers are being powered by gas turbines developed from the Concorde engine. Although pioneered by Britain, many other navies have adopted it as the prime means of propulsion.

The gas turbine has many distinct advantages. Its power-to-weight ratio is far superior to any other form of marine propulsion. Power for power, it takes up less space in a ship even than a conventional marine diesel engine, which is itself a great space saver. And it has the inestimable advantage for a warship that, from cold, it can develop full power within a very few minutes so that in an emergency a ship can get under way in a very short time, at full speed if necessary, without having to go through the long process of warming through the engines. Its main disadvantages, however, are its high cost (though this is modest compared with that of a nuclear reactor) and fuel consumption, and the fire risk caused by its highly volatile fuel.

It is a rough and ready rule that a warship's design is dictated largely by the weapons she carries rather than the other way round. This has posed some problems for modern naval architects ever since the missile rather than the gun became the main above-water weapon of all navies. Missile technology calls for extensive radar back-up both for detection of the enemy and for guidance to the target, and this in its turn means that a considerable weight has to be accommodated on and above the upper deck. To compensate for this extra weight the modern practice has been to substitute the lighter aluminium alloys for the heavier steel for all the vessel's superstructure, although in some warships even this is not enough to preserve their essential stability, making it necessary to carry additional ballast low down. Some small warships remain stable only by topping up their fuel tanks when half-empty, a requirement that drastically reduces their range. The new generation of warships will probably be built broader, sacrificing streamlining for the stability needed to carry extra armament for attack or defence.

Warships are designed and built to incorporate the lessons and the theories of naval warfare. Many of these lessons have had to be painfully re-learned over the past 20 years. In the Vietnam war, air attacks from offshore carriers proved so costly against sound AA defences that the US Navy recommissioned its 'Iowa' class battleships, to bombard inland targets with heavy-calibre shellfire. The Falklands War of 1982 proved a particularly hard school, showing that AA missile capacity can be costly and fallible alternative to carrier-borne airborne early warning and fighter cover. In the light of the Falklands experience the rapid-fire gatling gun, guided by its own radar, has been adopted as a potent counter to surface-skimming missiles of the Exocet type. Perhaps the most convincing warning against the dangers of modern 'technology mania' came in 1987. This was the use of contact mines, one of the oldest of all naval weapons, in the Iraq-Iran Gulf War. Only when several ships had fallen victim to this 'old technology' weapon did it emerge that the US Navy, the world's biggest, had virtually no conventional minesweepers for the location and removal of these simple but deadly weapons, which can be deployed wherever a small boat can venture. The new generations of warships will, no doubt, be better and even more efficient once these re-learned lessons have been thoroughly studied, analysed, and put into practice.

Left: A practice firing of the British Sea Slug surface-to-air guided missile from HMS *Kent*, one of four guided-missile destroyers of the 'County' class.

Below: HMS *Broadsword*, a Type-22 destroyer of the Royal Navy, armed with Exocet (surface-to-surface) and Sea Wolf (surface-to-air) missiles in addition to anti-submarine torpedoes.

Chapter Thirteen
Oil from the Seas

The tenfold rise in the price of crude oil over the last few years brought new problems to ship designers and builders. It meant that deposits of oil which were in difficult or inaccessible places, and therefore uneconomic in the days of cheap oil, became economic almost overnight. One of those difficult places was the North Sea, under which it was known that there were deposits of oil, and the rise in price made it apparent that there were good profits to be won if the difficulties of drilling and processing there could be overcome at not too large a cost.

There are three essential stages in the production of oil, whether below the sea or the land. The first and obvious one is to discover by a seismic survey the rock formations which indicate the probable presence of oil. At sea, this normally involves two ships, one fitted with seismic equipment for firing the charges, using compressed air instead of explosives to reduce the risk of killing too many fish, the other towing a string of microphones to record the echoes of the charges from the different rock formations. This process calls for exact navigation on the part of both ships since the readings must be related exactly to the seabed, even to within a few yards, in order to determine the exact position in which to drill. Special seismic survey vessels have been built to accommodate the equipment required for this first step in the discovery of oil.

With a potentially favourable seismic survey, the second stage is to drill an exploratory well to discover whether in fact the survey has been correct in forecasting the presence of oil and, if so, that the oil is of a quantity and quality worth recovering. It is at this stage that the costs of production begin to escalate at a prodigious rate, and an oil production company will expect to see at least ten years of prolific life from a well in order to justify the immense capital expenditure which is involved in recovering oil from fields under the sea.

Left: The Shell-Esso production platform Cormorant 'A' at the start of a long tow to Norway.

Two basic kinds of drilling rig are used today, a mobile jack-up rig which can be used in depths of water up to about 50 fathoms (90 m) and, for waters of greater depth, a self-propelled drilling ship or a semi-submersible rig. A jack-up rig has four legs with a drilling platform which can ride up and down them, a device developed as a result of experience in the Mulberry harbours erected for the invasion of Normandy in World War II. It is towed into position with its four legs raised, and when in the exact position the legs are lowered until they rest firmly on the seabed, the platform being lifted up the legs to the necessary height above sea level. The derrick which operates the drill is then erected on the platform, if it is not already in place, and drilling begins. The other type, drilling ship or semi-submersible, is not attached to the seabed with legs but is held in position by four or more anchors, together with an electronic monitor which adjusts the position automatically. This consists of a 'bleeper' placed in position on the seabed and instruments in the drilling ship or semi-submersible which listen continuously to the 'bleep' to detect every small change in position of the rig. If it does move, motors are automatically switched on to bring the rig back to its exact position. The drilling ship follows more or less the conventional hull shape of all ships, but adapted internally for its job of operating an oil drill, usually with the derrick amidships and, of course, the drill itself working through the ship's bottom. The semi-submersible is a specially designed drilling platform supported on large, tubular steel legs attached to pontoons, which are submerged to a depth of around 60 ft (18·3 m) and support the weight of the platform. They are very large and complex floating structures with all the necessary machinery for turning the drill and pumping the mud down the drill pipes, with full accommodation for the drilling crew and a deck for helicopters to land and take off. They represent the first large escalation of cost, for they can cost up to £20 million to build and £20,000 a day to operate. But they are

North Sea Oil-Rigs

Oil wells under the sea are no new phenomenon; there has been offshore production of oil for many years in relatively shallow waters. It is only in the last few years that the tenfold increase in the price of oil has made the exploration of deeper and less hospitable waters financially viable. The oil-producing companies have therefore been faced with new problems of constructing drilling and production rigs able to withstand greater extremes of wind and weather. The North Sea rigs illustrated here are the successful product of this engineering challenge.

The rig below is the *Ocean Benloyal*, a self-propelled Aker H-3 type twin-pontoon semi-submersible. It is used to drill exploratory wells to test for quality and quantity after a seismic survey has indicated a potential oilfield. Its drilling derrick reaches 160 ft (48 m) above deck level and it has accommodation for seventy-eight men. *Ocean Benloyal* is held in position by anchors, and can drill to a depth of 25,000 ft (7,620 m) in 1,200 ft (365 m) of water. The section diagram on the right gives some idea of the massive extent of a single oil-rig's possible field of drilling.

The illustration on the far right is B.P.'s *Forties Charlie*, a jacket rig which is fixed on the seabed after an exploratory rig has located a substantial oilfield. *Forties Charlie* has a deck area of 170 × 175 ft (52 × 53.5 m), stands in 416 ft (127 m) of water, and measures 285 ft (87 m) from sea-level to the top of the drilling derrick. It has accommodation for ninety-six people and a nominal production capacity of 125,000 barrels a day (1 barrel = 159 litres).

Above: The Shell-Esso Brent 'B' production platform during a North Sea storm with winds gusting up to 90 knots. The bottom of the platform is 75 ft (23 m) above sea level, which gives some indication of the height of the waves during the storm.

mobile and when sufficient exploratory wells have been drilled on one site to prove the extent and capacity of the field, they can be towed to other promising sites to continue the exploration work. When a field has proved itself worth developing, the modern drill stem can be made to operate outward into the seabed by means of ball and socket joints so that it can reach oil lying as much as two miles (3 km) from the site of the rig.

The design of a drilling rig, either fixed like a jack-up, or mobile like a semi-submersible, presents constant problems to the naval architect. For locations in areas such as the North Sea, where the weather is unpredictable and storms of considerable violence can spring up quite suddenly, the main problem is to build sufficient strength into the rig to withstand the pressures exerted at times by enormous waves and gales of 60 knots or more.

The final stage is the erection of production platforms to extract the oil and process it for transport to the refinery after the field has been proved and drilled. Although plans exist to use semi-submersible platforms to perform this part of the task, and indeed in very deep waters to do the job permanently underwater from production chambers on the seabed, almost all modern extraction is from platforms supported by concrete legs or piled steel jackets (scaffolding-like

structures) resting on the bottom.

Platforms on concrete legs have three of them, all hollow so that additional wells can be drilled through them. They are constructed ashore in their final, vertical position and then towed out by tugs, still upright, to the position in which they will operate, where they are sunk so that the concrete legs stand on the bottom with the actual platform well above sea level. They rely on their great weight to hold them fixed solidly to the seabed. Around the bottom of each leg is a cluster of storage tanks for the oil as it is forced out of the field, preparatory to its being processed on the platform to remove the gas and salt water that is dissolved in it. Some of the gas separated from the oil as it comes from the well can be used as fuel for the auxiliary machinery on the production platform, the remainder is flared off unless there is a sufficient quantity to make it worth piping ashore for commercial and domestic use.

Steel jacket platforms, also constructed ashore, are built in a dry dock lying on their side and resting on flotation tanks. When the dock is flooded on completion of the building, the platform is floated out on its tanks and again towed, still lying horizontally on its side, to its destination in the oilfields. On arrival, the flotation tanks are flooded, starting with those at the foot, so that it gradually tips upright and settles on the seabed. Once in position it is anchored to the bottom with steel piles driven through the feet of the uprights at each corner. The platform is then constructed on the top of the jacket with prefabricated parts lifted into position by cranes mounted on barges or ships.

A production platform is a vast structure. The platform itself, supported on top of its concrete legs or steel jacket, is the size of a large football ground. It is covered not only with all the machinery for drilling further wells and for the actual processing of the oil, but also with living accommodation for the platform crew, a mess hall and recreation room, facilities for a team of divers, and a helicopter deck for the daily delivery of supplies, the transference ashore of any sick or hurt members of the crew and the fortnightly relief and replacement of the crew. Some of the larger platforms also accommodate a small cinema, and all, of course, have a communications centre.

As with the drilling rigs, the complexity of the design and the inbuilt strength required cause many problems for the designers, virtually a complete departure from the design of a ship. It is the structural strength required, both to support the weight of the platform and to withstand the pressures of the elements, that makes the construction of a platform a real challenge to the skill of a designer. Although a great many of them have been built to service the many offshore oilfields around the world, only very occasionally does one hear of collapse due to a faulty design or damage caused by the failure of a platform to withstand the enormous stresses of rough seas and high winds.

The larger offshore oilfields are connected to an oil terminal or refinery ashore by a pipeline run along the seabed, an operation which requires specially designed ships to lay the pipes. Smaller fields pipe the processed oil either to a large tank on the seabed about a mile clear of the platform, or direct to a buoy known as a single buoy mooring. The seabed tank, if that is the method used, is also connected to a single buoy mooring. The distance of the buoy from the production platform is necessary to allow tankers, which come to collect the oil and take it to a terminal ashore, to have plenty of room to swing round the buoy clear of the platform while loading their cargo of oil. Unless the sea is very calm, it would be unsafe for a tanker to moor directly alongside a platform.

The whole business of extracting oil from an offshore field has given birth to a new generation of specialist ships and other craft designed purely for the purpose of servicing the industry. In addition to lifeboats for the emergency evacuation of a rig or platform, safety capsules have also been designed which are self-propelled and capable of going safely through a belt of fire on the sea should the oil escape and ignite. The laying of a pipeline, which consists of lengths of steel pipes welded together and covered with a coating of tar and cement, calls for a special pipe-laying barge, where the welding and coating is done, and a ship carrying a trenching machine which follows the barge. As the pipe is welded and coated it is paid out over the stern of the barge, and as it reaches the seabed the trenching machine takes it between two vertical arms and digs a trench in which the pipe rests, the movement of the sea filling the trench as the trenching machine moves on. Both these vessels are specially adapted to carry out this task.

There is a considerable variety of special support ships for the offshore oil industry, including converted trawlers on permanent standby to evacuate the platform crew in an emergency, supply and repair ships bringing essential stores and machinery or providing seaborne repair facilities, and specially designed fire-fighting vessels. Once an offshore site is in full production it becomes an economic necessity to keep it running at maximum capacity because of the heavy

Below: An aerial view of the accommodation rig *Treasure Finder* en route to its North Sea location alongside the Brent 'B' production platform. It provides facilities for rest and relaxation and has a medical centre with a flying-doctor service.

Above: An underwater construction support platform demonstrates its fire-fighting potential. Known as 'Uncle John', it is one of the most sophisticated support platforms in the world. In the background is the Brent 'D' production platform.

Right: *Semac I*, a semi-submersible pipe-laying barge engaged in laying a gas pipeline in the East Shetlands basin of the North Sea. In the background is the Cormorant 'A' production platform with a supply vessel (left) and a surveying ship (right).

highest rates of pay on board a production platform, any other methods of avoiding such lost working time are eagerly sought in a constant economic struggle to make a worthwhile profit from an oilfield.

One such answer is to use armoured diving suits with articulated joints modelled on those developed to recover the gold in the sunken liner *Egypt* in 1930–35. In these the diver works at normal atmospheric pressure and so is not affected by compression disease. But they are heavy, clumsy suits with very limited movement and, although tools can be operated through the articulated joints by remote control inside the suit, there is a limit to the number of repair operations which can be performed by the diver inside. Miniature two-man submarines offer more facilities for submerged repairs, adjustments and inspections, and like the armoured suit the divers inside work in a normal atmospheric pressure. They are much more mobile and are equipped with a variety of tools designed to be able to carry out most of the predictable tasks which can be expected in such a submerged installation, all of them remotely controlled from inside the submarine. These small submarines are, again, a legacy of World War II experience, their prototypes being the British X-craft and the German Biber boats.

Nevertheless, there will always be some tasks below water which only the individual diver can perform. Modern diving techniques enable these divers to work at depths greatly beyond those achieved in the years between the wars, and with the presence of a diving bell for periods of rest and sustenance, individual divers can remain operational for long periods at a time. There are some tasks, too, which call for the use of free divers with the normal aqualung equipment, such as period inspection of the rigs and platforms for signs of corrosion or malfunction or excessive growth of weed and barnacles.

Drilling rigs and production platforms fixed to the seabed with concrete legs or steel jackets can hardly be designated as ships, although they are generally built in shipyards or equivalent establishments and call for the knowledge and expertise of naval architects and marine engineers. A better case can perhaps be made for classing semi-submersible rigs as ships in spite of their non-shiplike appearance, for they are at least free-floating with a capability of self-propulsion within a very limited compass. But the whole offshore industry of winning oil from below the seas is essentially a maritime concept in its execution and support back-up, and calls in large measure for the skills and experience of men whose knowledge is of the techniques that apply to ships and the sea.

capital cost involved in the development of a difficult site under the sea in comparison with the generally easier sites on land. In a great many cases these vessels are adaptations of existing ships to the specialized services required, but some are designed and built from the keel up for particular oilfield duties.

The most interesting of the specialized vessels are probably the miniature submarines which many oil companies use today in place of divers, or in collaboration with them. All complicated underwater systems, such as those established for the offshore extraction of oil, require constant inspection and repair. Some of these systems are laid at a depth of as much as 150 fathoms (274 m), where the pressures are very high, calling in the case of individual divers for a long period in a decompression chamber, sometimes for as much as a week, to avert the danger of compression sickness, or the 'bends'. Such long periods of decompression obviously limit the diver's time of working on the seabed, and since they earn the

Epilogue
Beyond the Horizon

Looking back over the development of the ship from its earliest days, perhaps the most striking feature is how soon man hit upon the best overall hull shape for the ship. In very broad terms there is not a great deal of difference between the early Egyptian trading boats or their war galleys and the warships and merchant vessels of today, as far as the general shape of the hull is concerned. This would seem to indicate that there is little room for any radical advance in the hull design of ships, except in those cases where ships are built purely for specialized tasks, such as fast ferries using the hydrofoil principle. But in small ways there may well be design advances to be made on the more or less standard hull design of today. Who, a few years ago, would have thought of adding a large bulbous protrusion to the bows of a ship as an aid to efficiency? Yet this is what a bulbous bow does, giving a smoother passage of water along a ship's sides, therefore causing less resistance to her forward movement and reducing fuel consumption. At today's high fuel costs even a small saving is attractive to every commercial user of ships, so all the new designs of merchant ships of any size today incorporate the bulbous bow.

Another innovation of ship design in the years following World War II is the ship stabilizer, first introduced by the shipbuilding firm of Denny-Brown in the 1930s. It has a particular relevance to large ships, particularly liners, although it is fitted in some smaller vessels where extra stability is required. One of the first of the big liners to fit Denny-Brown stabilizers was the *France*. Their object is to reduce rolling at sea to a minimum, and this is achieved by fitting one or two retractable fins of aerofoil design on each side of the ship. They are pivoted at the base and act in very much the same way as the hydroplanes of a submarine. They are automatically controlled by gyroscopes, and as the ship

begins to roll the stabilizing mechanism automatically adjusts the angle of the fin to counteract the roll. In narrow channels or in harbour the stabilizing fins are retracted into spaces inside the hull below the waterline. Ship stabilizers are today fitted to most liners, some warships (where they provide a steadier gun platform, especially in smaller warships when operating in a seaway) and some fishing vessels, particularly those which do their fishing off the south-west coast of Africa where the sea conditions often produce excessive, and sometimes dangerous, rolling. In these smaller vessels one stabilizer is normally sufficient to control the rolling, and it is non-retractable. It can be fitted on either side of the vessel as circumstances and design dictate. In addition to their anti-roll properties, always appreciated by passengers prone to seasickness, stabilizers have a bearing on the economics of running a ship. A ship which is rolling heavily increases her resistance to forward movement through the water, thus slowing herself down, but if the rolling can be controlled she can maintain her speed with a lower consumption of fuel, or make a better speed for the voyage with the same consumption.

It is no loss that the other type of movement of a ship in a seaway, longitudinal pitching, cannot be automatically controlled except by the exertion of some force so gigantic as to be impossible to produce. All ships pitch when steaming into a head sea, and this is a big factor in ensuring the safety of their construction. If a ship were to be held rigid in these conditions she would be subjected to intolerable hull strains, and the seas would sweep over her with such force that they could damage, or even carry away, her bridge and superstructure.

Another post-war invention is the fitting of one or two lateral thrust propellers, often described as 'bow thrusters', driven by an auxiliary engine at right angles to the fore and aft line of a ship. Today most big ships, and many ferries, have bow thrusters as an aid to manoeuvrability in narrow waters and in ports. The lateral thrust

Left: The container ship *Table Bay*. The bulbous bow is a modern innovation which eases the flow of water along the hull and reduces fuel consumption.

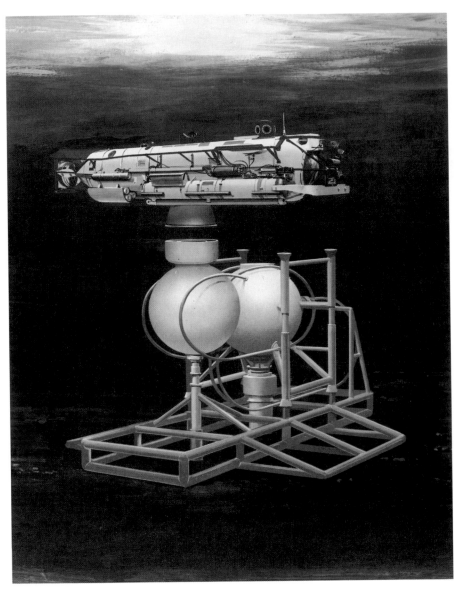

Above: Artist's impression of a diver lock-out submersible, in effect a midget submarine, mating onto a work chamber on the seabed.

tankers and container ships, but the practice continues to spread in general cargo ships. Again, efficiency is the key; the easier handling of cargo in loading and unloading, the chances that this affords for the more efficient use of the ship's crew, even the ability to work the ship with a smaller crew than in the past. These are some of the things which the shipowner of today is looking for and which keep the naval architect on his toes.

As we have seen, nuclear propulsion of ships was born out of the research into the atomic bombs which were dropped on Japan at the end of World War II. It has proved to be of extreme value for warships, having now been operated by them on a growing scale for thirty years without any serious mishap. It has provided the only solution to the dream of the true submarine, one which can operate submerged for long periods without needing to come to the surface to recharge batteries or renew the internal air supply. It has been proved, too, in surface warships where the advantages of an immense radius of action without the need to refuel are obvious. Although it is a costly system of propulsion to instal, one would have thought that its many and great advantages would have made it commercially attractive to the shipowner.

An attempt was made by the United States in 1962 to demonstrate its commercial possibilities with the building of the *Savannah*, a cargo ship of 22,000 tons fitted with a nuclear propulsion engine which gave her 21 knots on her trials, a very good speed for a merchant ship. Although only built for demonstration purposes and never operated as a commercial venture, she was not a success and was very quickly withdrawn and laid up. Germany built and launched a nuclear-powered cargo/passenger liner in 1968, the *Otto Hahn*, but she, too, has not caught the attention of modern shipowners as the way into the future.

The Russians have been more successful in their adoption of nuclear propulsion for icebreakers on the northern sea route between Novaya Zemlya and the Bering Sea, north of Siberia. The first of them, the *Lenin*, was commissioned in 1959 and was built with three nuclear reactors as her power plant. She was followed by the *Arktika*, which in August 1977 penetrated as far north through the ice as the Pole itself. Icebreakers, of course, are very specialized ships, only of real commercial interest if they can open up, and keep open, new and shorter sea routes between East and West, like for example the Arctic Ocean–Pacific Ocean route north of Russia or the notorious North-West Passage from Atlantic to Pacific north of Canada. With their nuclear-powered icebreakers the Russians have been able to keep open, at least during the

propeller is housed in a tunnel which runs laterally through the forward part of the ship below the waterline and, as it revolves, it draws water from one side of the ship and thrusts it out on the other, creating a turning force which assists sideways movements by pushing the bow round. Some ships also have a similar tunnel aft which acts as a stern thruster, so that when both are used simultaneously the ship can come alongside a harbour jetty broadside on. Many large ships can, with the aid of bow and stern thrusters, enter and leave port without having to call on the assistance of harbour tugs, an expense well worth saving in the modern economic climate of the shipping industry.

Any further innovations are most likely to take place inside the hull, however. Already, in the past two or three decades, there have been considerable changes, the main one being the move of the bridge superstructure from amidships to aft to permit a more sensible arrangement of the holds. This is particularly the case in summer months, their northern sea route, but so far no attempts have been made to open up the Atlantic–Pacific North-West Passage. There should, in theory at least, be no real difficulty in keeping this route open for at least a part of each year, given sufficient engine power such as a modern installation can provide and the strength of modern steels to withstand the forces entailed in breaking through the ice. Who can foretell how much that greatly shorter sea route between East and West might mean as an economic stimulus to increased world trade? It is a possibility for the future and if it were to come about, naval architects would be called upon to design, perhaps, a new breed of specially strengthened and equipped ships to take advantage of the new routes.

Apart from such specialized uses, and in spite of the wealth of experience gained from its naval operation, nuclear propulsion has not been seriously considered as a commercial proposition, even in the largest ships. The initial installation is very expensive, and the shielding which must enclose the reactor is massive and heavy, but one would think that the advantages of being able to operate a ship for up to two years without the need of refuelling her would outweigh the costs of installation and make this form of propulsion an attractive alternative for shipowners continually faced with spiralling increases in the cost of conventional fuel. The main reason against its installation in merchant ships lies in the size and political clout of the anti-nuclear lobby and the reluctance of many commercial ports around the world to accept and handle ships with this form of propulsion in the face of public disapproval and fears of radioactive leakages. Until or unless that element of public opinion changes, it is unlikely that commercial operators would risk the banning of their ships from many of the ports they serve.

Another form of ship propulsion, largely rejected commercially in spite of naval enthusiasm for its use, is the gas turbine. Its advantages lie in its

Below: The German nuclear-powered merchant ship *Otto Hahn* lying in Hamburg harbour. Nuclear propulsion has not yet proved itself as an economic method of propulsion for seaborne trade.

Right: The giant Russian icebreaker *Lenin* is one of the few non-military ships which justify the vast expense of nuclear propulsion. The power is needed to punch a way through the ice in order to keep open the northern sea route from Novaya Semlya to the Bering Sea.

weight and space-saving properties and its ability to produce full power within minutes of starting from cold – important assets for a warship. No other means of propulsion can equal its power output in relation to its overall weight. But additional speed, except in certain ships or short-haul passages, such as passenger and car ferries, is not so important commercially on long-haul voyages as fuel economy, and the gas turbine is a heavy 'gas guzzler'. Apart from specialized fields when speed is economically important, the gas turbine would therefore appear to have little commercial future in merchant shipping.

During the early 1970s four large 31,000-ton container ships were built, powered by gas turbines, to provide a fast transatlantic service to compare with that of the big passenger liners. They achieved a service speed of 28 knots, but when the price of oil rocketed in the middle and end of that decade, they were proved uneconomic and the gas turbines were run at reduced power to save fuel, providing a speed of 18 knots. Today the ships have been withdrawn from service so that their gas turbines can be replaced with diesel engines, an eloquent indication that speed in merchant ships can be too expensive in economic terms.

In the field of marine engineering the technological advances in the design and performance of steam and diesel engine propulsion have been enormous, and it is in the nature of all progress that these advances will continue. They are, between them, the most economical of all means of propulsion, with the steam turbine the more popular for the larger ships. In earlier years, as ships grew larger, the single engine developed

into two, three, and four to drive that number of propellers; today more and more big ships are reverting to the single propeller without much loss of speed and with much greater fuel efficiency. This has been made possible by the design of engines with greater power output than was thought feasible ten or twenty years ago. Because diesel fuel is very costly, the tendency today is to produce engines with a longer stroke, which makes them slow revving and enables them to burn a heavier and less refined oil. In this way the essential power is maintained at a reduced fuel cost. In some smaller ships these engines are used with controllable-pitch propellers, which simplify the overall control of the ships as they are operated directly from the bridge. Although some shipowners today look upon these propellers as an expensive luxury, others have discovered that the extra control they confer has resulted in a saving of engine-room staff. As experience with them builds up, they may well be more widely adopted.

It is in this aspect of ship management, the more economic use of crews, that the greatest changes have been seen in the last few years, and this process is likely to continue well into the future as new techniques are evolved. Automation in ships is a relatively new technology, but already it has drastically reduced the large crews which were carried on board during the days when much of the essential work on board was performed by manual labour. Today much of it is done by machines which are remotely controlled, not necessarily by human decisions but by electronic sensors which adjust to optimum efficiency. The days of the fully automatic ship with minimal crew have not yet arrived, and probably never will, but every advance in automation pays a dividend in the reduction of operational costs through the more economic use of manpower on board.

One small experiment carried out in Japan, which at first might look like a partial return to the practices of days long past, may well have a considerable influence on modern design. About three years ago a Japanese shipyard, Nippon Kokan, built a small tanker to which they fitted square sails controlled by a computer. The sails are spread, furled, and trimmed to the wind entirely by the computer, which decides when the wind is strong enough and blowing in a direction which will help the ship along. After several voyages over the course of a year, the tanker has cut her fuel costs by just over ten per cent without any loss of service speed or efficiency. The idea may look a little far-fetched, but the figures speak for themselves and the saving of fuel by using the wind when it is favourable may

Left: This jack-up rig was fitted with 200-ft (61-m) sails to assist it on its voyage from Louisiana to the Esso-Shell Leman Bank gasfield, near Great Yarmouth, England. With one tug towing the rig, the sails shortened the voyage by five days.

Below: The Japanese tanker *Shinaitoku Maru* is fitted with computer-controlled square sails for setting when the wind is favourable. A saving of ten per cent in fuel costs has been achieved without loss of speed or efficiency.

well prove an example that others will be tempted to follow.

Today, as for the last hundred years, steel remains the principal material for the construction of ships, though invariably welded instead of rivetted as in past years. It has some drawbacks, as it is prone to rust and corrosion, and it is heavy in comparison with some of the light alloys now available, which have great resistance to corrosion and can be welded as easily as steel. The reason for its almost universal use in preference to alloys lies in the comparative costs of the two materials, for aluminium alloys are still very expensive. Some small craft, mainly yachts, have been built of aluminium alloy and have been very successful, but these are the toys of the rich who are not concerned with the economics of shipbuilding for commercial purposes. There have been suggestions that a ship's hull built of these alloys could be additionally used as a means of trapping solar energy to provide extra energy for propulsion, but this is probably to approach the land of make-believe. Unless the cost of these alloys can be considerably reduced, which seems unlikely in the foreseeable future, steel is likely to remain unchallenged as the material for the building of ships. Glass reinforced plastic, so widely used for small craft today, has the strength, lightness, and complete resistance to corrosion that makes it an ideal material for shipbuilding, but it can never compete in the large shipbuilding industry because, by reason of its quick-setting property, hulls made of it have to be moulded as a whole and cannot be built in sections and subsequently joined together. This limits its practical use to hulls of less than 100 ft (30·5 m) overall.

It has been seen in a previous chapter how two closures of the Suez Canal have influenced the size of oil tankers, making it economically necessary to build very large tankers to carry immense cargoes on the longer sea passages. It has been seen, too, how the present glut of oil all over the world has caused many of these very large tankers to be laid up until the world demand picks up again. There are many who believe that world demand will never pick up enough in the future to justify these immense ships and that the price increases over the last few years have made nations, and individuals, so conservation-conscious that adequate world distribution can be assured more economically by tankers of moderate size. Others believe that the opposite scenario could well be the correct one, that political uncertainties among the Middle East oil producers may well produce a world shortage and that the very

large tanker will again come into its own in the economic transport of large cargoes of oil from the more distant fields, such as Alaska and the East Indies.

There is one aspect of the very large tanker which could well lead to a change in design. A ULCC, fully loaded, will have a draught of around 65 ft (20 m) or more (the *Seawise Giant*, for example, the biggest ship in the world, draws 98 ft /29·8 m when fully loaded), and there are in the world very few oil terminal ports which can guarantee that depth of water at the bottom of the tide. As a result it is often necessary for such tankers to lie off their ports of arrival in deep water and pump enough of their cargoes into smaller tankers until the reduction of draught makes it possible for them to enter and discharge the remaining oil direct. To make these harbours capable of handling such large ships direct would entail an immense and continuous programme of dredging, and therefore one might expect to see large tankers of the future built with separate sections which on arrival off a terminal could be floated off independently and towed in for delivering the oil. The ship herself would remain anchored in deep water, saving her owners the

cost of harbour dues which, being calculated on tonnage, are quite considerable for big ships.

It has been reported that one tanker design, for a ship even bigger than the *Seawise Giant*, incorporates a hinge device halfway down her length to enable her to ride more easily over waves at sea. If true, this would appear to be harking back to 1863 when such a ship, named the *Connector*, was built on the Thames at Blackwall (see p. 234). That ship did not work because the strain on the 'hinges' was too great when she rolled, but perhaps with modern engineering skills and the strength of modern metals it is a possibility

The world's largest tanker, *Seawise Giant*, of 564,763 deadweight tons. She has been converted from another tanker by the insertion of an additional midship section. Constructed in Japan, she is shown in this photograph in two parts ready to be joined together. On completion she will have an overall length of 1,504 ft (458·5 m).

today. She will be a novel ship if built.

A post-war development, designed to operate among the smaller ports of the world, is the stowage of independent barges or lighters within a ship's hull for ocean transport to smaller destinations where they can be floated off for direct delivery of cargoes. The best-known systems are LASH (Lighter Aboard Ship), BACAT (Barge aboard Catamaran) and SeaBee (Sea Barge). All operate on similar principles, though with different methods of loading and unloading. In the LASH system, loaded lighters, each of about 400 tons deadweight, are floated into the open stern of a single deck carrier. The lighters are lifted with a 500-ton travelling gantry crane and carried by it to their stowage position in the ship. On arrival off the port of discharge the reverse process unloads the lighters to be towed into port. BACAT, like LASH, has barges which are floated into the stern and positioned so that they then bed down onto a metal transporter, which can be drawn up to the final stowage position. The transporters are also given lateral movement by wheels operating on a rail so that the barges, on reaching their stowage level, can be moved sideways to enable them to be stowed abreast

within the hull of the catamaran. SeaBee is much the same as LASH except that the carrier ship normally has three decks and a 2,000-ton capacity elevator platform. The barges are larger than the lighters used in LASH, each with a capacity equal to thirty-six standard containers. When loaded the barges are towed, two at a time, to the open stern of the carrier ship and floated above the elevator platform. This lifts them to the level of the deck where they are to be stowed; then they are winched onto a wheeled transporter and drawn into their final position for the voyage. A typical SeaBee ship is the *Almeria Lykes*, which with a gross tonnage of 21,667 can carry thirty-eight barges stowed on her three decks. On the upper deck stowage, the individual barges can carry additional containers on their own decks.

These new developments are still in their infancy, but the ability to carry small cargoes to a number of adjacent ports and even deliver them, if required, to destinations served by rivers or canals, carries with it the promise of considerable expansion. It also brings within the range of seaborne trade a large number of small ports too shallow to accommodate ships of any size.

Below: A cargo barge carrier and dock ship, familiarly known as a 'SeaBee'. Barges loaded with up to thirty-six standard containers each are floated into the stern dock. They are then lifted on a 2,000-ton capacity elevator platform to the correct deck level, where they are winched onto a wheeled transporter on deck tracks for stowage. On arrival at their destination the reverse procedure floats them out for local dispersal. There is room on board for thirty-eight barges.

It seems likely that, in the not too distant future, naval architects will be confronted with the problems of extended exploitation of the seabed and its resources. Some of the problems of oil exploration and production from undersea fields have been examined in the previous chapter, but with the price of oil already very high and tending always to rise higher, it makes economic sense to the oil companies to exploit possible sources at depths of water too deep for the erection of a fixed production platform. One solution is the use of semi-submersible production platforms on the same principle as the semi-submersible drilling rig; another is the use of individual wellhead chambers positioned on the seabed above the wells and serviced by a capsule lowered from a ship on the surface. An umbilical cord brings fresh air pumped from above so that the crew can work in normal atmospheric pressure inside the chamber. Relief crews travel up and down in the service capsule.

A more ambitious production scheme is for the use of fixed chambers anchored on the bottom. Wells are drilled by a semi-submersible rig in which the drill string passes through the fixed chamber and drills the wells below it. When the oil begins to flow it is processed inside the chamber and the waste gas led to a flare-stack which takes it above sea level for burning off. The oil, when processed inside the chambers, is pumped to a module on the seabed made up of several cells, and from these is led to a single buoy mooring for collection and transport ashore by tankers. There are living quarters in the chambers and periodic relief of the crew is by mini-submarine which homes in to an access hatch much as a capsule connects with an orbiting laboratory in space. Air inside the chambers is at normal atmospheric pressure.

Oil is not the only source of wealth below water. In many areas of the ocean, the bed is strewn with nodules of valuable minerals, mainly manganese, and plans are afoot to recover them, perhaps by some sort of trawl, perhaps by other means. But collecting them, by whatever means are ultimately employed, will call for ships specially adapted for the process, another future task to test the skills of the naval architect and the shipbuilder.

For many years there have been those who prophesy a commercial future for the submarine. Speeds underwater can be very much higher than speeds on the surface, without any of the stresses suffered by the surface ship as she pounds into a heavy sea at speed. There is no rolling or pitching under water, and no inherent difficulties in the design or construction of a submarine able to carry an economic cargo. Navigation below water with an inertial system

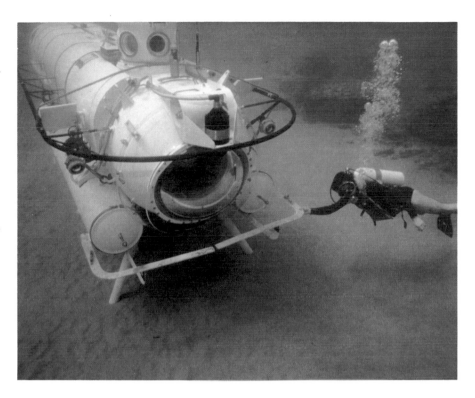

is just as exact as navigation on the surface. Trans-ocean voyages could be made at speeds in excess of 30 knots with much less wear and tear on the hull. But the sort of submarine which might have this sort of commercial future is inevitably nuclear-powered – the conventional battery-powered submarine has no such capability – and the reluctance of so many ports to give access to any ship with a nuclear installation would appear to be a complete bar to any development along those lines.

There are many directions in which ships can develop in the future, largely dependent on the nature and condition of world trade as it expands through the years ahead. New products of industry often call for new means of transport, and ships are no exception to this demand. Perhaps the one stable condition of advance in the design and building of ships is economic reality. Throughout the centuries in which the ship has developed, there has been no lack of enterprise on the part of owners, designers, and builders to try to produce the best vessel for each particular task in view. Many of the dreams they have had have come true, some have ended in failure. But for all of them, successful or not, the urge to create has been guided by an economic need. It is still so today, although the risks of failure are much reduced. Feasibility studies, the testing of models, advances in technology and computer analysis are the new tools which guide the ship-builders of today, so that very few vessels are built now or will be built in the future without the fore-knowledge that their economic success in their particular fields is virtually assured.

Above: A diver from a lock-out submersible. With the considerable development of underwater exploration for oil and gas, divers are needed for the continuous inspection of production rigs to ensure their safety and proper maintenance.

Some Maritime Definitions

ARTICLES The conditions of service signed by a seaman in the merchant service when joining a ship. They normally set out rates of pay, scale of victualling, hours of work, etc., and, signed also by the ship's master, form a contract binding on both sides. The ship's discipline on board is based on the articles and the master has the right of punishment when the articles are transgressed.

BEAUFORT SCALE A scale indicating the varying states of wind and sea first developed by Sir Francis Beaufort when he was Hydrographer of the British Navy between 1829 and 1855. The wind scale varies from 0, calm, to 12, hurricane, and each number, as it indicates a rising wind strength, is accompanied by a description of the sea state produced by a wind of that strength. The Beaufort Scale has been universally adopted as a quick and accurate means of general weather measurement. A similar scale is used to indicate the state of the sea based on the height of the waves. It varies from 0, flat calm, to 9, waves with a mean height of over 45 ft (14 m).

BILGE The almost horizontal floor of a ship on either side of her keel. The point where the hull starts to round upwards from its flattish bottom is known as the turn of the bilge.

BILGE KEELS Steel-plate projections running fore and aft along each side of a ship's hull just below the turn of the bilge, also known as docking keels. They were first introduced in the design of Brunel's *Great Eastern* in 1854 as a roll-damping device but their main use today is to take the weight of a ship on the launching ways as she is being built and to support the ship on lines of chocks when she enters a dry dock.

BOTTOMRY A mortgage raised on a ship by her master when he is out of contact with her owners and needs to raise money for repairs or to complete a voyage. Money raised by a bottomry bond must be used only for the exact purpose stated, and the bond takes priority over all other mortgages on a ship.

BURTHEN The older term for expressing the carrying capacity of a ship, based on the number of tuns (casks) of wine she could stow in her holds. See also TON, TONNAGE.

CLASSIFICATION The degree of seaworthiness of a ship as determined by a survey on her construction and the size (scantlings) of the materials used in her construction. An original classification lasts for a definite period of years and a ship must be resurveyed when this period expires if she is to retain her classification. After a disaster,

such as fire or shipwreck, another survey is required to re-establish her classification. The best known body which issues ships' classifications is Lloyd's Register of Shipping, which has committees for this purpose in every maritime nation in the world.

DRAUGHT Sometimes written as draft, the depth of water which a ship draws, obviously varying according to her load. When loaded down to her Plimsoll Line she is said to be at her deep load draught. Most ships have draught marks painted on both sides of the bow and stern, normally in Roman figures, each figure indicating 1 ft (30 cm) of draught measured to the bottom of the painted figure.

FLAGS OF CONVENIENCE A term applied to ships registered in certain small countries by owners who are not nationals of those countries. The practice started during the shipping slump of 1920–30 when some owners wished to operate their ships without the need to submit them to the inspections and regulations of the recognized maritime countries. The practice grew considerably after the Second World War when many Greek and Italian shipowners bought up war surplus tonnage and registered it in Panama, Honduras, Liberia, or Costa Rica, thus avoiding most of the conditions imposed by the main maritime nations, particularly in seaman's rates of pay, and also paying minimum taxes. Until about 1960 many of these ships were sub-standard, but by then such large profits had been made that the older ships were replaced by modern ones as good as any in the world.

At the same time Liberia became what was known as a 'flag of necessity' for many U.S. ships, reflecting the American stake in the international oil industry and her inability to compete economically because of the high rates of pay of American seamen in comparison with those of other nations. As a world maritime power the U.S. recognized the strategic need to maintain large tanker and cargo fleets on the world's trade routes, which added very considerably to the tonnage being operated under flags of convenience. While the real ownership of such ships is disguised, approximately half are U.S.-owned and many of the rest U.S.-financed.

GUNWALE (pron. gunnel) The thick plank of wood used to cover the tops of the timbers in a wooden ship.

KNOT The unit of speed of a ship at sea, one knot being a speed of one nautical mile an hour. Because of the difference in length between a nautical mile and a land mile, one knot at sea is equivalent to 1·15 m.p.h. (1·85

km/h) on land. The name comes from the early forms of speed measurement at sea when a wooden board to which a line was attached was cast overboard and the ship's speed estimated from the amount of line which ran out during a given period. After the adoption of the nautical mile during the fifteenth century as the unit of distance at sea, the line was marked with knots spaced uniformly in the same proportion to a nautical mile as was the running time of a sandglass to an hour. The smallest sandglasses issued to ships ran for about 30 seconds, so the knots were placed at intervals of 47 ft 3 in, approximately the same proportion to a nautical mile as was 30 seconds to an hour. The number of knots which ran out while the sand in the glass emptied itself gave the ship's speed in nautical miles an hour and was always reported as so many knots.

LLOYD'S An association of marine underwriters whose origin lies in a daily meeting of London merchants in Edward Lloyd's Coffee House in the City of London. It has a continuous history of marine underwriting from 1601 to the present day. It is also a centre of marine intelligence of the daily movements of merchant ships, marine casualties, etc. published every day in *Lloyd's List*.

In 1760 a number of Lloyd's underwriters formed a society to draw up rules regarding the construction of merchant ships. Known as Lloyd's Register of Shipping, the rules cover the size (scantlings) of the materials used in the construction, method of building, etc., and it issues Lloyd's classifications for all ships built to these rules. It publishes annually a list of all ships which are still afloat and have received the Lloyd's classification. See also CLASSIFICATION.

NAUTICAL MILE The unit of distance used at sea, being the length of an arc on the earth's surface subtended by an angle of one minute of latitude at the earth's centre. Because the earth is not a perfect sphere this length varies from place to place, being shortest at the equator and longest at the poles because the earth is flattened across the polar caps. The arithmetical mean of a nautical mile measured at the equator and one measured at the poles is 6,077 ft (1,852 m) but for the purpose of ships' navigation this figure is rounded up to 6,080 ft (1,853 m). Thus the nautical mile differs considerably from the land mile of 5,280 ft (1,609 m).

PLIMSOLL LINE A series of six lines painted on the sides of all British, and many foreign, merchant ships to show the maximum depths to which a ship may be loaded in various conditions. The six lines indicate the depth of loading in tropical fresh water, fresh water, tropical seawater, summer seawater, winter seawater, and winter North Atlantic. The Plimsoll Line is accompanied by a circle with a horizontal line through the centre and letters indicating the registration society; in all British ships and many foreign ones the letters are LR for Lloyd's Register.

The Plimsoll Line became compulsory in Britain under the terms of the Merchant Shipping Act of 1876 after a long parliamentary struggle by Samuel Plimsoll, M.P., who was campaigning against the so-called 'coffin ships', vessels often unseaworthy and overloaded and heavily insured against loss. Violent opposition to the parliamentary campaign was mounted by many shipowners who saw in the proposed legislation a threat to their livelihood by limiting the loading of their ships to below their total capacity.

PROPELLER The rotating screw of a powered ship which forces her through the water. The earliest propellers, introduced in 1835 – 40, had two blades, long and thin like early aircraft propellers, but with the building of larger ships and more research in hydrodynamics, three-, four-, five-, and six-bladed propellers have been introduced, with greater efficiency in the shape and the pitch of the blades.

The pitch of a propeller is the distance which one revolution moves the ship forward in still water. A recent innovation is the hydraulically operated variable-pitch propeller. This allows the angle at which the blades are set on the shaft to be altered while the ship is still in motion, giving the captain on the bridge control of his ship's movements from full speed ahead to full speed astern without the need of stopping and restarting the engine or altering the speed at which it is running. The advantage of the variable pitch propeller, besides giving a quicker and more flexible control of the ship's movement through the water, is that the engine can be run at the constant speed at which it performs most efficiently and economically.

RULE OF THE ROAD An internationally agreed set of 31 rules compiled by the International Convention for Safety of Life at Sea, which lay down the required conduct of ships at sea to prevent collisions between them. The rules are divided into six main groups which cover such points as the lights and shapes to be carried by night or day so that vessels and their employment, such as fishing, etc., can be recognized; sound signals in fog; steering and sailing rules to keep ships apart; distress signals; etc.

The most important group of rules are those which lay down the required conduct of ships approaching each other when there is a danger of collision if they maintain their original courses. They indicate which ship has the right of way in such circumstances and which has to give way so that collision is avoided. In general, under the Rule of the Road, ships keep to the right when at sea.

SEPARATION ZONES The introduction of one-way lanes for ships in narrow waters and channels which carry heavy traffic. As an example, the English Channel, which is the main waterway between northern Europe and the rest of the world, has separation lanes in which all eastbound traffic uses a lane off the coast of France and all westbound traffic one off the coast of England. The lanes are monitored by radar stations along the coast and ships are warned when there is one proceeding in the wrong lane.

STEEVE The angle made by the bowsprit of a sailing ship in relation to the level of the deck; a high-steeved bowsprit is one which is well cocked up towards the vertical.

TIMBERS The ribs of a ship, connected at their lower end to the keel and at their upper end to the deckbeams, which give the hull of a ship its shape and its strength. In steel ships they are more usually known as frames.

TON The unit of measurement of the capacity of a ship, being 100 cu ft (2·83 m³) of her internal volume. The origin of this measurement was the tun, a cask holding 252 old gallons of wine, and a ship's tunnage was measured by the number of tuns of wine she could hold. See also BURTHEN, TONNAGE.

TONNAGE A measurement used to indicate the capacity of a merchant ship for carrying passengers and/or cargo. The original measurement of capacity was the number of tuns (casks) of wine which a ship could stow in her holds but as ships grew larger during the sixteenth and seventeenth centuries with the growth of seaborne trade, it became necessary to devise a new and more accurate method of measurement on which the harbour dues payable by ships using them could be calculated. The formula agreed by shipowners and harbour officials was the product of length multiplied by breadth multiplied by depth of hold to give an internal capacity in cubic feet, and this was then divided by 100 to provide a figure known as tonnage on which harbour dues were calculated.

As ships developed through the years, becoming larger with finer lines, this formula was revised in 1773 to provide a more accurate tonnage measurement. Known as the Builders' Old Measurement, the new formula was much more complicated, but served its purpose well until, during the nineteenth century, iron, and later steel, became the accepted building material for ships, introducing an entirely new design of hull to which the Builders' Old Measurement had little relevance.

With these new ship designs a system was adopted of calculating from internal measurements the actual capacity in cubic feet of the hull below the upper deck and dividing the result by 100 to give a gross tonnage figure. But since this gross figure bore little relation to a ship's actual carrying capacity, a second figure was calculated on the same formula in which allowance was made for all space below the upper deck – boiler rooms, engine rooms, bunkers, living spaces, etc. – which could not be used for the stowage of cargo, and this figure gave the net tonnage. Both these figures, gross and net, are known as register tons as they are entered on the ship's certificate of registration. Harbour dues, salvage and towage dues, and light and buoyage dues are calculated on a ship's net register tonnage although merchant ships are normally quoted for size on their gross register tonnage.

Another tonnage calculation, known as displacement tonnage, is measured by the volume of water a ship displaces with her fuel tanks or bunkers full and all stores on board. This again is calculated in cubic feet but is divided by 35 as this volume of sea water weighs one ton. The size of warships is always indicated by their displacement tonnage.

Deadweight tonnage is the tonnage of cargo carried on board a ship to trim her down to her Plimsoll Line. It is measured in cubic feet by the difference between the volume of water displaced when she is unloaded but with fuel tanks or bunkers full and stores aboard and that displaced when she is down to her Plimsoll Line. The difference is, as in displacement tonnage, divided by 35. The size of oil tankers is often designated by their deadweight tonnage.

TRINITY HOUSE The body in England and Wales which is responsible for the erection and maintenance of lighthouses, lightships, buoys, and other aids to navigation around the shores. It is also the licensing authority for pilots. It was founded by King Henry VIII in 1517 as a guild to encourage the 'relief, increase, and augmentation of the shipping of this our realm of England', and its duties were extended by Henry's daughter, Queen Elizabeth I, to the erection of seamarks to aid ships in their inshore navigation. In 1604 the guild was reorganized into Elder and Younger Brethren, of whom the former are responsible for the day-to-day duties of Trinity House and also act as nautical assessors in the Admiralty Division of the High Court. There are thirteen Elder Brethren, eleven elected from the merchant service and two appointed by the Royal Navy.

Other nations have their own authorities who are responsible for the lighting and buoyage of their shores.

WALE An additional thickness of timber which was bolted to the sides of wooden ships to provide protection where required. A wale running the whole length of the ship just below the gunwale on both sides of the vessel protected the hull when lying alongside the quay where the rise and fall of the tide might cause damage to the hull planking by rubbing against the piers. In wooden warships wales were fixed between each row of gunports to protect the portlids from damage when coming alongside an enemy ship to board her. Shorter wales, known as chainwales, were fixed opposite each mast to prevent the shrouds rubbing against the gunwale.

Bibliography

Abell, Sir W. S. *The Shipwright's Trade* (Cambridge University Press, 1948)

Anderson, R. & R. C. *The Sailing Ship* (Evelyn, London 1971)

Archibald, E. H. H. *The Wooden Fighting Ship in the Royal Navy* (Blandford, London 1968)

Barnaby, K. C. *Basic Naval Architecture* (Hutchinson, London 1963)

Bathe, B. W. *Seven Centuries of Sea Travel* (Barrie & Jenkins, London 1972)

Bonsor, N. R. P. *The North Atlantic Seaway* – Vol. I (David & Charles, Newton Abbot 1975)

Bradford, E. *Southward the Caravels* (Hutchinson, London 1971)

Brinnin, J. M. *The Sway of the Grand Saloon* (Macmillan, London 1971; Delacorte Press, New York 1971)

Butler, T. Harrison *Cruising Yachts, Design and Performance* (R. Ross, Southampton 1945)

Chapman, F. H. *Architectura Navalis Mercatoria* – 3 vols (Svenska, Stockholm 1768; Adlard Coles, London 1971)

Corlett, E. *The Iron Ship: History and Significance of Brunel's 'Great Britain'* (Moonraker Press, London 1975)

De Mierre, H. C. *Clipper Ships to Ocean Greyhounds* (Harold Starke, London 1971)

Dugan, J. *The Great Iron Ship* (Hamish Hamilton, London 1953)

Dunn, L. *The World's Tankers* (Harrap, London 1956)

Emmons, F. *The Atlantic Liners 1925 – 1970* (David & Charles, Newton Abbot 1972)

Gibbs, C. R. V. *Passenger Liners of the Western Ocean* (Staples Press, London 1957)

Grant, Sir A. *Steel and Ships* (Michael Joseph, London 1950)

Griffiths, M. *Man the Shipbuilder* (Priory Press, London 1973)

Hardy, A. C. *Book of the Ship* (Sampson Low, Morston, London 1949)

Herrmann, P. *Conquest by Man* (Hamish Hamilton, London 1954)

Hobbs, E. W. *Sailing Ships at a Glance* (Architectural Press, London 1925)

Humble, R. *Aircraft Carriers – the Illustrated History* (Michael Joseph, London 1982)

Humble, R. (Ed.) *Naval Warfare – an Illustrated History* (Orbis, London 1983)

Hurd, Sir A. (Ed.) *Britain's Merchant Navy* (Odhams Press, London 1943)

Hyde, F. E. *Cunard and the North Atlantic 1840 – 1973* (Macmillan, London 1975)

Jobe, J. (Ed.) *The Great Age of Sail* (Patrick Stephens, London 1967; Viking Press, New York 1971)

Johnson, R. F. *The 'Royal George'* (Charles Knight, London 1971)

Kemp, P. (Ed.) *Oxford Companion to Ships and the Sea* (Oxford University Press, London 1976)

Kihlberg, B. *The Lore of Ships* (Heinemann, London 1964)

Landström, B. *Sailing Ships in Words and Pictures* (Allen & Unwin, London 1969)

Longridge, C. N. *Anatomy of Nelson's Ships* (P. Marshall, London 1955)

Lyon, D. & H. *World War II Warships* (Orbis, London 1976)

McKay, R. *Some Famous Sailing Ships and their Builder: Donald McKay* (7C' Press, New York 1970)

McDowell, W. *The Shape of Ships* (Hutchinson, London 1961)

MacIntyre, D. *The Adventure of Sail 1520 – 1914* (Paul Elek, London 1970; Random House, New York 1970)

Moore, J. E. *Warships of the Royal Navy* (Jane's, London & New York 1981)

Parkes, O. *British Battleships* (Seeley Service, London 1957)

Preston, A. *Sea Combat off the Falklands* (Willow Books, London 1981)

Rowland, K. T. *Steam at Sea* (David & Charles, Newton Abbot 1970)

Selincourt, A. de, *The Book of the Sea* (Eyre & Spottiswoode, London 1961)

Smith, E. C. *A Short History of Naval and Marine Engineering* (Cambridge University Press, 1938)

Spratt, H. P. *The Birth of the Steamboat* (Griffin Press, London 1958)

Spurling, J. & Lubbock, A. B. *Sail: the Romance of the Clipper Ships* (Blue Peter Publications, London 1927)

Tavernier, B. *Great Maritime Routes: an Illustrated History* (Macdonald, London 1972)

Watts, C. J. *Practical Yacht Construction* (R. Ross, Southampton 1947)

Wettern, D. *The Decline of British Seapower* (Jane's, London 1982)

Index

Acknowledgments

Admiralty Experiment Works: 177; American Museum in Bath: 184; Archivo B: 53; Associated Press: 257 (bottom); Beken of Cowes: 211, 277 (bottom); Bergens Sjofartsmuseum: 41 (top); C Bevilacqua: 22, 65, 79 (bottom), 188; Biblioteca Nacional, Madrid: 52; Bibliothèque Nationale, Paris: 74 (top), 86 (bottom), 120; Biblioteca Nazionale, Venice: 92; Bodleian Library: 60; A Bollo: 19 (top); Borras Edistudio: 14; British Library: 4–5, 63; British Museum: 85, 88 (bottom), 145; David Brown Gear Industries Ltd: 293 (bottom); Brunel University Library: 154 (top), 168 (left and right); Cees van der Meulen: 257 (top); Cement and Concrete Association: 282 (top); Central Office of Information: 290 (bottom); Chambre de Commerce de Boulogne: 273 (top); Chicago University: 16 (top and bottom); Richard Cooke: 288 (bottom); A C Cooper: 20 (bottom), 99 (bottom), 136 (bottom), 155, 201, 203, 210 (top); G Costa: 39 (top and bottom), 41 (bottom), 48, 70–1, 72, 91 (bottom), 116 (top), 117, 124 (bottom), 125, 128 (bottom), 178–9; G Dagli Orti: 70, 79 (top), 81; Daily Telegraph Colour Library/Mike Hardy: 276 (top left); Daily Telegraph Colour Library/P Ward: 262 (top left); Daily Telegraph Colour Library/ J Young: 292 (top right); Deutsches Archaologisches Institut, Rome: 32, 33; Deutsches Schiffahrtsmuseum, Bremen: 57 (bottom); C M Dixon: 26 (bottom), 27, 35, 37; Laurence Dunn Collection: 220, 221 (bottom), 224 (top), 255, 261 (top); Earl Beatty Collection: 233; Esso Petroleum Co. Ltd: 173 (bottom), 307 (top); Robert Estall: 78; Mary Evans: 36 (top), 194, 195 (bottom); Fathy: 15; Finnish Tourist Board UK Office: 274; W Forman: 38–9, 42, 42–3, 49 (top and bottom); Fox Photos: 247; Gilardi: 34–5 (bottom); Globtik Tankers Ltd: 264; Goole Shipbuilders Ltd: 272 (top right); Handford Photography: 310 (bottom); Robert Harding Associates: 8–9; Michael Holford: 9 (top and bottom), 25, 50–1, 64, 144 (top); Robert Hunt Picture Library: 226 (bottom), 236–7, 238, 245; ICP: 258–9; IGDA: 20 (top), 24, 26 (top), 62, 82 (top and bottom), 83 (left), 84, 87 (bottom), 128 (top); Illustrated London News: 182 (top and bottom), 234; Imperial War Museum: 136 (top), 179, 217 (top), 225 (bottom), 226 (top), 228 (top), 229, 239, 240 (top and bottom), 241 (top and bottom), 242 (top and bottom), 244 (top and bottom), 246, 252, 253; Istanbul University Library: 55; Lessing/Magnum: 12–13; Library of Congress, Washington: 1, 185 (top), 230–1; Jan Lukas: 6; William Macquitty: 134 (right); Mansell Collection: 86 (top), 235 (bottom); Mariner's Museum, Virginia: 153, 198 (top); Maritiem Museum 'Prins Hendrik', Rotterdam: 66; Masters and Fellows of Magdalene College, Cambridge: 93 (bottom), 96; F Arborio Mella: 74 (bottom); Merseyside County Museum: 150–1 (bottom); Metropolitan Museum, New York: 198 (inset); Musée de la Marine, Paris: 26 (middle), 111 (top), 118 (bottom), 119, 127, 164; Museum of City of New York/Byron Collection: 175 (top); Mystic Seaport, Connecticut: 196–7; National Archaeological Museum, Athens: 16–17; National Archives, Washington: 135 (top); National Gallery, London: 140–1, 161; National Maritime Museum, London: 80, 88 (top), 98, 99 (top), 103, 104–5, 106–7, 108–9 (top), 111 (bottom), 112–13 (bottom), 113, 116 (bottom), 118 (top), 121, 123 (top), 130–1, 132 (top and bottom), 133, 137, 138, 142–3, 143 (bottom), 148 (top and bottom), 149, 151,152 (top), 158, 159 (top and bottom), 160, 165, 166, 169, 172–3, 173 (middle), 174 (top and bottom), 175 (bottom), 176, 189, 191, 200, 202 (top and bottom), 204, 205, 209 (top and bottom), 212, 213, 217 (bottom), 219, 221 (top and middle); National Museet, Copenhagen: 22–3, 40–1; National Portrait Gallery, London: 97 (top); Naval Photographic Center, Washington: 285 (bottom), 286–7; Nippon Kokan KK: 307 (bottom), 308–9; Novosti: 306; N R Omell: 102; Orion Press: 272 (left); Orbis: 54–5, 61 (courtesy of Dean and Chapter, Winchester/ E A Sollars), 76, 77, 93 (top right), 97 (bottom), 154 (bottom), 162 (bottom); Overseas Containers Ltd: 269 (top), 271 (top), 302–3; P & O Photo Library: 146–7, 167 (top and bottom); Peabody Museum, Massachusetts: 198 (middle left), 199, 210 (bottom); Photri: 271, 283, 284, 289; R Pittaglia: 36–7; Popperfoto: 183, 185 (bottom), 186–7 (top and bottom), 215, 228 (bottom), 235 (top), 248, 254, 256, 260–1 (bottom); Port of London Authority: 268 (bottom), 270 (top); Press Association: 290 (top), 291 (top right); Publifoto: 218; F Quilici: 126–7; Real Photos: 249 (top); Reproduced by gracious permission of HM The Queen: 91 (top); Reale Accademia di San Fernando, Madrid: 87 (top); Rex Features: 293 (top); B Richner: 109, 124 (top), 278; Rijkesmuseum, Amsterdam: 101; A Rizzi: 54 (top), 75 (top), 83 (right); Roger-Viollet: 73; Rolls-Royce: 292; Ronan Picture Library: 149 (inset), 162 (top); John Ross: 10 (top and bottom), 11; San Francisco Maritime Museum: 208; Scala: 34–5 (top), 57 (top), 59; Science Museum, London: 12, 13, 67, 75 (bottom), 122, 129, 144 (bottom), 150 (top), 152 (bottom), 170, 190, 190 (inset), 192, 193 (top and bottom), 214; Shell Photo Service: 294–5, 298 (top), 299 (bottom), 300 (top), 301; Staatsarchiv Hamburg: 56, 57 (top and middle); Submarine Museum, Connecticut: 195 (top); Sutcliffe Gallery: endpapers; Titus: 19 (bottom); John Topham Picture Library: 265; US Navy: 227; US Navy Photo/MARS, Lincs.: 289 (top); Universitets Oldsaksamling, Oslo: 44 (left and right); Vasa Museum, Stockholm: 112–3 (top); Vatican Museum: 31 (top); P A Vicary/Maritime Photo Library: 163, 225 (top), 232–3; Vickers Ltd: 224 (bottom); VO Offshore Ltd: 304 (top left), 311 (top right); Vosper Thornycroft (UK) Ltd: 279 (bottom); Woodmansterne: 123 (bottom), 134 (left), 139; Zefa/Helmut Adam: 305 (bottom); Zefa/M. Pitner: 263; Zefa/Skyphotos: 266–7.